الفقه الإسلامي

500

Questions and Answers On Islamic Jurisprudence

Compiled and translated by:
Muhammad M. Abdul-Fattah

Qadeem Press

Qadeem Press

Qadeem Press Edition
Breathing Life into Forgotten Pages
www.qadeempress.com

Reprinted by Qadeem Press in 2025

Find our titles on your favourite online bookstore using the keyword 'Qadeem Press'

500

Questions and Answers On Islamic Jurisprudence

Compiled and translated by:

Muḥammad M. Abdul-Fattah

Edited by:

Reima Y. Shakeir

Contents

Preface

Almighty Allah has revealed the Qur'ān to His Prophet Muḥammad and inspired the *Shar'ī* to him to serve, along with the Qur'ān, as the main and primary sources of the religion of Islam. *Fiqh* or Islamic Jurisprudence can be described as one of the basic digests or products of these two sources, as it covers knowledge which encompasses many aspects of the Muslim's life both secularly and religiously.

Being keen to propagate religious knowledge in general especially among the English-speaking Muslims, We introduce to the readers this book which presents **500 questions** and provides answers to these questions in a simple manner which is apt to facilitate an easy understanding of the main sections of *Fiqh* from *Ṭahārah* (purification) to *mīrāth* (inheritance). Moreover, these questions cover the basic information related to each section as well as hundreds of the most questionable matters which Muslims inquire about daily or occasionally.

We thanks everyone who has helped in preparing, translating, editing, or publishing this book, or during any stage of work. We also invoke Allah to make this effort purely exerted for His Sake and to bless and reward all those who have participated in preparing it to be in this hopefully comprehensive form.

Qadeem Press

Introduction

All praises are due to Allah, Lord of the worlds, and peace and blessings be upon His Prophet Muḥammad, his household, his Companions, and whoever follows them on the path of guidance until the Day of Resurrection.

Allah has gifted some people with knowledge so that other people can ask them about what they may need to know concerning their religious life and their worldly affairs in general. *Fiqh* represents a basic and fundamental core of religious knowledge in Islam and in its general meaning it can denote "understanding" of the religion as an entire entity.

In order to help Muslims to understand their religion well through *Fiqh*, we have compiled a big number of questions along with their answers concerning the various sections of *Fiqh*, including purification, prayer, *Zakāh* (obligatory alms), fasting, *Ḥajj* (pilgrimage), *ʿUmrah* (minor pilgrimage), marriage, separation between spouses, oaths, vows, food, drinks, clothing, adornment, crimes, legal punishments, blood money, jurisdiction, dealings and transactions (with their various sections such as partnership, crop-sharing, mortgaging, etc.), and inheritance. These questions and answers cover the basic information related to each section as well as many of the most questionable matters that may not be included in the books which deal with *Fiqh* in general. This book also includes questions which are related to the surfacing changes in modern life, especially in subjects dealing with *Ribā* (usury), prayer shortening when traveling by air, hunting with rifles, the obligatory alms due in shares, brokerage, and many other critical matters.

We have mainly depended on the Qurʾān and the *Sharʿī*, as well as on the views of the leading Imāms of *Fiqh* especially Imām Mālik, Imām Abū Ḥanīfah, Imām Ash- Shāfiʿī, and Imām Aḥmad Ibn Ḥanbal.

For making things easy for our readers, we have inserted a glossary of Arabic terms at the end of this book. In this glossary we present an outlined yet conclusive definition of each term, aiming to help our readers to have a better knowledge of the Arabic *Shar'ī* terms which are mentioned in the different parts of the book. And important still, because this book deals with *Fiqh* and because of its inclusive and various contents, there are a good number of defined terms that may be met in any other book which has something to do with Islamic studies.

Also, for facilitating the job of keeping up with the Arabic transliterated terms, we have attached a table of transliteration at the end of the book.

Finally, we ask Allah to make this effort purely exerted for His Sake and to make it easy for as many Muslims as possible to benefit from it. Amen!

Purification (*Ṭahārah*)

Q. No. (1): What is the difference between physical or tangible purification (*Ṭahārah Ḥaqīqiyyah*) and legal or intangible purification (*Ṭahārah Ḥukmiyyah*)?

A: Faqīhs have divided purification into two sections:

1. Physical or tangible purification (*Ṭahārah Ḥaqīqiyyah*), which is purifying oneself from rea l existent impurity, such as that is found on the body, in a place, or on clothes.

2. Legal or intangible purification (*Ṭahārah Ḥukmiyyah*), which is purifying oneself from intangible impurity, by performing ablution or taking a bath. And Allah knows best.

Q. No. (2): With what should a Muslim purify himself?

A: Originally, purification is to be applied by means of pure water, as Almighty Allah states.

﴿وَأَنزَلْنَا مِنَ ٱلسَّمَآءِ مَآءً طَهُورًا ﴿٤٨﴾﴾

"And we send down pure water from the sky." [TMQ 25:48]

Water can also be used for purifying filthy garments and places. The Prophet (PBUH) is narrated to have said,

"Water is pure, and nothing makes it impure except that which changes its taste, colour, or smell."[1]

When water is not available it is sufficient that one substitutes it with *tayammum* (dry ablution), for Almighty Allah says,

﴿ فَلَمْ تَجِدُواْ مَآءً فَتَيَمَّمُواْ صَعِيدًا طَيِّبًا فَٱمْسَحُواْ بِوُجُوهِكُمْ وَأَيْدِيكُمْ ﴾

---

[1] Narrated by Ibn Mājah.

"... and you find no water, perform tayammum with clean earth and rub therewith your faces and hands..." [TMQ:4:43]

And, Allah knows best.

Q. No. (3): What are the kinds of water?

A: There are three kinds of water:

1. **Pure and purifying water**, which removes *Ḥadath* and impurity.

2. **Pure yet not purifying water**. This means that it is not valid to use it for ablution or *Ġhusl* though it is pure. An example of this is the water that has already been used in ablution.

3. **Impure water**, which a Muslim is not allowed to use for purification or removing impurity.

The first kind of water is the absolute water, that is, water which is pure in its own right and can be used for purifying other things, such as the water of rain, ice, and hail, as well as the water of springs, wells, rivers, groundwater, and seawater.

The second kind of water, which is pure yet not purifying, is like the water which a man used in ablution or *Ġhusl* when there was not any tangible impurity on his body, because if there was any such impurity the water would lose the characteristic of being pure. This indicates that this water is still pure in itself, as it was used for ablution on a clean body, but it is not purifying, that is, it is not suitable for ablution or for any other form of ritual purification for a second time, because it has become void of the characteristic of being a ritually purifying water, for it has already been used as such and thus cannot be used again for the same purpose.

The third kind of water, which is the impure water, is the water which is afflicted by impurity when its quantity is little and this impurity changes some of its qualities such as taste, colour, or smell.

It is not valid to use such water for ritual purification or removing impurity in general. And, Allah knows best.

Q. No. (4): What are the conditions of the validity of ablution?

A: These conditions can be listed as follows:

1. Washing the face once.

2. Washing the two hands up to the two elbows one time.

3. Rubbing the head (with one's wet hands) one time.

4. Washing the two feet with the two ankles one time. And, Allah knows best.

Q. No. (5): What are the acts of the *Shar'ī* related to ablution?

A: There are many acts of the *Shar'ī* related to ablution.

Below are some of them.

1. Pronouncing *tasmiyah* at the beginning of ablution by saying *Bismi-llāhi-raḥmānir-raḥīm* (In the Name of Allah, the All-Merciful, the Ever-Merciful)".

2. Washing the two hands up to the two wrists three times.

3. Rinsing the mouth three times.

4. Rinsing the nose three times.

5. Using *Siwāk*, for the Prophet (PBUH) said,

"*Siwāk* is a means of purifying the mouth and a means of satisfying the Lord."[1]

6. Starting with the organs on the right side, by washing the right organ before the left one.

---

[1] Narrated by An-Nasā'ī.

7. Running one's fingers through one's beard by passing water on to the roots of the beard hair.

8. Running one's fingers through the fingers of one's hands and feet.

9. Starting the rubbing of the head with the forelock, that is, from the upper part of the head following the forehead.

10. Rinsing the nose and the mouth with the right hand. And, Allah knows best.

Q. No. (6): What are the proprieties of ablution?

A: For considering the etiquettes and proprieties of ablution the Muslim should bear the following in mind:

1. Not to use a large amount of water.

2. Not to wash the organ in question more than three times.

3. To embrocate his organs.

4. Not to seek the help of anyone else to perform the acts of ablution for him except when disable to do that himself.

5. To say after finishing his ablution, "I testify that there is no god but Allah, and I testify that Muḥammad is His servant and His Messenger," as recommended by the Messenger of Allah (PBUH) in a Ḥadīth narrated by Muslim and others.

And, Allah knows best.

Q. No. (7): How is ablution nullified?

A: There are certain things that nullify ablution. They can be pinpointed in brief as follows.

1. Urine and excrement and whatever goes out of stool and urine ducts such as pre-seminal fluid (*madhy*) and wind.

2. Sleeping. If a man sleep lying, this nullifies ablution, yet if a man sleeps while sitting in such a way that makes him control his openings, his ablution is not invalidated because of that.

3. Vomiting a quantity contained in the mouth. If the quantity vomited is little, ablution is not nullified by that. This "little" quantity has been estimated by some Faqīhs to be less than a quantity that fills the mouth such as eructation with which some water or food goes out of the stomach.

4. The egression of blood when it flows out of the body or when it is a lot to the extent that its "flows" out.

5. Loud laughter nullifies ablution and therefore nullifies prayer. This is according to Abū Ḥanīfah. Smiling, however, does not affect either of them. On the other hand, Ash-Shāfiʿī and Aḥmad maintain that laughing does not invalidate ablution because it is not part of the *Ḥadath* that affects it. And, Allah knows best.

Q. No. (8): What is the *Sharʿī* ruling concerning arrangement when performing the acts of ablution?

A: Some Faqīhs consider arrangement when performing the acts of ablution to be one of the "conditions" that must be met for the validity of ablution. This arrangement is to be considered by washing the face first of all then the hands up to the elbows then rubbing the head then washing the feet with the ankles. This is obligatory according to Ash-Shāfiʿī and Aḥmad while Abū Ḥanīfah says that it is an act of the *Sharʿī*. And, Allah knows best.

Q. No. (9): What is the *Sharʿī* ruling concerning *Muwālāh* or continuation when performing ablution?

A: *Muwālāh* is to "continue" washing the specified organs of ablution one after the other immediately, or in other words to wash the following organ before the previous one dries. Scholars have differed concerning this matter, as some of them consider it to be an obligation while some others regard it as an act of the *Shar'ī*. And Allah knows best.

Q. No. (10): What is the *Shar'ī* ruling concerning any object that prevents water from reaching any of the specified organs of ablution?

A: One of the conditions that must be fulfilled for the validity of ablution is that none of the organs which water must reach is to be covered with anything that prevents water from reaching it, such as wax, blacktop, dough, as well as the substances that many women put on their nails in what is known as "manicure" and "pedicure". Moreover, and important still, as long as ablution is not valid because of such things, also prayer is not valid if performed with an ablution performed while the organs specified in it are covered with any of them. And, Allah knows best.

Q. No. (11): What is the *Shar'ī* ruling concerning a man who doubts if he is still in a state of ablution or not?

A: If a man performs ablution, then doubts if it has been invalidated or not, he is to deal with the matter according to the principle of "certainty," that is "Certainty does not fade away because of doubt". In other words, he remains in a state of ablution, in spite of his doubts, unless he becomes "certain" that he has been afflicted with a *Ḥadath*.

The same ruling applies if he is afflicted with *Ḥadath,* then doubts if he has performed ablution or not: the ruling here is that he is "certainly" in a state of *Ḥadath*, and so it is not permissible for him to perform prayer until he performs ablution. This is simply because "doubt" here is concerning *Ḥadath*, which invalidates ablution, and not concerning ablution itself.

The original proof in this regard is the Ḥadīth narrated by Al-Bukhārī and Muslim on the authority of Abdullāh Ibn Zayd, who said,

"Someone complained to the Prophet (PBUH) about (the case of) a man who imagines, while performing prayer, that he has been afflicted by something (i.e., *Ḥadath*), and he (PBUH) said, 'He must not leave (the prayer) unless he hears a sound or finds wind (i.e., smells wind).[1][2]

And, Allah knows best.

Q. No. (12): To what extent does sleeping nullify ablution?

A: Sleeping nullifies ablution if man is wholly engaged in it to the extent that he cannot realize whether something, such as wind, has gone out of him or not. It has been narrated on the authority of Safwan Ibn 'Assal, may Allah be pleased with him, who said,

"The Messenger of Allah (PBUH) commanded that if we are travelling, we should not take off our *khuffs* for three days along with their nights except because of *Janābah*, yet (not) because of excrement, urine, and sleeping."[3]

Thus, the Prophet (PBUH) put sleeping, urine, and excrement on the same footing. However, sleeping does not invalidate ablution absolutely as pin-pointed above. And, Allah knows best.

Q. No. (13): Does touching one's genitals nullify ablution absolutely?

A: Touching one's genitals nullifies ablution only if it is done without something that prevents direct touching with the skin. So, there is no harm if a person touches his genitals with a handkerchief, for example, in between.

Also, there is no harm if a woman touches the genitals of her husband, or her own anus, or the genitals of her child, because there is no proof in this connection. And, Allah knows best.

---

[1] i.e., unless he makes sure that he has passed wind, whether audible or inaudible.
[2] Narrated by Al-Bukhārī and Muslim.
[3] Narrated by At-Tirmidhī.

Q. No. (14): When is ablution desirable and not obligatory?

A: It is desirable, and not obligatory, for the Muslim to perform ablution for the following things:

1. For mentioning Allah, Glory be to Him, or, in other words, for saying or reciting any item of *dhikr*. This includes recitation of the Qurʾān.

2. For sleeping, because the Prophet (PBUH) said,

"If you (are about to) go to your bed (to sleep), perform ablution as you do for prayer..." to the end of the Ḥadīth.[1]

3. For having intercourse with one's wife again before performing *Ġhusl*, as well as for eating, drinking, or sleeping when being in a state of *Janābah*. It has been narrated on the authority of ʿĀʾishah, may Allah be pleased with her, that, "whenever the Prophet (PBUH) was in a state of *Janābah* and wanted to eat or sleep, he would perform ablution as he would do for prayer."[2] It has also been narrated on the authority of Abū Saʿid, may Allah be pleased with him, that the Prophet (PBUH) said,

"If any one of you has intercourse with his wife, then wants to do that again, let him perform ablution."[3]

4. Before performing *Ġhusl*, for it has been narrated that ʿĀʾishah, may Allah be pleased with her, said,

"Whenever the Messenger of Allah (PBUH) performed *Ġhusl* because of *Janābah*, he would wash his hands three times and perform ablution just as he would do for prayer. Then he would run (the fingers of) his hand through his hair, and when he felt that he had

---

[1] Narrated by Al-Bukhārī, Muslim, and others.
[2] Narrated by Al-Bukhārī, Muslim, and others.
[3] Narrated by Muslim, and others.

watered his skin he would pour water upon it three times then wash his whole body."[1]

5. For each prayer, because the Prophet (PBUH) used to do so, as narrated on the authority of Barīdah, may Allah be pleased with him.[2]

6. Whenever one is afflicted by something that nullifies one's ablution. It has been narrated that the Prophet (PBUH) heard the sound of Bilal's shoes in Paradise just in front of him, and he asked him, "For what did you precede me to it (Paradise)?" He said, "O Messenger of Allah! I never pronounced adhan except that I performed two *Rak'ahs* and I never had Ḥadath except that I performed ablution after it." Thereupon the Prophet (PBUH) said, "It is for that (that you preceded me)."[3]

7. For vomiting, because it has been narrated on the authority of Abū Darda', may Allah be pleased with him, that once the Messenger of Allah (PBUH) vomited and broke his fasting then performed ablution.[4] And, Allah knows best.

Q. No. (15): What are the things that make *Ġhusl* obligatory?

A: There are three things that make *Ġhusl* obligatory:

Janābah, menstruation, and postnatal bleeding.

1. *Janābah*

A Muslim becomes in a state of *Janābah* when he ejaculates semen as a result of lust even without copulation, as when semen goes out of the body on looking at or touching one's wife. This necessitates *Ġhusl* as unanimously agreed upon by scholars.

---

[1] Narrated by Al-Bukhārī, Muslim.
[2] Narrated by Muslim and others.
[3] Narrated by Al-Bukhārī and Muslim
[4] Narrated by At- Tirmidhi and Abū Dāwūd.

2. Menstruation

Whenever a woman menstruates then her menstruation period comes to an end, she must perform *Ġhusl* and no prayer that she performs is valid until she does so.

3. Postnatal bleeding

Whenever the bleeding happening during what is known as postpartum period ceases, any woman with this condition must perform *Ġhusl*, because she is jurisprudentially treated the same as a woman who has menses. And, Allah knows best.

Q. No. (16): How should *Ġhusl* because of *Janābah*, menstruation, or postnatal bleeding be performed?

A: It is "obligatory" as far as *Ġhusl* because of *Janābah* is concerned to rinse one's mouth and nose and wash one's "whole" body. As for the *Shar'ī*, a Muslim who is to perform *Ġhusl* should perform ablution first of all, just as he does for prayer. After that he should wash his whole body, letting water cover his head and all the parts of his body. Nevertheless, it will be sufficient if he washes his body without starting with ablution, simply because *Ġhusl* is what is required in this regard. Yet, he will have then neglected something better and more adequate.

Ġhusl because of menstruation or postnatal bleeding is the same as *Ġhusl* because of *Janābah* but the following things are to be considered as well:

1. To use soap and other such means of cleaning with water.

2. It is desirable for woman to undo her braids when performing *Ġhusl* because of menses to make sure that water has reached the roots of hair.

3. It is also desirable for her, after finishing *Ġhusl*, to get a perfumed piece of cloth and follow the trace of blood with it until the unpleasant smell fades away. And, Allah knows best.

Q. No. (17): What are the desirable forms of *Ġhusl*?

A: There are certain cases in which *Ġhusl* is performed as an act of the *Shar'ī* and not as a religious obligation. These are the cases in which the Prophet (PBUH) encouraged Muslims to perform *Ġhusl* yet without making that obligatory. They are as follows:

1. *Ġhusl* for Friday.

2. *Ġhusl* for any of the two Muslim feasts, namely, 'Idul- Fiṭr (Fast-breaking Day) and 'Idul- Aḍḥā (Sacrifice Day).

3. *Ġhusl* for entering into the state of *Iḥrām* for performing *Ḥajj* or *'Umrah.*

4. *Ġhusl* for entering Mecca.

5. *Ġhusl* for standing on *'Arafah.*

6. *Ġhusl* after washing the body of a dead person.

7. *Ġhusl* for every time a Muslim has intercourse with his wife.

8. *Ġhusl* after fainting. And, Allah knows best.

Q. No. (18): What is lawful and what is prohibited concerning *Ḥayḍ* and *nifās*?

A: The following rulings must be considered as far as menstruation and postnatal bleeding are concerned:

1. It is prohibited for a husband to have intercourse with his wife during menses or postnatal bleeding.

2. No woman in either of the two states is allowed to perform prayer or observe fasting.

3. No woman having menses or postnatal bleeding is to recite the Qur'ān.

4. Such a woman is not allowed to enter the mosque or circumambulate the Sacred House.

5. A woman is not in a state of purification or *Ṭahārah* as long as she is afflicted by menstruation or postnatal bleeding, because either of these two anti-purification states lasts until the menstruation or postnatal bleeding ends.

6. Either of the two states necessitates *Ġhusl* on its expiry.

7. Menstruation is the sign with which a girl is recognized as having reached the age of puberty. And, Allah knows best.

Q. No. (19): What is *Istiḥāḍah* and what is the *Shar'ī* ruling concerning it?

A: *Istiḥāḍah* is that a woman undergoes vaginal bleeding at times other than those known for menstruation and postnatal bleeding or at a time connected to either of them, and it results from the cutting of a blood vessel and so the blood is red and the bleeding resulting from this does not stop except when this cutting has been cured.

A woman who has such *Istiḥāḍah*- based bleeding is regarded as being in a state of purification, and so she can perform prayer and observe fasting as unanimously agreed upon by scholars. It is also worth mentioning that her husband can have intercourse with her as long as this takes place at a time other than that of menstruation, as maintained by most scholars.[1] And, Allah knows best.

Q. No. (20): Does woman unfasten her hair when performing *Ġhusl*?

A: It is generally obligatory that the person performing *Ġhusl* let water reach all parts of his or her body including the roots of hair of the head and that of the beard. However, if a woman's hair is plaited,

[1] See *Al-Mughnī*, 1/339.

she does not have to unfasten her plaits. Rather, it is permissible for her to pour water on her head on condition that it reaches the roots of her hair. This is derived from the Ḥadīth narrated on the authority of Umm Salamah, may Allah be pleased with her. She said,

"I said, 'O Messenger of Allah! I fasten the plaits of (the hair of) my head, so should I unfasten it when performing *Ġhusl* because of *Janābah*?' He said, 'It is only sufficient for you to pour on your head three handfuls of water then pour water on the rest of your body and thus you will be purified." [1]

Faqīhs refer the permissibility of keeping plaits unfastened to the difficulty it causes on the part of women, unlike the beard as it is not difficult to let water reach its root. And, Allah knows best.

Q. No. (21): What is the *Shar'ī* ruling concerning intercourse that takes place between a man and his immature wife or between a woman and her immature husband? Must they perform *Ġhusl*?

A: Ibn Qudamah has mentioned in his *Al-Mughnī* that Imām Aḥmad maintains that in either of the two cases mentioned in the question both the man and the girl and the woman and the boy must perform *Ġhusl*. Imām Aḥmad commented, "Would 'Ā'ishah not perform *Ġhusl* whenever the Prophet (PBUH) copulated with her?"[2] meaning when she was still a child. And, Allah knows best.

Q. No. (22): What is the *Shar'ī* ruling concerning a woman whose husband had intercourse with her then her period started before performing *Ġhusl*?

A: She does not have to perform *Ġhusl* because of *Janābah* yet when she performs *Ġhusl* after the end of her menses, she should perform it "once" for "both" menstruation and *Janābah*, "intending" this before starting the *Ġhusl*. This is the view of Imām Aḥmad.[3] However,

---

[1] Narrated by At-Tirmidhī.
[2] See *Al-Mughnī*, 1/206.
[3] See *Al-Mughnī*, 1/210.

some scholars, like *An-Nakha'i*, say that she must perform *Ġhusl* for *Janābah* then perform it after the end of her menses. Some others maintain that it is obligatory upon her to wash her vagina only. Still, Aḥmad's view is the correct one. And, Allah knows best.

Q. No. (23): What is prohibited as far as a person is in a state of *Janābah*?

A: It is prohibited for a person who is in a state of *Janābah* to do five things:

1. To perform prayer whether it is obligatory or voluntary, because Almighty Allah says,

﴿ وَإِن كُنتُمْ جُنُبًا فَٱطَّهَّرُواْ ﴾

"*... If you are in a state of Janābah, purify yourself (bathe your whole body) ...*" [TMQ: 5:6]

Allah also says,

﴿يَـٰٓأَيُّهَا ٱلَّذِينَ ءَامَنُواْ لَا تَقْرَبُواْ ٱلصَّلَوٰةَ وَأَنتُمْ سُكَـٰرَىٰ حَتَّىٰ تَعْلَمُواْ مَا تَقُولُونَ وَلَا جُنُبًا إِلَّا عَابِرِى سَبِيلٍ حَتَّىٰ تَغْتَسِلُواْ ﴿٤٣﴾﴾

"*you who believe! Approach not prayer when you are in a drunken state until you know (the meaning) of what you utter, nor when you are in a state of Janābah (and have not yet taken a bath) except when traveling on the road, till you wash your whole body....*" [TMQ: 4:43]

2. To circumambulate the *Ka'bah*, because the Prophet (PBUH) said,

"*Ṭawāf* (circumambulation round the *Ka'bah*) is like prayer, yet you do not speak during it, so let him whoever speaks (during *Ṭawāf*) say nothing but good."[1]

---

[1] Narrated by At-Tirmidhī

3. To stay in a mosque in general or for *I'tikāf*, because the Prophet (PBUH) said,

"Verily, I do not allow a woman during her menses or a person in a state of *Janābah* to (enter or stay in) a mosque."[1]

4. To recite the Qur'ān whether from a *Muṣḥaf* or by heart, because it has been narrated on the authority of 'Alī, may Allah be pleased with him, that nothing would hinder the Prophet (PBUH) from the Qur'ān except *Janābah*.[2]

5. To touch or carry a *Muṣḥaf*, because an honourable Ḥadīth reads,

"...and that no one should touch (a book containing) the Qur'ān except a purified person (i.e., in a state of purification)."[3]

Nevertheless, it is permissible for a person in a state of *Janābah* to say any other item of *dhikr* such as invocation, because it has been narrated on the authority of 'Ā'ishah, may Allah be pleased with her, that "the Messenger of Allah (PBUH) used to remember Allah in all conditions,"[4] meaning in all times and conditions, whether he was in a state of ablution or purification in general or not. And, Allah knows best.

Q. No. (24): What are the proprieties of answering the call of nature in Islam?

A: The following proprieties and morals are to be considered whenever a person wants to pass urine or evacuate the bowls:

1. To keep himself away from people's sight, especially if he is in the open as in a desert. It has been narrated on the authority of Jābir,

---

[1] Narrated by Abū Dāwūd
[2] Narrated by Abū Dāwūd and Ibn Mājah
[3] Narrated by Mālik, and it was part of the letter sent by the Prophet (pbuh) to the people of Yemen
[4] Narrated by Muslim.

may Allah be pleased with him, that "whenever the Prophet (PBUH) wanted to excrete, he would go off where nobody would see him"![1]

2. To seek refuge with Allah in the way specified by the Prophet (PBUH) before sitting to relieve oneself. It has been narrated on the authority of Anas Ibn Mālik, who said,

"Whenever the Prophet (PBUH) (was about to) enter the *Khalā'* (the place where people relieve themselves), he would say, 'O Allah! I seek refuge with You from the males and females of devils!"[2]

It has also been narrated that whatever (PBUH) went out of the *Khalā'*, he would say, (O Allah), Forgive me.[3]

The wisdom behind this is that the places where people answer the call of nature are mostly visited by devils, as narrated by Ibn Mājah, so the Muslim should seek refuge with Allah from their evil. On the other hand, he asks Allah to forgive him on leaving such places because he has neglected remembering him (orally) during his stay there.

3. To enter with the left foot and leave with the right one, as a way of following the example of the Prophet (PBUH) who, as narrated on the authority of Hafsah, may Allah be pleased with her, "used to make his right (hand) for his food, drink, and clothes and his left (hand) for things other than that".[4]

4. Not to enter such places with whatever thing in which or on which Allah is mentioned, such as a *Muṣḥaf* or a ring on which Allah's name is carved. It has been narrated on the authority of Anas, may Allah be pleased with him, that "the Prophet (PBUH) wore a ring on which

---

[1] Narrated by Abū Dāwūd and Ibn Mājah.

[2] Narrated by At-Tirmidhī.

[3] Narrated by At-Tirmidhī.

[4] Narrated by Abū Dāwūd. The quotation means that the right foot and the left one is used in the same way as the right hand and the left hand.

'Muḥammad is the Messenger of Allah' was carved, and he used to take it off whenever he entered the *Khalā'*.[1]

5. To protect himself against the drizzle of urine. It has been narrated on the authority of Ibn ʿAbbās, who said,

"Once the Prophet (PBUH), while passing through one of the graveyards of Medina or Mecca heard the voices of two persons who were being tortured in their graves. The Prophet (PBUH) said, 'These two persons are being tortured not for a major sin (to avoid).' The Prophet (PBUH) then added, 'Yes, (they are being tortured for a major sin). Indeed, one of them never saved himself from being soiled with his urine while the other used to go about with calumnies (to make enmity between friends).' The Prophet then asked for a green leaf of a date-palm tree, broke it into two pieces, and put one on each grave. On being asked why he had done so, he replied, 'I hope that their torture might be lessened, until these get dried."[2]

6. Not to speak or mention Allah with the tongue when relieving oneself, for it has been narrated on the authority of Ibn ʿUmar, may Allah be pleased with him, that "a man came to the Prophet (PBUH) while passing urine and saluted him yet the Prophet (PBUH) did not salute him back until he performed ablution."[3] Therefore, no one is to reply to a salutation, repeat what the *Mu'adhdhin* says, or praise Allah if he sneezes while answering the call of nature.

7. It is legally detestable (*Makrūh*) for the Muslim to answer the call of nature on the road or in the shadow. Imām Muslim has narrated that the Prophet (PBUH) said, "Be on your guard against the two curse bringers." The listeners asked, "And what are the two curse bringers?" He (PBUH) said, "(They are done by) a person who

---

[1] Narrated by Ibn Mājah.
[2] Narrated by Al-Bukhārī and Muslim
[3] Narrated by Muslim and Abū Dāwūd

evacuates the bowls on the road of people or (a person who does so) in the shadow they (shade themselves in)."

8. To invoke Allah after relieving himself. It has been narrated on the authority of ʿĀʾishah, who said, "Whenever the Messenger of Allah (PBUH) went out of the *Khalāʾ*, he used to say, '(O Allah!) Forgive me!"[1] According to another narration, the Muslim can say on leaving this place, "Praise be to Allah Who has taken harm away from me and protected me (from evil)!"[2]

9. Not to face the *qiblah* or turn his back toward it, because the Prophet (PBUH) said, as narrated on the authority of Jābir, may Allah be pleased with him,

"Whenever any one of you sits to answer the call of nature, let him not face the *qiblah* or turn his back toward it."[3]

10. It is legally detestable for the Muslim to urinate while standing except when necessary. It has been narrated on the authority of ʿĀʾishah, who said,

"Do not believe whoever tells you that the Messenger of Allah (PBUH) urinated while standing. He never urinated except while sitting."[4]

And, Allah knows best.

Q. No. (25): A woman does not perform prayer during her menses, but is it obligatory on her to make up for these prayers after her period has ended?

A: No woman must make up for the prayers she did not perform during her menses or postnatal bleeding, however she, who

---

[1] Narrated by At-Tirmidhī.
[2] Narrated by Ibn Mājah.
[3] Narrated by At-Tirmidhī.
[4] Narrated by At-Tirmidhī. "This Ḥadīth according to ʿĀʾishah is the best and most authentic (proof) in this regard."

commented, must make up for the fasting she did not observe during menses or postnatal bleeding. It has been narrated that ʿĀʾishah, may Allah be pleased with her, said,

"Any one of us (women) would have menses and we would be commanded to make up for (the unobserved) fasting yet we were never commanded to make up for (the unperformed) prayers."[1]

And, Allah knows best.

Q. No. (26): What should a woman do if her postnatal bleeding exceeds forty days then her normal period of menstruation starts?

A: In this case the bleeding during this "normal" period is treated as that of menses. However, if the postnatal bleeding exceeds forty days and does not coincide with her normal period of menstruation, this bleeding after forty days is to be treated as *Istiḥāḍah* in which her husband can have intercourse with her and she must resume performing prayers with a new ablution for each prayer.[2] And, Allah knows best.

Q. No. (27): How should man deal with his wife during her menses?

A: It is lawful for the man whose wife is menstruating to sleep with her in one bed and to play with her and enjoy all the parts of her body with the exception of what is between the navel and the knees. This is the view adopted by Abū Ḥanīfah, Mālik, and Ash-Shāfiʿī. It has been narrated that ʿĀʾishah, may Allah be pleased with her, said, "Whenever any one of us (i.e., the Prophet's wives) was menstruating and the Messenger of Allah (PBUH) wanted to have sex with her, he would order her to wrap herself then he would have sex with her." She added, "But who amongst you would control himself as the Prophet (PBUH) would?"[3] Having sex in this narration refers to such things as caressing, kissing, and the like, but not

---

[1] Narrated by Al-Bukhārī, Muslim, and At-Tirmidhī

[2] See Al-Mughnī, 1/346.

[3] Narrated by Muslim.

intercourse. However, some Faqīhs regard it as lawful that man enjoys all the parts of his wife's body except her vagina because the Prophet (PBUH) said, "Do everything except copulation."[1] Yet still, the view of the majority (i.e., the one adopted by the three Imāms above) is better for those who want to guard themselves against wrong, for it is difficult for many men to control themselves when being so close to this (temporarily) prohibited place in their women's bodies. And, Allah knows best.

Q. No. (28): If a woman's period starts shortly before the afternoon, for example, and she has not performed the *'Aṣr* Prayer yet, is it obligatory that she makes up for the *Zuhr* Prayer when the period comes to an end?

A: Yes, she must make up for this prayer, because it was obligatory before her period started. It other words, this prayer was to be performed obligatorily, and she was obliged not to perform it because her menses started. Therefore, the *Zuhr* Prayer remains obligatory unlike the *'Aṣr* Prayer that follows it along with the other Prayers until the end of the period. Moreover, she must make up for this *Zuhr* Prayer simply because she witnessed (at least the beginning of) its due time when she was still in a state of purification, that is, her period had not started when the time of the *Zuhr* Prayer became due. And, Allah knows best.

Q. No. (29): If a woman's period expires shortly before the afternoon, for example, and when she has performed *Ġhusl* the time of the *'Aṣr* Prayer becomes due, is it obligatory that she makes up for the *Zuhr* Prayer?

A: Yes, she must perform the *Zuhr* Prayer in this case. Not only this, if a woman's period of menstruation or postnatal bleeding expires before sunset, she must perform "both" the *Zuhr* Prayer and the *'Aṣr* Prayer of the day in question. Likewise, if the period comes to an end

[1] Narrated by Al-Bukhārī and Muslim

before dawn, she must perform "both" the *Maghrib* Prayer and the *'Ishā'* Prayer of the night in question. This is because the time of the second prayer is to be the time of the first one (in the pinpointed pairs of prayers) when there is an excuse. This is the view adopted by the majority of scholars including Mālik, Ash-Shāfi'ī, and Aḥmad, as mentioned by Ibn Taymīyah in his *Fatāwā*.[1] And, Allah knows best.

Q. No. (30): What is the period of wiping over *khuffs*?

A: The period of wiping over *khuffs* is three days with their nights for a traveller and one day with its night for a person in residence. And, Allah knows best.

Q. No. (31): What are the conditions of wiping over *khuffs*?

A: There are certain conditions that must be met by those who want to wipe over *khuffs*. They can be summarized in the following points:

1. To wear them while being fully purified, that is, after performing ablution and washing the feet.

2. To wipe over the surface of the *khuffs*.

3. The *khuff* must not contain any holes through which a part of the foot can be seen.

4. The *khuff* must cover the foot up to the part over the ankle.

5. The person who is to wear *khuffs* must not be in a state of *Janābah*. And, Allah knows best.

Q. No. (32): How should the Muslim wipe over *khuffs*?

A: According to the *Shar'ī*, the Muslim should start wiping over *khuffs* by placing his right hand on the right *khuff* and the left hand on the left *khuff* then he should stretch his hands over his *khuffs* up to the leg. And, Allah knows best.

---

[1] See Ibn Taymīyah, *Majmū' al-Fatāwā*, 2/434.

Q. No. (33): Is it permissible to wipe over socks just like *khuffs*?

A: It is permissible to wipe over socks if they are thick, or made of leather, or if the upper part or the lower part of them are covered with leather, as they will be then like *khuffs*. It has been narrated by At-Tirmidhī that the Prophet (PBUH) performed ablution and wiped over socks. In a word, it is permissible to wipe over socks if they are "thick," for, with this thickness, they resemble *khuffs*. And, Allah knows best.

Q. No. (34): What are the conditions of wiping over socks?

A: 1. They must be thick enough that the person who is wearing them can walk while wearing them (alone).

2. They must cover the feet up to the ankles.

3. One must wear them when being in a state of purification (i.e., in a state of ablution).

4. Wetness must not reach the feet on wiping over them, because it is not lawful to do washing and wiping together.

5. They must not contain any holes through which the feet can be seen. Accordingly, it is not permissible to wipe over thin socks because they are in no way like *khuffs*. And, Allah knows best.

Q. No. (35): When does wiping over *khuffs* become invalidated?

A: Wiping over *khuffs* or thick socks is invalidated whenever the ablution performed by the person who is wearing them is nullified, as well as when the period specified by the Legislator comes to an end. This period is three days with their nights for a person on a journey and one day and one night for a person who is in residence, that is, who is not on a journey. It is also invalidated by taking off one of the two *khuffs* or socks, and when the person wearing them becomes in a state of *Janābah*. And, Allah knows best.

Q. No. (36): What is the *Shar'ī* ruling concerning wiping over bandages?

A: For the same purpose of making things easy for the Muslim, Islam allows him to wipe over bandages because, under such circumstances, the bandaged wounds need cicatrisation and recovery, and this requires that they should not be washed with water every now and then. That is why the Prophet (PBUH) allowed 'Alī, may Allah be pleased with him, to wipe over the bandage when his wrist was broken on the Day of Uhud. And, Allah knows best.

Q. No. (37): What is the difference between wiping over *khuffs* and wiping over bandages?

A: Ibn Qudamah has mentioned in his Al-Mughnī that there are five differences between wiping over *khuffs* and wiping over bandages, as follows:

1. It is not permissible to wipe over the bandage except when it is harmful to remove it. This is not the case with *khuffs*.

2. The whole bandage must be wiped over, unlike *khuffs*.

3. It is permissible to wipe over the bandage without specification of time.

4. One can wipe over the bandage in a case of major purification, as in *Ġhusl*, unlike wiping over *khuffs* which is done only in the case of ablution.

5. It is not a condition that the bandage must be set in a state of purification, because of the Ḥadīth narrated on the authority of Jābir concerning the man whose head was broken.[1] And, Allah knows best.

---

[1] See Al-Mughni, 1/278. The Ḥadīth referred to above has been narrated by Abū Dāwūd and it reads that Jābir ibn 'Abdullāh, may Allah be pleased with him, said, "We were on a journey when the head of a man from among us was broken with

Q. No. (38): What are the reasons for which *tayammum* becomes permissible?

A: It is permissible to switch to *tayammum* for the following reasons:

1. If water is not available.

2. If a person is afflicted by a disease or a surgery because of which water becomes harmful.

3. If the water available is too cold to the extent that it causes harm and there is nothing to heat it with.

4. If a person needs the water available to drink when he is on a journey or in a place where he does not find water, or if he is imprisoned and cannot perform ablution because of the prison guards. In any of such cases, he is allowed to perform *tayammum* because it goes under the same ruling of not finding water. And, Allah knows best.

Q. No. (39): What are the conditions of *tayammum*?

A: The following conditions must be met so that *tayammum* can be valid:

1. Intention, by intending to remove *Ḥadath* or to perform something that makes one allowed to perform prayer.

2. The earth used for *tayammum* must be clean.

---

a stone. Then that man had a wet dream, so he asked his fellows, 'Do you know if I have a legal excuse (with this condition) to perform *tayammum*? They said, 'We do not know any legal excuse (which justifies that) as you can use water. Therefore, the man performed *Ġhusl* and died (as a result of that). When we came (back) to the Messenger of Allah (pbuh), he was told about that, so he said. "They killed him! May Allah hill them! Why did they not ask (about what they did not know) as they did not know (it)? The only remedy of ignorance is to inquire. It would have been sufficient for him to bandage his wound with a piece of cloth then pass a wet hand on it and wash the rest of his body."

3. There must be no water, or it is available, but the Muslim cannot use it because of illness or any tantamount harm such as extreme cold. And, Allah knows best.

Q. No. (40): How should the Muslim perform *tayammum*?

A: First of all, the person who is to perform *tayammum* must intend that he will remove his *Ḥadath* then recite *tasmiyah*. After that he must strike clean earth with both his hands and rub his whole face with both of them then strike the earth again and rub his forearms up to the elbows. Interestingly enough, the elbows are required here because *tayammum* is like ablution.

The majority of scholars maintain that two strikes are required for *tayammum*: one with which one rubs one's face and one with which one rubs one's hands up to the elbows. Yet still, some scholars view that it is permissible to do only one strike with which one rubs one's face and hands, and this is the view adopted by Al-Bukhārī and Aḥmad, yet the first view, of the majority of scholars, is preponderant and better for those who take precautions and guard themselves against wrong. And, Allah knows best.

Q. No. (41): How is *tayammum* nullified?

A: *Tayammum* is nullified by anything that nullifies ablution because it is an alternative to it. Therefore, if a person sleeps, urinates, evacuates the bowls, or passes wind, his *tayammum* is nullified. It is also invalidated whenever a person who has lost water finds it; the general rule in this connection is: whenever water is found, *tayammum* is nullified. And, Allah knows best.

Q. No. (42): What is the said or earth which is stipulated for the validity of *tayammum*?

A: The said or earth which is stipulated for the validity of *tayammum* is pure or clean dust and things that belong to the earth such as sand, stones, and milled or ground stones. Almighty Allah says, ...

perform tayammum with clean earth... (Qur'ān: 4: 43) Lexicologists have unanimously maintained that the Arabic term "said" (translated in the Qur'ānic quotation as "earth") refers to (the material constituting) the surface of the earth whether it consists of dust or anything else. Accordingly, if it is not easy for an ill person to find dust for his *tayammum*, he can wipe the dust over the wall beside him or on the ground if it is not made of wood and use this dust for his *tayammum*. The same ruling is effective on the part of an imprisoned person. And, Allah knows best.

Q. No. (43): Is *tayammum* an alternative to ablution in everything?

A: *Tayammum* is an alternative to ablution and *Ġhusl* and, consequently, it is lawful for a Muslim in a state of *tayammum* to do whatever he is allowed to do after performing ablution or *Ġhusl*, such as performing prayer, touching the *Muṣḥaf*, and circumambulating the Ka bah. Also, it is not a condition that the Muslim performs it during the due time of a prayer, and he can perform, with one performance of *tayammum*, whatever prayers he wishes be they obligatory or voluntary. This is because *tayammum* is equal to ablution: it validates what ablution validates and is invalidated by the same things that invalidate ablution. And, Allah knows best.

Q. No. (44): What is the *Shar'ī* ruling concerning *Khitān* or circumcision, particularly for woman?

A: Circumcision is one of the five practices which are characteristics of Fiṭrah (i.e., natural disposition). It has been narrated on the authority of Abū Hurayrah, may Allah be pleased with him, that the Messenger of Allah (PBUH) said,

"Five practices are characteristics of Fiṭrah: circumcision, shaving the pubic hair, cutting the moustache short, clipping the nails, and depilating the hair of the armpits."[1]

Generally speaking, it is an obligation on the part of men and a desirable, noble deed on the part of women.

One of the proofs which confirm that circumcision is (at least) "legal" for women is that it has been narrated on the authority of ʿĀʾishah, may Allah be pleased with her, that the Messenger of Allah (PBUH) said,

"If the two circumcised organs meet, *Ġhusl* becomes obligatory."[2]

It is crystal clear that the two organs in question are man's penis and woman's vulva, and this proves that women used to be circumcised. There are other Ḥadīths which, though graded as being of weak chains of transmitters, have been authenticated by Al-Albani, the well-known scholar of Ḥadīth. An example of these Ḥadīth is the one narrated by Abū Dāwūd on the authority of Umm ʿĀṭiyyah, may Allah be pleased with her, that the Prophet (PBUH) said to a woman who used to circumcise women in Medina,

"Do not wear out[3], for this is more preferable to a woman and more likeable to a husband."

After all, the minimum (reasonable) degree in judging the issue of circumcision as far as women are concerned is that it is "desirable" for them. And, Allah knows best.

---

[1] Narrated by Al-Bukhārī.

[2] Narrated by Ibn Mājah and others.

[3] i.e., do not exaggerate in cutting the part to be circumcised.

Prayer (Ṣalāh)

Q. No. (45): Upon whom is prayer obligatory?

A: Prayer is obligatory on whoever is Muslim, mature, sane, and witnesses the due time of prayer. Also, as far as woman is concerned, she must be neither menstruating nor in postnatal condition (*nifās*). And, Allah knows best.

Q. No. (46): What are the conditions of prayer?

A: There are seven conditions or *Shurūṭ* on which the validity of prayer depends and thus if any one of them is not met prayer becomes invalid. These seven conditions are to be considered "before" performing prayer, as the conditions that must be considered "inside" prayer are called pillars or *Arkān*. Both pillars and conditions of prayer are obligations that must be fulfilled. Below are the conditions that must be fulfilled before performing prayer.

The first condition is that the Muslim must be in a state of purification, and this means that he must not be in a state of *Ḥadath* whether it is minor, as when he has passed urine for example, or major as when he is a state of *Janābah*.

The second condition is that the Muslim must be free from impurity, that is, his body and clothes must be clean and so must be the place on which he will perform prayer.

The third condition is that the Muslim must cover his *ʿAwrah* or the private parts that must be covered including his genitals.

The fourth condition is that the Muslim must face the direction of the *qiblah*, that is, his face and chest must be toward its direction.

The fifth condition is that the Muslim must make sure that the stated time of prayer has become due, and thus it is not valid that he performs prayer before or after its stated time.

The sixth condition is intention.

And Allah knows best.

Q. No. (47): What are the pillars of prayer?

A: As pinpointed in the previous answer, the conditions of prayer are the obligations that must be fulfilled "before" entering to prayer, whereas its pillars are the obligations that are to be fulfilled "inside" it. Below are the pillars or the basic elements of which prayer consists, as follows.

The first pillar is *Takbīrat al-Iḥrām* or the act of *Takbīr* that is said at the very beginning of prayer and by which all the sayings and acts which are not related to prayer become prohibited.

The second pillar is standing, yet it is a pillar as far as obligatory prayers are concerned for those who are able to do it. However, he who is not able to stand in prayer, because of a surgery or any other cause, can perform prayer according to his capability, whether sitting on a chair or lying down on a bed.

The third pillar of prayer is recitation. It is enjoined upon a performer of prayer to recite while standing *Al-Fātiḥah* (the opening chapter of the Qur'ān) and after that he may recite any other part of the Qur'ān.

The fourth pillar is bowing down or *Rukūʿ* after finishing recitation. The prescribed act of bowing down is considered to be done properly when the Muslim bends in such a manner that his hands reach his knees; so, if he just lowers his head and does not bend along with his back, his bowing down is not valid and consequently his prayer is not valid.

The fifth pillar of prayer is raising one's head and standing straightly after bowing down.

The sixth pillar is prostration, which is placing one's face including the nose on the ground. This prostration is to be done twice in each *Rak'ah* as follows: the Muslim must prostrate and remain quiet in that position then sit and remain quiet in that position then prostrate again and remain quiet in that position.

The seventh pillar of prayer is the sitting between the two prostrations. According to the *Imāms* of *Fiqh*, this is an obligation which is to be done for separating the two prostrations. Yet, it should be known that, as narrated on the authority of *Al-Barā'*, may Allah be pleased with him, "the standing, the bowing, the standing after bowing, the prostration, and the sitting in between the two prostrations as done by the Messenger of Allah (PBUH) was approximately equal (in duration)."[1]

The eighth pillar is the last sitting with *tashahhud*, and it is an obligation as unanimously agreed upon by Faqīhs, as prayer is not valid without it.

The last sitting is the one after the second *Rak'ah* in the *Fajr* Prayer, after the third *Rak'ah* in the *Maghrib* Prayer, and after the fourth *Rak'ah* in the *Zuhr*, *'Aṣr*, and *'Ishā'* prayers. The first sitting is that is done after performing the first two *Rak'ahs* in the *Zuhr*, *'Aṣr*, *Maghrib*, and *'Ishā'* prayers.

The ninth pillar is *Salām* or *Taslīm*, which is the salutation made after finishing what is known *as As-Ṣalāh al-Ibrāhīmiyyah* or the *Ibrāhīmi* Invocation of Blessings, and it is recited after the *tashahhud* referred to at the end of the previous pillar. After saying *As-Ṣalāh al-Ibrāhīmiyyah* a performer of prayer makes two *Taslīmahs* or salutations, one while looking on his right side and the other on his left side, each with the words, "*As-salāmu 'alaykum wa raḥmatullāh* (Peace and Allah's Mercy be upon you)."

---

[1] Narrated by Al-Bukhārī.

The tenth pillar of prayer is the arrangement of pillars, that is, to start with *Takbīrat al-Iḥrām*, or the act of *Takbīr* that is said at the very beginning of prayer, then the recitation then bowing down then prostration two times with the sitting between the two of them then standing for the second *Rakʿah* and so on until the Muslim finishes his prayer with the *Taslīm*. This arrangement of the pillars is itself a pillar as unanimously agreed upon by scholars.

Q. No. (48): The acts of the *Sharʿī* related to prayer?

A: There are certain acts of the *Sharʿī* that a performer of prayer should do and preserve so that Allah may reward him for that. However, if he does not do them, his prayer will be valid though it will not be performed quite correctly; that is, typically according to the *Sharʿī*. These acts are as follows:

1. Raising hands at the beginning of prayer opposite to the shoulders in such a manner that the ends of the fingers are opposite to the upper part of the ears and the palms are. opposite to the shoulders. To consider the *Sharʿī* exactly in this regard, the raising of the hands should coincide with *Takbīrat al-Iḥrām*.

2. Joining hands, and to consider the *Sharʿī* exactly in this regard the Muslim should put his right hand on the left one above the navel or below the chest.

3. *Istiftāḥ*, or the invocation with which the Muslim commences his prayer after *Takbīrat al-Iḥrām*.

4. Saying *amin* (amen) after finishing the recitation of *Al-Fātiḥah* whether the performer of prayer is leading people or led by someone.

5. Reciting something from the Qurʾān after *Al-Fātiḥah*.

6. Saying *Takbīr* on moving from one act to another.

7. *Tasbīḥ* in bowing and prostration, by saying "*Subḥāna rabbīya-l-ʿaẓīm* (Glory be to my Lord, the Greatest) in bowing and "*Subḥāna rabbīya-l-aʿlā* (Glory be to my Lord, the Highest)" in prostration three times each.

8. Spreading the fingers apart and placing the hands on the knees in bowing.

9. Invoking Allah between the two prostrations.

10. Placing the hands on the thighs on saying *tashahhud*.

11. Pointing with the forefinger on saying "*ʾAshhadu allā ilāha illā-llāh* (I testify that there is no god but Allah)". After that the forefinger is to be lowered.

12. Invoking blessings on the Prophet (PBUH). This is the invocation of blessings known as *As-Ṣalāh al-Ibrāhīmiyyah* which is said after *tashahhud*. It is an act of the *Sharʿī* according to the majority of Faqīhs, yet some followers of Abū Ḥanīfah maintain that it is an obligation without which prayer is invalid.

13. Invoking Allah before *Salām* (salutation) at the end of prayer.

And, Allah knows best.

Q. No. (49): What are the things detested in prayer?

A: There are certain things that should not be done in prayer, and in spite of the fact that these things do not invalidate prayer they reduce the reward of it. These things are as follows:

1. Performing prayer while being prompted by the call of nature.

2. Playing with one's beard or one's body.

3. Raising one's sight toward the sky.

4. Looking hither and thither in prayer.

5. Keeping one's hand on one's waist in prayer, because this contradicts the morals that must be considered in prayer.

6. Performing prayer while feeling sleepy.

7. Raising one's head after bowing or prostration before the Imām.

8. Stretching one's forearms on the ground while prostrating.

9. Reciting something from the Qur'ān while bowing or prostrating.

10. Prostrating on the forehead only without the nose.

11. *Sadl* or wrapping oneself in one's garment while one's hands are inside the garment, because the Prophet (PBUH) forbade *Sadl* in prayer and that one should cover one's mouth while performing prayer.[1]

12. Removing pebbles and levelling sand while performing prayer on the ground.

13. Performing prayer in improper clothes.

14. Performing prayer in brocaded clothes or clothes containing something that distracts one from one's prayer.

15. Performing prayer in congregation after eating garlic or anything which has a detestable smell.

16. It is detestable for men to clap the hands in prayer, unlike women.

17. It is detestable for whoever leads people in prayer to prolong recitation or prayer as a whole. And, Allah knows best.

Q. No. (50): When and where is it detestable to perform prayer?

A: It is detestable to perform prayer at three times, as follows:

---

[1] Narrated by At-Tirmidhī.

1. When the sun begins to rise until it is fully up.

2. When the sun is at its height at midday until it passes over the meridian.

3. When the sun draws near to setting until it sets.

It is detestable to perform prayer at any of these times because the sun-worshipers worship it during them so Muslims have been forbidden to perform prayer at these times so that they may not do something that those polytheists do. There are other times at which it is detestable to perform voluntary prayers, as follows: after performing the obligatory prayer of the *ʿAṣr* and after performing the obligatory prayer of the *Fajr*.

As it is detestable for the Muslim to perform prayer at certain times, it is also detestable for him to perform it in certain places. This detestability may be either because these places are dirty, such as bathrooms and dunghills, or because it is dangerous to perform prayer therein, such as the pens of camels, for camels often bolt and may tread on the person who may be performing prayer in their place. The detestability in question may moreover be due to the sanctity of the place, such as the roof of the *Kaʿbah*.

And, Allah knows best.

Q. No. (51): What are the things which invalidate prayer?

A: There are certain things that invalidate prayer and necessitate that whoever does any of them must repeat the prayer. These things are as follows:

1. Eating and drinking invalidate prayer because a performer of prayer is having a confidential talk with his Lord while performing prayer and eating and drinking violate the essence of this talk.

2. Speaking while performing prayer invalidates it whether the person does this intentionally or forgetfully, because talking to people is not fitting during it as the Prophet (PBUH) said.[1]

3. Doing a great deal of action or making consecutive movements nullify prayer because it then becomes similar to playing and amusement and contains no submissiveness.

4. Laughing, especially loudly, invalidates prayer as unanimously agreed upon by Faqīhs.

5. Neglecting any of the conditions or pillars of prayer[2] nullifies prayer because these pillars and conditions are obligations that must be considered. And, Allah knows best.

Q. No. (52): What is the *Shar'ī* ruling concerning a person who neglects prayer?

A: Whoever neglects prayer because he denies it is a disbeliever, as agreed upon by scholars. Yet still, a person may neglect prayer while believing in it and that it is an obligation (*fard*), but he has neglected it out of laziness or because he has been distracted from performing it by something which is not considered by the Sharī'ah to be a legal excuse. Some Ḥadīths have stated explicitly that such a person has become a disbeliever and that he must be executed. For example, it has been narrated by Aḥmad and others that the Prophet (PBUH) said,

"Between man and disbelief is negligence of prayer."[3]

---

[1] Narrated by Muslim.
[2] Revise the conditions and pillars of prayer in some preceding answers in this part of the book.
[3] Narrated by Muslim

It has also been narrated on the authority of Ibn ʿAbbās, may Allah be pleased with him, that the Prophet (PBUH) said that "whoever neglects the obligatory prayer it is legal to shed his blood."[1]

However, many scholars, including Abū Ḥanīfah, Mālik, and Ash-Shāfiʿī, say that a person who neglects prayer not out of denial is not a disbeliever, yet he is dissolute (*Fāsiq*). Mālik, Ash- Shāfiʿī, and others maintain that such a person must be asked to repent and if he does not repent, he is to be executed, yet Abū Ḥanīfah says that he is not to be executed but to be punished with a discretionary punishment (*Taʿzīr*) and imprisoned until he performs prayer. And, Allah knows best.

Q. No. (53): What is the *Sharʿī* ruling concerning a person who does not know the *qiblah*?

A: If a person is bewildered concerning the *qiblah* while being on a journey or in a place away from people and he does not have any one whom he can ask about it, he should do his best to estimate its direction then perform prayer accordingly. Besides, he does not have to repeat the prayer if his estimation is proved to be wrong later on, simply because he is juristically ordered to seek to know the *qiblah* and he has already done that. And, Allah knows best.

Q. No. (54): What is the *Sharʿī* ruling concerning a person who performs a prayer before its due time, then realizes that?

A: In this case, he must repeat the prayer, because one of the conditions of prayer is that the Muslim must perform each prayer after its time has become due, and not before that. Almighty Allah says,

"*...Verily, prayer is enjoined on the believers at fixed hours.*" [TMQ: 4: 103]

And, Allah knows best.

---

[1] Narrated by Abū Ya'la

Q. No. (55): What should the Muslim do if he wants to join congregational prayer while the Imām is bowing?

A: In this case he must say *Takbīr*, as his first *Takbīrah* which is known as *Takbīrat al-Iḥrām*, while standing then say *Takbīr* again and bow. If he catches the bowing with the Imām while the latter is already bowing and manages to say even one *Tasbīḥah*,[1] then he will have caught the whole *Rak'ah*, otherwise, he will have missed the *Rak'ah*. A common mistake which many people commit in this context is that they say *Takbīrat al-Iḥrām* while bowing to make sure that they will catch the *Rak'ah* with the Imām, and even some of them say *Takbīr* only once for both *Takbīrat al-Iḥrām* and bowing. This invalidates prayer because it violates one of the pillars of prayer, namely "standing," for *Takbīrat al-Iḥrām* is to be said in the standing position. And, Allah knows best.

Q. No. (56): What is the *Shar'ī* ruling concerning a person who does not recite *Al-Fātiḥah* out of forgetfulness?

A: According to the Ḥanafīs, he must perform the two prostrations of forgetfulness at the end of the prayer, yet if he does not recite it on purpose, he must repeat the prayer. Most Faqīhs, however, maintain that recitation of *Al-Fātiḥah* is an obligation and without fulfilling it prayer is invalid, unless the performer of prayer is behind an Imām in a congregational prayer. It has been narrated on the authority of Jābir, may Allah be pleased with him, that the Prophet (PBUH) said,

"Whoever performs (even) one *Rak'ah* in which he does not recite the opening chapter of the Book, has not performed (it validly), unless he is (performing prayer) behind an Imām."[2]

And, Allah knows best.

---

[1] *Tasbīḥah* in this position of bowing down is to say. *Subḥāna rabbīyal-'aẓīm* (Glory be to my Lord, the Greatest).
[2] Narrated by At-Tirmidhī.

Q. No. (57): On how many organs must a performer of prayer prostrate?

A: Prostration must be performed on seven organs. The Prophet (PBUH) said, "I have been commanded to prostrate on seven bones,"[1] and these seven bones are the (extremities) of the two feet, the two knees, the two hands, and the face; and the face includes both the forehead and the nose, And, Allah knows best.

Q. No. (58): What is the best formula of invoking blessings on the Prophet (PBUH) in prayer?

A: The best formula of invoking blessings on the Prophet (PBUH) and which is known as *As-Ṣalāh al-Ibrāhīmiyyah* is the following one, as narrated by Muslim and An-Nasā'ī: "*Allāhumma ṣalli ʿalā Muḥammad wa ʿalā āli Muḥammad. Kamā ṣallayta ʿalā Ibrāhīm wa ʿalā āli Ibrāhīm. Wa bārik ʿalā Muḥammad wa ʿalā āli Muḥammad. Kamā bārakta ʿalā Ibrāhīm wa ʿalā āli Ibrāhīm fi-l-ʿālamīn. Innaka ḥamīdun majīd.* (O Allah! Send *Ṣalāh*[2] on Muḥammad and on the family of Muḥammad as You sent *Ṣalāh* on Ibrāhīm (Abraham) and on the family of Ibrāhīm. And bless Muḥammad and the family of Muḥammad as You blessed Ibrāhīm and the family of Ibrāhīm in the worlds. Verily, you are Praiseworthy and Honourable.)" And, Allah knows best.

Q. No. (59): What is the *Sharʿī* ruling concerning the first sitting in prayer?

A: The first sitting in prayer is the one done after the first two *Rakʿahs* of a prayer consisting of three or four *Rakʿahs*. Generally, this sitting is an act of the *Sharʿī* according to most Faqīhs but some Faqīhs, like Abū Ḥanīfah, says that it is a Wājib (duty) of prayer and if anyone forgets it, he must perform the two prostrations of

---

[1] Narrated by Muslim.

[2] Here: graces, honours, blessings, mercy, etc

forgetfulness. A performer of prayer says *tashahhud* in this sitting yet does not say *As-Ṣalāh al-Ibrāhīmiyyah.*[1] And, Allah knows best.

Q. No. (60): What is the *Sharʿī* criterion concerning movement in prayer?

A: Faqīhs maintain that moving in prayer is considered to be legally much (*Kathīr*) if it makes people think that the person who does such moving is not in prayer. Some Faqīhs have estimated this "much moving" to be three frequent movements. However, there is no harm with such movements as gesturing, scrubbing one's skin, or making one or two steps forward for straightening rows. By the same token, looking around in prayer does not invalidate it, yet turning around in such a manner that one's chest becomes away from the *qiblah*, does. And, Allah knows best.

Q. No. (61): What is the *Sharʿī* ruling concerning a person who neglects something that is meant for the perfection of prayer?

A: If a person neglects something which is meant for the perfection of prayer such as the invocation of *Istiftāḥ* and raising one's hands on saying the first *Takbīr*, his prayer is valid yet the reward for it is decreased because of that. Besides, such things do not necessitate any prostration for forgetfulness. And, Allah knows best.

Q. No. (62): Should the Muslim stand up before prostrating for forgetfulness?

A: No standing is required before performing the two prostrations of forgetfulness at the end of prayer, and the Muslim can perform them while sitting then makes the *Taslīm* or salutation. The Prophet (PBUH) said,

---

[1] See the Glossary.

"If any one of you does not know how many (*Rak'ahs*) he has performed, three or four, let him perform two prostrations while sitting."[1]

And, Allah knows best.

Q. No. (63): Is it obligatory upon boys to perform prayer?

A: It is not obligatory upon boys and children in general to perform prayer, but they should be taught how to perform it so that they can be ready for performing it perfectly and properly when it becomes obligatory upon them. The Prophet (PBUH) said,

"Command your children to perform prayer when they become seven years old, beat them for (neglecting) it when they become ten years old, and arrange their beds (in such a manner that makes them sleep) separately."[2]

And, Allah knows best.

Q. No. (64): What is the number of the obligatory prayers and what is the due time of each one?

A: Allah has prescribed upon Muslims five prayers to be performed obligatorily during daytime and night. They are the *Fajr* Prayer, the *Zuhr* Prayer, the *'Aṣr* Prayer, the *Maghrib*, Prayer, and the *'Ishā'* Prayer.

There is a stated time for each prayer and the Muslim must perform it during this fixed time. It has been narrated on the authority of 'Abdullāh Ibn 'Amr, may Allah be pleased with him, that the Messenger of Allah (PBUH) said,

"The time of the Zuhr Prayer is when the sun passes the meridian and a man's shadow is the same (length) as his height, (and it lasts)

---

[1] A part of a Ḥadīth narrated on the authority of Abū Hurayrah. See Fath al-Bārī, 2/99.

[2] Narrated by Aḥmad and others

as long as the time for the *'Aṣr* Prayer has not come; the time for the *'Aṣr* Prayer is as long as the sun has not become pale; the time of the Maghrib Prayer is as long as the twilight has not ended; the time of the *'Ishā'* Prayer is up to the middle of the average night; and the time of the *Ṣubḥ* (Morning) Prayer is from the appearance of dawn, as long as the sun has not risen. But when the sun rises, do not perform prayer, for it rises between the horns of the devil."[1]

And, Allah knows best.

Q. No. (65): What is the *Shar'ī* ruling concerning a person who forgets a prayer or sleeps without performing it?

A: The Prophet (PBUH) said,

"He who sleeps without performing a prayer or forgets it, should perform it when he remembers it, for that is (considered) its due time."[2]

And, Allah knows best.

Q. No. (66): What is the *Shar'ī* ruling concerning the performance of prayer after the *Ṣubḥ* Prayer and the *'Aṣr* Prayer?

A: The majority of scholars maintain that it is permissible to "make up for" a missed prayer at these times because the Prophet (PBUH) said that he who sleeps without performing a prayer or forgets it, should perform it when he remembers it, for that is considered its due time."[3] On the other hand, some of the Companions, including 'Alī, Abū Hurayrah, and Ibn 'Umar, may Allah be pleased with them, view that it is legally detestable to perform a "voluntary" prayer at these two times. Mālik and Abū Ḥanīfah adopt the same opinion while Ash- Shāfi'ī says it is permissible to perform a prayer that has some legal purpose such as the prayer that is to be performed after

---

[1] Narrated by Muslim.
[2] Narrated by At-Tirmidhī.
[3] Narrated by At-Tirmidhī.

ablution, as an act of the *Sharʿī*. As for the Ḥanbalīs, they say it is prohibited to perform any voluntary prayer at these two times. And, Allah knows best.

Q. No. (67): What is the wording of *Adhān*?

A: There are three ways for saying *Adhān* according to the texts and narrations available in this regard, but before mentioning these ways, we shall list the words of *Adhān* as separated yet arranged groups of words. In other words, below are the groups of words which constitute *Adhān* listed according to the order in which they are said but without repetition:

(a) *Allāhu akbar* (Allah is the Greatest).

(b) *ʾAshhadu allā ilāha illā-llāh* (I testify that there is no god but Allah).

(c) *Ashhadu anna Muḥammadan rasūlullāh* (I testify that Muḥammad is the Messenger of Allah).

(d) *Ḥayyi ʿalā-ṣ-ṣalāh* (Come to Prayer).

(e) *Ḥayyi ʿalā-l-falāḥ* (Come to success).

(f) Then another *Allāhu akbar* as an independent item of *Adhān*, that is, it is not a repetition of the first *Allāhu akbar.*

(g) *La ilaha illā-llah* (There is no god but Allah).

Now let us list the three ways known for saying *Adhān*, as follows:

1. To say *Allāhu Akbar* four times then say the remaining groups of words of the *Adhān* twice for each except the last group of words, namely "*La ilaha illā-llah*". However, there is no *Tarjiʿ*[1] when saying the *Shahādatan* (the second and the third items in the list). This is according to the narration of Abdullāh Ibn Zayd in which he

---

[1] *Tarji* is to utter the two testifications of faith (*Shahādatan*) twice for each quietly before uttering them, also twice for each, loudly. The *Shahādatan* is the testification (i) that there is no god but Allah and (ii) that Muḥammad is the Messenger of Allah (i.e., the second and the third items in the list above).

mentioned that he was taught that *Adhān* on a vision then recited it to the Prophet (PBUH) who ordered him to teach it to Bilal.[1] In the same narration 'Umar Ibn al-Khaṭṭāb, may Allah be pleased with him, told the Prophet (PBUH) that he had seen the same vision as Ibn Zayd's. Thus, this way of *Adhān* consists of fifteen groups of words with the pinpointed repetition.

2. To say *Allāhu akbar* four times then use *Tarji'* when saying the *Shahādatan* then say the remaining words as in the first way above. This way consists of nineteen groups of words with the pinpointed repetition, the addition being because of *Tarji'*. It has been narrated by At-Tirmidhī and others that Abū Mahdhurah, may Allah be pleased with him, said that the Prophet (PBUH) taught him *Adhān* as comprising nineteen (groups of) words.

3. To say *Allāhu akbar* only twice then use *Tarji'* when saying the *shahadatān* then say the remaining words as in the first way above. This way consists of seventeen groups of words. It has been narrated by Muslim on the authority of Abū Maḥdhūrah that the Prophet (PBUH) taught him *Adhān* as follows: *Allāhu akbar* twice, *'Ashhadu allā ilāha illā-llāh* twice, *Ashhadu anna Muḥammadan rasūlullāh* twice. Then he (PBUH) taught him to say *Ashhadu an lā ilāha illā-llāh* twice then *Ashhadu anna Muḥammadan Rasūlullāh* twice (in addition to the first saying of them, and this is what is meant by *Tarji'*). Then he taught him to say *Hayyi alas-Ṣalāh* twice then *Ḥayyi 'alā-l-falāḥ* twice then *Allāhu akbar* twice then *La ilaha illā-llah* once. And, Allah knows best.

Q. No. (68): What is the wording of *Iqāmah*?

A: First of all, the groups of words of which *Iqāmah* consists of are the same of which *Adhān* consists (as pinpointed in the previous answer) but there is an extra group of words in *Iqāmah*, namely "*Qad qāmati-s-salah* (Come to prayer)". Like *Adhān* again, there are three

[1] Narrated by Aḥmad, Abū Dāwūd, and others.

ways of saying *Iqāmah* according to the texts and narrations available in this connection, as follows:

1. To say *Allāhu akbar* four times then say each of the remaining items twice except the last one (*La ilaha illā-llah*). It has been narrated by Aḥmad and Abū Dāwūd on the authority Abū Maḥdhūrah that the Prophet (PBUH) taught him *Iqāmah* as consisting of seventeen (groups of) words: *Allāhu akbar* four times, *ʾAshhadu allā ilāha illā-llāh* twice, *Ashhadu allā ilāha illā-llāh, Ashhadu anna Muḥammadan rasūlullāh* twice, *Hayyi alas-Ṣalāh* twice, *Ḥayyi ʿalā-l-falāḥ* twice, *Qad qāmati-s-salah* (Come to prayer) twice, *Allāhu akbar* twice, and finally *La ilaha illā-llah* once.

2. To say *Allāhu akbar* twice both in the beginning and in the *Takbīr* before *La ilaha illā-llah*, and to say *Qad qāmati-s-Ṣalāh* also twice and say the remaining groups of words once for each. This counts eleven groups of words. It has been narrated on the authority of Abdullāh Ibn Zayd, also in the narration referred to in *Adhān* above, that he was taught *Iqāmah* like this: *Allāhu akbar* twice, *ʾAshhadu allā ilāha illā-llāh* once, *Ashhadu allā ilāha illā-llāh Ashhadu anna Muḥammadan rasūlullāh* once, *Ḥayyi ʿalā-ṣ-ṣalāh* once, *Ḥayyi ʿalā-l-falāḥ* once, *Qad qāmati-s-Ṣalāh* twice, *Allāhu akbar* twice, and finally *La ilaha illā-llah* once.

3. The third way of saying *Iqāmah* is like the previous one except for *Qad qāmati-s-Ṣalāh* which is to be said only once. This counts ten groups of words. And, Allah knows best.

Q. No. (69): What should be said during the *Adhān*?

A: It has been narrated by Al-Bukhārī and others that the Prophet (PBUH) said, "Whenever you hear the *Adhān*, say what the *Muʾadhdhin* says." However, when the *Muʾadhdhin* says, " *Ḥayyi ʿalā-ṣ-ṣalāh* (Come to Prayer)" and " *Ḥayyi ʿalā-l-falāḥ* (Come to success)," the Muslim should say, " *Lā ḥawla wa-lā quwwata illā bi-llāh-l-ʿaliyyi-l-ʿazim* (There is neither might nor power except with Allah, the Most High the Greatest)". This is according to a narration of Muslim and

Abū Dāwūd on the authority of Umar, may Allah be pleased with him. And, Allah knows best.

Q. No. (70): What should be said after the *Adhān*?

A: It has been narrated by Muslim on the authority of ʿAbdullāh Ibn ʿAmr, may Allah be pleased with him, that the Messenger of Allah (PBUH) said,

"When you hear the *Mu'adhdhin*, repeat what he says then invoke a blessing on me, for everyone who invokes a blessing on me will receive ten blessings from Allah; then beg from Allah for me the *Wasīlah* (literally meaning "means"), which is a rank in Paradise fitting for only one of Allah's servants, and I hope that I may be that one. For, whoever asks that I be given the *Wasīlah* will be assured of my intercession."

And, Allah knows best.

Q. No. (71): What should the *Mu'adhdhin* consider before and while pronouncing *Adhān*?

A: First of all, he should intend that his pronunciation of *Adhān* is purely for the sake of Allah and for helping Muslims to know that the time of the prayer in question is due. He should also be in a state of *Ṭahārah* or purification. He should moreover face the *qiblah*, raise his voice, and not speak to others while pronouncing *Adhān*. This is "generally" what the *Mu'adhdhin* should consider. And, Allah knows best.

Q. No. (72): Is it obligatory that the person who has pronounced *Adhān* pronounces *Iqāmah* as well?

A: This is not obligatory, for it is permissible, as agreed upon by scholars, that *Iqāmah* be pronounced whether by the *Mu'adhdhin* or by anyone else. Yet, it is more becoming that the person who has pronounced *Adhān* pronounces *Iqāmah* as well. At-Tirmidhī has stated that most scholars apply this. And, Allah knows best.

Q. No. (73): What is the time that is to be considered between *Adhān* and iqamah?

A: Generally speaking, as there is no "authentic" text that defines a certain period to be considered in this regard, it is recommended that people wait between *Adhān* and *Iqāmah* for a time which is enough for getting ready for the prayer and a during which people can gather to perform the prayer together, as mentioned by Ibn Battal. And, Allah knows best.

Q. No. (74): When exactly should people stand for prayer when *Iqāmah* has been pronounced?

A: Mālik says in his Muwattā' that there is no specified time for that, and he adds that it is according to people's estimation especially that there may be among them someone ill or heavy. Any way, it has been narrated by Ibnul-Mundhir that Anas, may Allah be pleased with him, used to stand up for the prayer when the person who would be pronouncing *Iqāmah* said, "*Qad qāmatiṣ-ṣalāh* (Come to prayer)". And, Allah knows best.

Q. No. (75): Can anyone other than the regular *Mu'adhdhin* of a mosque pronounce *Adhān*?

A: It is not permissible for anyone to do so except after taking permission from this regular *Mu'adhdhin*, or when the latter does not come to the mosque and the people fear that they should miss the time suitable for pronouncing *Adhān*. And, Allah knows best.

Q. No. (76): When does prostration of forgetfulness become incumbent?

A: Generally speaking, prostration of forgetfulness becomes obligatory if a performer of prayer does an act that is an addition or an increase to prayer itself, yet this act is one of the acts of prayer, as to perform an "extra" act of bowing or prostration. It has been narrated on the authority of Abdullah Ibn Mas'ud, may Allah be pleased with him, that once the Messenger of Allah (PBUH) performed five *Rak'ahs* in the *Zuhr* Prayer, so he was asked, "Is there an increase in the prayer?" The Prophet (PBUH) said, "And what is it?" They said, "You have performed five *Rak'ahs.*" So, he (PBUH) bent his legs and performed two prostrations (of forgetfulness).[1]

Some Faqīhs maintain that prostration of forgetfulness also becomes obligatory if a performer of prayer does such acts as reciting the Qur'ān out loud in a prayer in which it is to be recited quietly, or if he neglects the first sitting for *tashahhud*, or any of such acts of the *Shar'ī* related to prayer.[2]

If, however, a performer of prayer neglects a pillar of prayer, that is an obligation, and does not set right what he has neglected, his prayer will be invalid and cannot be made up for through prostration of forgetfulness. An example of this is that he may forget to bow down or to prostrate.

A performer of prayer may neglect doing such things which are for the perfection of prayer such as the invocation of *Istiftāḥ* or raising of hands on saying the first *Takbīr* in prayer (*Takbīrat al-Iḥrām*). In this case, his prayer is valid, and he does not have to perform prostration of forgetfulness. However, the reward for such prayer may be decreased. And, Allah knows best.

Q. No. (77): Should a person performing prayer behind an Imām perform prostration for the forgetfulness of the Imām?

A: If the Imām forgets something in prayer, he is to perform the two prostration of forgetfulness and those he is leading in the prayer are to do the same because they must follow him in all the actions of prayer. This is because once the Prophet (PBUH) forgot to sit (after the second *Rak'ah*) so when he finished the prayer, he performed two prostrations and the people also performed the two

---

[1] Narrated by Al-Bukhārī.

[2] See Kifāyatu-l-Akhyār, 1/243, Al- Hidayah, 1/95, and Al-Mughnī, 2/403.

prostrations with him instead of the sitting he forgot.[1] And, Allah knows best.

Q. No. (78): Should a person performing prayer behind an Imām perform prostration for forgetfulness if he (the person) forgets something?

A: If a person forgets something in congregational prayer behind the Imām, he does not have to prostrate for forgetfulness nor does the Imām have to do so because of this person's forgetfulness. It has been narrated by Ad-Daruqutni in his Sunan on the authority of Ibn 'Umar, may Allah be pleased with him, that the Prophet (PBUH) said,

"No (prostration for) forgetfulness is required on the part of a person (who is performing prayer) behind an Imām. But, if his Imām forgets (something), he (the Imām) and those who are behind him shoulder (the liability of) this (and so they all prostrate for forgetfulness)."

And, Allah knows best.

Q. No. (79): Is it required to say *tashahhud* after the prostration of forgetfulness?

A: Abū Ḥanīfah maintains that if a person prostrates for forgetfulness, he should sit after it and say *tashahhud* again then make *Taslīm*, because the Prophet (PBUH) did that as narrated on the authority of Imran ibn Husayn, may Allah be pleased with him. Aḥmad and Ash-Shāfi'ī assert that if the prostration of forgetfulness is performed after *Taslīm*, he should sit and say *tashahhud* then make *Taslīm* all over again. And, Allah knows best.

Q. No. (80): What is the *Shar'ī* ruling concerning a person who forgets to do the first sitting in prayer then remembers it when he is still near to the position of sitting?

---

[1] Narrated by Al-Bukhārī.

A: In this case he should sit and say *tashahhud.* However, if he remembers it when he is nearer to the standing position, he is not to sit down yet he should prostrate for forgetfulness. This is what the Prophet (PBUH) said in the Ḥadīth narrated by Abū Dāwūd on the authority of Al-Mughīrah Ibn Shuʿbah, may Allah be pleased with him.[1] And, Allah knows best.

Q. No. (81): What is the *Sharʿī* ruling concerning a person who forgets to sit the last sitting and stands up for a fifth *Rakʿah* in a four-*Rakʿah* prayer?

A: In this case he must cancel this fifth *Rakʿah* and sit for *tashahhud* then prostrate for forgetfulness. This is to be applied if he does not prostrate in the fifth *Rakʿah*; for if he does, Abū Ḥanīfah maintains that his prayer becomes voluntary and thus he will have to add a sixth *Rakʿah* to the five *Rakʿahs.* Also, if he sits after the fourth *Rakʿah* for (a period) enough for *tashahhud* then stands for a fifth *Rakʿah* out of forgetfulness and prostrates in this fifth *Rakʿah*, he is to add another *Rakʿah* to these five *Rakʿahs.* In this way his prayer will be complete and the two *Rakʿahs* will be regarded as voluntary prayer for him, yet he should prostrate for forgetfulness. And, Allah knows best.

Q. No. (82): What is desirable for the Muslim to do in the prostration of recitation?

A: It is desirable for a person who prostrates for recitation to stand up then say *Allāhu Akbar* then fall prostrate then say *Allāhu akbar* again then stand up. According to Faqīhs, standing before and after prostration of recitation is desirable and *Takbīr* before and after it is an act of the *Sharʿī.* It is also desirable to say certain words along with the three *Tasbīḥahs* which are normally said in prostration. For example, he can say, "My face has prostrated for Him Who has

[1] Narrated by At-Tirmidhī and Abū Dāwūd.

created and shaped it and Who has cleft (places for) its hearing and its sight, with His Might and Power."[1] And, Allah knows best.

Q. No. (83): What is the distance of prayer shortening?

A: Scholars, including the Companions of the Prophet (PBUH), have differed concerning the distance of shortening prayer, to the extent that there are more than twenty views in this regard, as mentioned by Ibnul-Mundhir and others. Some say that the journey must be long enough so that the shortening of prayer on it can be valid; therefore, if a Muslim goes out of his town to a place which is ten or twenty kilometers far away from it, it is not valid that he shortens prayer. The late Faqīhs estimated the distance of such a journey to be eighty- four kilometers, which was then the distance of a three-day journey on camels and donkeys including the times of rest. This estimation may be backed by the narration stating that Ibn ʿAbbās, may Allah be pleased with him, used to shorten prayer in journeys with distances like that which is between Mecca and At-Ṭā'if and that which is between Mecca and Asāfan.[2] The distance between Mecca and At-Ṭā'if is about ninety kilometers. Accordingly, it is not permissible for anyone who is undergoing a short journey to shorten prayer.

To settle this difference, some scholars have stated that it is permissible for a person to shorten prayer if the distance of his journey is considered to be a distance of travel according to the language of the Arabs in which the Islamic Sharī'ah has been revealed. This view may be backed by the general meaning of the verse dealing with shortening of prayer:

﴿وَإِذَا ضَرَبْتُمْ فِي ٱلْأَرْضِ فَلَيْسَ عَلَيْكُمْ جُنَاحٌ أَن تَقْصُرُوا۟ مِنَ ٱلصَّلَوٰةِ ١٠١﴾

[1] Narrated by At-Tirmidhī
[2] Narrated by Mālik.

"And when you (Muslims) travel in the land, there is no sin on you if you shorten your prayer..." [TMQ 4: 101].

The wording of this verse indicates in general that it is permissible to shorten prayer during any "travel in the land" that is considered as such according to the Arabic language in which the verse was revealed. And, Allah knows best.

Q. No. (84): What is the period of prayer shortening?

A: A Muslim on a journey remains legally in a state of travel until he intends to "reside" in some place. According to Abū Ḥanīfah, the period for which he is to be in a state of travel is fifteen days. Ash-Shāfi'ī and Aḥmad, however, maintain that if he intends to reside in a place for four days, he should perform prayers in full, and if he intends to reside there for a period less than that he should shorten prayers. Moreover, Mālik, Ash- Shāfi'ī, and Aḥmad assert that if a Muslim "decides" to reside in a place for four days, he should perform prayers in full.

To settle this difference, in his Fatḥ al-Bārī Ibn Ḥajar has mentioned that Al-Bayhaqī gathered these different opinions together by saying: those scholars who say that the period is nineteen days have included the day on which a traveller enters to the place to which he travels and the day on which he departs it; those who say it is seventeen days have excluded these two days; and those who say the period is eighteen have included only one of them. As for the narration in which the narrator said that the period is fifteen days, perhaps he thought that the period was originally seventeen and he excluded both the day of arrival and the day of departure and so he mentioned the period as purely fifteen days.[1]

It is worth mentioning here that the difference between Faqīhs about the period of residence, in which a traveller can shorten

[1] Ibn Ḥajar, Fatḥ al-Bārī, 2/562.

prayers, is concerning a traveller who has intended and determined to stay in some place for a specific period. This is because a traveller may not intend or determine any residence, such as a person who is on an invasion in the Cause of Allah or a person who is on a mission in some place and does not know when it will end. Such travellers can shorten prayers even if their journeys last for months or years. And, Allah knows best. And, Allah knows best.

Q. No. (85): What is the *Shar'ī* ruling concerning shortening of prayer by a person who travels by air or by car?

A: It is permissible for a person who travels by car or by airplane to shorten prayer if the distance of his journey is considered to be a distance of travel according to the language of the Arabs in which the Islamic Sharī'ah has been revealed. This is to be applied even if he finishes this distance in an hour, because the *Shar'ī* criterion here is that the distance he covers is a distance with which he can shorten prayer whether he covers it on foot or by an airplane. After all, travel causes hardship in principle, and the ruling remains the same even if it does not cause such hardship on the part of some people. And, Allah knows best.

Q. No. (86): When exactly can a traveller start shortening prayer?

A: Whenever a traveller surpasses the buildings of the town he travels from, it is permissible for him to start shortening his prayer, and it is not a stipulation that he reaches the town to which he is traveling. It has been narrated that Anas, may Allah be pleased with him, said, "I performed the *Zuhr* Prayer with the Prophet (PBUH) in Medina as four *Rak'ahs* and the *'Aṣr* Prayer in Dhū al-Ḥulayfah as two *Rak'ahs*."[1] It has also been narrated that 'Alī, may Allah be pleased with him, left Kūfah and shortened prayer while seeing (its) buildings. On his way back someone said to him, "This is Kūfah," but he said, "No, until we enter it." That is to say, it was said to him that

---

[1] Narrated by Al-Bukhārī and Muslim.

he could perform prayer in full as they had reached Kūfah, but he said, "No, until we enter it," meaning that they were still legally allowed to shorten prayer because they were still in a state of traveling until they would be inside Kūfah. And, Allah knows best.

Q. No. (87): What is the *Shar'ī* ruling concerning the performance of voluntary prayer on a journey?

A: According to the majority of Faqīhs, it is not legally detestable for those who shorten prayer because of being on a journey to perform voluntary prayers, whether they are from the voluntary prayers which are regularly performed (*As-Sunan ar-Rawātib*) or from any other voluntary prayers. This is because the Companions of the Prophet (PBUH) used to perform voluntary prayers before and after the obligatory prayers while traveling.[1] It has moreover been narrated on the authority of Jābir, may Allah be pleased with him, that the Prophet (PBUH) would perform voluntary prayer while riding (his mount) facing a direction other than that of the *qiblah*.[2] To confirm not to repeat, this is the opinion adopted by the majority of Faqīhs. And, Allah knows best.

Q. No. (88): Can a traveller perform prayer behind a man in residence, that is, a man who is not a traveller?

A: It is permissible for a traveller to perform prayer behind a man who is not in a state of travel. There is no difference among Faqīhs concerning this point, and they have agreed that whenever a traveller performs prayer behind a man in residence, he must perform the prayer in full, without shortening. This means that he is not allowed to make *Taslīm* after two *Rak'ahs* to end his prayer shortened while the "resident" Imām completes the prayer in full. This is because the Prophet (PBUH) said,

[1] Narrated by Ibn Abū Shaybah.
[2] Narrated by Al-Bukhārī.

"An Imām (in prayer) is meant for nothing but to be followed. Therefore, if he says *Takbīr*, then say *Takbīr*; if he recites (the Qur'ān), then listen (to the recitation) carefully; and if he says *Takbīr* and bows, then say *Takbīr* and bow..."

to the end of the Ḥadīth.[1] This clearly indicates that if the Imām performs prayer in full, those led by him must follow him. And, Allah knows best.

Q. No. (89): Can a man in residence perform prayer behind another who is on a journey?

A: There is no difference among Faqīhs that a man in residence can perform prayer behind a man on a journey. However, in this case the Imām, who is a traveller, will perform two *Rak'ahs* then make *Taslīm*, because he will have then completed what is obligatory upon him. On the other hand, the man in residence, who is led by the traveller, will perform the prayer in full, because what is obligatory upon him is to perform four *Rak'ahs*. Furthermore, it is legally desirable for the "traveling" Imām to say after *Taslīm*, "Complete your prayer, for we are on a journey," as the Prophet (PBUH)[2] and his Companions[3] did.[4] And, Allah knows best.

Q. No. (90): Is it a stipulation for the validity of shortening of prayer on a journey that this journey should be for performing an act of obedience?

A: Some Faqīhs have stipulated that a man's journey should be for performing an act of obedience so that he can shorten prayer during it. This is because if it is for performing an act of disobedience, such as traveling for undertaking a prohibited deal in intoxicants and the like, then it is not permissible for whoever travels for such purposes

---

[1] Narrated by Al-Bukhārī and Muslim

[2] Narrated by Abū Dāwūd.

[3] Narrated by Mālik.

[4] For more details, see Al-Mughnī, 3/146.

to shorten prayer, because that will be a kind of "helping" him to disobey Almighty Allah. This is the view adopted by the majority of Faqīhs.

However, Abū Ḥanīfah and others maintain that a traveling Muslim can shorten prayer whether his journey is for obeying or disobeying Allah, because Almighty Allah did not restrict the ruling concerning shortening of prayer to obedience or disobedience when He said,

﴿وَإِذَا ضَرَبْتُمْ فِى ٱلْأَرْضِ فَلَيْسَ عَلَيْكُمْ جُنَاحٌ أَن تَقْصُرُوا۟ مِنَ ٱلصَّلَوٰةِ ﴿١٠١﴾﴾

"And when you (Muslims) travel in the land, there is no sin on you if you shorten your prayer..." [TMQ: 4: 101]

And, Allah knows best.

Q. No. (91): What are the prayers which are to be shortened on a journey?

A: Prayers which are to be shortened on a journey are the obligatory prayers which consist of four *Rak'ahs*, namely, the *Zuhr* Prayer, the *'Aṣr* Prayer, and the *'Ishā'* Prayer. Accordingly, there is no shortening in the *Fajr* Prayer or in the *Maghrib* Prayer. And, Allah knows best.

Q. No. (92): Why is it not permissible to shorten the *Fajr* Prayer or the *Maghrib* Prayer?

A: Ibn Qudāmah says in his Al-Mughnī there is no difference among scholars that there is no shortening in the *Fajr* Prayer and the *Maghrib* Prayer. This is because the *Fajr* Prayer consists of two *Rak'ahs*, and if it was to be shortened, it would be one *Rak'ah*, while there is no one *Rak'ah* prayer except the *Witr* Prayer. In the same way, the *Maghrib* Prayer, which consists of three *Rak'ahs*, is the *Witr* (odd) prayer of daytime (as the voluntary *Witr* Prayer is performed by night); and if one *Rak'ah* was to be shortened from the *Maghrib* Prayer, it would no longer be *Witr* (i.e., of an odd number of *Rak'ahs*).

Still, if two *Rak'ahs* were to be shortened from the *Maghrib* Prayer, the most of its *Rak'ahs* would be taken out.[1] And, Allah knows best.

Q. No. (93): What is the *Shar'ī* ruling concerning a person who misses a four-*Rak'ah* prayer then goes on a journey and a person who misses it while traveling then returns to his town before making up for it?

A: Whoever misses a four-*Rak'ah* prayer while traveling is to make up for it when he returns to his town as two *Rak'ahs*. If, however a person misses a four-*Rak'ah* prayer while residing in his town then travels and wants to make up for it on his journey, he is to perform it as four *Rak'ahs*, and it is not permissible for him to shorten it. This is because, in either case, he is to make up for the prayer in question by performing it as it was to be performed when he missed it: if it was to be performed as four *Rak'ahs* then he is to make up for it as four *Rak'ahs*, and if it was to be performed as two, he is to make up for it as two. And, Allah knows best.

Q. No. (94): Is it stipulated that a person on a journey "intends" to shorten prayer if he wants to perform prayer behind an Imām who has already started his prayer?

A: Intention is not a stipulation in this case, as this traveling person can perform prayer behind this Imām though he does not know whether he will shorten the prayer or perform it in full. Thus, the traveling person will shorten the prayer if the Imām shortens it, and he will perform it "in full" if the Imām does so. This is because shortening of prayer does not require an intention which is independent from that of the prayer itself. And, Allah knows best.

Q. No. (95): What is the *Shar'ī* ruling if a traveling person catches only two *Rak'ahs* with a "resident" Imām: should he complete the prayer to four *rak'ahs*?

---

[1] See *Al-Mughnī*, 3/121.

A: He must complete the prayer to four *Rak'ahs* because his Imām is "resident" and not in a state of traveling like him. It has been narrated by Al-Bayhaqī that Ibn 'Umar, may Allah be pleased with him, was asked about the case of a man who catches two *Rak'ahs* with resident people in congregation: should he complete the prayer or the two *Rak'ahs* are sufficient for him. Ibn 'Umar said, "He is to perform the prayer as they do," meaning "as a resident person and not as a traveller," and this requires the performance of prayer in full. And, Allah knows best.

Q. No. (96): Is it permissible for the Muslim to combine two prayers if he is in need to do so?

A: It is permissible for the Muslim to combine prayers if he is in need to do so provided that this be incidental and not used habitually. It has been narrated that Ibn 'Abbas, may Allah be pleased with him, said, "The Messenger of Allah (PBUH) combined the *Zuhr* and the *'Aṣr* prayers and the *Maghrib* and the *'Ishā'* prayers and there was neither fear nor rain." It was said to Ibn 'Abbās, "What did he mean by that?" He said, "He meant not to put his nation to difficulty."[1] And, Allah knows best.

Q. No. (97): What are the conditions of prayers combination?

A: The Faqīhs who adopt the view that it is permissible to combine prayers on a journey have stipulated that a traveller who wants to combine prayers must do the following:

1. He must "intend" the combination in question.

2. He must perform the *Zuhr* Prayer before the *'Aṣr* Prayer and the *Maghrib* Prayer before the *'Ishā'* Prayer, because the Prophet (PBUH) used to do that.

[1] Narrated by Muslim and others.

3. He must not perform any voluntary prayers between the two prayers he wants to combine. And, Allah knows best.

Q. No. (98): What are the conditions obligating the *Jumu'ah* Prayer?

A: The *Jumu'ah* Prayer is not a must upon every Muslim, for it is only obligatory only on whoever meets the following conditions:

1. Freedom.

2. Masculinity.

3. Puberty.

4. Not being in a state of travel.

5. Not being in a state of illness.

These five conditions must be met so that the Muslim can be legally asked to obligatorily attend the *Jumu'ah* Prayer. And, Allah knows best.

Q. No. (99): It is not incumbent upon women or those who are ill or on a journey to perform the *Jumu'ah* Prayer, but will it be instead of the *Zuhr* Prayer if they perform it?

A: If a woman, an ill person, or a traveller performs the *Jumu'ah* Prayer, through it is not obligatory upon any of them, that will be sufficient for him or her who performs it and thus they will not have to perform the *Zuhr* Prayer. This is because the *Jumu'ah* Prayer is not obligatory upon such persons for the sake of making things easy for them and not putting them to difficulty and hardship. Therefore, if they perform the *Jumu'ah* Prayer, that will be good for them because it is "originally" obligatory on Muslims in general. And, Allah knows best.

Q. No. (100): What is the *Shar'ī* ruling concerning the *Khuṭbah* (sermon) of the *Jumu'ah*?

A: Faqīhs unanimously agree that there must be a *Khuṭbah* or religious sermon for the *Jumuʿah* to be valid, and this view is adopted by the Four *Imāms.* This is because the Prophet (PBUH) never neglected the *Khuṭbah* under any circumstances, and also because Almighty Allah says concerning the *Jumuʿah*, "... come to the remembrance of Allah..." [TMQ: 62: 9] "Remembrance" here is meant for the *Khuṭbah* because it includes items of preaching and reminds Muslims of Allah's ordinances and forbiddances. Besides, it is the objective of the Muslims' gathering on this occasion in addition to the prayer itself.

The *Khuṭbah* of the *Jumuʿah* must contain items of preaching and guidance and not only items of praising Allah and invoking blessings on Prophet Muḥammad (PBUH), for a *Khuṭbah* with these items of praise and invocation only is not the religious *Khuṭbah* which is meant for this occasion of the *Jumuʿah*. However, it is permissible to start the *Khuṭbah* with such items of praise then preach the Muslims.

Also, the *Khuṭbah* of the *Jumuʿah* must not be prolonged so that it may not be a difficult act of worship for the Muslims attending it.

Another important aspect related to the *Khuṭbah* of the *Jumuʿah* is that it is desirable that the khatib (the Imām who delivers the sermon) sits for a short while during it and this makes it in the form of two connected sermons. This is what the Messenger of Allah (PBUH) used to do as narrated by Muslim on the authority of Jābir Ibn Samurah. Some Faqīhs have estimated the duration of this sitting between the two sermons to be as long as the time during which the chapter of Al-Ikhlāṣ (Qur'ān: 112) can be recited. This chapter consists only of fifteen words in Arabic.

Yet still, it may be important to mention here that some Faqīhs maintain that it is a stipulation for the validity of the *Khuṭbah* of the *Jumuʿah* that it consists of two parts, that is to say it must be two sermons with the sitting required between them. This view is adopted by Aḥmad, yet the majority of Faqīhs view that it is "permissible" that the *Jumu'ah* has one sermon, but it is "better" to deliver two sermons. And, Allah knows best.

Q. No. (101): What is the *Shar'ī* ruling concerning "speaking" while the *Khuṭbah* or sermon of the *Jumu'ah* is being delivered?

A: It is legally forbidden for the Muslim to speak while the *Khuṭbah* of the *Jumu'ah* is being delivered, because it is then that he must listen to the Imām while delivering this very special religious talk. This serves more than one goal: not to distract neither the Imām nor the other worshipers and to benefit from the *Khuṭbah* when listening to it carefully. It has been narrated on the authority of Abū Hurayrah, may Allah be pleased with him, that the Prophet (PBUH) said,

"If you say to your fellow (Muslim) on Friday 'Listen!" (While the Imām is delivering the *Khuṭbah*), you will have committed a mistake,"[1]

meaning: you will have said an unbefitting word and thus deserved punishment, or you will have lost the reward of the *Jumu'ah*. At-Tirmidhī has stated that most scholars maintain that it is detestable for the Muslim to speak while the Imām is delivering the *Khuṭbah* of the *Jumu'ah*, but they allow that someone may tell him to keep silent only by gesturing.

In this connection, some scholars, including Aḥmad, say that it is permissible to reply to the greeting of a Muslim while the *Khuṭbah* is being delivered, whereas some others, including Ash- Shāfi'ī, maintain that this detestable. And, Allah knows best.

Q. No. (102): What is the *Shar'ī* ruling concerning the undertaking of business during the time of the *Jumu'ah*?

---

[1] Narrated by *Al-Bukhārī* and Muslim

A: Faqīhs have agreed that undertaking business is forbidden during the time of the *Jumuʿah* because Almighty Allah says,

﴿يَٰٓأَيُّهَا ٱلَّذِينَ ءَامَنُوٓاْ إِذَا نُودِيَ لِلصَّلَوٰةِ مِن يَوۡمِ ٱلۡجُمُعَةِ فَٱسۡعَوۡاْ إِلَىٰ ذِكۡرِ ٱللَّهِ
وَذَرُواْ ٱلۡبَيۡعَۚ ٩﴾

"You who believe (Muslims)! When the call is proclaimed for the prayer on the day of Friday (Jumuʿah Prayer), come to the remembrance of Allah and leave off business (and every other thing)." [TMQ: 62:9]

The Muslim is forbidden to undertake any business during this time so that he may not be distracted from this prayer by it. Ibn ʿAbbās said that business is prohibited when the call for the *Jumuʿah* Prayer is being pronounced, and Ibn Ḥajar agrees with him, yet he says that it is permissible though detestable to undertake business during the first *Adhān* of the *Jumuʿah.* [1]And still, most Faqīhs, including Mālik and Ahamd, view that any business undertaken during the time of the *Jumuʿah* Prayer is false and thus it must be cancelled. Whereas, some others, including Ath-Thawri and some followers of Abū Ḥanīfah, say that it is not false, yet it is an act of disobedience and whoever does that must repent to Allah. And, Allah knows best.

Q. No. (103): What is the *Sharʿī* ruling concerning a person who catches one *Rakʿah* from the *Jumuʿah* Prayer?

A: Most scholars maintain that whoever catches one *Rakʿah* from the *Jumuʿah* Prayer is to join to it another *Rakʿah* and his *Jumuʿah* will be valid. However, whoever catches with the Imām the prostration of the second *Rakʿah* or *tashahhud*, is to perform four *Rakʿahs* as a *Zuhr* prayer for it will not be a valid *Jumuʿah.* The Prophet (PBUH) said,

"Whoever catches a *Rakʿah* from the Jumuʿah Prayer or any other prayer, will have caught (that) prayer."[2]

---

[1] See *Fatḥ al-Bārī*, 2/391.
[2] Narrated by Ibn Mājah

The Ḥanafīs however maintain that whoever catches the *tashahhud* will have caught the *Jumuʿah* Prayer, and so he is to complete the prayer as two *Rakʿahs*, but he will have lost a better reward. They have quoted the following Ḥadīth as a proof: "When the prayer is started, do not run for it but just walk for it calmly and perform (with the Imām) whatever you catch (from it) and complete whatever is missed,"[1] and in another narration he (PBUH) said, "... and make up for whatever you miss." And, Allah knows best.

Q. No. (104): What is the *Sharʿī* ruling about performing prayer after the *Jumuʿah* Prayer?

A: It is an act of the *Sunnah* that the Muslim performs two or four *Rakʿahs* after the *Jumuʿah* Prayer. It has been narrated on the authority of Abū Hurayrah, may Allah be pleased with him, that the Prophet (PBUH) said,

"Whenever any one of you performs the *Jumuʿah* Prayer, let him perform four *Rakʿahs* after it."[2]

It has also been narrated that the Prophet (PBUH) would not perform any prayer after the *Jumuʿah* Prayer until he would leave (the place of prayer), then he would perform two *Rakʿahs*."[3] This means that whoever wants to perform four *Rakʿahs* after it can do so and whoever wants to perform two *Rakʿahs* can so, and this view has been attributed to Aḥmad. And, Allah knows best.

Q. No. (105): What is the *Sharʿī* ruling concerning perfuming and adorning oneself on Friday?

A: Friday is a day of feast for Muslims, and they gather on it to perform the *Jumuʿah* Prayer. That is why the Prophet (PBUH) encouraged the Muslim to wear for that his best clothes, to take a bath, to use *Siwāk*, and to apply the best perfume he can get. One of

---

[1] Narrated by Al-Bukhārī and Muslim.
[2] Narrated by Muslim.
[3] Narrated by Al-Bukhārī.

the Ḥadīths dealing with this matter is the Ḥadīth in which the Prophet (PBUH) said,

"This is a day of feast that Allah has made for Muslims. Therefore, whoever comes for the *Jumu'ah* Prayer should take a bath, and let him apply perfume if there is any, and use *Siwāk* (as well)."[1]

And, Allah knows best.

Q. No. (106): What should the Muslim do if it becomes too crowded in the *Jumu'ah* Prayer?

A: He can then bow and prostrate as best as he can even if this should be done on the back of his Muslim brother who is right before him in the prayer. It has been narrated that Umar, may Allah be pleased with him, said, "If it is too crowded, you can prostrate on your (Muslim) brother's back."[2] And, Allah knows best.

Q. No. (107): What is desirable for the Muslim to do on Friday in particular?

A: On Friday, it is desirable for the Muslim to invoke blessings much on the Prophet (PBUH). It has been narrated that the Prophet (PBUH) said,

"Verily, Friday is one of the best of your days. On it, Adam was created, on it he passed away, and on it (the trumpet) will be blown and (all humans) will swoon away (i.e., die right before Resurrection). Therefore, invoke blessings on me much on it, for verily your invoking blessings on me will be shown to me."

Those listening said, "O Messenger of Allah! How will our invoking blessings on you be shown to you when you will have deteriorated

---

[1] Narrated by Mālik and Ibn Mājah

[2] Narrated by Aḥmad and others.

(after death)?" He Prophet (PBUH) replied, "Verily, Allah has made it forbidden for the earth to eat the bodies of Prophets."[1]

It is also desirable that the Muslim recites the chapter of *Al-Kahf.* It has been narrated on the authority of Abū Sa'īd al-Khudrī, may Allah be pleased with him, that the Prophet (PBUH) said,

"Whoever recites the chapter of *Al-Kahf* on Friday, that will supply him with light (in the period) between the two (days of) Friday."[2]

meaning, that will supply him with light in the period between the Friday on which he recites this chapter and the next one.

It is moreover desirable for the Muslim to invoke Allah much on this day, trying to seek the hour in which Allah responds to invocations on Friday. The Prophet (PBUH) said,

"There is an hour on Friday and if a Muslim gets it while performing prayer and asks something from Allah, then Allah will definitely meet his demand."

He (PBUH) then pointed out the shortness of that time with his hands.[3] And, Allah knows best.

Q. No. (108): What should the Muslim recite from the Qur'ān in the *Fajr* Prayer on Friday?

A: It is desirable for the Muslim to recite from the Qur'ān in the *Fajr* Prayer on Friday as follows: to recite the chapter of As- Sajdah in the first *Rak'ah* and the chapter of Ad-Dahr (or Al-Insān) in the second *Rak'ah*. This is what the Prophet (PBUH) used to do as narrated by Muslim. And, Allah knows best.

Q. No. (109): What should the Muslim recite from the Qur'ān in the *Jumu'ah* Prayer?

---

[1] Narrated by Abū Dāwūd and An-Nasā'ī

[2] Narrated by Al-Hakim and others.

[3] Narrated by Al-Bukhārī and Muslim

A: It has been narrated by Muslim that the Prophet (PBUH) used to recite in the *Jumu'ah* Prayer: the chapter of Al- *Jumu'ah* and the chapter of *Al-Munāfiqūn.*

Q. No. (110): How should the Id (Feast) Prayer be performed?

A: The Id Prayer consists of two *Rak'ahs* yet it has special acts of *Takbīr* and there is a *Khuṭbah* or sermon to be delivered after it. This can be summarized in the following lines in a way that gathers all the considerable opinions in this connection together.

A performer of the Id Prayer starts by reciting the first *Takbīrah,* which is to say " *Allāhu akbar* (Allah is the Greatest)," and this first *Takbīrah* is called *Takbīrat al-Iḥrām.* After that he recites the invocation of *Istiftāḥ*, that is, the invocation with which prayer is commenced after the first *Takbīrah* and before recitation of *Al-Fātiḥah.* In this invocation he can say, "Glory be to You, O Allah, and to You be (all) Praise, and Blessed is Your Name, and Exalted is Your Majesty, and there is no god but You,"[1] or any other invocation in this regard.

After that he recites *Takbīr* with the words "*Allāhu akbar* " seven times according to Ash-Shāfi'ī and Aḥmad and three times according to Abū Ḥanīfah and Al-Thawrī, raising his hands with every *Takbīrah.* Then he seeks refuge with Allah from Satan, normally by saying, " *A'ūdhu bi-llāhi min ash-Shayṭān ir-Rajīm* (I seek refuge with Allah from Satan, the expelled [from His Mercy])." Then he recites *Al-Fātiḥah* and a chapter or some verses from the Qur'ān. According to the *Sunnah* of the Prophet (PBUH), it is recommended for him to recite the chapter of Al-A'lā (Qur'ān: 87) in the first *Rak'ah* and the chapter of Al-Ghāshiyah (Qur'ān: 88) in the second *Rak'ah*, for the Prophet (PBUH) used to do

[1] Narrated by Abū Dāwūd and At-Tirmidhī.

so as narrated on the authority of An-Nuʿmān Ibn Bashīr, may Allah be pleased with him.[1]

After that a performer of the Id Prayer performs the required bowing and prostration yet without specific items of dhikr. Then when he stands up for the second *Rakʿah* he says five *Takbīrahs* before reciting *Al-Fātiḥah* and after saying the *Takbīrah* required for standing for the second *Rakʿah.*

After that he recites *Al-Fātiḥah* and a chapter (such as the chapter of Al-Ghāshiyah as pinpointed earlier) or some verses from the Qurʾān then completes the second *Rakʿah* and sits for *tashahhud* then finishes the prayer with *Taslīm.* According to Abū Ḥanīfah, he is to say the required *Takbīrahs* after reciting *Al-Fātiḥah* and the Qurʾānic verses and before bowing.

After finishing the prayer, the Imām delivers two sermons between which he sits for a short while. When delivering the sermon after the prayer of the ʿIdul- Fiṭr, the Imām should encourage the Muslims to give in charity and work righteousness, and in the sermon of the ʿIdul- Aḍḥā prayer he should encourage them to offer sacrifice, explaining for them what they are to do exactly.

Finally, it is worth mentioning that Faqīhs have unanimously agreed that the sermon of the *Id* Prayer is to be delivered "after" performing the prayer, unlike the *Jumuʿah* sermon which is to be delivered "before" the prayer. And, Allah knows best.

Q. No. (111): Is it an act of the *Sunnah* that the Muslim performs voluntary prayer before or after the *Id* (Feast) Prayer?

A: On the contrary, according to the *Sunnah* on voluntary prayer is to be performed before or after the Id Prayer. It has been narrated by Muslim on the authority of Ibn ʿAbbās , may Allah be pleased with him, that the Messenger of Allah (PBUH) went out (for the ʿId

---

[1] Narrated by Ibn Mājah.

Prayer) on the Day of Sacrifice (ʿIdul- Aḍḥā) or the Day of Fast-breaking (ʿIdul- Fiṭr), and he performed two *Rakʿahs* but he did not perform any prayer before or after that. And, Allah knows best.

Q. No. (112): When can the Muslim perform prayer without facing the *qiblah*?

A: In principle, it is obligatory to face the *qiblah* when performing prayer. However, there are certain cases in which the Muslim can perform prayer without facing the *qiblah*. First, it is permissible for a person who is riding a mount (or any means of transportation) to perform "voluntary" prayer on his mount and his *qiblah* will be wherever his mount goes, for the Prophet (PBUH) would do so as narrated by Al-Bukhārī and Muslim on the authority of Amir Ibn Rabi'ah, may Allah be pleased with him. Secondly, a person who is in a state of fear, coercion, or illness can perform prayer without facing the *qiblah* if he is unable to face it.

Almighty Allah says,

﴿حَٰفِظُواْ عَلَى ٱلصَّلَوَٰتِ وَٱلصَّلَوٰةِ ٱلۡوُسۡطَىٰ وَقُومُواْ لِلَّهِ قَٰنِتِينَ ٢٣٨ فَإِنۡ خِفۡتُمۡ فَرِجَالًا
أَوۡ رُكۡبَانٗاۖ فَإِذَآ أَمِنتُمۡ فَٱذۡكُرُواْ ٱللَّهَ كَمَا عَلَّمَكُم مَّا لَمۡ تَكُونُواْ تَعۡلَمُونَ ٢٣٩﴾

"Guard strictly (the five obligatory) prayers especially the middle prayer (i.e., the best prayer - ʿAṣr). And stand before Allah with obedience (and do not speak to others during the prayers). And if you fear (an enemy), (perform prayer) on foot or riding. And when you are in safety, offer the prayer in the manner He has taught you, which you knew not (before)."
[TMQ: 2: 238-239]

Al-Bukhārī has narrated that Ibn 'Umar, may Allah be pleased with him, commented on the part and if you fear (an enemy), (perform prayer) on foot or riding saying, "(It means:) whether you are facing the *qiblah* or not facing it." And, Allah knows best.

Q. No. (113): What is the *Shar'ī* ruling concerning a person who does not know how to recite *Al-Fātiḥah* can he perform prayer without it?

A: Originally, no prayer is valid without *Al-Fātiḥah*, but Al- Khattābī' maintains that if a person does not know how to recite it, he can recite instead any other "seven verses" from the Qur'ān which he knows well. If he is unable to know any other part of the Qur'ān, he can switch to the items of *tasbīḥ*, *tahlīl*, and *taḥmīd* (see the glossary) which the Prophet (PBUH) has taught his *Ummah*. It has been narrated by Abū Dāwūd, At-Tirmidhī, An-Nasā'ī, and Al-Bayḥaqī that the Prophet (PBUH) taught a man prayer and said to him, "If you have (i.e., know) some (part) of the Qur'ān, recite (it), otherwise (worship Allah) with *tahmīd*, *Takbīr*, and *tahlīl* then bow down." And, Allah knows best.

Q. No. (114): What is the minimum limit of remaining quiet (or *ṭuma'nīnah*) in such positions of prayer as bowing and prostration?

A: Scholars have estimated the minimum of remaining quiet in the two pinpointed positions to be for a period enough for saying one *Tasbīḥah*. To remind our readers, the *tasbīḥ* which is traditional (*ma'thūr*) in the bowing position is to say "*Subḥāna rabbīya-l-'aẓīm* (Glory be to my Lord, the Greatest)," and the traditional *tasbīḥ* in the prostration position is to say "*Subḥāna rabbīya-l-a'lā* (Glory be to my Lord, the Highest)". And, Allah knows best.

Q. No. (115): What is the meaning of the word "*amin*" (usually translated as "*amen*") in "Arabic"?

A: It means "O Allah! (Please) answer (the invocation)!" It is said in general after finishing an invocation, yet it is said in special after finishing the chapter of *Al-Fātiḥah* in prayer, and it must be known that it is not a part of this chapter. And, Allah knows best.

Q. No. (116): Can a performer of prayer ask Allah to forgive him if he hears his Imām reciting a verse speaking about forgiveness for example?

A: Whenever the Muslim hears a verse speaking about mercy, he can ask Allah for His Mercy; if he hears a verse dealing with His Forgiveness, he can ask Him to forgive him; and whenever he hears a verse speaking about Hellfire, he can ask Allah to protect him from it, and so on. This is because the Prophet (PBUH) would do that as narrated by Muslim on the authority of Ḥudhayfah Ibn al-Yamān, may Allah be pleased with him. The Muslim can do that whether it is inside or outside prayer. And, Allah knows best.

Q. No. (117): In which prayers and *Rak'ahs* can a performer of prayer recite the Qur'ān out loud and where is he to recite it quietly?

A: According to the *Sunnah*, the Muslim can recite the Qur'ān out loud in the two *Rak'ahs* of the *Fajr* Prayer and those of the *Jumu'ah* Prayer, as well as in the first two *Rak'ahs* in the Maghrib and the *'Ishā'* prayers. He can also do so in the *'Id* Prayer, the Eclipse Prayer, and the *Istisqā'* Prayer. On the other hand, he is to recite the Qur'ān quietly in the *Zuhr* and the *'Aṣr* prayers, the third *Rak'ah* in the *Maghrib* Prayer, and the last two *Rak'ahs* in the *'Ishā'* Prayer. As for the rest of the voluntary prayers (*nawāfil*), he is to recite the Qur'ān quietly in those performed during daytime, yet he can recite it either quietly or out loud in those performed during the night. Interestingly enough, loud recitation is usually done by the Imām while those who are led by him listen to his recitation. And, Allah knows best.

Q. No. (118): Can a performer of prayer recite the Qur'ān while the Imām is reciting it out loud in a prayer in which the Qur'ān is to be recited out loud by the Imām?

A: He must listen to the recitation of his Imām and not recite with him. Almighty Allah says,

﴿وَإِذَا قُرِئَ ٱلْقُرْءَانُ فَٱسْتَمِعُوا۟ لَهُۥ وَأَنصِتُوا۟ لَعَلَّكُمْ تُرْحَمُونَ ٢٠٤﴾

"When the Qur'ān is recited, listen to it, and be silent that you may receive mercy." [TMQ: 7: 204]

And the Prophet (PBUH) said,

"An Imām (in prayer) is meant for nothing but to be followed. Therefore, if he says *Takbīr*, then say *Takbīr*; if he recites (the Qur'ān), then listen (to the recitation) carefully..."

to the end of the Ḥadīth.[1] And, Allah knows best.

Q. No. (119): What is the prostration of gratitude (*Sujūd ash-shukr*)?

A: Whenever you receive glad tidings that you have been bestowed with something good or that something bad has been taken away from you, it desirable that you fall prostrate for Almighty Allah as a way of thanking Him and showing gratitude to Him for that. It has been narrated by Abū Dāwūd and others on the authority of Abū Bakrah, may Allah be pleased with him, that whenever something good or pleasant happened to the Prophet (PBUH) he would fall prostrate to show gratitude to Allah, Glorified and Exalted be He. Important still, it is not a stipulation that a person who performs such prostration be in a state of ablution. And, Allah knows best.

Q. No. (120): What is the *Shar'ī* ruling concerning the performance of obligatory prayers in congregation?

A: The performance of obligatory prayers in congregation is a *Sunnah mu'akkadah* or an affirmed act of the *Sunnah.* As for performing voluntary prayers in congregation, it is allowed in general regardless of how many people join it.

The Prophet (PBUH) encouraged Muslims to perform prayers in congregation especially in the mosque. To illustrate this, he said, as narrated by Al-Bukhārī on the authority of Abū Hurairah,

---

[1] Narrated by Al-Bukhārī and Muslim.

"The prayer offered in congregation is twenty-five times more superior (in reward) to the prayer offered alone in one's house or in a business centre..."

On the other hand, the Prophet (PBUH) warned those who neglect performing prayer in the mosque in congregation, saying,

"By Him in Whose Hand my soul is, I was about to order (some Muslims) to collect firewood (fuel) and then order someone to pronounce the adhan for the prayer and then order someone to lead the prayer then I would go from behind and burn the houses of men who did not present themselves for the (obligatory congregational) prayer. By Him in Whose Hand my soul is, if any one of them had known that he would get a bone covered with good meat or two (small) pieces of meat present in between two ribs, he would have turned up (i.e., been present) for the *'Ishā'* Prayer."[1] And, Allah knows best."

Q. No. (121): What are the characteristics or qualities of a person who deserves most to lead people in prayer?

A: Who deserves most to lead people in prayer is the most versed in the Qur'ān among them. It has been narrated that the Prophet (PBUH) said,

"The one who is most versed in Allah's Book should lead people (in prayer). But if they are equally versed in reciting it, then the one who has most knowledge regarding the Sunnah; and if they are equal regarding the Sunnah, then the earliest one to emigrate; and if they emigrated at the same time, then the earliest one to embrace Islam. (And behold!) No man is to lead another in prayer where (the latter) has authority, nor (is he allowed) to sit in his place of honour in his house, without his permission."[2]

---

[1] Narrated by Al-Bukhārī and Muslim

[2] Narrated by Muslim, At-Tirmidhī, and others.

And, Allah knows best.

Q. No. (122): What is the *Shar'ī* ruling concerning *qunūt* in the *Witr* Prayer?

A: Firs of all, the *Witr* Prayer is a form of prayer that is performed in an odd number of *Rak'ahs*, and it is an affirmed act of the *Sunnah* (*Sunnah mu'akkadah*) which is to be performed every night.

It is desirable to make *qunūt* that is to invoke Allah in a certain way and a certain position in prayer in the *Witr* Prayer throughout the year. According to the *Sunnah, qunūt* in the *Witr* Prayer is to be made "before" bowing down and after recitation. This is what the Prophet (PBUH) used to do, as narrated on the authority of Ubayy Ibn Ka'b, may Allah be pleased with him.[1] This is unlike *qunūt* in an obligatory prayer, for it is made in such prayers "only" at times of catastrophes and it is to be made "after" bowing down and before falling prostrate, as narrated on the authority of Abū Hurayrah, may Allah be pleased with him.[2] The same ruling applies of course to the *Fajr* Prayer, and thus there is no *qunūt* that is to be made "especially" for this prayer, because that was not done during the time of the Prophet (PBUH) or any of the Rightly- guided Caliphs.[3] And, Allah knows best.

Q. No. (123): What is the *Shar'ī* ruling concerning the night prayer of Ramaḍān (*Tarāwīḥ*)?

A: The voluntary night prayers include the prayer known as *Tarāwīḥ* which is performed during the nights of Ramaḍān after the *'Ishā'* Prayer. The word *Tarāwīḥ* literally means "refreshments," and this goes with the purpose for which this prayer is performed at the

[1] Narrated by Abū Dāwūd.
[2] Narrated by Al-Bukhārī.
[3] See Musnad Aḥmad, 3/472. A narration confirming the same ruling has also been narrated by At-Tirmidhī, An-Nasā'ī, and Ibn Mājah.

nights of Ramaḍān, as it "refreshes" the Muslim's soul. The Prophet (PBUH) said about standing for prayer in Ramaḍān,

"Whoever establishes prayers during (the night of) Ramaḍān out of sincere faith and hoping for a reward from Allah, then all his previous sins will be forgiven."[1]

And, it is permissible for the Muslim to perform this prayer in congregation.

As for the number of *Rak'ahs* which are to be performed in this prayer, generally as pinpointed above, the Messenger of Allah (PBUH) would not perform more than eleven *Rak'ahs* voluntarily whether in Ramaḍān or in any other time, as narrated on the authority of 'Ā'ishah, may Allah be pleased with her.[2] It has also been narrated by Ibn Hibban on the authority of Jābir, may Allah be pleased with him, that the Prophet (PBUH) led them in eight *Rak'ahs* along with the *Witr*.

In addition to this, the people used to perform this prayer as twenty *Rak'ahs* during the times of Umar, Uthman, and 'Alī, as adopted by the Ḥanafīs and the Ḥanbalīs. Ash-Shafi`i and others also adopt this opinion as affirmed by At-Tirmidhī. However, Mālik says that this prayer consists of thirty-six *Rak'ahs* other than the two *Rak'ahs* known as the *shaf* and the odd *Rak'ah* (or *Rak'ahs*) of the *Witr*. To settle this matter, Ibn Hibban asserts that at the beginning the *Tarāwīḥ* prayer was eleven *Rak'ahs* then the people performed it as twenty *Rak'ahs* other than the *shaf* and the *Witr* yet they would recite in them from the Qur'ān less than what they used to recite in the eleven *Rak'ahs*. Then the recitation was curtailed while the number of *Rak'ah* was increased to thirty-six.

[1] Narrated by Al-Bukhārī and Muslim.
[2] Narrated by Al-Bukhārī and Muslim,

Finally, as some scholars maintain, the original number, i.e., eleven *Rakʿahs*, can be adopted because the Prophet (PBUH) used to do so when performing voluntary night prayers in general, yet there is no harm if the other numbers are applied. And, Allah knows best.

Q. No. (124): What is the Eclipse Prayer (*Ṣalāt al-Khusūf*) and how should it be performed?

A: The Eclipse Prayer is a *Sunnah muʾakkadah* which is to be performed both by men and by women. It is better to perform it in congregation, but it is permissible to perform it individually.

It consists of two *Rakʿahs* and each of the two *Rakʿahs* contains two acts of bowing and two acts of prostration. It is to be performed as follows:

1. Say *Takbīr* then recite *Al-Fātiḥah* and some part of the Qur'ān, prolonging the recitation.

2. Say *Takbīr* then bow down, prolonging your bowing.

3. Raise your body and say "*Samiʿa-llāhu liman ḥamidah. Rabbana wa laka-l-ḥamd* (Allah hears whoever praises Him. O Allah! Praise be to You!)"

4. Do not fall prostrate but recite while standing - *Al-Fātiḥah* and some part of the Qur'ān, prolonging your recitation yet make it a little bit shorter than your first recitation.

5. Say *Takbīr* and bow down, prolonging your bowing yet make it shorter than the first one.

6. Raise your body and say "*Samiʿa-llāhu liman ḥamidah. Rabbana wa laka-l-ḥamd.*"

7. Prostrate twice as you usually do in your prayer.

8. Stand up for the second *Rakʿah* and do in it as you did in the first one. And, Allah knows best.

Q. No. (125): What is the *Istisqā'* Prayer and how should it be performed?

A: It is an act of the *Sunnah* that the Muslim offers the *Istisqā'* Prayer when it stops raining and the land becomes dry. *Istisqā'* literally means "request for rain". In this prayer the Imām leads the people in two *Rak'ahs* for this purpose "of request for water" and invokes Allah and asks Him for forgiveness earnestly along with them. It has been narrated that Abdullāh Ibn Zayd, may Allah be pleased with him, said that the Prophet (PBUH) went toward the *Muṣallā* (place of prayer) and invoked Allah for rain, and that he faced the *qiblah* and offered two *Rak'ahs.*[1] And, Allah knows best.

Q. No. (126): What is the *Shar'ī* ruling concerning the Funeral Prayer (*Ṣalāt al-Janāzah*) and how should it be performed?

A: Almighty Allah holds a great and special position for the believer, so He has prescribed the Funeral Prayer or *Ṣalāt al-Janāzah* as a way through which his brothers in faith can invoke Allah for him and ask Him to forgive him. It is also a form of intercession (*shafā'ah*) done by the believers for their Muslim brothers and sisters after they die.

Ṣalāt al-Janāzah is a prescribed act of worship according to the Qur'ān and the *Sunnah*, and it is a *Farḍ kifāyah* or a collective obligation which, if done by some Muslims, the other Muslims are not legally asked to fulfil it.

To perform the Funeral Prayer, first of all, the *Janāzah* Muslims who want to perform the prayer are to stand in rows behind him. After that four *Takbīrahs*, that is, four acts of *Takbīr*, each with the words " *Allāhu akbar* " are to be said.

After the first *Takbīrah*, *Al-Fātiḥah* is to be recited quietly, even by the Imām. Interestingly enough, Ash-Shāfi'ī and Aḥmad maintain that it is obligatory to recite *Al-Fātiḥah* in the Funeral Prayer, unlike

---

[1] Narrated by Al-Bukhārī and Abū Dāwūd.

Mālik and Abū Ḥanīfah who view that it is "not" to be recited here because the Funeral Prayer is not like other forms of prayer which contain bowing and prostration. Any way, it is famous that *Al-Fātiḥah* is recited in this prayer, especially because it has been narrated by "Al-Bukhārī" that Ibn ʿAbbās, may Allah be pleased with him, once performed the Funeral Prayer in which he recited *Al-Fātiḥah,* then he said, "It is an act of the *Sunnah.*" Moreover, this is the same narration which Ash-Shāfiʿī has quoted to support his opinion that *Al-Fātiḥah* is to be recited in the Funeral Prayer.

After that the second *Takbīrah* is to be said and after it what is known as *As-Ṣalāh al-Ibrāhīmiyyah,* which is normally recited after *tashahhud* in normal prayer, is to be recited here in the Funeral Prayer after the second *Takbīrah. As- Ṣalāh Al- Ibrāhīmiyyah reads, "Allāhumma ṣalli ʿalā Muḥammad wa ʿalā āli Muḥammad. Kamā ṣallayta ʿalā Ibrāhīm wa ʿalā āli Ibrāhīm. ḥamīdun majīd.* (O Allah! Send *Ṣalāh*[1] on Muḥammad and on the family of Muḥammad as You sent *Ṣalāh* on Ibrāhīm (Abraham) and on the family of Ibrāhīm. And bless Muḥammad and the family of Muḥammad as You blessed Ibrāhīm and the family of Ibrāhīm in the worlds. Verily, you are Praiseworthy and Honourable.)"

After the third *Takbīrah,* a performer of the Funeral Prayer invokes Allah for the dead person, and it is better to use an invocation that is reported to have been said by the Prophet (PBUH) for the same purpose. For example, it has been narrated that Awf Ibn Mālik, may Allah be pleased with him, said,

"The Messenger of Allah (PBUH) led us in a funeral prayer, and I remember (the following words) from his invocation, 'O Allah! Forgive him (the dead person), have mercy upon him, give him peace, absolve him, receive him with honour, make his grave spacious. (O Allah!) Wash him with water, snow, and hail, and cleanse him from faults as You would cleanse a white garment from impurity. (O Allah!) Requite him with an abode more excellent than

---

[1] Here: graces, honours, blessings, mercy, etc

his (worldly) abode, with a family better than his family (in worldly life), and with a mate better than his mate (in it). (O Allah!) Admit him to Paradise and protect him from the torment of the grave and the torment of the Fire."[1]

Awf Ibn Mālik commented, "I earnestly desired that I were that dead person."

After the fourth *Takbīrah,* a performer of the Funeral Prayer invokes for the dead person, for himself, and for all the other Muslims, both those who are alive and those who are dead. He may say, "O Allah! Please do not put us to trial after him, do not deprive us of the reward of (invoking and performing prayer for) him, and forgive us and him." Then he makes *Taslīm* as he does in normal prayer, raising his voice while saying the salutation. And, Allah knows best.

---

[1] Narrated by Muslim.

Obligatory Alms (*Zakāh*)

Q. No. (127): How is it that wealth is a means and not a goal in Islam?

A: In Islam, wealth is a means and not a goal, in the sense that it is a means through which the Muslim seeks to obtain Allah's satisfaction by spending out of this wealth in His Cause. This is the best form of wealth, as it is earned through lawful. means and spent for religious purposes. On the other hand, there are people who take wealth as a goal giving no heed to how to gain it or where it is spent, legally or illegally. This is the worst form of wealth, as it is gained through illegal means and spent for illegal purposes. And, Allah knows best.

Q. No. (128): What is the *Shar'ī* ruling concerning withholding *Zakāh*?

A: Wealth is a divine favour and blessing in principle, yet it may become a trial and a cause of Allah's indignation if man does not fulfil the duty that he is obliged to fulfil concerning it, that is *Zakāh*. This is because *Zakāh* is a "right" that "must" be given to those who "deserve" it from among the poor and the needy, and no one is allowed to withhold this right.

Here is a Ḥadīth that indicates clearly the punishment of those who withhold *Zakāh*: It has been narrated by Al-Bukhārī on the authority of Abū Hurayrah, and in which the Prophet (PBUH) said,

"Any one whom Allah has given wealth but he does not pay its *Zakāh*, then, on the Day of Resurrection, his wealth will be presented to him in the shape of a bald-headed poisonous male snake with two poisonous glands in its mouth and it will encircle itself round his neck and bite him over his cheeks and say, I am your wealth; I am your treasure."

Then the Prophet recited this verse,

﴿وَلَا يَحْسَبَنَّ ٱلَّذِينَ يَبْخَلُونَ بِمَآ ءَاتَىٰهُمُ ٱللَّهُ مِن فَضْلِهِۦ هُوَ خَيْرًا لَّهُم ۖ بَلْ هُوَ شَرٌّ لَّهُمْ ۖ سَيُطَوَّقُونَ مَا بَخِلُوا۟ بِهِۦ يَوْمَ ٱلْقِيَٰمَةِ ۗ وَلِلَّهِ مِيرَٰثُ ٱلسَّمَٰوَٰتِ وَٱلْأَرْضِ ۗ وَٱللَّهُ بِمَا تَعْمَلُونَ خَبِيرٌ ﴿١٨٠﴾﴾

"And let not those who covetously withhold of that which Allah has bestowed on them of His Bounty (Wealth) think that it is good for them (and so they do not pay the obligatory Zakāh). Nay, it will be worse for them; the things which they covetously withheld shall be tied to their necks like a collar on the Day of Resurrection. And to Allah belongs the heritage of the heavens and the earth; and Allah is Well-Acquainted with all that you do."
[TMQ: 3: 180]

The verse has mentioned the "collar," which will be tied to the neck of whoever withholds *Zakāh*, and the Ḥadīth has clarified that it will be in the form of that huge "male snake," which will encircle itself round his neck. And, Allah knows best.

Q. No. (129): What are the conditions obligating *Zakāh*?

A: *Zakāh* is obligatory on whoever meets the following conditions: to be Muslim, to be free, to have the *Nisāb* (the minimal amount of wealth which obligates *Zakāh* as specified by the Sharīʿah), that a whole year passes while having the property, and not to be indebted.

The owner of the property must be Muslim, for this is a condition of legal responsibility or A payer of *Zakāh* must be free because a slave is himself owned by another person and it is known that a slave is possessed by his master along with whatever he himself possesses. It is also a condition that the Muslim should have the *Nisāb* so that it becomes obligatory upon him to pay *Zakāh* because *Zakāh* is obligatory on those who are rich, and not those who are poor, as the Prophet (PBUH) said,

"It is to be taken from their rich people to be (paid) back to their poor people."[1]

As for the passing of one year while having this *Nisāb*, this year is a Ḥijri one, which is counted according to lunar months. With this passing of a whole year, the Sharīʿah grants man the opportunity to increase his wealth through business and other lawful means, so that he can pay the *Zakāh* due on him from his profit.

Finally, a man must not be in debt for *Zakāh* to be due on him, because *Zakāh*, originally, is obligatory on the rich for supporting the poor and the needy, while an indebted man is himself poor and needy, and thus it cannot be due on him. And, Allah knows best.

Q. No. (130): Who are the recipients of *Zakāh* or what are categories of those who are to receive *Zakāh* legally?

A: The recipients of *Zakāh* are included in the following verse,

﴿ إِنَّمَا ٱلصَّدَقَٰتُ لِلْفُقَرَآءِ وَٱلْمَسَٰكِينِ وَٱلْعَٰمِلِينَ عَلَيْهَا وَٱلْمُؤَلَّفَةِ قُلُوبُهُمْ وَفِى ٱلرِّقَابِ وَٱلْغَٰرِمِينَ وَفِى سَبِيلِ ٱللَّهِ وَٱبْنِ ٱلسَّبِيلِ ۖ فَرِيضَةً مِّنَ ٱللَّهِ ۗ وَٱللَّهُ عَلِيمٌ حَكِيمٌ ﴿٦٠﴾ ﴾

"Alms-tax is only for the poor and the needy, for those employed to administer it, for those whose hearts are attracted ˹to the faith˺, for ˹freeing˺ slaves, for those in debt, for Allah's cause, and for ˹needy˺ travellers. ˹This is˺ an obligation from Allah. And Allah is All-Knowing, All-Wise." [TMQ: 9: 60]

This Qur'ānic verse lists the eight recipients of *Zakāh* or the eight categories of those who are to receive *Zakāh* legally. And, Allah knows best.

---

[1] A part of Ḥadīth narrated by Al-Bukhārī and Muslim.

Q. No. (131): What are the items of wealth in which *Zakāh* is due, what is the *Nisāb* of each item, and what is the amount that is to be paid as *Zakāh*?

A: The items of wealth in which *Zakāh* is due are the following:

1. Gold and silver

The *Nisāb* of gold is twenty *dinars* which equal eighty- five grams of 24-karat gold, or ninety-seven grams of 21-karat gold, or one hundred and thirteen grams of 18-karat gold.

The *Nisāb* of silver is two hundred dirhams which equal five hundred and ninety-five grams.

The amount of *Zakāh* due on any of these two currencies, as well as on any other currency such as riyal, dollar, and pound, is **2.5 percent**, on condition that the currency in question reaches the required *Nisāb* and a whole Ḥijri year passes while having it. And, the *Nisāb* of banknote is what equals the value of twenty *dinars* as pinpointed above.

2. Plants and fruits

It has been narrated on the authority of Abū Musa and Mu'adh, may Allah be pleased with both of them, that the Messenger of Allah (PBUH) sent them to Yemen to teach the people there their religion, and he (PBUH) ordered them not to take *Ṣadaqah* (*Zakāh*) except from the following four things: wheat, barley, dates, and raisins.[1]

The common denominator between these kinds is that all of them are food which can be stored, and that it is why rice, corn, and the like are included in these kinds. However, there is no *Zakāh* due for vegetables and fruits except for grapes and dates. This is according to the view adopted by the majority of scholars., including Mālik, Ash-Shāfiʿī, and Aḥmad: there is no *Zakāh* due for plants and fruits

---

[1] Narrated by Al- Hakim and Al- Bayhaqi.

except in the kinds that can be stored such as wheat and barley, provided that they reach the *Nisāb*; and there is no *Zakāh* in vegetables.

Zakāh is not obligatory as for any of the above-mentioned kinds except **when they reach five wasqs**: a *wasq* equals sixty *Sā*'s and a *Sā*' equals three kilograms approximately.

If any of the plants for which *Zakāh* is obligatory is irrigated through rain and the like, then **one tenth** (1/10th) is due for it as *Zakāh*; and if it is irrigated through machines and the like, then **a half of tenth** (1/20th) is due for it.

3. Cattle

It is well known that cattle, or *An'ām* in Arabic, is a term which generally refers to beasts which are raised for meat and dairy products, and this includes camels, cows, and sheep, yet this excludes beasts such as donkeys and mules because they are not for eating.

For *Zakāh* to be obligatory in cattle, the following conditions must be met:

1. The cattle must be let to pasture freely most of the year.

2. A whole year must pass while having the cattle in question.

3. The number of the cattle must reach the *Nisāb* determined by the Sharī'ah.

As for the *Nisāb* of cattle and the amount due for every type, it can be pinpointed as follows:

(a) Camels:

No *Zakāh* is due in camels if they are less than five, because the Prophet (PBUH) said,

"No *Zakāh* is due for less than five camels."[1]

The amount of *Zakāh* due for camels can be listed in figures as follows:

The number of the camels	**The *Zakāh* due for it**
5- 9	1 sheep
10- 14	2 sheep
15- 19	3 sheep
20- 24	4 sheep
25- 35	1 *bint makhāḍ* (one-year-old she- camel)
36- 45	1 *bint labūn* (two-year-old she-camel)
46- 60	1 *ḥiqqah* (three-year-old she-camel)
61- 75	1 *jadh'ah* (four-year-old she-camel)
76- 90	2 *bint labūns*
91- 120	2 *ḥiqqah*
121 or more	1 *bint labūns* for every 40 camels and 1 *ḥiqqah* for every 50 camels

(b) Sheep:

No *Zakāh* is due for a sheep if they are less than forty.

The amount of *Zakāh* due for sheep can be listed in figures as follows:

The number of sheep	**The *Zakāh* due for it**
40-120	1 sheep
121-200	2 sheeps
201-300	3 sheeps
300 or more	1 sheep for every 100 sheeps

[1] Narrated by Al-Bukhārī and Muslim.

(c) Cows:

No *Zakāh* is due in cows if they are less than thirty.

The amount of *Zakāh* due in cows can be listed as follows:

The number of cows	The *Zakāh* due for it
30-39	1 *tābī*ʿ (1 year old calf) or 1 *tābīʿah* (1 year old cow)
40-49	1 *mūsinnah* (two years old cow)
60	Two *Tabi*ʿʿs

After that for every thirty cows one *tābī*ʿ is to be paid and for every forty cows one *mūsinnah* is to be paid.

In other words, you can start with the number seventy (being 40+30), as follows: for seventy cows one *mūsinnah* and one *Tabi*ʿʿ are to be paid, for eighty cows two *mūsinnahs* are to be paid, for ninety cows three *Tabi*ʿʿs, for one hundred cows two *Tabi*ʿʿs and one *mūsinnah*, and so on. This means that the obligatory amount changes in every extra ten cows from *tābī*ʿ to *mūsinnah* and vice versa. This is what scholars have unanimously agreed upon according to the narrations available in this regard.

4. *Rikāz* and minerals

Rikāz is a term that refers to treasures buried before the Islamic era. A person may find such *Rikāz* without cost. Islam ordains that a person who finds it must pay **one fifth** of it immediately after finding it without waiting for a year or consideration for a certain *Nisāb*. It has been narrated on the authority of Abū Hurayrah, may Allah be pleased with him, that the Messenger of Allah (PBUH) said, "... And one fifth of *Rikāz* (is to be given as *Zakāh*)."[1] The same ruling applies

[1] Narrated by Al-Bukhārī and Muslim.

to metals or minerals, including everything of the kind that is taken out of the earth such as gold, silver, iron, lead, and copper.

Yet still, if a person finds the *Rikāz* in his own land, then there is no *Zakāh* due for it, as maintained by Abū Ḥanīfah. Ash-Shāfi'ī and Aḥmad, however, view that *Zakāh* is due in whatever metal that is procured out of the earth, and the amount of *Zakāh* here is 2.5 percent of the extracted metal, just like the amount ordained in gold and silver. And, Allah knows best.

Q. No. (132): What is the *Shar'ī* ruling concerning business material or *'Urūḍ at-Tijārah* as far as *Zakāh* is concerned?

A: Business material, or *'Urūḍ at-Tijārah* as expressed in Arabic, is a term that covers whatever man has prepared for marketing and intends to obtain profit through undertaking business on it. Scholars have unanimously agreed that *Zakāh* is due on such business material. This includes lands that a person buys for selling it as a material of business and not to construct a building on it to dwell in. It also includes rice, sugar, lentils, leathers, cars, clothes, and any other stuff in which people trade in. Their value is to be estimated at the end of the year, that is after the passing of a whole Ḥijri year, and *Zakāh* is to be paid for them if they reach the *Nisāb* of gold and silver (as pinpointed in the previous answer). This is because they are regarded as money, and they are utilized with the purpose of profiting.

In his *Al-Fatāwā*, Shaykh Shaltūt says that the majority of the scholars of the Muslim *Ummah*, including the early and the late ones, have maintained that *Zakāh* is obligatory due for business material as long as their value reaches the monetary *Nisāb* (of gold and silver). However, the estimation of the value should not include the value of the shop in which the business is handled nor the stable furniture which is used for undertaking this trade.[1] And, Allah knows best.

[1] See Shaltūt, *Al-Fatāwā*, 121

Q. No. (133): When exactly is *Zakāh* to be paid?

A: The majority of scholars maintain that *Zakāh* becomes due "once" a whole Ḥijri year has passed while having the *Nisāb*. This is because delaying it causes harm to those to whom it is to be paid and, besides this, it is probable that a person may lose his wealth before paying the *Zakāh* due for it and thus the right of the poor will be lost as a result; and still, he will remain legally liable for this *Zakāh*. The Muslim should also remember here that any *Zakāh* which is mixed with property ruins this property, as explicitly stated in the Ḥadīth narrated on the authority of 'Ā'ishah who said that the Prophet (PBUH) said, "No *Ṣadaqah* (i.e., *Zakāh*) is mixed with property except that it ruins it."[1] That is why it must be paid once it becomes due and no delay is allowable. And, Allah knows best.

117Q. No. (134): What is the *Shar'ī* ruling concerning the payment of *Zakāh* to one's relatives?

A: It is not permissible to pay *Zakāh* to one's ancestors and descendants, nor is it permissible for a husband to give *Zakāh* to his wife or for a wife to give *Zakāh* to her husband. Yet, it is permissible to give *Zakāh* to relatives other than these, such as brothers and sisters, provided that they legally deserve to receive it, like being poor for example. By ancestors we mean one's father and mother as well as one's grandfathers and grandmothers, and by descendants we mean one's sons and daughters as well as one's grandsons and granddaughters. This is because it is obligatory upon the Muslim to provide for them if they have no income from which they can spend on themselves. If a payer of *Zakāh* gave *Zakāh* to any of these relatives, it would be as if he himself had benefited from that *Zakāh* as he would not have to spend on them as ordained by the Sharī'ah. And, Allah knows best.

---

[1] Narrated by Al-Bukhārī and Ash-Shāfi'ī.

Q. No. (135): Is it permissible to give *Zakāh* to a strong young man who can earn his livelihood?

A: It is not permissible to give *Zakāh* to such a person because the Prophet (PBUH) said,

"*Ṣadaqah* is not lawful for a rich person or for a stout strong person."[1]

This is because if it was permissible to give him *Zakāh*, he would get accustomed to laziness and depending on such an easy source of income, while our religion stimulates Muslims to work and never be lazy or indolent. And, Allah knows best.

Q. No. (136): Is it permissible to give *Zakāh* to a young person?

A: It is permissible to pay *Zakāh* to people who are young and people who are old. This includes an orphan who has no property and a young child whose father is poor. However, in this case, *Zakāh* is to be given to the legal guardian (*Walī*) who is in charge of the affairs of this orphan or child; and if he has no legal guardian, *Zakāh* is to be paid to whoever may be responsible for him such as his mother, as maintained by Aḥmad Ibn Hanbal. Still, it is permissible to give *Zakāh* to a discerning boy who can distinguish between what is good and what is evil and who is able to spend the money given to him properly.[2] And, Allah knows best.

Q. No. (137): Is it obligatory that the Muslim gives the *Zakāh* due for *'Urūḍ at-Tijārah* or business material in the form of money, or is it permissible to give *Zakāh* out of the material itself?

A: It is permissible to give the *Zakāh* due for business material from the material itself. It has been narrated that Samurah Ibn Jundub, may Allah be pleased with him, said,

---

[1] Narrated by Abū Dāwūd and At-Tirmidhī.

[2] See *Al-Mughnī*, 4/97.

"The Messenger of Allah (PBUH) used to order us to give out *Ṣadaqah* (meaning *Zakāh*) from (the material) which we used to prepare for trading."[1]

It is also permissible to estimate the value of this material and pay the *Zakāh* due for it in the form of money. It has been narrated on the authority of Abū ʿAmr Ibn Ḥamās who said that his father said,

"I used to sell leather, pots, and bowls, and once ʿUmar Ibn al-Khaṭṭāb passed by me and said, Pay the *Zakāh* due for your property.' I said, 'O Commander of the Believers! They are just leather and pots! He said, 'Estimate (their value) then pay the *Zakāh* due for them."[2]

And, Allah knows best.

Q. No. (138): What are the things for which *Zakāh* is not obligatory?

A: No *Zakāh* is due for any of the necessary things which man always needs and uses in his life. Faqīhs have stated that no *Zakāh* is due for a house which is used for lodgement, nor for the furniture of such a house, nor for clothes which one wears, nor for one's car which is used for personal transportation, nor for the machines used in factories and the like, nor for any other thing which is used in a similar way and for similar purposes. In a word, *Zakāh* is not to be paid for these things as long as they are not used for "profiting". And, Allah knows best.

Q. No. (139): Is it valid to count debt as part of the *Zakāh* which is to be paid?

A: If a person is indebted to another yet he is poor and cannot pay the debt back, it is not valid for the creditor to count this debt as part of *Zakāh* which he is to pay. This is because the property in question does not actually exist and thus it cannot be counted as

---

[1] Narrated by Abū Dāwūd and At-Tirmidhī.

[2] Narrated by Aḥmad, Ash-Shāfiʿī, and others.

part of the *Zakāh*. In his *Al-Fiqh ash-Sharī' al-Muyassar, As-Sabūni* suggests that to solve this problem, the creditor can pay a certain sum of money to the indebted person while intending that this money is from the *Zakāh* due on him then tells the indebted person to pay the debt back from this money. Another possible solution is that the creditor sends part of the *Zakāh* money to the indebted person with another one and the latter tells the indebted person that he can pay his debt back from this money which Allah has bestowed upon him. In this way, the indebted person will "own" the money and thus it will be valid for the creditor to take that money as a payment of the debt he owes that poor person.[1] And, Allah knows best.

Q. No. (140): Is it obligatory that the giver of *Zakāh* tells the person to whom he gives it that it is *Zakāh*?

A: On the contrary, he should not tell him that the money he is giving to him is *Zakāh* so that he may not break his heart and hurt his feelings. It is enough that the payer of *Zakāh* "intends" that what he is giving to that person is part of the *Zakāh* due on him, for actions are judged only according to intentions. He may also present that *Zakāh* to him in the form of a gift or a present or brotherly aid while intending that it is part of the *Zakāh*. This will be sufficient for him, and Allah knows best.

Q. No. (141): What is the *Shar'ī* ruling concerning a person who pays the *Zakāh* due on him to a person then discovers later on that this person is rich?

A: The payment of *Zakāh* in this case is legally sufficient and effective on the part of its payer and he does not have to pay it again to a poor person, because what is "obligatory" in this connection is to pay the *Zakāh* due on him to a person whom he thinks to be poor or needy according to his personal reasoning, and he has already fulfilled this

---

[1] See *Al-Fiqh ash-Sharī' al-Muyassar*, 2/144.

duty, so what he has done is sufficient for him. This is further because it may not be easy to make out those who are to be legally regarded as rich and those who are to be legally regarded as poor. Thus, if he thinks that a certain person is poor, it is permissible for him to pay *Zakāh* to this person, and it is not stipulated that he should ask him whether he is poor or not, yet he may ask others about him.

This may be indicated by what has been narrated on the authority of Abū Hurayrah, may Allah be pleased with him, that the Messenger of Allah (PBUH) said,

"A man said that he would surely give *Ṣadaqah* (alms) (to someone) but when he went out with his *Ṣadaqah* he put it at the hand of a rich man. The people started talking (to one another) that a *Ṣadaqah* had been given to a rich man! He (the man who gave it) said, 'O Allah! Praise be to You! (Has the *Ṣadaqah* been given) to a rich man?' Then someone came to him and said, your *Ṣadaqah* has been accepted (by Allah). As for the rich man, perhaps he will take an example (from this) and spend out of what Allah has bestowed on him."[1]

And, Allah knows best.

Q. No. (142): Is it permissible to move or carry *Zakāh* from one country to another?

A: It is permissible to move or carry the money or property assigned as *Zakāh* from one country to another, if the people in the other country need it more than the people of the country from which it is moved. This is because the Prophet (PBUH) said,

"It is to be) taken from their rich people to be (paid) back to their poor people."[2]

---

[1] Narrated by Al-Bukhārī, Muslim, and An-Nasā'ī.

[2] A part of Ḥadīth narrated by Al-Bukhārī and Muslim.

This means that *Zakāh* is to be taken from the rich among Muslims to be paid back to the poor also among Muslims. Muslims constitute one nation no matter where they are, and any place in which Muslims live is like a homeland for the other Muslims. Therefore, it is permissible for the Muslim to pay the *Zakāh* due for his wealth to the Muslims who may be in a place other than that in which he lives. However, if there are poor people in his place, it is legally detestable that he carries *Zakāh* to another place or country, because it is more becoming for a Muslim to fulfil the need of those who are close to him than to fulfil the need of those who are far away from him.

It has been narrated by Muslim on the authority of Jābir, may Allah be pleased with him, that the Prophet (PBUH) said to a man,

"Start with your own self and spend on yourself; and if anything is left, it is to be spent on your family; and if anything is left (after meeting the needs of the family), it is to be spent on your relatives; and if anything is left from your relatives, it is to be spent like this, and so on."

This Ḥadīth indicates the way how the Muslim should act concerning "spending" in general, and it may support the judgment that *Zakāh* can be moved from one place to another one where Muslims may be in more need for it. And Allah. knows best.

Q. No. (143): Give an example clarifying the way how the Muslim can pay the *Zakāh* due for his banknote?

A: First of all, you should know that the value of any banknote the Muslim may have is to be estimated with the value equal to the *Nisāb* of gold. If the value of this banknote amounts to the *Nisāb* of gold and a whole Ḥijri year passes while being in his possession, then the Muslim must pay *Zakāh* for it. The amount of *Zakāh* due for banknote is 2.5 percent, just like gold and silver.

Suppose that you have ten thousand pounds. To count the *Zakāh* due for this sum of money you should know first that the *Nisāb* of gold is eighty-five grams of 24-karat gold. If the value of one gram of this karat equals 30 pounds, then the *Nisāb* will be: 85 30 2550 pounds. This means that the money possessed (i.e., 10000 pounds) exceeds the *Nisāb*, and thus what is to be paid as *Zakāh* here is 2.5 percent of this sum of money: 2.5% of 10000 = 250 pounds. Thus, 250 pounds is the *Zakāh* amount that is to be paid for these ten thousand pounds. And, Allah knows best.

Q. No. (144): What is the description of the wealth which is legally regarded as "hoarded"?

A: Wealth that is legally described as "hoarded" is that whose *Zakāh* is not paid, whether it is gold, silver, banknote, or any other form of property for which *Zakāh* is due yet this *Zakāh* is not paid. Almighty Allah says,

﴿وَٱلَّذِينَ يَكۡنِزُونَ ٱلذَّهَبَ وَٱلۡفِضَّةَ وَلَا يُنفِقُونَهَا فِي سَبِيلِ ٱللَّهِ فَبَشِّرۡهُم بِعَذَابٍ أَلِيمٖ ٣٤﴾

"... And those who hoard up gold and silver and spend it not in the Way of Allah, announce unto them a painful torment." [TMQ: 9:34]

Ibn 'Umar, may Allah be pleased with him, said,

"If the *Zakāh* due for any of that (i.e., gold or silver) is paid, then it is not of the (prohibited) hoarding (of gold and silver), even if it is (kept) under seven earths; and whatever is seen of it (i.e., not hoarded) and the *Zakāh* due for it is not paid, then it is of the (prohibited) hoarding."[1]

And, Allah knows best.

Q. No. (145): It is a stipulation that for *Zakāh* to be due on a person he must not be indebted, but what if his wealth exceeds his debt?

---

[1] Narrated by 'Abd ar-Razzāq.

A: The Prophet (PBUH) said,

"There is no (due) *Ṣadaqah* (alms) except that which is (given) as a result of richness (or self-sufficiency)."[1]

That is why no *Zakāh* is due upon any indebted person as he then becomes himself poor and needs help to pay his debt back. Nevertheless, if the wealth he possesses exceeds his debt and this extra amount reaches the *Nisāb*, he must pay *Zakāh* for this extra property. It has been narrated that 'Uthman Ibn Affan, may Allah be pleased with him, said,

"This is the month of your *Zakāh* (i.e., Ramaḍān). Therefore, let him whoever is indebted pays his debt back then pay *Zakāh* for the rest of his property."

He said that in the presence of some Companions of the Prophet (PBUH) and none of them objected to what he had said, and that indicated that they agreed with him concerning his judgment.[2] And, Allah knows best.

Q. No. (146): What is the *Shar'ī* ruling concerning the payment of *Zakāh* due for the wealth of a child or an insane person?

A: The majority of scholars, including Mālik, Ash-Shafi`i, and Aḥmad, maintain that *Zakāh* is due for the property of a child and an insane person, and thus the legal guardian (*Walī*) of the child or the insane person must pay this *Zakāh*. They have quoted the following Ḥadīth to prove their view:

"Trade in the property of orphans. *Zakāh* does not consume it."[3]

---

[1] Narrated by Aḥmad, and Al-Bukhārī has narrated a wording similar to this one.
[2] See Al-Mughni, 4/264.
[3] Narrated by At-Tabarani.

They have also said that ʿĀʾishah, may Allah be pleased with her, used to pay the *Zakāh* due on some orphans who were under her patronage.

However, Abū Ḥanīfah asserts that *Zakāh* is not due for the property of a child or an insane person because neither of them is legally responsible (*mukallaf*) and sanity and puberty are stipulated for fulfilling an act of worship like *Zakāh*, just like Prayer. It has been narrated that Ibn ʿAbbās, may Allah be pleased with him, said,

"No *Zakāh* is obligatory upon a child until prayer is obligatory upon him."[1]

To settle this matter, it can be said that Abū Ḥanīfah's view may be more evident because the conditions obligating *Zakāh* are not met by the persons in question, yet still the view adopted by the majority of scholars is better for those who take precautions against wrong-doing. And, Allah knows best.

Q. No. (147): What is the *Sharʿī* ruling concerning the wealth gained during the year which is to pass while having the *Nisāb*?

A: One of the conditions obligating *Zakāh* is that a whole Ḥijri year must pass while having the *Nisāb*. However, it is not a stipulation that a year should pass for every property added to this *Nisāb*. Rather, it is sufficient to count the period of the year, which is to pass before paying the *Zakāh*, by defining a beginning and an end for it. For example, one may count one's *Zakāh in* the month of Ramaḍān every year. In this way the Muslim can count whatever property he can gain from the beginning of the year to its end. For instance, if you have five thousand pounds at the beginning of the year and you save two thousand pounds every month, thus accumulating to an extra twenty-four thousand pounds at the end of the year, then you have to pay *Zakāh* for the total sum you have at the end of the year

---

[1] Narrated by Ad-Daruqutni.

as follows: 5000 pounds possessed at the beginning of the year 24000 pounds saved throughout the year = 29000 pounds. 2.5 percent of 290000 725 pounds, and this is the *Zakāh* that is to be paid for the whole property. And, Allah knows best.

Q. No. (148): What is the *Shar'ī* ruling concerning a person who dies before paying the *Zakāh* due on him?

A: Whenever a person dies before paying the *Zakāh* due upon him, this *Zakāh* is to be paid before his debts are paid to the creditors if he is indebted - and also before dealing with legacies he may have bequeathed. However, Abū Ḥanīfah maintains that no *Zakāh* is to be paid out of the deceased person's property because *Zakāh* is an act of worship which is to be fulfilled with intention and no such intention can go out of a dead person, and thus no one can fulfil this act of worship in his stead. And, Allah knows best.

Q. No. (149): What is the *Shar'ī* ruling concerning voluntary alms paid by the heirs of a dead person?

A: It is permissible for the heirs of a dead person to give voluntary alms on his or her behalf and the reward of that will reach him or her. It has been narrated by At-Tirmidhī that a man said, "O Messenger of Allah! My mother is dead. Will it benefit her if I give out voluntary alms for her benefit?" He (PBUH) answered in the affirmative, so the man said, "So, I have a garden, and I call you to witness that I have given it in charity on her benefit." And, Allah knows best.

Q. No. (150): Is it valid to pay *Zakāh* before it is due?

A: The majority of Faqīhs, including Ash-Shāfi'ī, Aḥmad, and Abū Ḥanīfah, maintain that it is permissible to pay *Zakāh* before its time, because Ibn Mājah has narrated that Al-`Abbas, may Allah be pleased with him, asked the Messenger of Allah (PBUH) if he could pay his *Ṣadaqah* (*Zakāh*) before its time and he (PBUH) allowed him to do so.[1] This is permissible because it is considered a kind of "hastening" to do something good. And, Allah knows best.

Q. No. (151): How can the Muslim pay *Zakāh* for his business money?

A: A Muslim trader must make an inventory of his business material at the end of every year and count its value according to the prices of the time of counting, and not according to the time when he bought that material, because the value of things increases and decreases in accordance with the expensiveness and cheapness of things. After that he can pay the *Zakāh* due for this material if its value reaches the *Nisāb*. However, he must not include in the counting the value of the furniture, instruments, or machines used in his business, because they are not included in the stuff prepared for marketing. And, Allah knows best.

Q. No. (152): What is the *Shar'ī* ruling concerning the payment of *Zakāh* for diamonds, pearls, and peridot?

A: The majority of scholars have agreed that there is no *Zakāh* due for the afore-mentioned jewels and any other gems as long as they are used as adornment. Yet, if they are used for business or investment, then *Zakāh* is to be paid for them because they will then include in *'Urūḍ at-Tijārah* or business material, which includes everything that has been prepared for selling and profiting. Thus, their value is to be estimated at the end of the year then 2.5 percent of their value is to be paid as *Zakāh* if their value reaches the *Nisāb*. And, Allah knows best.

Q. No. (153): What is the *Shar'ī* ruling concerning the *Zakāh* due for debts which a Muslim owes people?

A: Scholars unanimously view that *Zakāh* is due for a debt on the creditor if it is acknowledged by the indebted person and he is trustworthy. However, Ash-Shāfi'ī says that the creditor must pay

---

[1] Narrated by Ibn Mājah and At-Tirmidhī.

the *Zakāh* due for the debt even before taking it back because he has the ability to take it back, whereas Abū Ḥanīfah and Aḥmad maintain that it is not obligatory upon the creditor to pay the *Zakāh* due for the debt except when he has already got it as he can then pay the *Zakāh* due for the debt including the *Zakāh* due for the previous years through which he did not take it back.

If the debt is with an insolvent person or with a person who denies the debt or postpones it every now and then, then no *Zakāh* is due for such a debt on the creditor until he gets it, and then he can pay *Zakāh* for it as due for only one year and no *Zakāh* is due for the previous years. This is because if *Zakāh* was due for them, it would be another tribulation on the part of the creditor added to the tribulation of owing such an insolvent person or a person who denies his right to it. And, Allah knows best.

Q. No. (154): Is *Zakāh* due for horses and slaves?

A: The majority of Faqīhs view that no *Zakāh* is due for horses and slaves unless they are used as business material. This is because horses are originally used for racing and slaves for service and thus both are included in the things which are necessary and important for man's use. Scholars have proved this opinion with a number of texts. For example, it has been narrated by Al-Bukhārī and Muslim on the authority of Abū Hurayrah, may Allah be pleased with him, that the Messenger of Allah (PBUH) said,

"No *Ṣadaqah* (*Zakāh*) is due upon the Muslim for his slave or his horse."

However, Abū Ḥanīfah asserts that *Zakāh* is due for horses if they are males and females, because they can propagate with this characteristic, especially with the fact that Abū Dāwūd has narrated on the authority of Jābir, may Allah be pleased with him, that the Prophet (PBUH) said,

"One *dīnār* is due (as *Zakāh*) for every horse that pastures freely."

Still, the opinion of the majority of scholars that no *Zakāh* is due for horses absolutely - is more evident because the hadiths backing it are mentioned in the Two Ṣaḥīḥs of Al-Bukhārī and Muslim.[1] And, Allah knows best.

Q. No. (155): Is it valid to pay the *Zakāh* due for camels from the male camels?

A: Only female camels or she-camels are to be paid as *Zakāh* for camels, because the hadiths defining the *Zakāh* due for them mention only female camels. Al-Bukhārī has narrated that Anas, may Allah be pleased with him, said, "When Abū Bakr sent me to (collect *Zakāh* from) Bahrain, he wrote to me the following: (and what he wrote to him included the following,)"... For every five camels one sheep is to be paid, and if they are between twenty-five to thirty-five camels, one *bint makhāḍ* (one-year-old she-camel) is to be paid; and if they are between thirty-six to forty-five (camels), one *bint labūn* (two- year-old she-camel) is to be paid; and if they are between forty- six to sixty (camels), one *ḥiqqah* (three-year-old she-camel) is to be paid; and if the number is between sixty-one to seventy-five (camels), one *jadh'ah* (four-year-old she-camel) is to be paid..." to the end of the narration. However, both male and female cows and sheep can be paid as *Zakāh* for cows and sheep, also because the wording of the texts defining *Zakāh* for them includes both of them. And, Allah knows best.

Q. No. (156): What is the *Shar'ī* ruling concerning a collector of *Zakāh* who takes the best of the cattle as *Zakāh* and leaves the other camels, cows, or sheep for the payer of *Zakāh*?

A: It is not permissible for a collector of *Zakāh* to select the best camels, cows, or sheep and take them as *Zakāh because* the Prophet (PBUH) forbade this, for it causes harm to the owner of the cattle. Rather, he should select the cattle on a scale of the average of what

---

[1] See *Fatḥ al-Bārī*, 3/327.

is good and what is bad among the animals in question. It has been narrated by Al-Bukhārī and Muslim on the authority of Ibn ʿAbbās, may Allah be pleased with him, that when the Messenger of Allah (PBUH) sent Mu'adh, may Allah be pleased with him, to Yemen, he said (to him),

"You are going to people of a (Divine) Book. First of all invite them to worship Allah (alone) and when they come to know Allah, inform them that Allah has enjoined on them five prayers in every day and night; and if they start offering these prayers, inform them that Allah has enjoined on them *Zakāh*, and it is to be taken from the rich amongst them and given to the poor amongst them; and if they obey you in that, take *Zakāh* from them and avoid (i.e., do not take) the best property of the people as *Zakāh*."

In another Ḥadīth the Prophet (PBUH) said,

"Whoever deals with *Ṣadaqah* (*Zakāh*) excessively is like a person who withholds it."[1]

meaning that whoever takes from it what exceeds the due. amount of *Zakāh* is as sinful as a person who does not pay the due *Zakāh*. And, Allah knows best.

Q. No. (157): What is not valid to be taken in *Zakāh*?

A: Just as the Sharīʿah forbids that a collector of *Zakāh* takes the best of the property of the *Zakāh* payer as *Zakāh*, it also forbids that the *Zakāh* payer gives what is bad in his property as *Zakāh*. For example, the Prophet (PBUH) said concerning the *Zakāh* due for cattle,

"No old (animal whose teeth have dropped because of old age) is to be taken out as *Ṣadaqah* (*Zakāh*) nor an imperfect (animal is to be taken out for that)."[2]

---

[1] Narrated by Ibn Mājah and others.
[2] Narrated by At-Tirmidhī and Abū Dāwūd.

At-Tirmidhī has stated that Az-Zuhrī says that a collector of *Zakāh should* divide the sheep into three categories: one containing the best of them (in terms of quality), one containing the medium of them, and one containing the worst of them. After that he should take the medium of them as *Zakāh.*[1] And, Allah knows best.

Q. No. (158): What is the *Zakāh* due for honey?

A: Faqīhs have differed concerning the question whether there is any *Zakāh* due for honey or not. There are two views in this regard: the first view is that *Zakāh* is due for honey and its amount is one tenth, just as the case with plants and fruits. This opinion is adopted by the Ḥanafīs and the Ḥanbalīs, who have quoted certain hadiths to prove their view. For instance, it has been narrated on the authority of Ibn ʿUmar, may Allah be pleased with him, that the Messenger of Allah (PBUH) said,

"In every ten canteens of honey one canteen is due (as *Zakāh*)."[2]

The second view is that no *Zakāh* is due for honey, because it resembles the silk that comes out of silkworms. This opinion is adopted by the Shāfiʿīs and the Mālikīs, who have quoted the following narration to prove their view: it has been narrated that Nafi` said,

"Umar Ibn Abdul-Aziz asked me about the *Ṣadaqah* (*Zakāh*) due for honey and I said to him, 'We do not have any honey so that we can give *Ṣadaqah* (*Zakāh*) out of it. Yet still, Al-Mughīrah Ibn Ḥakīm has told us that no *Ṣadaqah* (*Zakāh*) is due for honey.' 'Umar commented, "This is an acceptable just (ruling).' Then he sent a message to the people (i.e., to his rulers as he was the Caliph then) that no *Zakāh* was to be collected from the people for that."[3]

---

[1] Name of At- Tirmidhi, 3/19.

[2] Narrated by At-Tirmidhī

[3] Narrated by At-Tirmidhī

The first view adopted by the Ḥanafīs and the Ḥanbalīs is stronger because it secures more benefit for the poor and because it resembles the plants and fruits that come out of the earth. After all, Almighty Allah says,

﴿ وَمَآ أَنفَقْتُم مِّن شَىْءٍ فَهُوَ يُخْلِفُهُۥ وَهُوَ خَيْرُ ٱلرَّٰزِقِينَ ٣٩ ﴾

"... and whatsoever you spend of anything (in Allah's Cause), He will replace it. And He is the Best of providers." [TMQ: 34: 39]

And, Allah knows best.

Q. No. (159): What is the *Shar'ī* ruling concerning the *Zakāh* due for what is taken out of the sea?

A: The majority of Faqīhs maintain that no *Zakāh* is due for whatever is taken out of the sea, such as fish, pearls, corals, ambergris, etc., because Al-Bukhārī has narrated that Ibn `Abbas, may Allah be pleased with him, said,

"Ambergris is not included in *Rikāz* (here *Rikāz* can be translated as "ore"), as it is something that the sea throws out."

And, Allah knows best.

Q. No. (160): Is there any *Zakāh* due for property that is usurped, stolen, or lost?

A: The majority of Faqīhs maintain that no *Zakāh* is due for any property that has been usurped, stolen, or lost, because it is, with this condition, out of the possession the person who possessed it once, and so he cannot get any growth or investment out of it. Whereas Mālik says that he must pay *Zakāh* for it for one year when he gets it back.

The first view is more correct and more evident, because such property is out of his possession and when he gets it back, he just starts dealing with it as a newly possessed thing, and thus *Zakāh* will be due for it after a year passes from the time, he gets that usurped, stolen, or lost property. And, Allah knows best.

Q. No. (161): Is "intention" obligatory on paying *Zakāh*?

A: *Zakāh* is an act of worship, and so it is stipulated that whoever is to pay it must "intend" that what he is going to pay is *Zakāh*, while seeking to get reward from Allah for that. Almighty Allah says,

﴿وَمَآ ءَاتَيۡتُم مِّن رِّبٗا لِّيَرۡبُوَاْ فِيٓ أَمۡوَٰلِ ٱلنَّاسِ فَلَا يَرۡبُواْ عِندَ ٱللَّهِۖ وَمَآ ءَاتَيۡتُم مِّن زَكَوٰةٖ تُرِيدُونَ وَجۡهَ ٱللَّهِ فَأُوْلَٰٓئِكَ هُمُ ٱلۡمُضۡعِفُونَ ٣٩﴾

"And that which you give in gift (to others), in order that it may increase (your wealth by expecting to get a better one in return) from other people's property, has no increase with Allah, but that which you give in Zakāh seeking Allah's Countenance then those, they shall have manifold increase." [TMQ: 30: 39]

Also, the Prophet (PBUH) says in the well-known Ḥadīth which has been narrated on the authority of Umar, may Allah be pleased with him,

"Actions are but by intention and every man shall have but that which he intends..."[1]

Interestingly enough, Mālik and Ash-Shāfi'ī stipulate that "intention" must be determined at the time when *Zakāh* is paid, while Abū Ḥanīfah maintains that intention can be determined either at the time when *Zakāh* is paid or when the person "sets aside" the amount due in his property as *Zakāh*. Aḥmad, however, says that it is permissible to determine intention a short time before paying it. And, Allah knows best.

Q. No. (162): Is it permissible to pay *Zakāh* before the end of the year that is stipulated to pass while having the *Nisāb*?

---

[1] Narrated by Al-Bukhārī and Muslim.

A: The majority of Faqīhs view that it is permissible to do so because it is a way of "hastening" to do something good and beneficial for the recipients of *Zakāh*. Almighty Allah says,

﴿ فَٱسْتَبِقُوا۟ ٱلْخَيْرَٰتِ ۚ إِلَى ٱللَّهِ مَرْجِعُكُمْ جَمِيعًا فَيُنَبِّئُكُم بِمَا كُنتُمْ فِيهِ تَخْتَلِفُونَ ﴿٤٨﴾ ﴾

"... so, strive as in a race in good deeds. The return of you (all) is to Allah; then He will inform you about that in which you used to differ."

[TMQ: 5:48]

To prove their view, the majority of Faqīhs have quoted what has been narrated by Abū Dāwūd and others that Ibn 'Abbās, may Allah be pleased with him, asked the Messenger of Allah (PBUH) to permit him to pay the *Zakāh* due on him before the passing of the (required) year as a way of hastening to do good, and he (PBUH) allowed him to do so.[1] Mālik, however, maintains that the payment of *Zakāh* is not legally sufficient unless a whole year passes as ordained by the Prophet (PBUH).[2] And, Allah knows best.

Q. No. (163): What is the *Shar'ī* ruling concerning the payment of the "value" of what is due for *Zakāh*?

A: The majority of Faqīhs maintain that it is permissible for a payer of the *Zakāh* due for items of *Zakāh* (other than money), such as cattle, gold, silver, etc., to pay the value of such items of *Zakāh* in the form of money. This is because the purpose of paying *Zakāh* is to give the recipient of *Zakāh* what is sufficient to fulfil his needs. Therefore, as it is permissible to do that with dates, camels, and gold, for instance, it is also possible that this be accomplished through the monetary value of these things. Among the proofs which the majority of scholars have used to prove their view is the narration

---

[1] Narrated by Abū Dāwūd and others.

[2] This is in narrated with the same meaning by Ibn Mājah and Al-Bayhaqi.

of Al-Bukhārī that Mu'adh, may Allah be pleased with him, asked the people of Yemen to bring him clothes as *Ṣadaqah* (*Zakāh*) instead of barely and corn because that, he said, was "easier for them and better for the Companions of the Prophet (PBUH) in Medina".

On the other hand, Ash-Shāfiʿī views that it is not permissible to pay the value of an item of *Zakāh* instead of the item itself except when the item or its kind is not available, because this is what the Muslim should do as a way of acting upon the textual ordinances in this regard. It has been narrated by Abū Dāwūd and Ibn Mājah that when the Prophet (PBUH) sent Mu'adh to Yemen, he said to him,

"Take (as *Zakāh*) grains from grains, sheep from sheep, camels from camels, and cows from cows."

In the light of the items of proof presented by the majority of Faqīhs and their justification of this judgment that what matters here is to bring about what is beneficial for the recipients of *Zakāh*, it becomes clear that their view is more correct and more evident. And, Allah knows best.

Q. No. (164): Is it a stipulation that *Zakāh* be paid to all of the eight categories representing the recipients of *Zakāh*?

A: First of all, the eight categories representing the recipients of *Zakāh* are those mentioned in the Qur'ānic verse that reads,

﴿ إِنَّمَا ٱلصَّدَقَٰتُ لِلْفُقَرَآءِ وَٱلْمَسَٰكِينِ وَٱلْعَٰمِلِينَ عَلَيْهَا وَٱلْمُؤَلَّفَةِ قُلُوبُهُمْ وَفِى ٱلرِّقَابِ وَٱلْغَٰرِمِينَ وَفِى سَبِيلِ ٱللَّهِ وَٱبْنِ ٱلسَّبِيلِ ۖ فَرِيضَةً مِّنَ ٱللَّهِ ۗ وَٱللَّهُ عَلِيمٌ حَكِيمٌ ﴿٦٠﴾ ﴾

"As-Sadaqat (here it means Zakāh) are only for the poor, and the needy, and those employed to collect (the funds); and to attract the hearts of those who have been inclined (towards Islam); and to free the captives; and for those in debt; and for Allah's Cause, and for the wayfarer (a traveller who is cut

off from everything); a duty imposed by Allah. And Allah is All-Knower, All-Wise." [TMQ: 9: 60]

As for the question whether it is a stipulation that *Zakāh* be paid to all of these eight categories, the majority of Faqīhs maintain that it is permissible for a payer of *Zakāh* to pay it either to only one of these legally defined recipients or to all of them. This is because Almighty Allah has made *Zakāh* only for the pinpointed categories and a payer of *Zakāh* can pay it to all of them or to only one of them. The objective of paying *Zakāh* is to give to the needy what suffices their needs, as the Prophet (PBUH) said to Mu'adh, may Allah be pleased with him, when he sent him to Yemen, that *Zakāh* "is to be taken from the rich amongst them and given to the poor amongst them..."[1] In this Ḥadīth, the Prophet (PBUH) did not mention all the eight categories, so Faqīhs assert that it is permissible to pay *Zakāh* only to one category, or to all of the eight categories.

It is worth mentioning here that An-Nakha'ī says that if the *Zakāh*-oriented property is a large amount, it can be divided and distributed among the defined recipients, and if it is a small amount, it is permissible to give it only to one category.[2] And, Allah knows best.

Q. No. (165): Is it lawful to pay *Zakāh* to a rich man?

A: It is not lawful to give *Zakāh* to a rich man who possesses the *Nisāb* and thus he himself is legally asked to pay *Zakāh*. The Prophet (PBUH) said,

"*Ṣadaqah* (alms) is not lawful for a rich person or for a stout strong person."[3]

He also said,

---

[1] Narrated by Ibn Mājah and others.
[2] Al-Mughni, 4/128.
[3] Narrated by Abū Dāwūd and At-Tirmidhī.

"*Ṣadaqah* is not lawful for a rich person except when it is in Allah's Cause (i.e., for jihad-oriented objectives and the like), or (when it is paid to) a wayfarer, or (to) a poor neighbour to whom *Ṣadaqah* is given (by you) then he gives it (back) to you as a present or invites you (to share it with him)."[1]

And, Allah knows best.

Q. No. (166): Is it lawful to give *Zakāh* to a disbeliever?

A: It is prohibited to give *Zakāh* to a disbeliever, a *dhimmī* (a non-Muslim living under the protection of an Islamic government), or an atheist, because the Prophet (PBUH) said that *Zakāh* "is to be taken from the rich amongst them and be given to the poor amongst them,"[2] meaning that *Zakāh* is to be taken from the rich amongst Muslims and be paid back to the poor also amongst them, and thus non-Muslims are not to be given anything of it. Ibnul-Mundhir says, "All the scholars we have learned (religious and fight knowledge) from unanimously agree that no *dhimmī* is to be given anything from the property of *Zakāh*."

However, it is permissible to give such people voluntary alms because it has been narrated by Muslim that Asma' Bint Abū Bakr, may Allah be pleased with her, asked the Prophet (PBUH) whether she could keep the tie of kinship with her polytheist mother through some property and he (PBUH) said to her, "Yes, keep the ties of kinship with your mother." And, Allah knows best.

Q. No. (167): Is it lawful that one of the spouses pays *Zakāh* to the other?

A: It is not lawful that a husband gives *Zakāh* to his wife because it is obligatory upon him to spend on her, so if he gave her *Zakāh* it would be as if he paid it back to himself. This is the opinion adopted by all

---

[1] Narrated by Abū Dāwūd.
[2] Narrated by Ibn Mājah and others.

scholars as stated by Ibn Ḥajar in his *Fatḥ al-Bārī* where he also says that scholars have differed concerning the question whether it is lawful for a wife to give *Zakāh* to her husband: Ash-Shāfiʿī says that it is lawful because the Prophet (PBUH) allowed Zaynab, the wife of Ibn Mas'ud to spend on her husband, saying, "She will receive two rewards: a reward for (maintaining ties of kinship and a reward for *Ṣadaqah*."[1] Ash-Shāfiʿī commented, "This indicates that it is permissible for a wife to pay *Zakāh* to her husband." In contrast, Abū Ḥanīfah and Aḥmad maintain that this is not lawful because a wife's *Zakāh* that she pays to her husband goes back to her through what he spends upon her so it would be as if she did not pay it. Abū Ḥanīfah adds that the story mentioned in the narration quoted by Ash-Shafi`i is concerning voluntary alms.

Ibn Ḥajar also comments in *Fatḥ al-Bārī* that the justification that Zaynab's story was concerning voluntary alms can be identified more through the following narration of Al-Bukhārī: Abū Saʿid Al-Khudri, may Allah be pleased with him, said,

"On ʿIdul- Fiṭr (Fast-breaking Feast) or ʿIdul- Aḍḥā (Sacrifice Feast) the Messenger of Allah (PBUH) went out to the Muṣallā (prayer place). After finishing the prayer, he delivered a sermon and ordered the people to give alms. He said, 'O people! Give alms.' Then he went toward the women and said, 'O women! Give alms, for I have seen that the majority of the dwellers of Hellfire were (from amongst) you (women).' The women asked, 'O Messenger of Allah! What is the reason for it? He replied, 'O women! You curse frequently and are ungrateful to your husbands. I have not seen anyone more deficient in reasonability and religion (i.e., religiosity) than you. O women! Some of you can lead a cautious wise man astray." Then he left. And when he reached his house, Zaynab, the wife of Ibn Mas'ud, came and asked permission to enter. It was said, 'O Messenger of Allah! It is Zaynab.' He asked, 'Which Zaynab?' The

[1] Narrated by Al-Bukhārī. See *Fatḥ al-Bārī*, 3/328.

reply was that she was the wife of Ibn Mas'ud. He said, 'Yes, allow her to enter,' and she was admitted. Then she said, 'O Prophet of Allah! Today you ordered people to give alms, and I had an ornament and intended to give it as alms, but Ibn Mas'ud said that he and his children deserved it more than anybody else.' The Prophet replied, Ibn Mas'ud had spoken the truth. Your husband and your children have more right to it than anybody else."[1]

This narration indicates that the story in the other narration was concerning voluntary alms, and not concerning obligatory alms (*Zakāh*), especially with the fact that *Zakāh* is not lawful to one's children either, while the Prophet (PBUH) told her that her husband and "her children" had more right to it than anybody else. This further indicates that the view adopted by Abū Ḥanīfah and Aḥmad is preponderant and more evident concerning this issue. And, Allah knows best.

Q. No. (168): Why is it that *Zakāh* is not lawful for the household of the Prophet (PBUH)?

A: *Zakāh* is not lawful for the household of the Prophet (PBUH) because it represents people's "impurities," as the Prophet (PBUH) said,

"Verily, these alms (i.e., *Zakāh*) are the impurities of people, and they are not permissible for Muḥammad (PBUH) or for the family of Muḥammad."[2]

Explaining the meaning of "people's impurities," An-Nawawi says it means that *Zakāh* "washes" their impurities because it purifies their souls and property, as Almighty Allah says,

﴿خُذْ مِنْ أَمْوَٰلِهِمْ صَدَقَةً تُطَهِّرُهُمْ وَتُزَكِّيهِم بِهَا وَصَلِّ عَلَيْهِمْ ۖ ١٠٣﴾

[1] Narrated by *Al-Bukhārī*. See *Fatḥ al-Bārī*, 3/325.
[2] Narrated by Muslim.

"Take Ṣadaqah (alms) from their wealth in order to purify them and sanctify them with it..." [TMQ: 9: 103]

It is also important to mention in this context that the ruling of the prohibition under discussion was cancelled when *Ṣadaqah* was given to a person then that person gave "the same item of *Ṣadaqah*" to the Prophet (PBUH) "as a present". It has been narrated by Al-Bukhārī that once some meat was presented to the Prophet (PBUH) and ʿĀʾishah, may Allah be pleased with her, said to him, "This (meat) was given in charity to Barirah (slave-girl)." He said, "It is an object of charity for Barirah but a present for us." And, Allah knows best.

Q. No. (169): Is it permissible to give presents to the household of the Prophet (PBUH)?

A: Unlike *Zakāh*, it is permissible to give presents to the household of the Prophet (PBUH) because it has been narrated that people would offer presents to the Prophet (PBUH) and he would accept them. It has also been narrated that whenever something was offered to him, he would ask, "Is it (offered as) alms or (as) a present?" If they (those who had offered it) said that it was alms, he would not eat it, and if they said it was a present, he would eat it.[1] And, Allah knows best.

Q. No. (170): What are the conditions obligating *Zakātul-Fiṭr* or Fast-breaking Obligatory Alms, and what is the amount which is to be paid?

A: For *Zakātul-Fiṭr* to be obligatory certain conditions must be met. **The first** of these conditions is that the payer of this *Zakāh* must be Muslim because it is an act of worship which, as said by the Prophet (PBUH), is a means of purification for the fasting person, and Islamic fasting is not valid on the part of a disbeliever nor is he worthy of purification.

---

[1] Narrated by At-Tirmidhī and An-Nasāʾī.

The second condition in this regard is that a payer of Fast-breaking *Zakāh* must be free, because a slave is not legally asked to pay *Zakāh* as he and whatever his hands possess belong to his master. That is why the latter is to pay *Zakātul-Fiṭr* for his slave.

Another condition, which is set by Abū Ḥanīfah unlike Mālik, Ash-Shāfi'ī, and Aḥmad, is that the Muslim must have the *Nisāb* (of *Zakāh* in general) so that it can be obligatory upon him to pay this *Zakāh* of fast-breaking. In contrast, Mālik, Ash- Shāfi'ī, and Aḥmad maintain that *Zakātul-Fiṭr* becomes obligatory upon a person if he possesses what is more than the food needed for a day and its night, and it is not a stipulation that he possesses the *Nisāb* because this *Zakāh* is ordained as a way of helping the poor people, and whenever there is a poor person there is another one who is poorer than him. And, Allah knows best.

As for the amount of *Zakātul-Fiṭr*, the Sharī'ah has ordained that it is one *Sā'* of wheat, barley, dates, raisins, rice, corn, or any similar kind of grain which is used most by the people of a town as food. And, Allah knows best.

Q. No. (171): Is it permissible to pay *Zakātul-Fiṭr* before the time it is due?

A: The time in which *Zakātul-Fiṭr* becomes due is when the sun has set on the last day of the month of Ramaḍān, and that is why it is called *Zakātul-Fiṭr* or Fast-breaking *Zakāh*. It is obligatory to pay this *Zakāh* at least before going to attend the *Id* Prayer, because this is what the Prophet (PBUH) ordained in this regard: he said,

"Whoever pays it before (the Id) prayer, it will be an accepted *Zakāh* (from him); and whoever pays it after the prayer, it will be a (mere) act of charity."[1]

---

[1] Narrated by Abū Dāwūd and Ibn Mājah.

Faqīhs have unanimously agreed that it is permissible to pay *Zakātul-Fiṭr* one or two days before *'Idul- Fiṭr* (Fast- breaking Feast). This view is adopted by Mālik and Aḥmad, and Mālik narrated in his *Muwattā'* that Ibn 'Umar would send *Zakātul-Fiṭr* to the collector of *Zakāh* two or three days before *idul-Fitr*. Ash-Shāfi'ī and Abū Ḥanīfah say that it is even permissible to pay it from the first day in Ramaḍān because fasting is the cause of this *Zakāh* as it is a means of compensation for the deficiency that the fasting person may undergo. It has been narrated that Ibn 'Abbās , may Allah be pleased with him, said

"The Messenger of Allah (PBUH) enjoined *Zakātul-Fiṭr* as a means of purification for the fasting person from blunder and obscenity and as a means of feeding for the needy..."[1]

Scholars also say that as it is permissible for the Muslim to pay *Zakāh* in general before the passing of the year which is to pass while having the *Nisāb*, it is also permissible for him to pay *Zakātul-Fiṭr* even days before the day of the feast. They also say that it is "desirable" that the Muslim pays *Zakātul-Fiṭr* at the eve of the feast before going to perform the Id Prayer. And, Allah knows best.

Q. No. (172): Is it valid to pay the "value" of the items of *Zakātul-Fiṭr*?

A: The majority of scholars, including Mālik, Ash-Shāfi'ī, and Aḥmad, maintain that it is not permissible for the Muslim to pay the value of the items of *Zakātul-Fiṭr*, that is the value of dates, or barley, or raisins, etc. instead of the objects themselves. This is because he must pay exactly what the Prophet (PBUH) has specified for this *Zakāh*. It has been narrated by Abū Dāwūd that Messenger of Allah (PBUH) enjoined the payment of one *Sā'* of dates, or one *Sā'* of barley, or one *Sā'* of raisins as *Zakātul-Fiṭr* on every Muslim free or slave, male or female.

[1] Narrated by Abū Dāwūd and Ibn Mājah.

Abū Ḥanīfah and others, on the other hand, maintain that it is permissible for the Muslim to pay the value of the items of *Zakātul-Fiṭr* because this is easier and more helpful for the poor. The Prophet (PBUH) said,

"Make them in no need to ask (for people's help) on this day (of feast)."[1]

This, they say, can be achieved both with barley, dates, raisins, etc., and with their value. Thus, if a poor person needs food, he will make use of it, and if he needs new clothes, for example, especially for an occasion like the feast, he will use the money given to him as *Zakātul-Fiṭr* to buy what he needs. Abū Ḥanīfah has proved his opinion with textual proofs, such as the narration recorded in *Ad-Dāruqutni's Sunan* that when Mu'adh went to Yemen, he asked the people there to bring him clothes as *Ṣadaqah* (*Zakāh*) instead of barely and corn because that, as he said, was easier for them and better for the Emigrants in Medina.[2]

Abū Ḥanīfah's view is easier and more useful for the poor and his proofs are well-established and convincing. And, Allah knows best.

---

[1] Narrated by Al- Bayhaqi and others.

[2] Narrated by Ad-Daruqutni and Al-Bayhaqi.

Fasting (*Ṣiyām*)

Q. No. (173): How can it be confirmed that Ramaḍān has come?

A: The dawning of the month of Ramaḍān is legally confirmed and authenticated by seeing the crescent of this month. However, astronomic computations may be used sometimes just to give preponderance to some hypotheses concerning the seeing of the crescent over some other hypotheses. Still, such astronomic computations cannot be the only means through which the appearance of the crescent of Ramaḍān is legally established, as the Sharī'ah has made the "seeing" of the crescent the legal way to confirm its appearance which in turn confirms that the month of Ramaḍān has come or started.

The Prophet (PBUH) did not ask Muslims to resort to such computations yet simply ordained that we can start observing fasting if we see the crescent, otherwise we are not to observe any fasting. It has been narrated by Muslim on the authority of Abū Hurayrah, may Allah be pleased with him, that the Messenger of Allah (PBUH) said,

"Observe fast when you see it (the new moon of Ramaḍān) and break the fast when you see it (the new moon of Shawwāl), but if (the actual position of the month is) concealed from you (because the sky is cloudy), then count thirty days."

In the book *Al-Fiqh 'alā al-Madhāhib al-Arba'ah* (Islamic Jurisprudence According to the Four Schools), it is mentioned that the beginning of the month of Ramaḍān is confirmed through two things: first, by seeing its crescent, if the sky is free from things that may hinder this observation, such as clouds, smoke, dust, and the like; and second, by completing the month of Sha'bān (which is right before Ramaḍān) as thirty days, if the sky is not free from the pinpointed things that hinder seeing the crescent, because the Prophet (PBUH) said,

"Observe fast when you see it (the new moon of Ramaḍān) and break the fast when you see it (the new moon of Shawwāl)."

to the end of the Ḥadīth as mentioned above.

The Ḥadīth means that if the sky is clear, the fasting of Ramaḍān is contingent upon the seeing of the crescent and thus it is not permissible to start observing fast except when the crescent has already been seen. If however the sky is cloudy, the reference in this case is to be to the month of Sha'bān by completing the number of its days to thirty; and thus, if it is incomplete according to our reckoning, we will cancel that incompleteness by completing it, and if it is complete, then we must start observing fast.

Abū Ḥanīfah, Mālik, and Ash-Shāfi'ī adopt this rule while the Ḥanbalīs do not adopt the part concerning the cloudiness of the sky,[1] acting upon the wording of the Ḥadīth reading,

"Observe fast when you see it (the new moon of Ramaḍān) and break the fast when you see it (the new moon of Shawwāl), but if (the actual position of the month is) concealed from you, then take it into consideration."[2]

The Ḥanbalīs say that "take it into consideration" ("*uqdur lah*" in Arabic) means: take precautions by observing fast. The Ḥanbalīs moreover prove their view with the actual application of Ibn 'Umar on whose narration this Ḥadīth has been narrated, as when thirty days had passed from the month of Sha'bān, he would send someone to check if the crescent of Ramaḍān had appeared or not: if the person he sent saw the crescent Ibn 'Umar would observe fasting the

---

[1] i.e., the Ḥanbalīs do not adopt the rule that if the sky is cloudy Muslims are to complete Sha'bān as thirty days; and instead, they say that if the sky is cloudy Muslims are to observe fasting the next day.

[2] Narrated by Al-Bukhārī.

next day, and if the person did not see the crescent because of something that hindered that seeing, Ibn ʿUmar would observe fasting the next day as well; and, of course, if the person did not see the crescent while the sky was clear, Ibn 'Umar would not observe fast the next day. And, Allah knows best.

Q. No. (174): Is the testimony of only one person sufficient for authenticating the seeing of the crescent of Ramaḍān?

A: If the sky is cloudy or foggy leaving a hazy horizon or anything of the sort is hindering the seeing of the crescent, then the testimony of one person is sufficient for authenticating it's seeing. However, this person must be *ʿAdl* or upright, and this requires that he is a Muslim who is trustworthy and adherent to the instructions of Islam and is not known for dissoluteness or looseness. This is because the seeing of the crescent is one of the religious matters for which *ʿadalah* or uprightness is required.

However, if the sky is clear and nothing hinders seeing the crescent, then the testimony of a number of Muslims is required. This number is "two" according to Abū Ḥanīfah and Mālik. Ash- Shāfiʿī, on the other hand, asserts that the testimony of one upright person is sufficient for the seeing of the crescent. Ash- Shāfiʿī has proven this view with certain texts, as follows:

It has been narrated that Ibn ʿUmar, may Allah be pleased with him, said,

"The people went out to see the crescent and I told the Messenger of Allah (PBUH) that I had seen it, so he observed fast (according to my testimony) and ordered the people to observe fast (as well)."[1]

It has also been narrated that Ibn ʿAbbās, may Allah be pleased with him, said,

---

[1] Narrated by Abū Dāwūd

"A Bedouin came to the Messenger of Allah (PBUH) and said, 'I have seen the crescent of Ramaḍān.' He (PBUH) said to him, 'Do you testify that there is no god but Allah?" The man answered in the affirmative then he (PBUH) said, '(And) do you testify that Muḥammad is the Messenger of Allah?' He answered in the affirmative (as well), so he (PBUH) said, 'O Bilal! Call upon the people that they should observe fast tomorrow."[1]

An-Nawawi says that the correct view in this regard is that the testimony of only one upright person is sufficient as far as this is related to the crescent of Ramaḍān, unlike the case with the crescent of Shawwāl, which determines the fast breaking, for most scholars maintain that at least two upright persons are required for authenticating seeing it.

As-Sabūni has a comment that is worth mentioning here: he says that for authenticating seeing the crescent of Ramaḍān, the testimony of one upright person is sufficient due to the two narrations of Ibn 'Umar and Ibn ʿAbbās mentioned above. He adds that even if something wrong should happen in the testimony in question, there will be no harm if Muslims observe fast for a day extra to the days of Ramaḍān, unlike the case with Shawwāl, for a mistake in this connection may cause a decrease in the obligatory fasting of Ramaḍān. That is why the testimony of at least two upright persons is required for authenticating the seeing of the crescent of Shawwāl. And, Allah knows best.

Q. No. (175): Is the forecasting that the crescent has appeared by an astrologer legally considered?

A: Abū Ḥanīfah, Mālik, and Ibn Hanbal maintain that what is to be legally considered in this regard is "the seeing of the crescent" as determined by the Sharīʿah. For, astrologers' statements[2] are not

[1] Narrated by Abū Dāwūd and At-Tirmidhī.
[2] See *Al- Fiqh alal- Madhahib Al- Arba'ah*, 1/500.

exact even if they may be based on precise rules, simply because their views differ in most cases. Ash-Shāfiʿī however says that an astrologer's statement with regard to the seeing of the crescent can be legally considered on his own part as well as on the part of whoever believes him, yet still the rest of the people who do not believe him - do not have to observe fast according to his statement. And, Allah knows best.

Q. No. (176): What is the *Sharʿī* ruling concerning "seeking" the crescent?

A: It is a collective obligation or *farḍ kifāyah* that the Muslims seek to see whether the crescent of Ramaḍān - or that of Shawwāl - has appeared or not. As for the seeing of the crescent of Ramaḍān, it is to be sought at the sunset of the twenty-ninth of the month of Shaʿbān so that they can legally authenticate whether they are to observe fast the next day as being the first day in Ramaḍān or they must complete the days of Shaʿbān as thirty. And, by the same token, the seeing of the crescent of Shawwāl is to be sought at the sunset of the twenty- ninth of Ramaḍān. This is because Almighty Allah has connected fasting, as well as *Ḥajj* including the stay on *ʿArafah*, to the crescent. Allah says,

﴿هُوَ ٱلَّذِى جَعَلَ ٱلشَّمْسَ ضِيَآءً وَٱلْقَمَرَ نُورًا وَقَدَّرَهُۥ مَنَازِلَ لِتَعْلَمُوا۟ عَدَدَ ٱلسِّنِينَ وَٱلْحِسَابَ ۚ ٥﴾

"It is He Who made the sun a shining thing and the moon as a light and measured out its (their) stages, that you might know the number of years and the reckoning..." [TMQ: 10:5]

and says,

﴿۞ يَسْـَٔلُونَكَ عَنِ ٱلْأَهِلَّةِ ۖ قُلْ هِىَ مَوَٰقِيتُ لِلنَّاسِ وَٱلْحَجِّ ۗ ١٨٩﴾

"They ask you (O Muḥammad) about the new moons. Say: These are signs to mark fixed periods of time for mankind and for the pilgrimage..."

[TMQ: 2: 189]

Therefore, if Muslims neglect seeking the crescent all together, they become sinful for that, because it is something without which an obligation - i.e., the fasting of Ramaḍān cannot be fulfilled. After all, Almighty Allah says,

﴿ذَٰلِكَۖ وَمَن يُعَظِّمۡ شَعَٰٓئِرَ ٱللَّهِ فَإِنَّهَا مِن تَقۡوَى ٱلۡقُلُوبِ ٣٢﴾

"And whosoever honours the Symbols of Allah, then it is truly from the piety of the heart." [TMQ: 22: 32]

And, Allah knows best.

Q. No. (177): Is the difference of the place or places where the crescent of Ramaḍān can be seen legally considered?

A: The majority of scholars, including Abū Ḥanīfah, Mālik, and Ibn Hanbal, view that there is no consideration for this difference, and therefore if the seeing of the crescent of Ramaḍān is authenticated in an Islamic country all Muslims throughout the world must start observing fast, in compliance with the Prophet's order:

"Observe fast when you see it (the crescent of Ramaḍān) and break the fast when you see it (the crescent of Shaʿbān)."[1]

This is because the Prophet (PBUH) addressed "all" Muslims with this order, and not the Muslims of a particular country.

Ash-Shāfiʿī, on the other hand, maintains that the difference of the places where the crescent is seen can be legally considered. In other words, the seeing authenticated by the people of every country is legally considered on their part and they do not have to act according to the seeing of the people of another country, because

[1] Narrated by Al-Bukhārī and Muslim.

places where the crescent can be seen differ according to the countries to which these places belong. The Shāfi'īs prove their opinion with what Muslim has narrated on the authority of Kurayb, who said that he arrived in Ash-Shām when the month of Ramaḍān had commenced there. He saw the crescent (of Ramaḍān) on Friday then came back to Medina at the end of the month. Abdullah Ibn 'Abbās, may Allah be pleased with him, asked him (about the crescent of Ramaḍān), saying, "When did you see the crescent?" Kurayb said, "We saw it on the night of Friday." He said, "Did you see it yourself?" He answered, "Yes, and the people also saw it and they observed fast and Mu'awiyah also observed fast." Thereupon Ibn 'Abbās said, "But we saw it on Saturday night. So, we will continue to observe fast until we complete thirty (days) or we see it (the crescent of Shawwāl)." Kurayb said, "Is the seeing (of the crescent) by Mu'awiyah not valid for you?" He said, "No. This is how the Messenger of Allah (PBUH) has commanded us."[1]

As-Sabūni says that the view adopted by the majority of scholars is more evident and so are the items of proof they have presented, especially that it confirms the principle of unity among Muslims, in addition to the fact that nowadays it is very easy for all Muslim countries with the technological progress in telecommunications- to inform one another of the appearance of the crescent only a while after it has been confirmed in one of them. This is unlike the case with the early Muslims, as it would take a month, for example, for the people of Ash-Shām at that time to tell the people in Mecca of the witnessing of the crescent. This is apt to consolidate the principle of unity of worship among Muslims all over the world and helps them start the fasting and break it all together and consequently celebrate the Fast-breaking Feast also all together. And, Allah knows best.

---

[1] Narrated by Muslim and At-Tirmidhī

Q. No. (178): Is seeing the crescent during daytime legally considered?

A: There is no consideration for the witnessing of the crescent by daytime, for what is legal here is that it should be. seen at sunset, as ordained by the Prophet (PBUH). And, Allah knows best.

Q. No. (179): Is it stipulated that the Muslims observe fast according to the judgment of their ruler?

A: It is not stipulated that the Muslims start observing fast according to the judgment of their ruler. In other words, if a person sees the crescent of Ramaḍān for sure and tells the ruler about that yet the latter does not accept his testimony, it is obligatory that this person observes fast according to his own seeing of the crescent even if the rest of the people do not observe it. This is because the *Imāms* of *Fiqh* have unanimously agreed that whoever sees the crescent alone must observe fast accordingly, for Almighty Allah has ordained,

﴿فَمَن شَهِدَ مِنكُمُ ٱلشَّهۡرَ فَلۡيَصُمۡهُۖ ١٨٥﴾

"...So, whoever of you sights (the crescent on the first night of the month (of Ramaḍān), must observe fasts (during) that month..." [TMQ: 2: 185]

Still, if the ruler of a Muslim country judges that the seeing of the crescent has been authenticated, it is obligatory that all his Muslim subjects observe fast accordingly even if this should contradict the judgment of any one of them, because the ruler's judgment overrules the existence of any different opinions. And, Allah knows best.

Q. No. (180): How is it authenticated that the month of Shawwāl has commenced?

A: It is through the witnessing of the crescent of Shawwāl that Muslims can authenticate that this month has started and so they can break the fasting of Ramaḍān, otherwise they are to complete the days of Ramaḍān as thirty. It has been narrated by Muslim on the authority of Abū Hurayrah, may Allah be pleased with him, that the Messenger of Allah (PBUH) said,

"Observe fast when you see it (the new moon of Ramaḍān) and break the fast when you see it (the new moon of Shawwāl), but if (the actual position of the month is) concealed from you, then count thirty days."

If thirty days have passed from the month of Ramaḍān - according to the witnessing of the crescent testified at the beginning of the month - and the crescent of Shawwāl has not appeared yet, there are three views in this regard: the Ḥanafīs and the Mālikīs maintain that it is not lawful for Muslims to break their fast as long as the sky is clear. They add that accordingly those who testified that the crescent of Ramaḍān appeared on a certain night are to be belied and so Muslims. must observe fast the next day as being from the month of Ramaḍān. If, however the sky is unclear, Muslims must break the fast the next day which is thus counted as being the first of Shawwāl. The Shāfi'īs say that they must break the fast whether the sky is clear or not as long as the start of the fasting was testified by even one upright person, while the Ḥanbalīs view that they must break the fast if the start of the fasting was testified by two upright people yet they must observe fast on the thirty- first day if the start of the fasting was testified by one upright person.[1] And, Allah knows best.

Q. No. (181): What are the conditions obligating fasting?

A: In Islam, for the fasting of Ramaḍān to be obligatory on a person, he must be Muslim, sane, mature, sound (not ill), and resident (not in a state of travel). Besides, a woman, in addition to these

[1] See *Al- Fiqh alal- Madhahib Al- Arba'ah*, 1/502.

requirements, must not be in a state of menstruation or that of postnatal bleeding.

A person who observes fast must be a Muslim because a disbeliever is not qualified for worshiping Allah simply because he does not believe in Him in principle.

Sanity and puberty are required as well because they represent the basis on which legal responsibility is established. This is because neither an insane person nor a child is legally asked to perform any obligatory act of worship. Still, even though fasting is not obligatory upon children, their parents should command them to observe fasting, according to their capacity, so that they may become accustomed to it when it is time that they observe it obligatorily.

The Muslim must be sound - i.e., not ill- and resident - i.e., not in a state of travel or else fasting will not be obligatory upon him. Islam has allowed the ill person and the traveller to break fasting in Ramaḍān as a way of consideration for these special circumstances under which fasting may put him through more difficulty and hardship. However, such a person is to make up for the non-fast days by observing fast for the same number of days after Ramaḍān when he recovers from his illness, or his journey comes to an end.

Nevertheless, not every ill person is allowed to break fasting in Ramaḍān, for illness must be acute to an extent with which fasting causes harm to the person in question or prolongs the period of remedy. This can be realized through experimentation as well as by asking a trustworthy doctor.

Also, for a traveller to be permitted to break fasting his journey is to have the requirements that must be met for those who can shorten prayers while traveling. Some scholars have estimated the distance of such a journey to be not less than eighty-four kilometres while some others say that this is to be restricted to whatever distance with which the journey is considered to be one of "*safar*" or travel according to the Arabic language in which the verse of shortening prayer has been revealed. Also, according to the majority of scholars, not including the Ḥanafīs, this journey must be for fulfilling an act of obedience, such as acquisition of religious knowledge, and not for undertaking some illegal deed, such as trading in intoxicants. Moreover, the majority of scholars stipulate that the journey must be started before dawn, because if a person starts fasting with the rise of dawn, then goes on a journey, he is not allowed to break his fasting. The Ḥanbalīs do not stipulate this, but it is better for whoever goes on a journey during a day of fasting to complete his fast to avoid this difference of opinions.

A woman must not be menstruating or in a postnatal condition or else fasting will not be obligatory upon her. Rather, it is not valid for a woman in either of the two conditions to observe fast just as it is not permissible for her to perform prayer. This is because she is not in a state of purification (*Ṭahārah*). Therefore, if she observes fast, it is invalid and not to be counted as from the validly fasted days. This means that she must make up for the days during which she undergoes such a condition. And, Allah knows best.

Q. No. (182): What are the pillars of fasting?

A: There are three pillars of fasting and without these pillars fasting is not valid. They are as follows:

1. The first pillar is abstaining from eating, drinking, and sexual intercourse.

2. The second pillar of fasting is intention, that is, the Muslim must intend that he will observe fast before the rise of dawn. Intention is a pillar of fasting, especially the obligatory one, because this is required for distinguishing what is performed as an act of worship from what is done as a habit.

3. The third pillar of fasting is that a woman must not be menstruating or in a postnatal period. And Allah knows best.

Q. No. (183): What are the things allowed in fasting?

A: There are certain things which are allowed for the fasting person as they do not affect his fasting negatively. They are as follows.

1. Use *Siwāk*.

2. Applying kohl.

3. Taking a bath and performing ablution.

4. Rinsing the mouth and the nose.

5. Injection: It is permissible for a fasting person to get injected in the veins and bottom for alleviating the degree of temperature or pain, but this injection must not be for feeding.

6. Applying and smelling perfumes.

7. To delay taking the ritual bath of *Janābah*.

8. Eating, drinking, and having intercourse with one's wife until dawn.

9. To delay making up for the broken fasts in Ramaḍān until after the month of Shawwāl (which is right after Ramaḍān). And, Allah knows best.

Q. No. (184): What are the things that invalidate fasting?

A: There are certain things that invalidate fasting, and they are divided into two sections: (i) that which invalidates fasting and obligates making up (Qaḍā') and expiation (*Kaffārah*) and (ii) that which invalidates fasting and obligates making up only.

The first section: that which invalidates fasting and obligates making up and expiation.

The first section which obligates both making up for the invalidated fasts and expiation is intercourse which is done purposefully during any of the daytimes of Ramaḍān. This intercourse invalidates fasting and because of it both expiation and making up are obligatorily required. Making up is obligatory in this case because a fasting person who has intercourse breaks his fast because of this intercourse, and so he must make up for the broken fast by observing fast for one day instead of the day on which he has broken his fast. And expiation is obligatorily required for this act because intercourse violates the sanctity of this blessed month of Ramaḍān, as the person in question has purposefully broken his fast without forgetfulness, and so he is to be chastised with a punishment that is apt to reprimand him so that he may not do that again. This expiation is to do one of three things: emancipating a slave, observing fast for two consecutive months other than the day, which is to be made up for, or providing food to sixty poor people.

The second section: that which invalidates fasting and obligates making up only

The second section of the things that invalidate fasting is that which obligates making up only, and this section covers the following things:

1. Taking something that is not for feeding through the normal opening the mouth into the abdomen, such as swallowing a stone or dust.

2. Vomiting intentionally, by forcing food to come back out of the abdomen. However, if a person is overcome by vomiting that will not invalidate his fasting.

3. If a fasting person eats or drinks thinking that the sun has set or takes *Suḥūr* (pre-dawn meal) thinking that dawn has not risen yet then "realizes that he was mistaken," he - must make up for the fast in question yet he does not have to expiate for that because he did not mean to violate the sanctity of the month.

4. Masturbation, which is an intentional ejaculation of one's semen out of the body due to some means of stimulation such as kissing, touching, or caressing one's wife or masturbating with the hand.

5. If a fasting person cures a wound in his abdomen or head and the medicine reaches his abdomen or head, his fasting is invalidated because of that, and he must make up for that and no expiation is required.

6. Fasting is also invalidated by such things as using enema for anal injection and applying drops to the nose or the ears. This is because something that breaks fast has reached the inside of the body from a normal opening.

7. Menstruation (*Ḥayḍ*) and postnatal bleeding (*nifās*) invalidate fasting.

8. If a fasting person satisfies his sexual desire using his genitals yet incompletely, as when he has intercourse with a dead body or a beast,[1] his fasting is invalidated, and he must make up for the day in question without expiation. This is according to the majority of Faqīhs.

9. Incense, the smoke resulting from grilling and roasting, as well as that which results from smoking cigarettes and the like, all invalidate fasting if a fasting person smells them deeply and purposefully, and he must make up for the fast in question without expiation.

10. If a fasting person "intends" to break his fasting, his fasting is invalidated because of this intention even if he does not actually take anything that breaks fasting. And, Allah knows best.

Q. No. (185): What are the things detested in fasting?

---

[1] This is surely eccentric, yet it might happen.

A: There are certain things which are detested in fasting yet do not invalidate it. They are as follows:

1. Tasting food with the tongue for testing its saltiness and the like.

2. A mother's chewing food for her baby.

3. A husband's kissing his wife.

4. Doing something that may cause weakness, such as cupping.

5. Collecting saliva in the mouth then swallowing it.

6. Harvesting, i.e., it is detestable for a fasting person, unless it is necessary, to harvest plants lest some of the harvesting dust reach his throat as this may invalidate his fasting. And, Allah knows best.

Q. No. (186): What are the things desired in fasting?

A: There are certain things which are desirable as far as fasting is concerned, and they are also considered the proprieties of fasting. They are as follows.

1. Taking *Suḥūr* or pre-dawn meal.

2. Avoiding things and acts that contradict fasting, such as lying and talking nonsense.

3. Showing generousness and open handedness and studying the Qur'ān.

4. Breaking fast with dates.

5. Hastening to break the fast once the sun has surely set.

6. Invoking Allah on breaking fast.

7. Providing breakfast for others.

8. Invoking Allah for the person who offers breakfast.

9. Worship Allah intensely during the last ten nights of Ramaḍān. And, Allah knows best.

Q. No. (187): What are the benefits of fasting?

A: Fasting has many benefits both spiritually and physically. They can be summarized in the following points:

Fasting implants within the believer what may be called the natural endowment (*malakah*) of piety and helps him get accustomed to submissiveness and obedience to Allah, Glorified and Exalted be He. This in turn helps him keep straightforwardly to the path of Allah by behaving in accordance with His ordinances and forbiddances. This is because piety, which is grown in the believer's heart by means of fasting, exemplifies the meaning of committing to what Allah has ordained and avoiding what He has forbidden. It is in a word the quality which guarantees the believer's uprightness.

Fasting is a means of discipline through which the believer is taught how to "fear" Almighty Allah in one of the best ways of disciplining: when fasting, he can see food, drink, and his wife in front of him many times, but "each time" he restrains his hunger, thirst, or sexual lust for the sake of Allah. This moreover inculcates and implants in him the faculty of being patient, which in turn prepares him for enduring hardships in the Cause of Allah. That is why the Prophet (PBUH) said, "Fasting is a half of patience," as narrated by Ibn Mājah.

Fasting moreover helps man to be familiar with loving good for others and doing it to them and strengthens the passion of mercy and fraternity among Muslims. This in turn stimulates the tie of integrity and cooperation among them, as they invite one another to breakfast and pay the Fast-breaking *Zakāh* at the end of the month of fasting. This is also because the rich when fasting - can feel and actually estimate how hard and painful hunger and deprivation are to the poor.

Still, fasting renews the life of a fasting person, as it refreshes the cells of his body and allows his stomach and the rest of his digestion system to rest for some time during the period of fasting. In this way, by virtue of fasting the body gets rid of many of the excrements precipitated in it and the bad remains that may have been left behind in the stomach.

Thus, fasting is very important for man both spiritually and physically. And, Allah knows best.

Q. No. (188): What are the days on which fasting is prohibited?

A: The Islamic Shari ah has prohibited fasting on certain days, as follows.

1. The day of fast-breaking or the first day in the days of ʿIdul- Fiṭr (Fast-breaking Feast).

2. The Day of Sacrifice along with the three Days of *Tashrīq*: these are the days of ʿIdul- Aḍḥā (Sacrifice Feast) and the three days right after it.

3. It is prohibited to observe fasting on Friday alone.

4. It is prohibited to observe fasting on Saturday alone.

5. It is prohibited to observe fasting on the day of doubt, i.e., the day concerning which people doubt whether it is the last day in the month of Shaʿbān or the first day in the month of Ramaḍān. And, Allah knows best.

Q. No. (189): In addition to the days on which fasting is prohibited (as pinpointed in the previous answer), is there any other forms of forbidden fasting?

A: Along with the days on which fasting is forbidden, there are certain forms of fasting which Muslims are forbidden to observe. They are as follows:

1. A woman is forbidden to observe voluntary fasting without her husband's permission.

2. It is forbidden to observe fasting for the whole year.

3. It is forbidden to observe fasting continuously, i.e., by observing fasting for a whole day (24 hours) without breaking it when the sun sets and continuing fasting until the next day, thus observing fast for two consecutive days without breaking it even for an hour. This is called *Wiṣāl* or continuation. And, Allah knows best.

Q. No. (190): Is the Muslim recommended to observe fasting voluntarily on certain occasions or certain days?

A: The Muslim is recommended to observe fasting voluntarily on certain occasions and on certain days due to the great reward that he is supposed to receive by virtue of these fasts. These occasions and days can be listed as follows:

1. Six days from the month of Shawwāl.

2. The Day of Ashura' (the tenth of Al-Muharram).

3. The day of *ʿArafah.*

4. Observing fast during the month of Shaʿbān.

5. Mondays and Thursdays.

6. Three days every month.

7. Observing fast for one day and breaking it for another.

And, Allah knows best.

Q. No. (191): What is the day of doubt and what is the *Sharʿī* ruling as regards observing fast on it?

A: The day of doubt is the day concerning which people doubt whether it is the last day of the month of Shaʿbān or the first day in the month of Ramaḍān. It is prohibited that Muslims observe fast on this day so that they may not add an extra day to the fasting of Ramaḍān, as they are commanded to observe fast if they see the crescent of Ramaḍān; and, if they do not see it, they are not legally asked to observe any fasting the next day. It has been narrated on the authority of Ammar Ibn Yasir, may Allah be pleased with him, that "whoever observes fasting on the day of doubt will have disobeyed Abul-Qasim (i.e., Prophet Muḥammad), Allah's peace and blessings be upon him."[1]

However, some scholars, including Ibn 'Umar and Ibn Hanbal, say that it is permissible to observe fast on this day of doubt if the sky is unclear. And, Allah knows best.

Q. No. (192): What is the *Shar'ī* ruling concerning the fasting of a pregnant woman, a suckling woman, and old people?

A: The Sharī'ah allows a pregnant woman and a suckling woman to break the fast if they fear that fasting should harm them or their babies, but they must make up for the non-fast days later on. The same ruling applies to old people, male and female. Almighty Allah says in this regard,

﴿ وَعَلَى ٱلَّذِينَ يُطِيقُونَهُۥ فِدْيَةٌ طَعَامُ مِسْكِينٍ ﴿١٨٤﴾ ﴾

"And as for those who can fast with difficulty, (e.g., an old man, etc.), they have (a choice either to fast or) to feed a poor person (for every day)."

[TMQ: 2: 184]

It has been narrated by Al-Bukhārī on the authority of `Ata who said that he heard Ibn 'Abbās, may Allah be pleased with him, reciting the verse ... And as for those who can fast with difficulty, (e.g., an old man, etc.), they have (a choice either to fast or) to feed a poor person (for every day) then Ibn 'Abbās said,

[1] Narrated by At-Tirmidhī.

"It (this verse) has not been abrogated. It is about the old men and women who cannot observe fast: (they can break fast) and feed a poor person for every day (on which they break the fast)."

Abū Dāwūd has narrated that Ibn ʿAbbās said concerning the same verse that it concerns (along with the old people) the pregnant and suckling women if they fear (that fasting would harm them or their babies), so they can break fast and do the required feeding.

Ibn ʿUmar, may Allah be pleased with him, was asked about the ruling concerning a pregnant woman who fears that harm should afflict her baby. He said that she can break fast and feed a poor person one *mudd* of wheat for every day.[1]

Abū Ḥanīfah says that the pregnant and suckling women who fear such harm can break fast, but they should only do the required feeding and no making up is required. Whereas Ash- Shāfiʿī and Aḥmad say that if they fear that harm should afflict only their babies, they are to do the feeding along with the making up for the non-fast days; and if they fear that harm should afflict them along with the babies, then they are only to make up for the non-fast days. As for those who break the fast because of old age or because of an illness which is not supposed to be cured, they are to do the feeding only.[2] And, Allah knows best.

Q. No. (193): Was the verse ... *And as for those who can fast with difficulty, (e.g., an old man, etc.), they have (a choice either to fast or) to feed a poor person (for every day),* (Qur'ān: 2: 184) abrogated or not?

A: According to the majority of scholars, this verse was abrogated with the verse speaking about the fasting of Ramaḍān, namely with the part that reads.

---

[1] Narrated by Mālik and Al-Bayhaqi.

[2] See *Al-Mughnī*.

﴿ فَمَن شَهِدَ مِنكُمُ ٱلشَّهْرَ فَلْيَصُمْهُ ١٨٥ ﴾

"... So, whoever of you sights (the crescent on the first night of the month (of Ramaḍān i.e., is present at his home), he must observe fasts (during) that month..." [TMQ: 2: 185]

They prove this view with what has been narrated by Aḥmad and Abū Dāwūd on the authority of Mu'adh, who said,

"Allah enjoined fasting upon the Prophet (PBUH) and so He revealed the verses *(O you who believe! Observing fasting is prescribed for you as it was prescribed for those before you, that you may become pious...)* to the words ... *(And as for those who can fast with difficulty, (e.g., an old man, etc.), they have (a choice either to fast or) to feed a poor person (for every day),* [TMQ: 2: 183-184] Accordingly, people who wanted to observe fast did so and those who wanted (to break it) fed a poor person (for every non- fast day), and that was sufficient for them. After that Almighty Allah revealed the other verse (*The month of* Ramaḍān *in which was revealed the Qur'ān*), to the words ... *So whoever of you sights (the crescent on the first night of) the month (of* Ramaḍān *i.e. is present at his home), he must observe fasts (during) that month...*) [TMQ: 2:185] Allah thus confirmed fasting in it (Ramaḍān) on the part of whoever is resident (not on a journey) and sound (not ill), permitted that whoever is ill and on a journey (can break the fast in it), and confirmed (the ruling of) feeding (a poor person for every non-fast day) on the part of the old person who cannot observe fast."

Adversely, Ibn 'Abbās, may Allah be pleased with him, maintains that the verse mentioned in the question above was not abrogated, and that it contains an allowance (*Rukhṣah*) for the old person who observes fast with difficulty permitting him to break the fast and feed a poor person for every day without having to make up for the non-fast days. Ibn 'Umar is reported to have adopted the same view as well. And, Allah knows best.

Q. No. (194): Is it obligatory that a traveller breaks fast or is it just an allowance?

A: Scholars have unanimously agreed that it is permissible for a traveller to observe fast because Almighty Allah has permitted him to break it only not to put him to difficulty. Therefore, it is not obligatory that he breaks fast, and if he chooses to observe fast his fasting will be valid and sufficient, for it has been narrated by Al-Bukhārī that Ḥamzah Ibn ʿAmr al-Aslamī, may Allah be pleased with him, asked the Prophet (PBUH), "Should I fast while traveling?" The Prophet (PBUH) replied, "You may fast if you wish, and you may not fast if you wish." And, Allah knows best.

Q. No. (195): Which is better for a traveller: to observe fast or to break it?

A: Scholars have differed as to the question which is "better" for a traveller: to observe fast or to break it. Abū Ḥanīfah, Mālik, and Ash-Shāfiʿī assert that it is better for whoever can endure the difficulty of fasting on a journey to observe it, and that it is better for whoever cannot endure that to break the fast. This is because fasting is an obligation (*ʿazīmah*) and fast breaking is an allowance (*Rukhṣah*), and it is better to act upon obligations than to be keen on making use of allowances especially when this is unnecessary. The proponents of this view have quoted the following verse as proof.

﴿وَأَن تَصُومُواْ خَيۡرٞ لَّكُمۡ ١٨٤﴾

"... And that you fast, it is better for you if only you know." [TMQ: 2: 184]

Aḥmad, however, is of the opinion that feast breaking is better for a traveller because Almighty Allah likes that His servants make use of His allowances as He likes that they act upon His obligations.

Any way, it is better in all cases that a traveller breaks fast if it is difficult for him to observe it, both for the allowance mentioned in the verse and because it has been narrated on the authority of Ibn

ʿAbbās , may Allah be pleased with him, that once the Prophet (PBUH) headed for Mecca in Ramaḍān, and he observed fast until he reached Al-Kadid a place near to Usfan - where he broke fast and so did the people with him.[1] That was because fasting had then become difficult for his Companions, so he (PBUH) broke fast before them to encourage them to follow his example, especially that they had become so exhausted as indicated by another narration of Al-Bukhārī also on the authority of Ibn ʿAbbās. Moreover, Al-Bukhārī has narrated that once when the Prophet (PBUH) was on a journey he saw some people shading a man because of the heat of the sun, so he asked, "What is this?" They said, "(It is) a fasting person." Thereupon he (PBUH) said,

"It is not a sign of righteousness to observe fast while traveling."

And, Allah knows best.

Q. No. (196): What is meant by *"the white thread"* and the *"black thread"* *in the verse ... and eat and drink until the white thread of dawn appears to you distinct from the black thread..."* [TMQ: 2: 187]?

A: This is one of the wondrous and beautiful aspects of the Qur'ān, for in this verse "the white thread" is used to refer to the light of dawn and "the black thread" is used to refer to the darkness of night. This means: eat and drink until the light of dawn appears to you as distinguished from the darkness of night. There is an interesting story concerning this verse as narrated by Al-Bukhārī and Muslim. ʿAdiyy ibn Ḥātim, may Allah be pleased with him, said,

"When the verse ... *until the white thread of dawn appears to you distinct from the black thread...* was revealed, I took two (hair) strings, one black and the other white, and kept them under my pillow and went on looking at them throughout the night but could not make anything out of it. So, the next morning I went to the Messenger of

[1] Narrated by Al-Bukhārī.

Allah and told him the whole story. He explained to me, 'That verse means the darkness of the night and the whiteness of the dawn."

That was only a misunderstanding of the meaning of the verse. And, Allah knows best.

Q. No. (197): Why is it that expressing the intention regarding fasting with the tongue is an act of the *Sunnah* though intention is to be expressed in the heart?

A: Originally, intention is to be determined by the heart, but the majority of scholars maintain that it is an act of the *Sunnah* that the Muslim expresses his intention concerning fasting with his tongue as a way of following the example of *Ḥajj*. Thus, he may say for example, "I intend to observe fast tomorrow for the sake of Allah out of faith and seeking Allah's reward". Mālik, however, says that it is more becoming that the Muslim does not express his intention with regard to fasting with his tongue just as the case with the intention regarding prayer. And, Allah knows best.

Q. No. (198): Why is that woman makes up for the days she does not fast during her period of menstruation or that of postnatal bleeding yet does not make up for the prayers she does not perform under the same circumstances?

A: The Sharīʿah takes into consideration the housework and other such affairs that abstract woman most of the time, so it has exempted her from things that would add to her hardships. Consequently, because prayer is to be performed five times a day while fasting is to be observed only for one month a year, woman is to make up for the days she does not fast during her period of menstruation or that of postnatal bleeding. This is because there is no harm in making up for a few non-fast days, unlike making up for the non-performed prayers which are so many, especially with the fact that menstruation normally happens for a number of days every month.

To illustrate this, a woman may have a seven-day period of menstruation: if she were to make up for the prayers unperformed during these seven days, she would have to perform every obligatory prayer twice during the seven days next to the seven days constituting her period. By adding the physical hardship of menstruation, itself including cramps, nausea, headaches, etc., that may be undergone by women - to the hardship of performing normal prayers to the hardship of making up for a number of prayers equal to them, then we come to realize how difficult it would be for such a woman to endure this triple hardship every month. That is why Islam has exempted woman from making up for the prayers in question.

This example may be handled in a different way as follows: if this woman who has a seven-day period were to make up for the prayers she would not perform during this period, then she would have to make up for thirty-five prayers every month and four hundred and twenty prayers every year (7 days × 5 prayers = 35 prayers × 12 months = 420 prayers a year). Also, if a woman were to perform the prayers she would not perform during her postnatal bleeding, the maximum of which is normally forty days, she would have to make up for two hundred prayers (40 days x 5 prayers = 200 prayers) only for this period, bearing in mind that during her making up for them she would have to perform the normal prayers - which consist of an equal number - in addition to undertaking her numeral duties toward her husband and children. Almighty Allah says,

﴿ وَمَا جَعَلَ عَلَيْكُمْ فِي ٱلدِّينِ مِنْ حَرَجٍ ۚ ٧٨ ﴾

"And He has not laid upon you in religion any hardship." [TMQ: 22: 78]

How great, merciful, and easy our religion is! And, Allah knows best.

Q. No. (199): Is the expiation ordained for intercourse in fasting obligatory both on the part of man and on the part of woman?

A: This expiation becomes obligatory on the woman to whom the intercourse is done if she assented to the man in question. If however, that was done to her under coercion, then there is no expiation required on her part and only the man is to expiate. This is because it has been narrated that the Prophet (PBUH) said,

"My followers have been exempted from (the liability of errors they commit by) mistake, (out of) forgetfulness, or that which (they do) under coercion."[1]

Moreover, the expiation concerning intercourse is obligatory only if the intercourse is done intentionally. The same ruling applies if a husband has intercourse with his wife while she is sleeping. Mālik even maintains that in such cases the husband is to expiate twice, one for the violation he has committed during the fasting and one instead of his wife because he exercised his will on her by putting her through such a situation. And, Allah knows best.

Q. No. (200): What is the *Shar'ī* ruling concerning a woman who knows that the dawn has risen yet conceals this from her husband thus letting him have intercourse with her?

A: The author of *Al-Ikhtiyār* says that in this case the expiation of having intercourse while fasting is imposed upon her alone and her husband is not legally asked to expiate for that.[2] And, Allah knows best.

Q. No. (201): What is the *Shar'ī* ruling concerning a woman whose husband caresses her while she is fasting until she excretes *madhy* (here "womanly sexual secretions without an orgasm")?

A: If a man kisses and caresses his wife while she is fasting until she excretes *madhy*, she does not fall under any legal liability in this as far as the validity of her fasting is concerned.[3] The ruling however

---

[1] Narrated by Ibn Mājah.
[2] Al- Musili, Al- Ikhtiyar, 1/131
[3] See Jami' Ahkām al-Nisā', 2/361.

is different if the husband ejaculates or the wife has an orgasm as a result of such kissing or caressing, for this invalidates fasting and necessitates making up for the invalidated fast. And, Allah knows best.

Q. No. (202): What is the *Sharʿī* ruling concerning a person who invalidates his fasting with intercourse but not during the month of Ramaḍān?

A: No expiation is required on the part of whoever invalidates his fasting with intercourse during a month other than Ramaḍān, as when he is making up for a day that he did not fast in Ramaḍān or fasting as a performance of a vow. This is because the Prophet (PBUH) ordained expiation only on those who violate the sanctity of the month of Ramaḍān by having intercourse while fasting in it. This has been explicitly narrated in the two Ṣaḥīḥs of Al-Bukhārī and Muslim: when a man had intercourse with his wife (while fasting) in Ramaḍān, the Prophet (PBUH) ordered him to set a slave free, but the man told him that he could not do that, so he (PBUH) ordered him to observe fast for two consecutive months... to the end of the Ḥadīth. And, Allah knows best.

Q. No. (203): Is expiation required for things other than intercourse?

A: The Ḥanafīs and the Mālikīs maintain that expiation is obligatory upon a person who eats or drinks "intentionally" while fasting just like having intercourse because by doing so he violates the sanctity of the month of Ramaḍān. It is also because expiation is ordained as a way of atoning for the guilt of invalidating fasting, and this invalidation exists as a result of eating and drinking, especially with the fact that "fasting" is to "abstain" from eating, drinking, and having sexual intercourse. Thus, to invalidate fasting with one of them is equal to invalidating it with any of the others.[1] They have proved their view with what has been narrated that ʿAlī, may Allah

---

[1] See As-Samarqandī, Tuhfatul-Fuqahā' ", 1/535

be pleased with him, said, "Expiation is required for eating, drinking, and intercourse."[1] Moreover, Mālik has narrated in his *Muwattā'* that once a man broke fast in Ramaḍān and the Prophet (PBUH) commanded him to expiate.

The Shāfi'īs and the Ḥanbalīs, on the other hand, view that expiation is connected to intercourse only, because the text speaking about expiation concerned a Bedouin who had intercourse with his wife during the daytime of Ramaḍān. Besides, having intercourse while fasting in this month is such a heinous act that is not to be compared to eating and drinking.

To settle this difference of opinions, it may be said that the view adopted by the Ḥanafīs and the Mālikīs is more evident, and it may be added that the "desire" of eating and drinking is - in most cases and for many people - much stronger than sexual "desire". So, just as expiation is required because of intercourse, it is also required because of eating or drinking. And, Allah knows best.

Q. No. (204): What is the *Shar'ī* ruling concerning a person whose fasting has been invalidated while he is observing the fasting of Ramaḍān: can he act as a person who is not in a state of fasting?

A: Whenever a person's fasting is invalidated during Ramaḍān, he must abstain from the things from which he is to abstain as a fasting person until the end of the day, as a way of maintaining the sanctity of this great month. However, if this happens while a person is fasting in a month other than Ramaḍān, as when he is making up for the fast of Ramaḍān or performing a vow-based fasting, he does not have to abstain from the required things until the end of the day, as agreed upon by the Imāms of *Fiqh*. Still, the Mālikīs assert that he must abstain from these things until the end of the day if the fasting is for performing a named vow, such as making a vow that he will observe fast during the first ten days of the month of *Dhū al-Ḥijjah*,

---

[1] See Al-Ikhtiyār, 1/ 131.

for example, because this naming or specification gives the fasting sanctity similar to that of fasting in Ramaḍān. And, Allah knows best.

Q. No. (205): What is the *Shar'ī* ruling concerning a fasting person who donates blood?

A: Donating blood is like cupping, and it is detestable for a fasting person to do something that may make him weak to the extent that he may not be able to observe fasting for some time. This applies to cupping and donating blood, but the majority of scholars view that such acts do not invalidate fasting. It has been narrated by Al-Bukhārī on the authority of Ibn 'Abbās, may Allah be pleased with him, that the Prophet (PBUH) applied cupping while he was fasting. Al-Bukhārī has also narrated on the authority of Anas Ibn Mālik, may Allah be pleased with him, that they (the Companions) would not hold cupping as detestable for a fasting person, except for weakness, meaning it would be detestable to them if it caused weakness and feebleness. And, Allah knows best.

Q. No. (206): What is the *Shar'ī* ruling concerning a person who chews gum while fasting?

A: It is detestable for a fasting person to chew gum because this invalidates fasting if the chewing process causes some part of the gum to enter the belly or a substance in it to ooze and enter it. The majority of scholars maintain that such chewing, with which such things enter the belly, invalidates fasting.[1] And, Allah knows best.

Q. No. (207): Is it permissible for a woman who menstruates while fasting to eat or drink during the daytime?

A: Imām Mālik maintains that if a woman menstruates while fasting, she does not have to continue fasting until sunset. However, it is recommended for such a woman to conceal her breaking the fast from people especially children. And, Allah knows best.

---

[1] See *Al-Mughnī*, 3/109.

Q. No. (208): What is the *Shar'ī* ruling concerning a woman whose menstruation comes to an end during the daytime of Ramaḍān?

A: In this case she does not have to abstain from eating or drinking until the sun sets. Important still, if her husband returns from some journey while he is not fasting, he can have intercourse with her during the daytime of Ramaḍān.[1] And, Allah knows best.

Q. No. (209): What is the *Shar'ī* ruling concerning a woman whose menstruation ends before dawn, and she intends to observe fast the next day but does not take the ritual bath except after the rise of dawn?

A: The majority of scholars maintain that the fasting of such a woman is valid even though she did not take the ritual bath except after the rise of the dawn with which her fasting started.[2] And, Allah knows best.

Q. No. (210): What is the *Shar'ī* ruling concerning a woman who is to observe fast for two consecutive months as expiation: does her period of menstruation invalidate the required consecutiveness?

A: Generally speaking, those who are to observe fast for two consecutive months must observe that fast consecutively, in the sense that if the fast of even one day of them is broken the person in question will have to observe fast for two consecutive months from the very beginning. In the case of a woman, menstruation does not invalidate or break the consecutiveness required for this form of fasting. Mālik says that when her period starts, she is to stop fasting until the period ends and after that she is to observe fast adding the days she fasted before menstruation to those she will fast

---

[1] See *Al- Umm*, 2/62.

[2] See *Fatḥ al-Bārī*, 4/192.

after it and so on until she finishes the required two-consecutive-months fasting.[1] And, Allah knows best.

Q. No. (211): What is the *Sharʿī* ruling concerning a person who breaks fast out of forgetfulness?

A: Whoever eats or drinks out of forgetfulness while observing fast, his fast is valid and he does not have to make up for the fast in question. This is because the Sharīʿah considers the fasting person who eats or drinks out of forgetfulness as remaining in a state of fasting and that what he has eaten or drunk is a provision that Allah has bestowed upon him, and therefore no making up is required in consequence of this forgetfulness-based eating or drinking. This ruling applies whether the fasting in question is obligatory or voluntary.

It has been narrated by At-Tirmidhī on the authority of Abū Hurayrah, may Allah be pleased with him, that the Prophet (PBUH) said,

"Whoever eats or drinks (while fasting) out of forget- fulness is not to break his fast (because of this), for it is a provision which Allah has bestowed upon him."

It has moreover been narrated by Abū Dāwūd that Abū Hurayrah, may Allah be pleased with him, said,

"A man came to the Prophet (PBUH) and said, 'O Messenger of Allah! I ate and drank out of forgetfulness while I was fasting.' He (PBUH) said to him, 'Allah provided you with (that) food and (that) drink."

Thus, whoever eats or drinks out of forgetfulness while fasting is to complete his fasting because this does not affect his fasting negatively. And, Allah knows best.

---

[1] See *Al- Muwattā*ʾ, 1/317.

Q. No. (212): What is the *Shar'ī* ruling concerning a person who breaks fasting mistakenly?

A: A fasting person may break his fast mistakenly, as for example when he has breakfast thinking that the sun has set - without making sure of that then realizes later on that he was mistaken. Such a person must make up for the fast in question. Al-Bukhārī has narrated that Asma' Bint Abū Bakr, may Allah be pleased with her, said, "We broke our fast during the lifetime of the Prophet (PBUH) on a cloudy day and then the sun appeared." Hisham - the sub-narrator was asked, "Were they ordered to make up for that day?" He replied, "It had to be made up for."

The same ruling applies if the people of some place do not see the crescent of Ramaḍān because of fog or clouds and do not observe fast the next day which they come to know later that it was the first day of Ramaḍān. They must make up for this day as unanimously agreed upon by scholars. And, Allah knows best.

Q. No. (213): What is the *Shar'ī* ruling concerning a person who hears the *Adhān* of the *Fajr* Prayer while food is in his mouth?

A: In this case he must throw this food out of his mouth. The ruling applies if he hears the *Adhān* while having intercourse with his wife, as then he must stop doing so immediately. If he eats the food in his mouth, his fast will be broken because of that and thus he must make up for the fast. Still, if he continues having intercourse, he will have to make up for the broken fast and do the expatiation required upon those who break the fast with intercourse: emancipating a slave or observing fast for two consecutive months other than the day which is to be made up for, or providing food to sixty poor people. And it should be known that he must deal with these three things in arrangement, that is, he must start with the first one and if he cannot find a slave then he can switch to the next one and so on. This is because Almighty Allah has made it lawful for him to eat, drink, and have intercourse until the rise of dawn but he exceeded the prescribed limit and made use of that privilege for a time extra to the allowed one.

On the other hand, some scholars maintain that if a person is taking the pre-dawn meal (*Suḥūr*) and hears the *Adhān* of the *Fajr* Prayer while his food is in his hand, he can eat it because the Prophet (PBUH) allowed that as narrated by Abū Dāwūd and Al-Hakim.[1]

To avoid this difference of opinions and keep to the safe side, the Muslim can "finish" eating, drinking, or having intercourse with his wife "before" dawn "approaches". He can also avoid doing any of these things "right before" the rise of dawn. This is better for him, and Allah knows best.

Q. No. (214): What is the *Shar'ī* ruling concerning a person who dies without making up for certain fasts due on him?

A: Originally, fasting is a physical act of worship which the Muslim is to perform by himself and no one else is to perform it in his stead, as in the case with prayer. However, scholars have differed concerning a person who dies without making up for certain fasts that he had to make up for while he was alive.

The majority of scholars, including Abū Ḥanīfah, Mālik, and Ash-Shāfi'ī according to a famous report about him in this regard, maintain that a deceased person's *Walīyy* who is - normally one of his sons or his heirs in general is not to observe the fasts due on him on his behalf, yet he can present a *mudd* of food for every day on his behalf. They prove this opinion with what At-Tirmidhī has narrated on the authority of Ibn 'Umar, may Allah be pleased with him, that the Prophet (PBUH) said,

"Whoever dies while the fasting of one month is due on him, a poor person is to be fed for every day (of the thirty) on his behalf."

---

[1] See Fiqhus- *Sunnah* An- Nisa', p. 234.

On the other hand, Aḥmad and others view that it is permissible for the *Walīyy* of a deceased person to observe fasting on his behalf. They prove their view with a number of texts including the following one narrated by Al-Bukhārī and Muslim: ʿĀʾishah, may Allah be pleased with her, said that the Prophet (PBUH) said,

"Whoever dies while (some) fasting is due on him, his *Walī*yy can observe (the due) fast on his behalf."

Aḥmad has also proved his view with what he himself and others has narrated on the authority of Ibn ʿAbbās, who said,

"A woman came to the Prophet (PBUH) and said, 'O Messenger of Allah! My sister died while the fasting of two consecutive months was due on her.' In another narration she said, 'Can I observe fast on her behalf? - He (PBUH) said, "Tell me: if your sister was indebted (to someone), would you then pay her debt?" She answered in the affirmative and he (PBUH) said, "Then Allah's right is more worthy (of fulfilment than a human's)."

To settle this difference, it may be said that if the *Walīyy* is well-to-do yet weak or ill and cannot fast, then he can act according to the first opinion, that is to say he can pay a *mudd* of food for every day on the deceased person's behalf. If, however the *Walīyy* is strong yet poor, he can act according to the second opinion and observe fast for the required day or days. But still, it is mentioned in Sunan Abū Dāwūd that scholars have agreed that if a person broke fast due to illness or travel then did not neglect making up for that until he died, nothing is due on him and no feeding is required on his behalf.[1] And, Allah knows best.

Q. No. (215): Why is it desirable for the Muslim to study the religion and the Qur'ān during the month of Ramaḍān?

---

[1] Name of Abū Dāwūd, 2/792.

A: It is desirable for the Muslim to study the religion and the Qurʾān during the month of Ramaḍān simply because it is the month in which the Qurʾān was revealed, and the Qurʾān is the primary source of the religion along with the *Sunnah* of the Prophet (PBUH). Almighty Allah says,

﴿شَهۡرُ رَمَضَانَ ٱلَّذِيٓ أُنزِلَ فِيهِ ٱلۡقُرۡءَانُ هُدٗى لِّلنَّاسِ وَبَيِّنَٰتٖ مِّنَ ٱلۡهُدَىٰ وَٱلۡفُرۡقَانِۚ ١٨٥﴾

"The month of Ramaḍān in which was revealed the Qur'ān, a guidance for mankind and clear proofs for the guidance and the criterion (between right and wrong)." [TMQ: 2: 185]

It is also because the Prophet (PBUH) used to study the Qur'ān with Jibril (Gabriel) during Ramaḍān. That is why the Muslim should make of Ramaḍān a school in which he tries to acquire as much religious knowledge as possible, putting the Qur'ān on top of such blessed efforts.

It has been narrated that Ibn ʿAbbās, may Allah be pleased with him, said,

"The Messenger of Allah (PBUH) was the most generous of all the people, and he used to be more generous in the month of Ramaḍān when Jibril would meet him. Jibril used to meet him every night in Ramaḍān to study the Qurʾān carefully together. Thus, whenever he (PBUH) met Jibril, he would be more generous than the fast wind."[1]

Besides, it is quite significant for the Muslim to remember that the Prophet (PBUH) said, as narrated on the authority of Abū Hurayrah, may Allah be pleased with him,

"... He who treads a path in search of knowledge, Allah makes that path easy for him (so that it would) lead (him) to Paradise. Whenever a number of people assemble in one of the houses of Allah (mosques)

---

[1] Narrated by Al-Bukhārī and Muslim.

and recite the Book of Allah and learn and teach it (among themselves), tranquillity descends upon them, mercy covers them, the angels surround them, and Allah makes a mention of them in the presence of those near Him..."[1]

This means that recitation of the Qur'ān and knowledge: acquisition is recommended at all times, yet they are more desirable in the month of Ramaḍān in particular. And, Allah knows best.

Q. No. (216): How would Jibril (Gabriel) study the Qur'ān with the Prophet (PBUH) in Ramaḍān?

A: As narrated by Ibn Mājah on the authority of ʿĀʾishah, may Allah be pleased with her, Jibril, peace be upon him, used to study the Qurʾān with the Prophet (PBUH) once every Ramaḍān, but when it was the year in which he (PBUH) passed away he studied the Qur'ān with him twice. That was why the Prophet (PBUH) felt that he would die soon enough. And, Allah knows best.

Q. No. (217): What is the excellence of the Night of Decree (*Laylatul-Qadr*)?

A: The Night of Decree belongs to the blessed month of Ramaḍān in which the Qurʾān was revealed. Rather, it was the night in which Allah revealed this great light of guidance. Almighty Allah says about this night, glorifying and honouring it from among the other nights of the year,

﴿إِنَّآ أَنزَلۡنَٰهُ فِي لَيۡلَةِ ٱلۡقَدۡرِ ١ وَمَآ أَدۡرَىٰكَ مَا لَيۡلَةُ ٱلۡقَدۡرِ ٢ لَيۡلَةُ ٱلۡقَدۡرِ خَيۡرٞ مِّنۡ أَلۡفِ شَهۡرٖ ٣ تَنَزَّلُ ٱلۡمَلَٰٓئِكَةُ وَٱلرُّوحُ فِيهَا بِإِذۡنِ رَبِّهِم مِّن كُلِّ أَمۡرٖ ٤ سَلَٰمٌ هِيَ حَتَّىٰ مَطۡلَعِ ٱلۡفَجۡرِ ٥﴾

"Verily! We have sent it (this Qurʾān) down in the night of Al-Qadr (Decree). And what will make you know what the night of Al-Qadr (Decree) is? The

[1] Narrated by Muslim.

night of Al-Qadr (Decree) is better than a thousand months. Therein descend the angels and the Ruh (Jibril [Gabriel]) by Allah's Permission with all Decrees. Peace![1] Until the appearance of dawn."

[TMQ 97: 1-5]

That is why the Prophet (PBUH) encouraged Muslims to seize the opportunity of worshiping Allah in this night. He (PBUH) said,

"Seek the Night of Decree in the last ten (nights) of Ramaḍān."[2]

He also said,

"Whoever stands (in prayer during) the Night of Decree out of faith and hoping for (Allah's) reward, his previous sins will be forgiven for him."[3]

By connecting the last Ḥadīth with the verse quoted above, we know that worshiping Allah at the Night of Decree equals worshiping Him in more than eighty-three years and one third of a year. This further means that there is no other night that has the superiority and excellence of the Night of Decree in the sight of Allah. And, Allah knows best.

Q. No. (218): How is it that the Night of Decree is one of the special merits of the Muslim *Ummah*?

A: Al-Khattābi has stated that scholars unanimously agree that the Night of Decree is one of the special merits that Allah has bestowed upon the *Ummah* of Prophet Muḥammad (PBUH). This is first of all indicated by Allah's connecting it to the revelation of the Qur᾿ān:

﴿إِنَّآ أَنزَلۡنَٰهُ فِي لَيۡلَةِ ٱلۡقَدۡرِ ١﴾

---

[1] i.e., All that night, there is peace and goodness from Allah to His believing servants.

[2] Narrated by Al-Bukhārī.

[3] Narrated by Al-Bukhārī and Muslim.

"Indeed, I revealed it on the Night of Decree Verily! We have sent it (this Qur'ān) down in the night of Al- Qadr (Decree)." [TMQ: 97:1]

and the Qur'ān was revealed to the seal of all Prophets and Messengers, Muḥammad (PBUH). This makes the Night of Decree a special merit of his *Ummah*, which Allah has made the best of nations.

This excellence of the Night of Decree is further indicated by what Mālik has narrated in his *Muwattā'* that "the lifetimes of people before the Messenger of Allah (PBUH) were displayed to him, and it seemed that he regarded the lifetimes of his followers as short and so they would not perform as many (good) deeds as done by those who were given longer lifetimes before them. Therefore, Allah granted him the Night of Decree, which is better than a thousand months.

﴿وَمَآ أَدۡرَىٰكَ مَا لَيۡلَةُ ٱلۡقَدۡرِ ۝٢ لَيۡلَةُ ٱلۡقَدۡرِ خَيۡرٞ مِّنۡ أَلۡفِ شَهۡرٖ ۝٣﴾

"And what will make you know what the night of Al- Qadr (Decree) is? The night of Al-Qadr (Decree) is better than a thousand months."

[TMQ: 97: 2-3][1]

And, Allah knows best.

Q. No. (219): Why did Almighty Allah conceal the Night of Decree?

A: Almighty Allah has concealed this Night of Decree from the Muslim *Ummah* so that they can exert more efforts in worshiping Him for more nights in Ramaḍān, especially the last ten nights in which the Prophet (PBUH) told Muslims that this night is one of them, saying,

"Seek the Night of Decree in the last ten (nights) of Ramaḍān."[2]

---

[1] See Tafsīr Ibn Kathīr, 4/568.
[2] Narrated by Al Bukhārī.

And, Allah knows best.

Q. No. (220): Is there any sign that may indicate the Night of Decree?

A: Ibn Ḥajar has stated in his *Fatḥ al-Bārī'* that there are certain signs which indicate or characterize the Night of Decree. Some of these signs are as follows:

It has been narrated by Muslim that the sun rises with no rays in the morning of this night. Aḥmad has also narrated that this night is so clear that it seems that there is a shinning moon in it, and that it is still and fair, neither hot nor cold. And, it has been narrated by Ibn Khuzaymah that the angels are (spread) throughout the earth (in numbers) more than stones.[1] And, Allah knows best.

Q. No. (221): What are the sections of *I'tikāf*?

A: I'tikaf is divided into two sections: *I'tikāf* as an act of the *Sunnah* and i'tikaf as an obligation. *I'tikāf* as an act of the *Sunnah* is that which the Muslim performs voluntarily as a way of drawing near to Almighty Allah and seeking His reward, as well as of following the example of the Prophet (PBUH). This form of *I'tikāf* is a confirmed act of the *Sunnah* during the last ten days of Ramaḍān, for the Prophet (PBUH) used to practice it regularly during these days in particular. It has been narrated that Ibn 'Umar, may Allah be pleased with him, said,

"The Messenger of Allah (PBUH) used to practice *I'tikāf* during (all) the last ten (days) of Ramaḍān."[2]

I'tikaf as an obligation, however, is that which a Muslim has made obligatory upon himself by vowing, as when he says, for example, "I vow that I will perform *I'tikāf* for one day," whether he specifies that day or not. Such i'tikaf is obligatory because Almighty Allah says as a general rule, ... *and let them perform their vows...* [TMQ: 22: 29] Not

---

[1] See *Fatḥ al-Bārī*, 4/306.
[2] Narrated by Al-Bukhārī and Muslim

only this, it has been narrated on the authority of Ibn ʿUmar, may Allah be pleased with him, that his father ʿUmar Ibn al-Khaṭṭāb, may Allah be pleased with him, said to the Prophet (PBUH), "In (the pre-Islamic period of) ignorance I made a vow that I would confine myself in the Sacred Mosque (in Mecca)." He (PBUH) said, "Perform your vow."[1] And, Allah knows best.

Q. No. (222): What are the conditions of *i`tikaf*?

A: For the validity of *Iʿtikāf*, the following conditions must be met.

1. It is to be performed in a mosque where prayers are performed.

2. Intention is required, because *Iʿtikāf* is an act of worship, and no act of worship is to be performed without intention.

3. A woman must not be menstruating or in a postnatal condition, or else her i'tikaf will not be valid. And, Allah knows best.

Q. No. (223): What are the things which invalidate *Iʿtikāf*?

A: There are certain things that invalidate *Iʿtikāf*, as follows:

1. Having sexual intercourse intentionally invalidates *i'tikaf*, even if this should happen without ejaculation.
2. Defecting from Islam invalidates *Iʿtikāf* because this contradicts the nature of worship and *I'tikāf* is an act of worship.
3. If a person loses sanity either by becoming insane or as a result of drunkenness, his i'tikaf becomes invalid.
4. If a woman while being in a state of *Iʿtikāf* is menstruating or in a postnatal condition, her *Iʿtikāf* becomes invalid because of that.
5. Going out of the mosque where a person is performing *Iʿtikāf* invalidates his i'tikaf, if this is done without necessity. And, Allah knows best.

[1] Narrated by Al-Bukhārī.

Q. No. (224): What is desirable and what is detestable as far as *i'tikaf* is concerned?

A: A *muʿtakif* (a person who is practicing *Iʿtikāf*) is recommended to perform as many voluntary acts of worship during his *Iʿtikāf* as possible. This is because i'tikaf is an act of worship with which the Muslim confines himself in a mosque where he is supposed to draw nearer and nearer to Him. throughout the period of his i'tikaf, seeking His forgiveness and hoping for His blessings and rewards. Thus, it is desirable for a *muʿtakif* that he spends his time glorifying, praising, and praying to Almighty Allah. He can also recite as much as he can from the Qurʾān and invoke blessings on the Prophet (PBUH).

Along with this, it is detestable that a *muʿtakif* leaves the mosque during his i'tikaf to visit an ill person or witnessing a funeral procession, because this is not included in the necessities that justify his leaving the mosque, especially that a funeral procession can be witnessed by others. Moreover, it is forbidden that a *muʿtakif* - or any other person to sell or buy anything inside the mosque. Additionally, it is detestable for a *muʿtakif* to abstain from speaking thinking that this helps him to draw near to Allah. Abstaining from speaking in the meaning of fasting - has nothing to do with Islam. And, Allah knows best.

Q. No. (225): Where can woman perform *i'tikaf*?

A: Some Faqīhs maintain that *Iʿtikāf* in general is not valid except when performed in a mosque, and that this applies both to men and to women, because Almighty Allah has attached. i'tikaf to mosques when he said,

﴿وَلَا تُبَٰشِرُوهُنَّ وَأَنتُمۡ عَٰكِفُونَ فِي ٱلۡمَسَٰجِدِۗ ١٨٧﴾

"And do not have sexual relations with them (your wives) while you are in Iʿtikāf in the mosques." [TMQ: 2: 187]

Abū Ḥanīfah, however, views that it is an act of the *Sunnah* that a woman performs *I'tikāf* in her house because she must be covered from strangers' sight while sleeping and it is possible that she is uncovered during her sleep in the mosque if she performs *I'tikaf* there. To prove his view, Abū Ḥanīfah has sought proof with the fact that it is legally known and confirmed that it is better for a woman to perform prayer, which is greater than i'tikaf, in her house, and this makes it more becoming that she performs *I'tikāf* in her house. The Prophet (PBUH) said,

"... and their (women's) houses are better for them, if they but knew!"

Abū Ḥanīfah moreover proves his opinion with what has been narrated on the authority of 'Ā'ishah, may Allah be pleased with her, that the Prophet (PBUH) intended to practice *I'tikāf* and when he reached the place where he intended to perform *I'tikāf*, he saw some tents, and they were the tents of 'Ā'ishah, Hafsah, and Zaynab (the Prophet's wives). So, he said, "Have they intended to do righteousness by doing this?" And then he went away and did not perform *I'tikāf* (in Ramaḍān) but performed it in the month of Shawwāl for ten days.[1] This clearly indicates that the Prophet (PBUH) disapproved of his wives' hastening as in a race to perform *I'tikāf* with him in the mosque, and that is why he did not perform *I'tikāf* in Ramaḍān and performed it in the month of Shawwāl for ten days. This shows that it is detestable for a woman to perform *I'tikāf* in the mosque. This is the end of the review of Abū Ḥanīfah's view.

As for Ash-Shāfi'ī, he maintains that it is detestable for women to perform *I'tikāf* in a mosque where prayers are performed in congregation, while Aḥmad is of the opinion that it is permissible for a woman to perform i'tikaf in the mosque, yet this should be in the company of her husband.

---

[1] Narrated by Al-Bukhārī.

Thus, Faqīhs are agreed to the effect that it is permissible for woman to perform i'tikaf in the mosque in general, but Abū Ḥanīfah says this is detestable for her and so he prefers that she performs it in her house because it secures more "covering" for her. And, Allah knows best.

Ḥajj (Pilgrimage) And *'Umrah* (Lesser Pilgrimage)

Ḥajj (Pilgrimage)

Q. No. (226): When was *Ḥajj* prescribed for Muslims?

A: Scholars have differed about the time when *Ḥajj* was prescribed for the Muslim *Ummah*. Some say it was prescribed before the emigration (Ḥijrah) to Medina, but the famous view in this regard is the one confirming that *Ḥajj* was prescribed after the Prophetic emigration to Medina. Accordingly, some say it was prescribed in the fifth year after Ḥijrah and others that was in the eighth year after Ḥijrah, yet the famous view in this connection is that *Ḥajj* was prescribed during the sixth year after Ḥijrah.[1] And, Allah knows best.

Q. No. (227): What is the time of *Ḥajj*?

A: Almighty Allah says,

﴿ٱلْحَجُّ أَشْهُرٌ مَّعْلُومَٰتٌ ۚ ١٩٧﴾

"The Ḥajj (pilgrimage) is (in) well-known months..." [TMQ: 2: 197]

According to the view adopted by the majority of scholars, these "well-known months" are Shawwāl, Dhū al-Qa'dah, and the first ten days of Dhū al-Ḥijjah. However, some scholars, including Ibn Mas'ud, Ibn 'Umar, and Az-Zuhrī, maintain that these months are Shawwāl, Dhū al-Qa'dah, and the whole month of Dhū al-Ḥijjah.

This difference of opinion may be good for a Muslim who performs any of the duties related to *Ḥajj* after the Day of Slaughter or the tenth day of Dhū al-Ḥijjah. This is because his *Ḥajj* will be sound

[1] See Al-Ignā, 2/159

according to the view that the months of *Ḥajj* are Shawwāl, Dhū al-Qaʿdah, and the whole of Dhū al-Ḥijjah.

Equally important, it is not permissible to assume *Iḥrām* for *Ḥajj* before its stated months, that is, before the month of Shawwāl, the first of the months of *Ḥajj*, and this is the preponderant opinion in this concern, because the apparent meaning of the verse The *Ḥajj* (pilgrimage) is (in) well-known months... implies that *Ḥajj* is to be performed in, and not before, these well-known months. And, Allah knows best.

Q. No. (228): Is *Ḥajj* a physical act of worship or is it a fiscal one?

A: Acts of worship are either physical, such as prayer and fasting, or fiscal, such as *Zakāh* and voluntary alms (*Ṣadaqah*). *Ḥajj* has these two characteristics, that is, it is both physical and fiscal. To explain this, the pilgrim performs the *Manāsik* of *Ḥajj* using his body in doing so, and thus he assumes *Iḥrām* wearing the clothes specified for it, performs *Ṭawāf*, *Saʿy* between As-Ṣafā and Al-Marwah, staying at *ʿArafah*, throwing of pebbles, and the other duties of *Ḥajj*. He also spends out of his money to cover the expenses of the journey of *Ḥajj* as well as those of the *hady* required in this *Ḥajj*. That is why the reward of *Ḥajj* is great, and it is sufficient for a pilgrim to have the reward pinpointed by the Prophet (PBUH) in the Ḥadīth that reads,

"Whoever performs *Ḥajj* and neither has sexual relations (with his wife) nor commits sin, will return with his sins (forgiven and so he will be as sinless) as he was on the day his mother delivered him." [1]

Another Ḥadīth states,

"No reward is for a *Ḥajj* Mabrūr (i.e., *Ḥajj* which is done according to the Sunnah and is accepted by Allah) except Paradise."[2]

---

[1] Narrated by Al-Bukhārī, Muslim, and others
[2] Narrated by Al-Bukhārī, Muslim, and others

Both hadiths mean that these rewards are to be given to those who perform *Ḥajj* according to the instructions of the Sharīʿah. And, Allah knows best.

Q. No. (229): Why is it that the Muslim who wants to perform *Ḥajj* should earn his livelihood through lawful means?

A: The Messenger of Allah (PBUH) said,

"No reward is for a *Ḥajj* Mabrūr (i.e., *Ḥajj* which is done according to the Sunnah and is accepted by Allah) except Paradise."[1]

This simply means that any person who wants his *Ḥajj* to be *Mabrūr* must earn the money spent for this *Ḥajj* through lawful means. This is because Allah does not bless anything which depends on ill-gotten money, and the Prophet (PBUH) confirmed that Allah is Good (and Pure) and does not accept except that which is good (and pure). And, Allah knows best.

Q. No. (230): Why is it that *Ḥajj* is prescribed to be performed "only once" - as obligatorily by whoever is legally able to perform it?

A: The answer to this question may be provided by the following Ḥadīth: It has been narrated that Abū Hurayrah, may Allah be pleased with him, said,

The Messenger of Allah addressed us and said, 'O people! Allah has made *Ḥajj* obligatory for you; so, perform *Ḥajj*.' Thereupon a person said, 'O Messenger of Allah! (Is it to be performed) every year?' He (PBUH) kept quiet, and he (the man) repeated (these words) three times, whereupon the Messenger of Allah said, 'If I were to say Yes, it would become obligatory (for you to perform it every year) and you would not be able to do it. Then he (PBUH) said, leave me with what I have left to you, for those who were before you were destroyed because of excessive questioning and their opposition to their Prophets. So, whenever I command you to do anything, do it

---

[1] Narrated by Al-Bukhārī, Muslim, and others

as much as it lies in your power, and whenever I forbid you to do anything, then abandon it."[1]

The part that carries the exact answer to the question is the Prophet's statement, "and you would not be able to do it," which means that Allah wants to make things easy for people and not otherwise. Yet still, the Prophet (PBUH) allowed the Muslim to perform *Ḥajj* more than once voluntarily, as narrated by Abū Dāwūd on the authority of Al-Aqraʿ Ibn Ḥābis. And, Allah knows best.

Q. No. (231): What should the Muslim do before starting the journey for *Ḥajj* or *ʿUmrah*?

A: He should consider the following:

He should determine in his heart that this act of worship he is going to perform is purely for the sake of Allah. He should repent to Allah and give anything he may have taken unjustly to those who have the right to it. He should consult people who are qualified to give advice, and he should also perform the prayer of *Istikhārah.*

- He should choose righteous individuals to accompany him in this blessed travel.
- He should advise his family, acquaintances, and friends to be conscious of Allah.
- He should use for his *Ḥajj* or *ʿUmrah* money which has been earned through legal means.
- He should learn whatever he is supposed to need of the religious and *Sharʿī* rulings pertaining to travel, *Ḥajj*, and *ʿUmrah.* For this purpose, it is better that he seeks to be in the company of a well-versed scholar who can answer him properly whenever he needs to know anything in this connection. And, Allah knows best.

---

[1] Narrated by Muslim and An-Nasāʾī.

Q. No. (232): What should the Muslim do on starting the journey for *Ḥajj* or *ʿUmrah* and during it?

A: He is recommended to consider the following:

- It is desirable that he chooses Thursday to start the journey on. It is desirable that he performs two *Rakʿahs* before setting out.
- It is desirable that he says upon going out if his house, "In the Name of Allah! I depend on Allah, and there is neither might nor power except with Allah".
- It is desirable that he says when mounting the means of transportation that will get him to Mecca, "In the Name of Allah and praise be to Allah! Glory to Him Who has subjected this to us, and we could never have it (by our efforts); and verily, to Our Lord we indeed are to return! Praise be to Allah! Praise be to Allah! Praise be to Allah! Allah is the Greatest! Allah is the Greatest! Allah is the Greatest! Glory be to You, O Allah! I have wronged myself, so forgive me, for no one forgives sins but You!"
- It is desirable that he pays farewell to his near family and the other relatives and asks them to invoke Allah for him. He may also invoke Allah for them.
- He should not harm any of the people accompanying him. Rather, he should be helpful to them and advise them whenever they need his advice.

He can make use of the religious allowance related to prayer on journeys, i.e., to shorten the four-*Rakʿah* prayers. He may also combine the *Zuhr* Prayer and the *ʿAṣr* Prayer as well as the *Maghrib* Prayer and the *ʿIshāʾ* Prayer especially when necessary. And, Allah knows best.

Q. No. (233): What are the conditions obligating *Ḥajj*?

A: *Ḥajj* is obligatory upon whoever meets the following conditions:

1. **To be Muslim**, because a disbeliever is not qualified for worshiping Allah.

2. **To be mature**, because a boy is not legally responsible (*mukallaf*) because of his young age.

3. **To be sane**, because an insane person is incompetent while sanity is the basis of legal responsibility.

4. **To be free**, because a slave is always busy undertaking the affairs of his masters as a right upon him. Besides, he does not have money with which he would afford the expenses of *Ḥajj*.

5. **To be capable**, and capability or *istitā'ah* is established once the Muslim is physically and financially ready to go on such a journey of *Ḥajj* that is supposed to be hard and costly in most cases. This condition of capability is the primary condition of *Ḥajj* obligation because Almighty Allah says,

﴿وَلِلَّهِ عَلَى ٱلنَّاسِ حِجُّ ٱلْبَيْتِ مَنِ ٱسْتَطَاعَ إِلَيْهِ سَبِيلًا ۚ ﴿٩٧﴾﴾

"And Ḥajj (pilgrimage to Makkah) to the House (Ka'bah) is a duty that mankind owes to Allah, those who can afford the expenses (for one's conveyance, provision and residence)" [TMQ: 3: 97]

Therefore, whoever is ill or does not have the money that suffices the expenses of the *Ḥajj* journey, is regarded legally as incapable, and Allah does not burden a person beyond his scope.

If any of these five conditions is not met by a Muslim, *Ḥajj* is not obligatory upon him. And, Allah knows best.

Q. No. (234): What are the kinds of *nusuk* (the prescribed duties of *Ḥajj*)?

A: There are three kinds or forms of *nusuk*, i.e., the prescribed duties of *Ḥajj*, or in other words the prescribed duties of *Ḥajj* can be performed in any of three forms: *Ifrād, Tamattu', or Qirān*. Each item will be explained as follows:

1. ***Ifrād***: It literally means "setting aside" and it is that a person assumes *Iḥrām* from the *Mīqāt* - the place from which *Iḥrām* starts intending to perform *Ḥajj* "alone". He can say when intending to do so, "*Labbayka bi Ḥajj* (Here I am at Your service, [intending to perform] *Ḥajj*)" This person will remain in a state of *Iḥrām* until he stands on *'Arafah* and performs the throwing of pebbles at Al-'Aqabah then disengages himself from the state of *Iḥrām*. Then after performing the duties related to *Ḥajj*, he can perform *'Umrah* if he wishes to do so, and no *hady* will be obligatory upon him because of performing *Ḥajj* alone.
2. ***Tamattu'***: It literally means "enjoyment" and it is that a person assumes *Iḥrām* for performing *'Umrah* during the months of *Ḥajj* then performs *Ḥajj* during the same year in which he performed *'Umrah*. When starting to say *talbiyah*,[1] he says, "*Labbayka bi 'Umrah* (Here I am at Your service, [intending to perform] *'Umrah*)". This form is called *Tamattu'* or enjoyment because after finishing *'Umrah* the person in question becomes like the inhabitants of Mecca in the sense that it becomes lawful for him to wear normal clothes - other than those of *Iḥrām* - and to use perfume and have sexual relations with his wife, thus, "enjoying" after disengaging himself from the state of *Iḥrām* - the same things which a non- *muḥrim* - i.e., a person who is not in a state of *Iḥrām* - enjoys. Therefore, if a person performs *'Umrah* during the months of *Ḥajj* then performs *Ḥajj* during the same year, then he is a *Mutamatti'*, that is, a person who has performed the prescribed duties of *Ḥajj* in the form of *Tamattu'* as described

[1] *Talbiyah* is a formula that starts with the Arabic word "*Labbayka*" meaning "Here I am at Your service".

above. In this case, he is to slaughter a sheep which is a *hady* offered for showing gratitude to Allah because He has enabled him to perform two acts of worship during one journey.

3. ***Qirān***: It literally means "joining" or "connecting" and it is that a person assumes *Iḥrām* for performing both *Ḥajj* and *'Umrah*. He says when starting to say *talbiyah*, "*Labbayka bi Ḥajj wa 'Umrah* (Here I am at Your service, intending to perform] *Ḥajj* and *'Umrah*)".
   Talbiyah is a formula that starts with the Arabic word "*Labbayka*" meaning "Here I am at Your service".

Whoever assumes *Iḥrām* for performing both *Ḥajj* and *'Umrah* must remain in a state of *Iḥrām* until he finishes the duties of *Ḥajj* and *'Umrah* altogether. In other words, he must remain in a state of *Iḥrām*, no matter how long this may take, until he stands on *'Arafah*, goes down to Muzdalifah, performs the required throwing of pebbles at Al-'Aqabah, slaughters the required *hady*, then disengages himself from his *Iḥrām* by having the hair of his head shaved or shortened.

This form of *nusuk* is called *Qirān* because in it the pilgrim connects his performance of *'Umrah* to another of *Ḥajj* when starting to say *talbiyah*, thus intending to perform two acts of worship with one intention and on one journey. And, Allah knows best.

Q. No. (235): What are the pillars of *Ḥajj*?

A: There are four pillars of *Ḥajj*. Below are abridged definitions:

1. ***Iḥrām***

It literally means "consecration," and it is a state in which one is prohibited to practice certain deeds that are lawful at other times. The ceremonies of *'Umrah* and *Ḥajj* are performed during such a state. When one assumes this state, the first thing one should do is to mentally and orally express one's intention to assume this state for the purpose of performing *Ḥajj* or *ʿUmrah* or both of them. Then *talbiyah* is recited. Two sheets of unstitched clothes are the only clothes one wears in this state: (1) *Izār* (wrapper), which is worn below one's waist, and (2) *Ridāʾ* (garment), which is worn round the upper part of the body.

2. **Staying at *ʿArafah***

The second pillar of *Ḥajj* is to stay at the mountain of *ʿArafah* at Mecca beginning from the time after the noon of the ninth day in Dhū al-Ḥijjah until the rise of the dawn of the tenth day in the same month, i.e., the first of the days of ʻIdul-Adha (Sacrifice Feast).

3. ***Ṭawāf* or circumambulating the *Kaʿbah***

Ṭawāf literally means "circumambulation," and as far as *Ḥajj* is concerned it means "to circumambulate the *Kaʿbah*".

4. ***Saʿy* or going between As-Ṣafā and Al-Marwah**

The fourth pillar of *Ḥajj* is to go between the two mountains called As-Ṣafā and Al-Marwah in a certain way and for a specific number of times, as part of the prescribed duties of *Ḥajj*.[1] And, Allah knows best.

Q. No. (236): What are the *Mawāqīt* (times and sites) of *Iḥrām*?

A: *Mawāqīt* is the plural of the Arabic word "*Mīqāt*" which refers to the time when and the place where a pilgrim assumes *Iḥrām* for *Ḥajj* or *ʿUmrah* This means that *Mawāqīt* are divided into two sections: *al-Mawāqīt az-Zamāniyyah* or times and *al-Mawāqīt al-Makāniyyah* or sites where *Iḥrām* is assumed.

al-Mawāqīt az-Zamāniyyah refers to the times during which the duties or rituals of *Ḥajj* must be performed otherwise they will not be valid. The month of Shawwāl, the month of Dhū al-Qaʿdah, and ten days from the month of Dhū al-Ḥijjah represent the time or *al-Mīqāt az-*

---

[1] This is a brief description of the pillars of *Ḥajj* and more details about each pillar will be found in some coming answers

zamani during which those who want to perform *Ḥajj* can assume *Iḥrām*. *'Umrah* however can be performed throughout the year.

Al-Mawāqīt al-Makāniyyah refers to the sites where pilgrims assume *ihrām* for *Ḥajj* and *'Umrah*. These sites were defined by the Prophet (PBUH), and it is not permissible for any person who wants to perform *Ḥajj* or *'Umrah* to surpass them without *Iḥrām*. These sites are five, as follows:

1. The *miqāt* of the people of Medina is Dhū al-Ḥulayfah, and it is located four hundred and thirty kilo meters from Mecca. It is called now Bayar ʿAlī.

2. The *Mīqāt* of the people of Ash-Shām is Al-Juḥfah, and it is located one hundred and ninety kilo meters away from Mecca.

This place is now known as *Rābigh*, and it has become the *Mīqāt* of the people of Ash-Shām as well as those of Egypt and whoever passes by it after the sights of Al-Juhfah have been effaced. It is toward the north of Mecca.

3. The *Mīqāt* of the people of Najd is *Qarn al-Manāzil*, which is located ninety-four kilo meters away from Mecca toward the east.

4. The *Mīqāt* of the people of Yemen is Yalamlam, which is fifty-four kilo meters away from Mecca toward the south.

5. The *Mīqāt* of the people of Iraq is Dhatu Irq, which is ninety-four kilo meters away from Mecca north-eastward. And, Allah knows best.

Q. No. (237): What are the proprieties of *Iḥrām*?

A: There are certain proprieties and acts of the *Sunnah* related to *Iḥrām* and a pilgrim should consider them while being in the state of *Iḥrām*. They are as follows:

1. **Cleanliness**, by trimming nails, plucking out or shaving the hair of the armpit, clipping the moustache, performing ablution or taking a bath along with it for it is better.

2. **That the *Izār* (wrapper) and the *rida'* (garment) be white**, because white clothes are the dearest clothes in the sight of Allah.

3. **Perfuming one's body and clothes.**

4. **Performing two *Rak'ahs*.**

5. **Expressing intention**, by saying when intending to perform *Ḥajj* "I have intended to perform *'Umrah* and I have assumed *Iḥrām* for performing it for the sake of Allah, Glorified and Exalted be He," and saying when intending to perform *Ḥajj*, "I have intended to perform *Ḥajj* and I have assumed *Iḥrām* for performing it for the sake of Allah, Glorified and Exalted be He". If the Muslim intends to connect *Ḥajj* and *'Umrah* (*Qirān*), he can say, "I have intended to perform *Ḥajj* and *'Umrah* and I have assumed *Iḥrām* for performing them for the sake of Allah, Glorified and Exalted be He."

6. **To stipulate**, by saying, "If something stops me, I will finish my *Iḥrām* at any place where You stop me." This is according to Ash-Shāfi'ī and Aḥmad. On the other hand, Abū Ḥanīfah and Mālik assert that it is not lawful for a pilgrim to make such a condition as he must complete performing the prescribed duties of *Ḥajj* or *'Umrah* if he has started to perform them. They add that this stipulation was denied by Ibn 'Umar, may Allah be pleased with him. And, Allah knows best.

Q. No. (238): What are the things forbidden in *Iḥrām*?

A: There are certain things that a pilgrim is prohibited to do while being in the state of *Iḥrām*. They are as follows:

1. **Sexual relations** are prohibited in *Iḥrām* including intercourse itself and things that may lead to it such as kissing, caressing, and even a man's talking to his wife about things pertaining to

intercourse. 2. **A *muḥrim* is forbidden to commit any act of disobedience (*ma'ṣiyah*),** such as looking at a marriageable woman with lust, dissoluteness, looseness, and any other forbidden act.

3. **It is forbidden that a *muḥrim* disputes** with his fellow Muslims, his servants, or any other person.[1]

4. **It is prohibited for a *muḥrim* to wear stitched** clothes which are worn in normal cases such as shirts, trousers, jubbah, and the like.

5. **He is not to wear things such as turbans**, socks, and shoes.

6. **He is not to wear clothes scented** with perfumes.[2]

7. **A *muḥrim* is forbidden to conduct a marriage contract** whether it is for himself or for another one.

8. **Land-game (hunting) is forbidden for a *muḥrim*,** be it by killing, or slaughtering, or even showing the way to it.

9. **A *muḥrim* if forbidden to shave his head or clip his nails.** This ruling concerns the shaving of the hair of the head or that of any part of the body. And, Allah knows best.

Q. No. (239): What are the things allowed in *Iḥrām*?

A: There are certain things which the *muḥrim* is allowed to do, as follows.

---

[1] The original source in which these three things are forbidden is the verse that reads, *So, whosoever intends to perform Ḥajj therein (by assuming Iḥrām), then he should not have sexual relations (with his wife), nor commit sin, nor dispute unjustly during the Ḥajj...* [TMQ: 2: 195]

[2] About the items 4, 5, and 6, it has been narrated by Al-Bukhārī that Ibn Umar, may Allah be pleased with him, said, "A man asked the Prophet, 'What (kinds of clothes) should a *muḥrim* wear? He replied, 'He must not wear a shirt, a turban, trousers, a head cloak, or garment scented with saffron or wars (kinds of perfumes). And if he has no slippers, then he can use *khuffs* but the socks should be cut short so as to make the ankles bare."

1. **Taking a bath and changing the *Izār* (wrapper) or the *rida'* (garment)** required in *Iḥrām*.

2. **It is permissible for a *muḥrim* to shade himself** with things such as umbrellas, tents, and the like.

3. **A *muḥrim* is allowed to tighten a belt around his waist** to keep his money and precious possessions therein.

4. **A *muḥrim* can cover his face** in protection of dust, wind, and sand. This view has been attributed to Uthman Ibn Affan, may Allah be pleased with him, and Abū Ḥanīfah and Mālik assert that a *muḥrim* is not to cover his face.

5. **It is permissible for the *muḥrim* to pluck out a tooth**, apply cupping, and squeeze a pimple.

6. **A *muḥrim* is allowed to scratch his head and body**, but he should do that gently so that he may not remove any hair while doing so.

7. **A *muḥrim* can kill things that may harm him** such as snakes, scorpions, and rabid dogs.

8. **A *muḥrim* can punish his boy** and beat his servant.

9. **A *muḥrim* can carry and smell flowers**, because this is not part of the forbidden perfuming.

10. **A *muḥrim* woman who is in a state of menstruation or postnatal bleeding** can perform all the actions of *Ḥajj* and *'Umrah*, but she is not allowed to circumambulate the *Ka'bah* until the bleeding comes to an end.

11. **A *muḥrim* can receive medical treatment** with things that do not contain perfume, and no ransom (*fidyah*) is required for this. And, Allah knows best.

Q. No. (240): What should the Muslim do before assume *Iḥrām*?

A: If a Muslim intends to assume *Iḥrām* for *Ḥajj* or *'Umrah*, he should consider the following pieces of advice:

- He should accommodate himself with things that will help him cut his nails, trim his moustache, and remove the hair under his armpits and that which is in the pubic area. He may not take such things if he has already done this.
- He should take a bath and remove any dirt that may be attached to his body, but he may not take that bath if he cannot do so.
- In the case of a man, he is to take off all the stitched clothes he may be wearing. This includes hat, turban, trousers, and suit or jilbab (gown or loose garment). And he is to wear instead: (1) *Izār* (wrapper), which is worn below one's waist, and the other (2) *rida'* (garment), which is worn round the upper part of the body. It is desirable that the *rida'* and the *Izār* be white and clean whether they are new or not, yet he can wear whatever shoes he likes.
- In the case of a woman, she should only take off any face cover she may be wearing, yet she can cover her face, when necessary, as when marriageable men are passing by for example. A woman should also take off any gloves she may be wearing. After that she can wear what Muslim women normally wear to cover themselves according to the instructions of the Sharī'ah. Still, there is no specific colour of clothes that a *muḥrim* woman is recommended to consider, but shy is not recommended to wear flashy colours.
- After that the Muslim can assume *Iḥrām*. And, Allah knows best.

Q. No. (241): What is the *Shar'ī* ruling concerning a person who applies perfume out of forgetfulness or ignorance while being in a state of *Iḥrām*?

A: A person who is in a state of *Iḥrām* is forbidden to apply perfume to his body or clothes, and this applies both to men and to women. If a person does this forgetfully or out of ignorance then comes to know later on that he was mistaken, Ash-Shāfiʿī maintains that he must remove that perfume immediately and no expiation is required. Abū Ḥanīfah, Mālik, and Aḥmad however maintain that a *fidyah* (ransom) is required because of that. And, Allah knows best.

Q. No. (242): What is the *Sharʿī* ruling concerning a person who dies while being in a state of *Iḥrām* as far as perfume is concerned?

A: If a *muḥrim* dies, no perfume is to be applied to his water of *Ġhusl* (bathing) or to his shroud because he will be resurrected on the Day of Resurrection while reciting *talbiyah.*

It has been narrated by Al-Bukhārī that Ibn ʿAbbās, may Allah be pleased with him, said,

"While a man was riding (his mount) at Arafat, he fell down it and broke his neck (and died). The Prophet said, 'Wash him with water and sidr (extract of the leaves of lote-tree) and shroud him in two pieces of cloth, and neither perfume him nor cover his head, for he will be resurrected on the Day of Resurrection reciting *talbiyah* (i.e., like a pilgrim)."

And, Allah knows best.

Q. No. (243): What is the *Sharʿī* ruling concerning a person who commits any of the forbiddances of *Iḥrām*?

A: He is to do a penalty slaughtering as long as the forbiddance committed is not intercourse because the latter invalidates *Ḥajj*: if intercourse is done before the stay at *ʿArafah*, his *Ḥajj* will be invalidated because of that and he should slaughter a sheep; and if it is after the stay at *ʿArafah*, his *Ḥajj* will not be invalidated and he will have to offer a *badanah* (a camel, an ox, or a cow). Important still, once the *Ḥajj* is invalidated, he is to repeat it the next year. And, Allah knows best.

Q. No. (244): Does the situation differ if a woman menstruates before assuming *Iḥrām*?

A: If a woman menstruates before assuming *Iḥrām*, she should take a bath and clean herself then she can assume *Iḥrām* just like the other women who are not in a state of menstruation. And, Allah knows best.

Q. No. (245): What should a person who is traveling by air do concerning *Iḥrām* if he passes by a *Mīqāt*?

A: In this case he should assume *Iḥrām* while being in the plane and it is permissible for him to delay assuming *Iḥrām* until the plane lands in Jeddah airport because Jeddah is not a *Mīqāt* except for its citizens and whoever determines the intention of performing *Ḥajj* or *'Umrah* in it from among others. who are not from its citizens. And, Allah knows best.

Q. No. (246): What should a person who is traveling by air as in the previous question - do if he does not have the clothes of *Iḥrām*?

A: In this case he can keep his trousers yet take off his garment and wrap it around his shoulders and chest then assume *Iḥrām*. After that when he lands, he should wear the clothes of *Iḥrām* once he procures them and take off the trousers.

In the case of a woman, she has only to remove any face cover and gloves she may be wearing. And, Allah knows best.

Q. No. (247): What are the things that may perplex a *muḥrim* though they are permissible?

A: These things include the following:

- Taking a bath and changing the *Izār* or the *rida'*.

- Covering the face on the part of man when a strong dusty wind is blowing for example and covering it on the part of woman in the presence of marriageable men.
- Wearing *khuffs* by women. Tightening a belt around the waist for keeping one's money.
- Wearing a ring or a watch.
- Applying kohl.
- Shading oneself under an umbrella, a tent, a roof, or anything of the kind.
- Killing the harmful animals and birds such as the rabid dog and the kite as well as all that which is harmful. And, Allah knows best.

Q. No. (248): What is stipulated for whoever wants to perform *Ḥajj* on behalf of someone else?

A: Whoever wants to perform *Ḥajj* on behalf of someone else must have performed *Ḥajj* on behalf of himself. In other words, in order to perform *Ḥajj* for someone else the Muslim must perform the prescribed *Ḥajj* for himself first if he is legally capable to perform it. And, Allah knows best.

Q. No. (249): What should the pilgrim do when he reaches the Sacred Mosque?

A: When entering the Sacred Mosque, the pilgrim should start with his right foot and say,

"In the Name of Allah and blessings be upon the Messenger of Allah. I seek refuge with Allah the Greatest, with His Face the most honourable, and with His ancient dominion (before which there was no dominion), against Satan the expelled (from Allah's Mercy). O Allah! Open for me the gates of Your Mercy!"

This invocation is to be said when entering any mosque and not only the Sacred Mosque.

When he sees the *Ka'bah*, the pilgrim is recommended to raise his hands and say,

"O Allah! You are (the source of) peace and (so) peace is provided by You, so salute us, O our Lord, with peace!"

He can also say,

"O Allah! Increase the honour, greatness, tribute, dignity, and righteousness connected to this House, and increase the honour, greatness, and righteousness of whoever adds to its honour and tribute from among those who make pilgrimage to it (in the form of *Ḥajj*) or *'Umrah*!"

And, Allah knows best.

Q. No. (250): What is the *Shar'ī* ruling concerning the *Ḥajj* performed by a slave or a boy?

A: *Ḥajj* is obligatory upon whoever meets certain conditions. Among these conditions, is that he must be free and mature. This means that *Ḥajj* is not obligatory upon slaves or boys because a slave is always busy fulfilling the right of his master to his service and a boy is not legally responsible (*mukallaf*) because of his being under the age of puberty.

However, if a boy or a slave performs *Ḥajj*, his *Ḥajj* will be valid yet it will not suffice for the *Ḥajj* of Islam which is prescribed upon them when the slave becomes free and the boy mature. It has been narrated by At-Tabarani that the Prophet (PBUH) said,

"(Even) if a slave performs *Ḥajj* ten times, then is set free, he is legally asked) to perform the *Ḥajj* (prescribed by) Islam (upon whoever is able to perform it); and (even) if a boy performs *Ḥajj* ten times, then becomes mature, he is (legally asked) to perform the *Ḥajj* (prescribed by) Islam."

It is quite encouraging for those who like to let their boys perform *Ḥajj* to know that it has been narrated on the authority of Ibn ʿAbbās, may Allah be pleased with him, that a woman. displayed a boy to the Prophet (PBUH) and asked, "Can this (boy) perform *Ḥajj*?" He (PBUH) said, "Yes, and you will receive a reward (for that)."[1]

And, Allah knows best.

Q. No. (251): When is capability or *Istiṭāʿah* established as far as *Ḥajj* is concerned?

A: Capability or *Istiṭāʿah* is established once the Muslim is physically and financially ready to go on such a journey of *Ḥajj* that is supposed to be hard and costly in most cases. This also includes the safety of the journey. Accordingly, an ill person is not legally asked to perform *Ḥajj* until his illness is cured, nor is a poor person asked to perform it until he is financially able to do so. It has been narrated on the authority of Ibn ʿUmar, may Allah be pleased with him, that a man came to the Prophet (PBUH) and said, "O Messenger of Allah! What does obligate *Ḥajj*?" He (PBUH) replied, "(To have) provision and a means of transportation."[2]

It should be known that "provision" here is not to be secured for the person who wants to perform *Ḥajj* only, for he must secure provision - including the expenses of the journey for the whole travel, i.e., from his homeland to Mecca and from the latter to the former as well as for his family whom he must support during his travel.

Another condition is required on the part of woman: she must have a mahram (her husband or any of her unmarriageable male relatives) to accompany her. If she cannot find a mahram, she is not legally asked to perform *Ḥajj* until she finds one. The Prophet (PBUH) said,

---

[1] Narrated by Muslim and At-Tirmidhī.
[2] Narrated by At-Tirmidhī.

"It is not lawful for a woman who believes in Allah and the Last Day to go on a one-day-march journey except with a mahram."[1]

In another narration of Muslim, on the authority of Ibn ʿAbbās, the latter said that he heard the Messenger of Allah (PBUH) delivering a sermon and saying,

"No man is to be alone (in private) with a woman except with a mahram, and no woman is to travel except with a mahram."

A man stood up and said, "O Messenger of Allah! My woman (wife) has set out to perform *Ḥajj* and I have been assigned to take part in such and such an invasion." The Prophet (PBUH) said to him, "Go and perform *Ḥajj* with your woman (wife)." According to the apparent wording of this text, the Prophet (PBUH) did not specify the travel with a certain time or distance as in the first narration. And, Allah knows best.

Q. No. (252): It has been narrated that in the Farewell Pilgrimage- the Prophet (PBUH) commanded his Companions to cancel their *Ḥajj* and make it a *ʿUmrah*. Why was that?

A: This has been narrated by Muslim on the authority of Jābir Ibn Abdullah, may Allah be pleased with him. What matters here is that the Prophet (PBUH) did not order his Companions to do so to show that *Tamattuʿ* was better as some people think. Rather, he ordered them to do so to show the falsehood of a belief that was widespread during the pre- Islamic period; namely, that performing *ʿUmrah* during the months of *Ḥajj* was one of the most abominable acts. The Prophet (PBUH) wanted to show that such a belief was false and ridiculous, so he commanded that whoever among them had *hady* with him should put off his *Iḥrām* for *Ḥajj* and make it a *ʿUmrah* and he (PBUH) told them that were it not that he had already had *hady*

[1] Narrated by Al-Bukhārī and Muslim.

he would have done as he had ordered them to do, i.e., he would have put off his *Iḥrām* for *Ḥajj* and make it a *'Umrah* He (PBUH) said,

"If I had known beforehand what I have come to know afterwards, I would not have brought sacrificial animals and would have performed a *'Umrah* So, he who among you does not have the (required) sacrificial animals with him should put off his *Iḥrām* and make this a *'Umrah*."[1]

Another narration of Al-Bukhārī on the authority of Ibn 'Abbās records the wrong belief referred to above as adopted during the pre-Islamic period and how the Prophet (PBUH) commanded his Companions who did not have *hady* to cancel their *Ḥajj* and make it a *'Umrah* to show the fallacy of that pre-Islamic conviction. And, Allah knows best.

Q. No. (253): Was the Companions cancelling of *Ḥajj* specially pertained to them?

A: Some Faqīhs view that this cancelling of *Ḥajj* was specially pertained to the Companions, may Allah be pleased with them, as the Prophet (PBUH) ordered them to do so in order to uproot the wrong idea - referred to in the answer to the previous question from the heads of people so that they would perform *'Umrah* during the months of *Ḥajj* then enjoy whatever the non-*muḥrim* could enjoy including intercourse with women and perfuming. Those Faqīhs add that this ruling was not to be applied anymore after the rulings of the Sharī'ah had been settled and clarified. They moreover prove this view with the narration of Ibn Mājah that Abū Dharr, may Allah be pleased with him, stated that this cancelling of *Ḥajj* was in this particular case meant only for the Prophet's Companions. And in another narration of Ibn Mājah this time on the authority of, the latter said that he asked the Prophet (PBUH), "O Messenger of Allah! Is the cancelling of *Ḥajj* in *'Umrah* (i.e., making that *Ḥajj* a *'Umrah*)

[1] Narrated by Muslim

special for us or for people in general?" He (PBUH) replied, "*Rather, it is special for us?*"[1] And, Allah knows best.

Q. No. (254): Which is better: *Tamattu', Qirān, or Ifrād?*[2]

A: The Companions performed *Ḥajj* in different forms: some performed it as *Tamattu'*, some as *Ifrād*, and some as *Qirān*.

That is why Faqīhs have differed as to which of these three forms of *Ḥajj* is better.

Mālik and Ash-Shāfi'ī are of the opinion that *Ifrād* is better because with this form the pilgrim performs "all" the ceremonies of *Ḥajj* and *'Umrah* when performing them each alone. They prove their opinion with what Muslim has narrated on the authority of 'Ā'ishah, who said,

"We went out with the Prophet (PBUH) in the year of the Farewell Pilgrimage. Some of us assumed *Iḥrām* for *'Umrah*, some assumed it for *Ḥajj* and *'Umrah*, and some assumed it for *Ḥajj* (alone); and the Prophet (PBUH) assumed *Iḥrām* for *Ḥajj*. Those who assumed *Iḥrām* for *Ḥajj*, or (those who did so) to connect *Ḥajj* and *'Umrah*, did not disengage themselves (from their *Iḥrām*) until the Day of Sacrifice (the tenth day of Dhū al-Ḥijjah)."

This Ḥadīth states that the Messenger of Allah (PBUH) assumed *Iḥrām* for *Ḥajj* and not for *Ḥajj* and *'Umrah* or for *'Umrah* alone and this indicates that *Ifrād* is better.

Aḥmad however maintains that *Tamattu'* is better because the Prophet (PBUH) commanded his Companions, may Allah be pleased with them, to do it, and he would not command them to do except what was better for them. Aḥmad has proved his view with more than one item of proof, including the fact that the Prophet (PBUH) commanded his Companions to apply *Tamattu'* and expressed his

---

[1] See Sunan Ibn Mājah, 2/172.

[2] See the glossary of the book for the definition of each of the three terms.

sorrow for not being able to do like them because he had already had *hady* with him. This indicates the excellence of *Tamattu*ʿ. Aḥmad also says that unlike the other *Manāsik*, *Tamattu*ʿʾ is recorded in the Qurʾān; Allah says,

﴿وَأَتِمُّوا۟ ٱلْحَجَّ وَٱلْعُمْرَةَ لِلَّهِ ۚ فَإِنْ أُحْصِرْتُمْ فَمَا ٱسْتَيْسَرَ مِنَ ٱلْهَدْىِ ۖ ﴿١٩٦﴾﴾

"Whosoever performs the ʿUmrah in the months of Ḥajj, before (performing) the Ḥajj, he must slaughter a Hady such as he can afford."

[TMQ: 2: 196]

Still, Abū Ḥanīfah asserts that *Qirān* is better because it is hard and the harder an act of worship is the better its reward becomes. Also, it is better because the Prophet (PBUH) applied it. To prove that the Prophet (PBUH) applied *Qirān*, Abū Ḥanīfah has quoted more than one Ḥadīth, including what Muslim has narrated on the authority of Anas who said that he heard the Prophet (PBUH) saying, *"Labbayka bi Ḥajj wa ʿUmrah* (Here I am at Your service, (intending to perform) *Ḥajj* and *ʿUmrah*)."

Ibn Ḥajar has stated that it can be derived from the available narrations in this regard that the Prophet (PBUH) applied *Qirān* - meaning that he attached *ʿUmrah* to *Ḥajj* - after assuming *Iḥrām* for *Ḥajj* alone.[1]

It can also be added that the Prophet (PBUH) wished he could apply *Tamattu*ʿ, as he had ordered his Companions to do, to appease their hearts as they were sad because of not being. able to do as he (PBUH) was doing. And, Allah knows best.

Q. No. (255): What is the time of *talbiyah*?

A: The pilgrim starts reciting *talbiyah* at the time when he assumes *Iḥrām* and continues reciting it (on the occasions on which it is recited) until the time of the throwing of pebbles at Al-`Aqabah on

---

[1] *Fatḥ al-Bārī*, 3/427.

the Day of Sacrifice and he should stop reciting it after throwing the first pebble. As for *'Umrah*, the Muslim is to recite *talbiyah* until he touches the Black Stone. And, Allah knows best.

Q. No. (256): What does the *Sunnah* ordain concerning the wording of *talbiyah*?

A: It is an act of the *Sunnah* that the Muslim recites *talbiyah* according to what has been authentically attributed to the Prophet (PBUH) in this regard. He (PBUH) used to say in his *talbiyah*,

"*Labbayka-bi-Ḥajjwa-'Umrah-Labayk-allāhumma-labbayk. Labbayka lā sharīka laka labbayk. Inna-l-ḥamda wa-n-ni'mata laka-wa-l-mulk,lā-sharīka-lak.* (Here I am at Your service, O Allah! Here I am at Your service! Here I am at Your service, you have no partner, Here I am at Your service! Verily, praise is due to You and blessings and sovereignty belong to You, (and) You have no partner!)" And, Allah knows best.

Q. No. (257): What are the conditions of staying at *'Arafah*?

A: There are two conditions that must be met for the duty of staying at *'Arafah* to be valid and properly performed:

1. That the staying be at the land representing *'Arafah* during the time specified for that as maintained by the majority of scholars, i.e., from the time after the noon of the ninth day in Dhū al-Ḥijjah until the rise of the dawn of the tenth day in the same month.

2. That the person who stays at *'Arafah* be legally qualified for worship. And, Allah knows best.

Q. No. (258): What are the proprieties of staying at *'Arafah*?

A: These proprieties can be listed as follows:

1. To take a bath at Namirah with the intention of taking that bath for the sake of staying at *'Arafah*.

2. Not to enter the land of *ʿArafah* except after combining the *Zuhr* and the *ʿAṣr* prayers.

3. To attend the two sermons delivered on this occasion and combine the *Zuhr* and the *ʿAṣr* prayers.

4. To hasten to stay at *ʿArafah* immediately after performing the two prayers.

5. Not to observe fasting on this day of staying because this is better for the pilgrim as it helps him to invoke Allah eagerly.

6. To be in a state of *Ṭahārah* or purification. Purification is "required" in *Ḥajj* and *ʿUmrah* only for *Ṭawāf* and the two *Rakʿahs* related to it.

7. To stay at *ʿArafah* while facing the direction of the *qiblah*.

8. To stay at it with a heart void of any worldly affair that may distract the pilgrim from invocation.

9. To be keen on staying at the spot where the Prophet (PBUH) stayed, that is, at the rocks located at the lower part of the mount of *Ar- Raḥmah*.

10. To be keen on invoking Allah, showing submission to Him, and asking Him for forgiveness throughout the stay at *ʿArafah*, and to recite *talbiyah* and verses from the Qur'ān. And, Allah knows best.

Q. No. (259): Is it stipulated that a pilgrim should be in a state of *Ṭahārah* (purification) for the ritual stay at 'Arafah?

A: It is not stipulated that a pilgrim be in a state of purification for performing the ritual stay at *ʿArafah* in *Ḥajj*, nor is it stipulated that he should face the *qiblah* while doing that. It has been narrated that the Prophet (PBUH) said to ʿĀ'ishah, may Allah be pleased with her, when she was menstruating,

"Do whatever the pilgrim does except that you should not circumambulate the House (i.e., the *Kaʿbah*) until you have washed yourself (i.e., performed *Ġhusl* at the end of the menstruation)."[1]

And, Allah knows best.

Q. No. (260): Is it obligatory to spend the night at Muzdalifah until dawn?

A: Faqīhs have differed concerning the time for which the pilgrim should stay at Muzdalifah. Abū Ḥanīfah says that it is obligatory to spend the night at Muzdalifah until the dawn of the Day of Sacrifice. Therefore, if he leaves Muzdalifah before dawn, he is to do a penalty slaughtering. Abū Ḥanīfah's proof in this regard is that the Prophet (PBUH) stayed at Muzdalifah until the rise of the dawn of the Sacrifice Day, and he (PBUH) performed the *Fajr* Prayer there then headed for *Mīnā* before sunrise. Thus, it is a must that the pilgrim does as the Prophet (PBUH) did.

Ash-Shāfiʿī and Aḥmad assert that it is sufficient that a pilgrim spends the night at Muzdalifah until after midnight, and there is nothing required if he leaves after that for *Mīnā*.

The third opinion in this connection is that it is sufficient that the pilgrim spends part of the night at Muzdalifah in as much as he dismounts there, takes some rest, and performs prayer. Therefore, if he just passes by it and does not dismount, he is to do a penalty slaughtering. The proof of this view is that the Prophet (PBUH) permitted some weak men, women, and children to leave Muzdalifah during the night and this indicates that the period those people had spent at Muzdalifah was sufficient for spending the night until dawn. It has been narrated by Al-Bukhārī that Ibn ʿAbbās, may Allah be pleased with him, said,

---

[1] Narrated by Muslim.

"I was one of the weak people from among the Prophet's family whom he let proceed (to *Mīnā*) at the night of Muzdalifah."

And, Allah knows best.

Q. No. (261): What is the *Shar'ī* ruling about combining two prayers at Arafat and Muzdalifah?

A: The pilgrim combines the *Zuhr* Prayer and the *'Aṣr* Prayer at *'Arafah* as *Jam' Taqdīm* (advancement combination) by performing the *Zuhr* Prayer as two *Rak'ahs* then the *'Aṣr* Prayer also as two *Rak'ahs* with one *adan* and two pronouncements of *Iqāmah*. This combination is done for the sake of *Ḥajj* and the Prophet (PBUH) applied it. That it is better for the pilgrim as with this combination he has more time in which he can invoke Allah and recite different items of dhikr in this blessed and special situation at *'Arafah*.

Also, the pilgrim combines the *Maghrib* Prayer and the *'Ishā'* Prayer as *Jam' Ta'khīr* (delay combination) at Muzdalifah. Thus, he does not perform the *Maghrib* Prayer at *'Arafah* but delays it until he performs it with the *'Ishā'* Prayer at Muzdalifah with one pronouncement of *Iqāmah* for each, but there is no harm if he performs both prayers with one pronouncement of *Iqāmah* as it has been mentioned in some narrations that the Prophet (PBUH) did that. It has been narrated by Muslim that Ibn 'Umar, may Allah be pleased with him, said,

"The Messenger of Allah (PBUH) combined the Maghrib Prayer and the *'Ishā'* Prayer at Jam (i.e., Muzdalifah) without prostration between the two (i.e., he did not offer any supererogatory prayer between them). He performed the Maghrib Prayer as three *Rak'ahs* and the *'Ishā'* as two, with one *Iqāmah*."

And Al-Bukhārī has narrated that Ibn 'Umar, may Allah be pleased with him, said,

"The Prophet (PBUH) combined the Maghrib Prayer and the *'Ishā'* Prayer at Jam, each with one *Iqāmah*, and he did not glorify Allah between the two (i.e., he did not offer any supererogatory prayer between them)."

This means that combining the two prayers with two pronouncements of *Iqāmah* is better. And, Allah knows best.

Q. No. (262): What is the *Shar'ī* ruling concerning a pilgrim who performs the *Maghrib* Prayer at *'Arafah* during its due time?

A: According to the *Sunnah*, the *Maghrib* Prayer is to be combined with the *'Ishā'* Prayer at Muzdalifah after finishing the stay at *'Arafah*. Yet, if a pilgrim performs the *Maghrib* Prayer at *'Arafah* during its due time, his prayer is valid, but he will have done something against the *Sunnah*, as maintained by Mālik, Ash-Shāfi'ī, and Aḥmad.

Abū Ḥanīfah and Ath-Thawri however affirm that that will not be sufficient for him, and he is to repeat the prayer because the Prophet (PBUH) combined the two prayers the *Maghrib* and the *'Ishā'* so it became one of the rituals of *Ḥajj*, and he (PBUH) ordered Muslims to learn the *Manāsik* of *Ḥajj* and *'Umrah* from him. Moreover, it has been narrated by Al-Bukhārī and Muslim that Usamah Ibn Zayd, may Allah be pleased with him, said,

"The Prophet (PBUH) descended from *'Arafah* and when he reached the mountain pass (before Muzdalifah) he dismounted and urinated then performed a light ablution. I said, 'O Messenger of Allah! Prayer!' He said, Prayer is ahead of you.' Then he mounted (his she-camel) and when he reached Muzdalifah *Iqāmah* was pronounced, and he (PBUH) performed the *Maghrib* Prayer (leading the people in it). Then *Iqāmah* was pronounced (again) and he (PBUH) performed the *'Ishā'* Prayer (leading the people in it as well) and did not perform any (voluntary) prayer between the two prayers..."[1]

to the end of the Ḥadīth. The words "Prayer is ahead of you indicate that this prayer (the *Maghrib*) is to be performed at Muzdalifah. And, Allah knows best.

Q. No. (263): Why is it recommended that the pilgrim who performs the *Fajr* Prayer at Muzdalifah should perform it at the beginning of its stated time?

A: If a pilgrim performs the *Fajr* Prayer at Muzdalifah, it is recommended that he performs it at the beginning of its due time so that he can have more time in which he can invoke and glorify Allah at *Al-Mash'ar al-Ḥarām*, because Almighty Allah says,

So, when you disperse from those whom you know, remember God at the Sacred Land and remember Him as He has guided you, even if you were before him among those who went astray.

﴿ فَإِذَآ أَفَضۡتُم مِّنۡ عَرَفَٰتٖ فَٱذۡكُرُواْ ٱللَّهَ عِندَ ٱلۡمَشۡعَرِ ٱلۡحَرَامِۖ وَٱذۡكُرُوهُ كَمَا هَدَىٰكُمۡ وَإِن كُنتُم مِّن قَبۡلِهِۦ لَمِنَ ٱلضَّآلِّينَ ١٩٨ ﴾

"Then when you leave Arafat, remember Allah (by glorifying His Praises, i.e., prayers and invocations, etc.) at the Mash'ar al-Ḥarām. And remember Him (by invoking Him for all good, etc.) as He has guided you, and verily, you were, before, of those who were astray." [TMQ: 2: 198]

Besides, it has been narrated by Muslim on the authority of Jābir, may Allah be pleased with him, that

"When the Prophet (PBUH) came to *Mash'ar al-Ḥarām* (i.e., the mountain located at Muzdalifah), he faced the direction of *qiblah*, invoked Him (Allah), glorified Him (with *Takbīr*), and pronounced His Oneness (with "*Lā ilāha illā-llāh* (There is no god but Allah)"). He

[1] Narrated by Al-Bukhārī and Muslim.

(PBUH) continued standing until daylight was very pronounced (in the sky)."

And, Allah knows best.

Q. No. (264): Is it permissible for women and the weak people to start throwing pebbles from the time after midnight on the eve of the Sacrifice Day?

A: It is permissible for women and the weak people to do so because it has been narrated by Al-Bukhārī that Asma' Bint Abū Bakr, may Allah be pleased with her, stated that the Prophet (PBUH) allowed women and the disabled to do that. And, Allah knows best.

Q. No. (265): Is it recommended that the pilgrim says certain words when throwing pebbles?

A: The pilgrim continues reciting *talbiyah* until he throws *Jamrat al-ʿAqabah* on the Day of Sacrifice, as he then stops reciting *talbiyah* and switches to *Takbīr*. It has been narrated by Al-Bukhārī on the authority of Ibn 'Abbas, may Allah be pleased with him, that Usamah rode behind the Prophet. (PBUH) (on the prophet's she-camel) from *ʿArafah* to Muzdalifah then he (PBUH) let Abul-Fadl ride behind him from Muzdalifah to *Mīnā*, and both of them said that the Prophet (PBUH) continued reciting *talbiyah* until he threw the *Jamrah* (*Jamrat al-ʿAqabah*).

According to the *Sunnah*, the pilgrim is to recite *Takbīr* while throwing each pebble. It has been narrated on the authority of Ibn ʿAbbās, may Allah be pleased with him, that Abul-Fadl said,

"I left Arafat with the Messenger of Allah (PBUH), and he continued reciting *talbiyah* until he threw *Jamrat al-ʿAqabah* (where-upon he would be) reciting *Takbīr* with every pebble..."[1]

---

[1] Narrated by Ibn Khuzaymah.

It has also been narrated that Abdullah Ibn Mas'ud and Ibn ʿUmar, may Allah be pleased with both of them, used to say on throwing *Jamrat al-ʿAqabah*, "O Allah! Make it a *Ḥajj Mabrūr* (i.e., *Ḥajj* which is done according to the *Sunnah* and is accepted by Allah) and praiseworthy endeavour!"

Moreover, `Ata' says, "When you are to throw (pebbles), recite *Takbīr* making (each) *Takbīrah* follow (each act of) throwing." And, Allah knows best.

Q. No. (266): Why is it that woman is forbidden from having the hair of her head shaved?

A: It is not permissible for a woman to have the hair of her head shaved though it is permissible for men (rather obligatory upon them) to have their hair shaved or cut short- for *Ḥajj* or *ʿUmrah* simply because a woman's hair is an integral part of her beauty and if this hair is shaved that will be a sort of "disfigurement," which may cause her husband to dislike her or even divorce her. And, Islam does not mean to harm women or enjoin things that may cause such disfigurement or marital disunion.

It has been narrated by At-Tirmidhī that ʿAlī, may Allah be pleased with him said,

"The Messenger of Allah (PBUH) has forbidden that a woman should have (the hair of) her head shaved."

It has also been narrated by Abū Dāwūd on the authority of Ibn ʿAbbās, may Allah be pleased with him, that the Prophet. (PBUH) said,

"Women are not (legally asked) to shave (the hair of their heads), and it is only that they are (asked) to shorten (that hair)."

The amount that is to be shortened from a woman's hair is what equals a fingertip, i.e., two centi-meters, as judged by Ibn ʿUmar, may Allah be pleased with him. And, Allah knows best.

Q. No. (267): What are the forms of *Ṭawāf*?

A: There are four types or forms of *Ṭawāf*:

1. ***Ṭawāful- Qudūm* (arrival circumambulation)**

The first thing that a pilgrim does when he enters the Sacred Mosque is to circumambulate the *Ka'bah*. This circumambulation is called *Ṭawāful-Qudūm* or arrival circumambulation, because it is the first thing that a pilgrim performs from among the *Manāsik* or the prescribed duties of *Ḥajj*.

2. ***Ṭawāful-Ifāḍah* (leaving circumambulation)**

Ṭawāful- Ifāḍah or leaving circumambulation is one of the pillars of *Ḥajj* and without it the latter is not valid. It is to be performed during the time starting from the midnight of the eve of the Sacrifice Day after "leaving" *'Arafah* and staying at Muzdalifah.

The time of this *Ṭawāf* ends with the third day of the days of Sacrifice Feast ('Idul- Aḍḥā) according to Abū Ḥanīfah, and thus if it is delayed a penalty slaughtering is required because the duties of *Ḥajj* end with the third day of the days of Sacrifice Feast. According to Mālik, the time of *Ṭawāful-Ifāḍah* ends with the end of the month of Dhū al-Ḥijjah. Aḥmad, however, maintains that the time of this *Ṭawāf* is limitless, so it will be valid if a pilgrim performs it at any time until the end of the year.

3. ***Ṭawāful- Wadā'* (farewell circumambulation)**

Ṭawāful-Wadā' or farewell circumambulation is performed before leaving Mecca and it is obligatory according to the majority of Faqīhs, and thus a penalty slaughtering is required if it is neglected. This is because the Prophet (PBUH) enjoined it both through words and through personal application.

It is worth mentioning here that a menstruating woman is exempt from this farewell circumambulation.

4.*Ṭawāfut-Tatawwu* (voluntary circumambulation)

This is the *Ṭawāf* that is performed voluntarily and not as an obligation.

And, Allah knows best.

Q. No. (268): What are the conditions of *Ṭawāf*?

A: For the validity of *Ṭawāf* certain conditions must be met, as follows.

1. A person who is to perform *Ṭawāf* must be in a state of purification.

2. He must cover his awrah (private parts).

3. *Ṭawāf* must be performed in seven complete rounds.

4. He must commence the *Ṭawāf* from position of the Black Stone and end it also at its location.

5. The *Ka'bah* must be on the left side of the person who performs *Ṭawāf*.

6. *Ṭawāf* is to be performed outside the *Ka'bah*.

7. A person who performs *Ṭawāf* should do the seven rounds of *Ṭawāf* consecutively. This seventh condition must be met for *Ṭawāf* to be valid according to Mālik and Aḥmad yet there is no legal liability if the rounds are not done exactly consecutively - i.e., if they are separated by waiting for a short time due to tiredness or some other excuse such as illness. The Ḥanafīs and the Shafi is however say that performing the seven rounds consecutively is an act of the *Sunnah*. And, Allah knows best.

Q. No. (269): What are the acts of the *Sunnah* related to *Ṭawāf*?

A: There are certain acts of the *Sunnah* pertaining to *Ṭawāf*.

They may be outlined as follows.

1. Kissing the Black Stone.

2. *Idtiba* or uncovering the right hand is an act of the *Sunnah*, and the pilgrim is to do that while performing the *Ṭawāf* related to *ʿUmrah* and every *Ṭawāf* after which there is *Saʿy* or going between As-Ṣafā and Al-Marwah) in *Ḥajj*.

3. Ramal or moving quickly in the first three rounds of *Ṭawāf*.

4. Touching the Yemenite Corner while saying *Takbīr*.

5. Invoking Allah beside the two corners - the Yemenite Corner and the Black Stone with what has been attributed to the Prophet (PBUH) in this connection. It has been narrated by Ibn Mājah on the authority of Abū Hurayrah, may Allah be pleased with him, that the Prophet (PBUH) said,

"Seventy angels have been charged with it (the Yemenite Corner). So, whoever says, 'O Allah! I ask You for forgiveness and wellbeing in worldly life and the Hereafter. Our Lord! Give us in this world that which is good and in the Hereafter that which is good, and save us from the torment of the Fire!' the angels say, 'Amin (Amen!)"

6. Concerning the two *Rakʿahs* related to *Ṭawāf*, it is an act of the *Sunnah* that the Muslim recites the chapter of *Al-Kāfirūn* in the first *Rakʿah* and the chapter of *Al-Ikhlas* in the second *Rakʿah*. And, Allah knows best.

Q. No. (270): Why is it that certain women can be exempted from *Ṭawāful-Wadāʿ* or farewell circumambulation?

A: To make things easy for Muslim women, the Shariah has excluded a woman who is menstruating or has postnatal bleeding from performing *Ṭawāful-Wadāʿ* or farewell circumambulation so that her family and companions may not be harmed because of the delay if she waits until her bleeding stops and then performs that *Ṭawāf*. The relationship between women and men is also taken into consideration as the latter may dislike women or dislike to accompany them.

There are certain items of proof which indicate that such. women are excluded from farewell circumambulation. For example, it has been narrated by Al-Bukhārī that ʻĀʼishah, may Allah be pleased with her, said that Safiyyah Bint Huyayy (the Prophet's wife), may Allah be pleased with her, got her period (after performing *Ṭawāful-Ifāḍah* leaving circumambulation]). ʻĀʼishah added that she told the Prophet (PBUH) that Safiyyah had got her period, and he (PBUH) said, "Will she detain us?" But ʻĀʼishah said that she then told him (PBUH) that Safiyyah performed *Ṭawāful-Ifāḍah* then her menstruation started. Thereupon he (PBUH) allowed her to depart. In another narration of Al-Bukhārī the Prophet (PBUH) asked Safiyyah, "Did you not perform *Ṭawāf* of the *Kaʻbah* on the Day of Sacrifice (i.e., *Ṭawāful-Ifāḍah*)?" Safiyyah replied in the affirmative, so he (PBUH) said to her, "There is no harm for you to proceed on with us."

These texts and others indicate that *Ṭawāful-Wadāʻ* is cancelled on the part of any woman who is in a state of menstruation or postnatal bleeding. Thus, she can leave Mecca without paying farewell to the *Kaʻbah* through this *Ṭawāf* if her family are in a hurry and want to leave soon. And, Allah knows best.

Q. No. (271): Is it obligatory that the Meccan pilgrims perform farewell circumambulation?

A: No farewell circumambulation is required on the part of the people of Mecca simply because paying farewell is done by those who are to "leave" the place for their homelands while the people of Mecca will stay in it, so they do not need to pay farewell. In addition to this, there is no say after farewell. circumambulation nor is there *Iḥrām* before it, so the pilgrim can pay farewell to the House while wearing his normal clothes - and not those of *Iḥrām* - then leave for his homeland. And, Allah knows best.

Q. No. (272): How many times is *Ṭawāf* to be performed by a person who applies *Qirān*?

A: A person who applies *Qirān* performs *Ṭawāf* only one time and performs say between As-Ṣafā and Al-Marwah only one time as well, according to the majority of scholars. This is because At-Tirmidhī has narrated on the authority of Jābir Ibn `Abdullah, may Allah be pleased with him, that the Messenger of Allah (PBUH) performed *Ḥajj* and *'Umrah* together and performed *Ṭawāf* only one time for both of them.

Abū Ḥanīfah however maintains that a person who applies *Qirān* is to perform *Ṭawāf* twice one for *Ḥajj* and one for *'Umrah*, and that he should do the same with *Sa'y*. In this way, he says, each act of worship of the two will be performed perfectly. It has been narrated that Ibn Mas'ud, may Allah be pleased with him, said, "A person who applies *Qirān* is to perform *Ṭawāf* twice and say twice." Another narration of At-Ṭaḥāwī states that 'Alī, may Allah be pleased with him, gave the same judgment when he said to Abun-Nadr, "Pour a utensil of water upon yourself then assume *Iḥrām* for both of them (i.e., *Ḥajj* and *'Umrah*) and perform *Ṭawāf* once for each." And, Allah knows best.

Q. No. (273): What is ramal and what is *idtiba*?

A: Ramal is to move quickly during the first three circuits of *Ṭawāf* then walk at a normal pace during the other four circuits, while *idtiba* is that the pilgrim uncovers the right hand also while performing *Ṭawāf*.

Ramal and *idtiba* are not obligations as they are acts of the *Sunnah* which are desirable for the pilgrim to consider when performing *Ṭawāful-Qudūm* (arrival circumambulation), unlike *Ṭawāfut- tatawwu* (voluntary circumambulation) and *Ṭawāful-Wadā'* (farewell circumambulation). This is according to what the Prophet (PBUH) prescribed and did. And, Allah knows best.

Q. No. (274): What is *At-Taḥallul al-Awwal* (the first putting off) and what is *At-Taḥallul ath-Thānī* (the second putting off)?

A: When the pilgrim throws Jamrat al-ʿAqabah (the Big Jamrah), it becomes lawful for him to do any of the things which have been forbidden for him during his *Iḥrām* except for intercourse. Thus, once he throws this Jamrah he can have the hair of his head shaved or shortened and this is called *At-Taḥallul al-Awwal* or the first putting off of *Iḥrām* with which the pilgrim can wear normal clothes, apply perfume, cut his nails, trim his Mustache, wear a turban, etc., yet he is not allowed to approach women sexually. However, when he performs *Ṭawāful-Ifāḍah* (leaving circumambulation), everything becomes allowed including intercourse, and this is called *At-Taḥallul ath-Thānī* or the second putting off of *Iḥrām* or *at- Taḥallul al-akbar* or the major putting off of *Iḥrām*. And, Allah knows best.

Q. No. (275): What is the *Sharʿī* ruling concerning a pilgrim who has intercourse with his wife before *Ṭawāful-Ifāḍah* (leaving circumambulation)?

A: If a pilgrim has intercourse with his wife before *Ṭawāful- Ifāḍah*, he must slaughter a camel or a cow, and the slaughtering of a sheep will not be sufficient. More important, if he has intercourse with her before the stay at *ʿArafah*, his *Ḥajj* will be invalidated because of that. And, Allah knows best.

Q. No. (276): What is the *Sharʿī* ruling concerning a person who is in doubt concerning the number of circuits in *Ṭawāf*?

A: In this case he should base the counting of the number of circuits on the lesser number. In other words, if he is in doubt whether he has performed four or five circuits for example, he should count the circuits performed as being four and not five then complete the *Ṭawāf* until he finishes the required seven circuits. If, however he doubts the number of circuits after finishing the *Ṭawāf*, he is not legally asked to do anything. And, Allah knows best.

Q. No. (277): What is the *Shar'ī* ruling concerning the performance of two *Rak'ahs* after performing *Ṭawāf*?

A: According to Abū Ḥanīfah and Ash- Shāfi'ī, after performing *Ṭawāf* the Muslim must perform two *ra'kahs* behind the Maqam of Ibrāhīm or in any other place in the Sacred Mosque, because the Prophet (PBUH) used to perform two *Rak'ahs* after every *Ṭawāf* he performed. It has been narrated by Al-Bukhārī on the authority of Az-Zuhrī who said that the Prophet (PBUH) never performed seven circuits of *Ṭawāf* except that he performed two *Rak'ahs* (after that). It has also been narrated by Al-Bukhārī that Ibn 'Umar, may Allah be pleased with him, used to perform two *Rak'ahs* after every *Ṭawāf*.

On the other hand, Aḥmad and Mālik maintain that the performance of these two *Rak'ahs* after *Ṭawāf* is an act of the *Sunnah* just like any other voluntary act of worship.

It may be said that the first opinion that the performance of these two *Rak'ahs* is an obligation is more evident because the Prophet (PBUH) never neglected them. It can also be added that it is desirable that the Muslim recites the chapter of *Al-Kāfirūn* in the first *Rak'ah* and the chapter of *Al-Ikhlas* in the second because the Prophet (PBUH) did that. And, Allah knows best.

Q. No. (278): Is it permissible for a person to perform *Ṭawāf* as seven circuits followed by another seven and so on?

A: There is no harm if a person performs seven circuits of *Ṭawāf* then another seven circuits for a number of times, and after finishing that he can perform two *Rak'ahs* for each *Ṭawāf*. Thus, if he performs twenty-one circuits, for instance, he is to perform six *Rak'ahs*: two for each seven circuits.[1] And, Allah knows best.

Q. No. (279): What is the *Shar'ī* ruling concerning a person who performs *Ṭawāf* while riding a mount?

---

[1] See *Al-Mughnī*, 5/233.

A: If a person has some legal excuse that prevents him from performing *Ṭawāf* on foot, such as illness or weakness, it is permissible for him to perform *Ṭawāf* riding some mount or carried by someone. It has been narrated by Al-Bukhārī and Muslim on the authority of Umm Salamah, may Allah be pleased with her, that she complained to the Prophet (PBUH) that he had been afflicted by some illness and he said to her,

"Perform *Ṭawāf* behind the people (performing it) while you are riding (some mount)."

She said that she did as he said.

An-Nawawi has commented on this Ḥadīth saying,

"The Prophet (PBUH) ordered her to perform *Ṭawāf* behind the people for two reasons: (i) women are to keep away from men while performing *Ṭawāf*, and (ii) if she did that while being near to the people (by performing *Ṭawāf* amongst them for example), her mount might harm them."[1]

And, Allah knows best.

Q. No. (280): What is the *Shar'ī* ruling concerning the performance of *Ṭawāf* by a person who is afflicted by an infectious disease such as leprosy?

A: It has been narrated by Mālik in his *Muwattā'* that once 'Umar Ibn al-Khaṭṭāb, may Allah be pleased with him, passed by a leprous woman who was circumambulating the House. He said to her, "O female slave of Allah![2] Do not harm people! If you sat in your house, it would be better for you!" The woman stayed in her house. Later on, when Umar had died, a man passed by her and said, "The man who prevented you (from going out and performing *Ṭawāf*) has died,

---

[1] See his commentaries on the Ḥadīth No 1276 in Ṣaḥīḥ Muslim.

[2] By this he meant to start the talk with her in a gentle way so that she might not feel hurt because of what he would say after that.

so get out." She said, "By Allah, I would not obey him when he was alive and disobey him when he is dead!"

It is worth mentioning here that 'Umar, may Allah be pleased with him, said those words to the woman while considering the interest of Muslims and acting upon the Prophet's words,

"Flee away from a leper as you would flee away from a lion."

As, Umar never meant to insult that Muslim woman. And, Allah knows best.

Q. No. (281): What is the *Shar'ī* ruling concerning men's performing *Ṭawāf* with women?

A: It is permissible that men perform *Ṭawāf* with women, but women should maintain an appropriate distance from men so that they may not intermingle with them. This is because Islam is a religion of modesty and purity and even when performing an act of worship is it not permissible that men and women intermingle. That is also why the Prophet (PBUH) commanded that women should stay behind men in congregational prayer. It has been narrated by Al-Bukhārī on the authority of Ibn Jurayj that 'Ā'ishah, may Allah be pleased with her, used to perform *Ṭawāf* while isolating herself from men, and that once a woman said to her, "Come on, O Mother of the Believers! Let us touch the Black Stone!" and 'Ā'ishah refused to go with her. And, Allah knows best.

Q. No. (282): Is it detestable to perform prayer after *Ṭawāf* when the sun is rising?

A: If a person performs *Ṭawāf* after the *Fajr* Prayer, it is permissible for him to perform the two *Rak'ahs* of *Ṭawāf* after the prayer because it is obligatory according to the preponderant view in this concern. He can also delay these two *Rak'ahs* until about twenty minutes after the sun rises, for it is detestable to perform prayer when the sun rises. It has been narrated by Al-Bukhārī that 'Urwah Ibnuz-Zubayr said that once ʻĀʼishah, may Allah be pleased with her, saw some people circumambulating the House after the *Ṣubḥ* (Morning) Prayer and after that they sat to listen to the preacher until the sun started to rise. Thereupon they stood up to perform prayer, so ʻĀʼishah commented, "They sat until the time in which performing prayer is detestable had come then they stood up to perform prayer!" Al-Bukhārī has also narrated on the authority of Ibn ʻUmar, may Allah be pleased with him, that he heard the Prophet (PBUH) forbidding that prayer be performed when the sun rises or when it sets. In addition to this, Ibn Abū Shaybah has narrated that ʻĀʼishah, may Allah be pleased with her, said,

"If you want to circumambulate the House after the Fajr Prayer or the *ʻAṣr* Prayer delay the (two-*Rakʻah*) prayer (related to *Ṭawāf*) until the sun sets or until it rises, then perform two *Rakʻahs* for each seven circuits (of *Ṭawāf*)."[1]

Still, it is worth mentioning in this connection that the author of *Fatḥ al-Bārī* has stated that the majority of the Prophet's Companions and those who came after them maintain that it is permissible to perform prayer after *Ṭawāf* at any time. He has added that some of them view that it is detestable to perform such prayer (of *Ṭawāf*) because of the generality of forbidding prayer after the *Ṣubḥ* Prayer and the *ʻAṣr* Prayer[2], and this view has been adopted by Abū Ḥanīfah and Mālik.[3] And, Allah knows best.

Q. No. (283): Is it permissible to perform prayer inside the *Kaʻbah*?

---

[1] See *Fatḥ al-Bārī*, 3/489.

[2] This forbiddance is recorded in the Ḥadīth narrated by Al-Bukhārī and Muslim; it reads, "There is no prayer after the *Fajr* Prayer until the sun rises, and there is no prayer after the *ʻAṣr* Prayer until the sun sets."

[3] See *Fatḥ al-Bārī*, 3/489

A: The Messenger of Allah (PBUH) entered the *Ka'bah* and performed prayer therein, and thus it is permissible for Muslims to perform prayer inside it as unanimously agreed upon by scholars. It has been narrated by Al-Bukhārī and Muslim that Abdullah Ibn 'Umar, may Allah be pleased with him, said,

"The Messenger of Allah (PBUH) entered the *Ka'bah* along with Usamah Ibn Zayd, Bilal, and 'Uthman Ibn Talhah and closed the door and stayed there for some time. I asked Bilal when he came out, 'What did the Prophet do?' He replied, 'He offered prayer with one pillar to his left and one to his right and three behind. In those days the *Ka'bah* was supported by six pillars."

Therefore, it is permissible to perform prayer inside the *Ka'bah* whether this prayer is obligatory or voluntary. It is also possible that the Muslim enjoys the merit of performing prayer inside the *Ka'bah* by performing it inside the *Ḥijr*[1] of Isma'il (Ishmael) because it is part of the *Ka'bah*.

It has been narrated that the Prophet (PBUH) said to 'Ā'ishah, may Allah be pleased with her,

"O 'Ā'ishah! If your people had not been recently polytheists, I would have demolished the *Ka'bah*, and would have brought it to the level of the ground, and would have constructed two doors, one facing the east and the other one to the west, and would have added to it six cubits of space from the *Ḥijr*, for the Quraysh reduced it when they rebuilt it."[2]

It has also been narrated y At-Tirmidhī that 'Ā'ishah, may Allah be pleased with her, said,

"I would like to enter the House and perform prayer therein, so the Messenger of Allah (PBUH) took my hand and let me enter the *Ḥijr*

---

[1] The *Ḥijr* is the unroofed portion of the Kā'bah which is at present in the form of a compound toward the northwest of the Kā'bah
[2] Narrated by Muslim.

and said, '(You can) perform prayer in the *Ḥijr* if you want to enter the House (and perform prayer in it), because it is a piece from the House, but your people reduced it when they rebuilt the *Ka'bah* and thus separated it from the House."

And, Allah knows best.

Q. No. (284): What are the conditions of *Sa'y*?

A: There are certain conditions that must be met for the *Sa'y* or going between As-Ṣafā and Al-Marwah to be valid, as follows.

1. To walk between As-Ṣafā and Al-Marwah in seven phases which are counted as follows: the going from As-Ṣafā to Al- Marwah is to be counted as one phase and the return from Al- Marwah to As-Ṣafā is to be counted as another, and so on until the seven phases are done.

2. To start with As-Ṣafā and end with Al-Marwah in the first, third, fifth, and seventh phases and to start with Al- Marwah and end with As-Ṣafā in the second, fourth, and sixth phases.

3. The say is to be performed after *Ṭawāf* which is performed as a pillar of *Ḥajj* or after *Ṭawāful-Qudūm* (arrival circumambulation).

4. The say is to be performed in the masa or the place of say, that is, between the mountain of As-Ṣafā and the mountain of Al-Marwah.

And, Allah knows best.

Q. No. (285): What are the acts of the *Sunnah* related to say?

A: There are certain acts of the *Sunnah* pertaining to say between As-Ṣafā and Al-Marwah. They can be summarized as follows.

1. That a man - and not a woman - mounts up As-Ṣafā and Al-Marwah as high as the stature of an erect man and sees the *Ka'bah*, because the Prophet (PBUH) towered up these two mountains until he saw the *Ka'bah*, as narrated by Muslim.

2. The person who performs say should be in a state of purification.

3. He should walk at a normal pace whether at the beginning or at the end of the *Sa'y.*

4. To invoke Allah with words with which the Prophet (PBUH) invoked Him while performing say. It has been narrated by Muslim that in the Farewell Pilgrimage the Prophet (PBUH) towered up As-Ṣafā until he saw the House, then he faced the *qiblah* and said,

"There is no god but Allah, alone. He has no partner. Sovereignty and praise are due to Him and He is on all things Omnipotent. There is no god but Allah, alone. He fulfilled His promise, granted His servant victory, and defeated the Confederates alone."

And, Allah knows best.

Q. No. (286): What are the obligations of *Ḥajj*?

A: The obligations or *Wājibat* of *Ḥajj* are the things that a pilgrim must do during his *Iḥrām*. They are as follows:

1. To assume *Iḥrām* from the specified *Mīqāt.*
2. To stay at *'Arafah* until the nightfall.
3. To spend the night at Muzdalifah.
4. To spend the night at *Mīnā* during the three nights of *Tashrīq*, i.e., the second, the third, and the fourth nights of the days of 'Idul- Aḍḥā or Sacrifice Feast.
5. To throw pebbles.[1]

---

[1] In *Ḥajj*, the pilgrim must throw pebbles in certain numbers and in a certain way on the Day of Sacrifice and the Days of *Tashrīq*.
The time of throwing pebbles on the first day which is the Day of Sacrifice - starts with sunrise and extends to sunset, yet it is an act of the *Sunnah* that it is done at forenoon. On the second and the third days of 'Idul- Aḍḥā pebbles are to be thrown from the time after the sun passes the meridian- that is to say at noon until sunset. And there is no harm if the throwing is delayed until the night because of crowdedness.
Faqīhs have agreed to the effect that the required throwing is not permissible except with stones, or anything related to the origin of earth. The number of

6. To shave or shorten the hair, and this is to be done after throwing the pebbles at Jamratul-`Aqabah "in *Ḥajj*" and after finishing the say between As-Ṣafā and Al-Marwah "in *ʿUmrah.*
7. To perform farewell circumambulation. And, Allah knows best.

Q. No. (287): What are the acts of the *Sunnah* related to *Ḥajj*?

A: There are many acts of the *Sunnah* pertaining to *Ḥajj*. The following may be the most important among them.

1. *Ifrād:*

Literally meaning "setting aside," *Ifrād* is that a person assumes *Iḥrām* from the *Mīqāt* - the place from which *Iḥrām* starts intending to perform *Ḥajj* "alone," then after performing the duties related to *Ḥajj* he can perform *ʿUmrah* if he wishes to do so, and no *hady* will be obligatory upon him because of performing *Ḥajj* alone.

2. ***Talbiyah***

---

pebbles which are to be thrown on the Day of Sacrifice and the Days of *Tashrīq* amounts to seventy pebbles if the pilgrim does not hasten to leave in two days and wants to do what is better; and the number is forty-nine if he hastens to leave in two days.

These pebbles are to be thrown as follows:

1. On the first day of the ʿIdul- Aḍḥā days the pilgrim throws seven pebbles only after sunrise at *Jamratul- Aqabah* (the Big Jamrah).

2. On the second day of the ʿIdul- Aḍḥā days he throws twenty-one pebbles after the sun passes the meridian. He starts with the Small Jamrah and throws seven pebbles then throws other seven pebbles at the Medium Jamrah then throws seven pebbles as well after noon at Jamratul- Aqabah.

3. On the third day the pilgrim throws twenty-one pebbles at the Small Jamrah, then the Medium Jamrah, then the Big Jamrah, each with seven pebbles. The time of this throwing starts after the sun passes the meridian, that is, at noon. With this third day the total number of the pebbles thrown is forty-nine (7+21 +21=49). If the pilgrim stays until the fourth day at Mina, he is to throw twenty-one pebbles as well. With the pebbles thrown on the fourth day the number of the pebbles becomes seventy (7+21+ 21+ 21 70), and this is perfect and better for the pilgrim.

Talbiyah is an act of the *Sunnah* in *Ḥajj* except when throwing pebbles as then *Takbīr* is to be recited instead of it.

3. ***Ṭawāful- Qudūm*** (arrival circumambulation)

This *Ṭawāf* is one of the acts of the *Sunnah* related to *Ḥajj* and it is some sort of salutation to the Sacred Mosque.

4. **The two *Rak'ahs* of *Ṭawāf***

This is one of the well-known acts of the *Sunnah* as far as *Ḥajj* is concerned.

5. **To spend the night of *'Arafah* at *Mīnā.***

6. ***Ṭawāful-Wadā'* or farewell circumambulation** is an act of the *Sunnah* according to Mālik. And, Allah knows best.

Q. No. (288): What is the *Iḥṣār* or "prevention" because of which it becomes lawful for a *muḥrim* to put off *Iḥrām*?

A: In principle, Almighty Allah has commanded that all the ceremonies of *Ḥajj* and *'Umrah* must be performed properly and completely, and that we are to offer *hady* if something prevents us from completing them. He says,

﴿وَأَتِمُّوا۟ ٱلْحَجَّ وَٱلْعُمْرَةَ لِلَّهِ ۚ فَإِنْ أُحْصِرْتُمْ فَمَا ٱسْتَيْسَرَ مِنَ ٱلْهَدْيِ ۖ ١٩٦﴾

"And perform properly (i.e., all the ceremonies according to the ways of Prophet Muḥammad), the Ḥajj and 'Umrah (i.e., the pilgrimage to Makkah) for Allah. But if you are prevented (from completing them), sacrifice a Hady (animal, i.e., a sheep, a cow, or a camel, etc.) such as you can afford"

[TMQ: 2: 196]

When a person is prevented from completing *Ḥajj* or *'Umrah*, he is called "*muḥṣar*" (prevented) and the state in which he becomes then is called "*Iḥṣār*" (prevention). This *Iḥṣār* happens when a person is prevented from completing the *Manāsik* because of illness or an enemy who is waiting to harm him, for example. In this case this *muḥṣar* or prevented person is allowed to put off *Iḥrām* and slaughter a sheep for example, and this is what is meant by Allah's words in the verse quoted above... But if you are prevented (from completing them), sacrifice a Hady such as you can afford...

Essential still, the least form of *hady* is one sheep yet it is better to slaughter a cow or a camel. Slaughtering a sheep - and not a camel or a cow - is sufficient because Almighty Allah says, ... sacrifice a *Hady* such as you can afford... meaning: sacrifice whatever you can afford from among the animals that can be slaughtered to be offered as presents to the Sacred House of Allah.[1] This ruling applies whether the pilgrim has already got the *hady* with him or not and whether the *Iḥrām* is for *Ḥajj* or *ʿUmrah*. And, Allah knows best.

Q. No. (289): Where is the *Iḥṣār* oriented *hady* to be slaughtered?

A: All forms of slaughtering which are required in *Ḥajj* and *ʿUmrah* including those related to *Tamattuʿ*, *Qirān*, or penalty slaughtering are to be executed inside the *Haram* so that the poor of the *Haram* can eat from the meat of the slaughtered animals. The *Haram* here refers to Mecca and the areas around it such as *Mīnā*, Muzdalifah, and the places where gaming (hunting) is prohibited.

However, scholars have differed concerning the place where the slaughtering related to *Iḥṣār* (explained in the answer to the previous question) can be done. The majority of scholars - including Mālik, Ash-Shāfiʿī, and Aḥmad - maintain that it is to be done at the place of *Iḥṣār*, i.e., where the pilgrim has been prevented from completing *Ḥajj* or *ʿUmrah*. They add that it makes no difference whether the place of *Iḥṣār* is inside the *Haram* or not. On the other hand, Abū Ḥanīfah asserts that this slaughtering of *Iḥṣār* is not to be executed except inside the *Haram* because Almighty Allah says,

---

[1] This is the literal meaning of "hady" as it is the meaning of "hadiyyah" or present.

﴿لَكُمۡ فِيهَا مَنَٰفِعُ إِلَىٰٓ أَجَلٖ مُّسَمّٗى ثُمَّ مَحِلُّهَآ إِلَى ٱلۡبَيۡتِ ٱلۡعَتِيقِ ٣٣﴾

"In them (cattle offered for sacrifice) are benefits for you for an appointed term, and afterwards they are brought for sacrifice unto the ancient House."

[TMQ: 22: 33]

Abū Ḥanīfah says that the words ... and afterwards they are brought for sacrifice unto the ancient House means that they are to be brought to the place in which they are to be sacrificed, and this place is "the ancient House" which refers to the *Haram.*

The preponderant view concerning this matter - and Allah knows best - is that of the majority, because the Messenger of Allah (PBUH) became in a state of *Iḥṣār* in Al- Ḥudaybiyyah when the polytheists prevented him from entering Mecca, so he slaughtered the *hady* in Al- Ḥudaybiyyah, which is not part of the *Haram.* Besides this, the words ... and afterwards they are brought for sacrifice unto the ancient House may concern people who are not in a state of *Iḥṣār*, as they can reach the *Haram*, unlike those who are prevented from doing so. And, Allah knows best.

Q. No. (290): What are the conditions obligating the slaughtering related to *Tamattu*'?

A: There are five conditions which obligate the slaughtering related to *Tamattu*', as follows:

1. That the pilgrim performs *'Umrah* before *Ḥajj*, so if he performs *Ḥajj* then *'Umrah* he is not a *Mutamatti*'".

2. That he assumes *Iḥrām* for *'Umrah* during the months of *Ḥajj*: Shawwāl, Dhū al-Qa'dah, and ten days from Dhū al-Ḥijjah.

3. That he performs *Ḥajj* during the same year in which he performed *'Umrah*, because Almighty Allah says, "*...whosoever performs the 'Umrah in the months of Ḥajj, before (performing) the Ḥajj, he must slaughter a Hady such as he can afford...*" [TMQ: 2: 196]

4. That the pilgrim is not one of the people of Mecca, because Almighty says in the same verse quoted above, "*this is for him whose family is not present at Al-Masjid al-Ḥarām (i.e., non-resident of Makkah)*".

5. That he assumes *Iḥrām* for *Ḥajj* from Mecca, so if he returns to the *Mīqāt* and assumes *Iḥrām* from it for *Ḥajj* he will not have to sacrifice any *hady*, according to the view of Ash-Shāfiʿī. Abū Ḥanīfah however says that he will have to sacrifice the *hady* unless he returns "to his homeland".

These are the conditions which, if met, the pilgrim in question must sacrifice *hady* for applying the form of *Ḥajj* known as *Tamattuʿ*. And, Allah knows best.

Q. No. (291): What are the characteristics of the Sacred Mosque?

A: There are many characteristics of the Sacred Mosque.

The following may be the most important of them.

- A prayer performed in it is better than a hundred thousand prayers performed in any other mosque.

- It is the best area of land on earth. It is the *qiblah* of all Muslims throughout the world.

-It is an obligation that the Muslim makes pilgrimage to it.

-Whoever enters it is safe and secure.

-Paradise is the reward of whoever visits it with a pious heart and a pure intention.

-Whoever intends inside it to commit some sin is to be punished for that, as Almighty Allah says, "*And whoever inclines to evil actions therein or to do wrong, him We shall cause to taste a painful torment.*" [TMQ: 22:25]

-Its trees and grass are prohibited for *muḥrims* and non- *muḥrims* even the people of the *Haram*.

-Its game is prohibited for all people including the people of the *Haram.*

-Whoever acts against the religion of Islam is to be prevented from entering it, according to the view of the majority of scholars.

-Its pickings are not lawful for whoever finds them and intends to possess them, but it is permissible to pick up such gleanings for the purpose of searching for those who possess them.

-It is prohibited to bury the body of a polytheist in it. It is the place specified for sacrificing *hady.*

-It is "not detestable" to perform voluntary prayer in it at "any" time. This ruling applies to Mecca and all the area constituting the *Haram.*

-No *hady* is required on the part of the person who applies *Tamattuʿ* or *Qirān* if he is from its people. In it there is the well of Zamzam whose water is sufficient as food and remedy.

-In it the Revelation was sent down on the Prophet (PBUH).

-In it Abrahah and his soldiers the People of the Elephant were defeated.

-It was where the journey of *Al-Isrāʾ wa-l-Miʿrāj* (The Nocturnal Journey and the Ascension) started.

-In it the moon was cleft asunder to be a proof of the truthfulness of the Prophet (PBUH), as the people of Mecca requested Prophet Muḥammad to show them a miracle, so he showed them the splitting of the moon.

-In it was the greater conquest when the idols were destroyed, and falsehood vanished.

-In its precincts Prophet Muḥammad (PBUH) was born.

These may be the most important characteristics of the Sacred Mosque. And, Allah knows best.

Q. No. (292): What is the difference between the known days (*Ayyām Maʿlūmāt*) and the appointed days (*Ayyām Maʿdūdāt*)?[1]

A: Almighty Allah says,

﴿لِّيَشۡهَدُواْ مَنَٰفِعَ لَهُمۡ وَيَذۡكُرُواْ ٱسۡمَ ٱللَّهِ فِيٓ أَيَّامٖ مَّعۡلُومَٰتٍ عَلَىٰ مَا رَزَقَهُم مِّنۢ بَهِيمَةِ ٱلۡأَنۡعَٰمِۖ ٢٨﴾

"That they may witness things that are of benefit to them (i.e., reward of Ḥajj in the Hereafter, and also some worldly gain from trade, etc.), and mention the Name of Allah on appointed days (Ayyām Maʿlūmāt), over the beast of cattle that He has provided for them (for sacrifice)."

[TMQ: 22: 28]

Almighty Allah also says,

﴿۞وَٱذۡكُرُواْ ٱللَّهَ فِيٓ أَيَّامٖ مَّعۡدُودَٰتٖۚ فَمَن تَعَجَّلَ فِي يَوۡمَيۡنِ فَلَآ إِثۡمَ عَلَيۡهِ وَمَن تَأَخَّرَ فَلَآ إِثۡمَ عَلَيۡهِۖ لِمَنِ ٱتَّقَىٰۗ وَٱتَّقُواْ ٱللَّهَ وَٱعۡلَمُوٓاْ أَنَّكُمۡ إِلَيۡهِ تُحۡشَرُونَ ٢٠٣﴾

"And remember Allah during the appointed days (Ayyām Maʿdūdāt). But whoever has to leave in two days, there is no sin on him and whosoever stays on, there is no sin on him, if his aim is to do good and obey Allah (fear Him) and know that you will surely be gathered unto Him."

[TMQ: 2: 203]

[1] According to many of those who have translated meanings of the Qur'ān into English, both *ayyam ma'lumat* and *ayyam ma'dudat* are translated as "appointed days" as in the translation of the meaning of the two verses to follow. Thus, "the known days" for the first and "the appointed days" for the second can be regarded as literal translation of each term, just to distinguish between them.

The *Ayyām Maʿlūmāt* are the first ten days of the month of Dhū al-Ḥijjah and the last of them is the Day of Sacrifice, whereas the *Ayyām Maʿdūdāt* are the three days following the Day of Sacrifice.

According to another interpretation, the *Ayyām Maʿdūdāt* are the three days following the Day of Sacrifice while the *Ayyām Maʿlūmāt* are the Day of Sacrifice and two days after it. This has been attributed to Ibn ʿUmar, may Allah be pleased with him. And, Allah knows best.

Q. No. (293): What is the excellence of performing prayer in the Sacred Mosque, the Prophetic Mosque, the Aqsa Mosque, and Quba' Mosque as distinguished from the other mosques?

A: It has been narrated by Aḥmad and Ibn Mājah on the authority of Jābir, may Allah be pleased with him, that the Messenger of Allah (PBUH) said,

"A prayer performed in this mosque of mine is better than a thousand prayers performed in any other mosque except the Sacred Mosque, and a prayer performed in the Sacred Mosque is better than a hundred thousand prayers performed in any other mosque."

It has also been narrated by At-Tabarani and Ibn Khuzaymah on the authority of Abū-Darda', may Allah be pleased with him, that the Prophet (PBUH) said,

"A prayer performed in the Sacred Mosque equals a hundred thousand prayers; a prayer performed in my mosque equals a thousand prayers; and a prayer performed (in the Aqsa Mosque) in Jerusalem equals five hundred prayers."

And, it has been narrated by At-Tirmidhī on the authority of Usayd Ibn Zahir Al-Ansari, may Allah be pleased with him, that the Messenger of Allah (PBUH) said,

"A prayer performed in the mosque of Quba' is like (performing) a *ʿUmrah.*"

And, Allah knows best.

Q. No. (294): What are the things by which a woman is marked with regard to *Ḥajj* and *'Umrah*?

A: Woman is marked by the following things:

-She is not forbidden to wear stitched clothes like men. and thus, she can assume *Iḥrām* while wearing her normal clothes except for the face cover and gloves.

-It is permissible for her to wear *khuffs*. She is not to uncover her head.

-She must have a mahram to accompany her.

-She does not apply ramal or *idtiba* while performing *Ṭawāf.*

-She does not move quickly between the two green flags in the masā (place of Sa'y).

-She does not raise her voice with *talbiyah*.

-She needs the permission of her husband to perform voluntary *Ḥajj*, yet she can perform the obligatory *Ḥajj* without his permission if he prevents her.

-It is not permissible for woman to have the hair of her head shaved, and she is only asked to cut a part equal to a fingertip (two centimeters) from her hair.

-She does not touch the Black Stone if it is surrounded by men.

- If she is overtaken by menstruation, she can perform all the *Manāsik* except for *Ṭawāf* which she delays until her menstruation is over.

-She is exempted from *Ṭawāful- Wadā'* or farewell pilgrimage if she is afflicted by menstruation or postnatal bleeding.

-This is in general what differentiates women from men as far as *Ḥajj* and *'Umrah* are concerned.

And, Allah knows best.

Q. No. (295): What is the difference between *hady* and *fidyah*?

A: *Hady* (sacrificial animal) may be obligatory as in the case of *Tamattu'* or *Qirān*, and *hady* here is a sheep or one seventh of a cow or one seventh of a camel. *Hady* may also be an act of the *Sunnah*, and there is no limit of this form of *hady* as the Muslim can slaughter for the poor of the *Haram* whatever he wants of *hady*. According to the *Sunnah*, whoever presents *hady* is recommended to eat of its meat whether is it is obligatory or an act of the *Sunnah*.

Fidyah (ransom) however is a penalty slaughtering which is prescribed upon any pilgrim who commits any of the things. forbidden in *Iḥrām* or neglects any duty related to *Ḥajj*. This also includes the *fidyah* referred to in the following verse,

﴿ وَلَا تَحْلِقُوا۟ رُءُوسَكُمْ حَتَّىٰ يَبْلُغَ ٱلْهَدْىُ مَحِلَّهُۥ ۚ فَمَن كَانَ مِنكُم مَّرِيضًا أَوْ بِهِۦٓ أَذًى مِّن رَّأْسِهِۦ فَفِدْيَةٌ مِّن صِيَامٍ أَوْ صَدَقَةٍ أَوْ نُسُكٍ ۚ ﴿١٩٦﴾ ﴾

"And do not shave your heads until the Hady reaches the place of sacrifice. And whosoever of you is ill or has an ailment in his scalp (necessitating shaving), he must pay a Fidyah (ransom) of either observing Sawm (fasts) or giving Ṣadaqah (charity) or offering sacrifice". [TMQ: 2:196]

And, Allah knows best.

Q. No. (296): What is the amount of *fidyah* required for committing one of the forbiddances of *Iḥrām* and that which is required for neglecting one of the duties of *Ḥajj*?

A: The answer to this question can be presented in the following points:

1. If a pilgrim man or woman removes hair or nails or applies perfume, and if a man wears stitched clothes or covers his head, and if a woman wears gloves or a face cover, one *fidyah* is required for "each" of these forbidden things. This *fidyah* is to slaughter a sheep, or to feed six poor people, or to observe fast for three days. The pilgrim can choose between these three alternatives.

2. If the pilgrim neglects one of the duties of *Ḥajj*, such as throwing pebbles and spending the night at Muzdalifah and *Mīnā*, a penalty slaughtering is required for this. If he cannot afford it, he can observe fast for ten days three of which are done during *Ḥajj* and seven when he returns to his homeland, and if he cannot observe the three-day fast during *Ḥajj*, he can observe it along with the other seven days when he returns home.

And, Allah knows best.

Q. No. (297): What is the excellence of the first ten days of Dhū al-Ḥijjah?

A: There are a number of hadiths that indicate the excellence of the first ten days of Dhū al-Ḥijjah. For example, it has been narrated by At-Tabarani on the authority of Ibn ʿAbbās, may Allah be pleased with him, that the Prophet (PBUH) said,

"There are no days on which doing righteous deeds is dearer to Allah, Glorified and Exalted be He, than these days (meaning the ten days of Dhū al-Ḥijjah)."

Those listening said, "O Messenger of Allah (PBUH)! Not even jihad in the cause of Allah?" He (PBUH) said,

"Not even jihad in the cause of Allah, except for a man who goes out with (the intention of dedicating) his soul and property then come back with nothing."

It has moreover been narrated that Anas Ibn Mālik, may Allah be pleased with him, stated,

"It was said that each day of the ten days (of Dhul- Hijjah) is equivalent to a thousand days and that the day of *'Arafah* is equivalent to ten thousand days,"

meaning in excellence.

That is why it is desirable that the Muslim performs as many acts of worship as possible during these days. And, Allah knows best.

Q. No. (298): If a man wants to perform *Ḥajj* or *'Umrah* and wears the clothes of *Iḥrām* in the airplane yet he does not know the *Mīqāt* where he should assume *Iḥrām*: can he delay assuming *Iḥrām* until he reaches Jeddah?

A: If a person intends to travel by air for performing *Ḥajj* or *'Umrah*, he can take a bath in his house and wear the *Izār* and the *rida'* if he wants, and when he is a short distance far away from the *Mīqāt* he can assume *Iḥrām*.

If, however he does not know the *Mīqāt*, he can ask the pilot or one of those on board if any of them is well-known for his knowledge and experience in this regard. And, Allah knows best.

Q. No. (299): If a person intended to perform *Ḥajj* and travelled by air for doing so yet did not assume *Iḥrām* until he reached Jeddah where he assumed it, is there any expiation for that?

A: First of all, whenever such a person lands in Jeddah and he is one of the people of Ash-Shām or Egypt, he is to go to Rabigh and assume *Iḥrām* there and not in Jeddah itself. Also, if he comes from Najd and does not assume *ihrām* until he lands in Jeddah, he is to go to *As-Sayl* - which is *Wādī Qarn* - and assume *Iḥrām* there.

If, however such a person assumes *Iḥrām* in Jeddah and does not go to the pinpointed place, he is to slaughter a sheep in Mecca and distribute it among the poor. He can also offer one seventh of a camel or one seventh of a cow to compensate for what he has committed. And, Allah knows best.

Q. No. (300): If a person assumes *Iḥrām* for *Ḥajj* and *'Umrah* together (i.e., applies *Qirān*) and after performing *'Umrah* he puts off his *Iḥrām*, will he be considered a *Mutamatti'*?

A: Yes, if he assumes *Iḥrām* for *Ḥajj* and *'Umrah* as *Qirān* and performs *Ṭawāf* and *Sa'y* then makes it a *'Umrah* he is a *Mutamatti'* and in this case he is to sacrifice the *hady* required for *Tamattu'*. And, Allah knows best.

Q. No. (301): What is the *Shar'ī* ruling concerning a person who intends to perform *Ḥajj* alone (i.e., as *Ifrād*) yet makes it *Tamattu'* when he reaches Mecca by performing *'Umrah* then putting off *Iḥrām*?

A: He can do so, that is, he can perform *'Umrah* then put off *Iḥrām* then assume *Iḥrām* for *Ḥajj*, and in this case, he will have to sacrifice the *hady* required for *Tamattu'* because what he has done is *Tamattu'*. And, Allah knows best.

Q. No. (302): Is there any specific formula with which the person can express intention for performing *Ḥajj* if he intends to perform it on behalf of someone else?

A: Intention is originally determined in the heart, and thus this person can determine in his heart that the *Ḥajj* he is going to perform is on behalf of such and such person. He can also express this intention with words by saying, "O Allah! Here I am at Your service for performing *Ḥajj* on behalf of so and so." Besides, when he performs the duties of *Ḥajj*, he does not need to express that what he is doing is on behalf of the person in question, as the first intention is general and suffices for all the duties and acts related to *Ḥajj*. In a word, after determining or expressing the intention on assuming *Iḥrām*, he performs the duties of *Ḥajj* just as he would do for himself. And, Allah knows best.

Q. No. (303): What is the *Shar'ī* ruling concerning a person who cuts a tree in the *Haram*?

A: If a person cuts a big tree in the *Haram,* he is to slaughter a badanah, and if it is a small one, he is to slaughter a sheep. Yet it is permissible to cut the branches that hinder people's path and harm them. It is also permissible to cut what is grown by man. And, Allah knows best.

Q. No. (304): What are the boundaries of the Meccan *Haram*?

A: The boundaries of the Meccan *Haram* are as follows: Al-Jiʿrānah eastward, Ash-Shumaysī westward, At-Tanʿīm northward, Wādī Nakhlah north-eastward, and Adah southward. Interestingly enough, there are visible flags that refer to the boundaries of the *Haram*.

And, Allah knows best.

Q. No. (305): What is the *Sharʿī* ruling concerning a *muḥrim* whose hair falls when he is performing ablution?

A: There is no harm in this as long as he does not cause the hair to fall deliberately. For, if he causes his hair to fall on purpose or cuts his hair while being in a state of *Iḥrām*, he will have committed one of the forbidden things related to *Iḥrām*. In this regard, it should be known that there is dead hair that. falls down while the person moves his hair when performing ablution or taking a bath, and there is no harm in this. And, Allah knows best.

Q. No. (306): Can a person assume *Iḥrām* while wearing socks and gloves?

A: It is not permissible for a person to be in a state of *Iḥrām* while wearing socks, nor is it permissible for him to wear. *khuffs* unless he cannot find shoes, because the Prophet (PBUH) said,

"Whoever does not find shoes can wear khuffs, and whoever cannot find *Izār* can wear trousers."

This Ḥadīth is unanimously agreed upon as authentic.

As for woman, there is no harm if she wears *khuffs* or socks while being in a state of *Iḥrām* because they secure more covering for her body. But she can let down her clothes so that they may cover her feet and then she will not need to wear socks or *khuffs*.

Still, it is not permissible neither for man nor for woman to wear gloves while being in a state of *Iḥrām* because the Prophet (PBUH) said concerning a *muḥrim* woman,

"A woman must not wear a face cover or gloves."[1]

As this is forbidden for women, it is more becoming that it is forbidden for men as well. That is why the Prophet (PBUH) said regarding the man who died while being in a state of *Iḥrām*,

"Wash him with water and sidr (extract of the leaves of lote-tree) and shroud him in two pieces of cloth, and neither perfume him nor cover his head, for he will be resurrected on the Day of Resurrection reciting *talbiyah* (i.e., like a pilgrim)."

This has been narrated by Al-Bukhārī on the authority of Ibn `Abbas, may Allah be pleased with him. And, Allah knows best.

Q. No. (307): Should a person who has assumed *Iḥrām* for *'Umrah* keep marching until he performs *'Umrah* or can he dismount for some time to rest a bit then proceed?

A: It is not obligatory that such a *muḥrim* keeps marching until he performs *'Umrah* Rather, he can rest on his way in whatever rest house he wants as long as he needs to do so, while being in a state of *Iḥrām*. And, Allah knows best.

Q. No. (308): What is the *Shar'ī* ruling concerning a person who cannot wear the clothes of *Iḥrām* because he is paralyzed?

---

[1] Narrated by Al-Bukhārī.

A: If a person cannot wear the *Iḥrām* clothes because of such a disability, he can wear whatever clothes that suit his condition, but he should slaughter a sheep and distribute it among the poor, or feed six poor people giving a half of *Sāʿ* of food to each or observe fast for three days. This is how scholars have judged comparing this case with having the hair of the head shaved because of some legal excuse; Almighty Allah says,

﴿ وَلَا تَحْلِقُوا۟ رُءُوسَكُمْ حَتَّىٰ يَبْلُغَ ٱلْهَدْىُ مَحِلَّهُۥ ۚ فَمَن كَانَ مِنكُم مَّرِيضًا أَوْ بِهِۦٓ
أَذًى مِّن رَّأْسِهِۦ فَفِدْيَةٌ مِّن صِيَامٍ أَوْ صَدَقَةٍ أَوْ نُسُكٍ ﴿١٩٦﴾ ﴾

"And do not shave your heads until the Hady reaches the place of sacrifice. And whosoever of you is ill or has an ailment in his scalp (necessitating shaving), he must pay a Fidyah (ransom) of either observing Sawm (fasts) or giving Ṣadaqah (charity) or offering sacrifice." [TMQ: 2:196]

The Prophet (PBUH) explained that the fast that is to be observed as ordained in this verse is for three days, that the *Ṣadaqah* mentioned in the verse is feeding six poor people giving a half of *Sāʿ* of food to each, and that the sacrifice is to be offered by slaughtering one sheep. And, Allah knows best.

Q. No. (309): Is it forbidden that the *muḥrim* perfumes his body?

A: What is forbidden as far as perfuming in *Iḥrām* is concerned is that the *muḥrim* applies it to the clothes of *Iḥrām*, i.e., the *Izār* and the *rida'*. However, according to the *Sunnah*, he can apply perfume to his body including his head, beard, armpits, etc. And, Allah knows best.

Q. No. (310): What is the *Sharʿī* ruling concerning a person who came to Mecca for something other than *Ḥajj* and *ʿUmrah* then wanted to perform *Ḥajj* or *ʿUmrah*?

A: A person may come to Mecca to visit a relative of his for example then he may wish to perform *Ḥajj* or *ʿUmrah* There is no problem in this but he should consider certain things: if it is *Ḥajj* that he wants to perform, he can assume *Iḥrām* for it from the place where he is whether he is in Mecca or its suburban; and if it is *'Umrah* he is to go outside the Haram to assume *Iḥrām* for *'Umrah.* He can go to *At-Tan'īm* to do so because when 'Ā'ishah, may Allah be pleased with her, wanted to perform *'Umrah* the Prophet (PBUH) ordered her to go out to *At-Tan'īm* to assume *Iḥrām* for it. And, Allah knows best.

Q. No. (311): What is the *Shar'ī* ruling concerning a person who has a wet dream while performing *Ḥajj*: does this invalidate his *Ḥajj*?

A: Having a wet dream does not invalidate *Ḥajj* or *'Umrah* and whoever has such a dream while being in a state of *Iḥrām* is to perform *Ġhusl* for *Janābah* if he finds semen, and no *fidyah* is required for that because he did not have the wet dream on his own accord. And, Allah knows best.

Q. No. (312): What is the *Shar'ī* ruling concerning a person who performs *Sa'y* before *Ṭawāf* in *Ḥajj*?

A: He does not have to repeat the say because it has been narrated by Abū Dāwūd on the authority of Usamah ibn Sharik who said that he set out with the Prophet (PBUH) for performing *Ḥajj*. The people would come to him and one of them would say, "O Messenger of Allah! I performed *Sa'y* before *Ṭawāf*," or that he did one thing before or after another, and he (PBUH) would say "*There is no harm (in this).*"

And, Allah knows best.

Q. No. (313): What is the *Shar'ī* ruling concerning a person who performed *Ṭawāf* and did not perform *Sa'y* thinking that it was not obligatory then after five days he was told that he should have performed say: is it permissible for him to perform *Sa'y* without performing *Ṭawāf* before it?

A: If a person does not perform say after *Ṭawāf* thinking that it is not obligatory then someone tells him that he should have performed say, he is to perform say only and there is no need for performing

Ṭawāf before it. This is because it is not stipulated that say must be performed immediately after *Ṭawāf*. Even if that person delayed say on purpose, there is no harm, yet it is better that say be performed after *Ṭawāf*. And, Allah knows best.

Q. No. (314): What is the *Shar'ī* ruling concerning a person who forgetfully wears stitched clothes without having the hair of his head shaved or shortened then remembers that he has not had his hair shaved or shortened?

A: In this case he is to take off the stitched clothes once he remembers that then he should have the hair of his head shaved or shortened then wear the stitched clothes again. Also, if he forgetfully or ignorantly has his hair shaved or shortened while wearing stitched clothes, that will be sufficient, and he will not have to repeat the shaving or shortening. After all, he must take off the stitched clothes so that he can have his hair shaved or cut short while being in a state of *Iḥrām*' because stitched clothes contradict *Iḥrām*.

And, Allah knows best.

Q. No. (315): What is the *Shar'ī* ruling if *Iqāmah* is pronounced for prayer while a person is performing *Ṭawāf* or *Sa'y*?

A: in this case he can join the prayer then complete his *Ṭawāf* or say starting from the point he had reached before joining the prayer.

And, Allah knows best.

Q. No. (316): What is the *Shar'ī* ruling concerning a man who touches a marriageable woman while performing *Ṭawāf*?

A: If a man touches the body of a marriageable woman while performing *Ṭawāf* due to crowdedness, this does not affect his *Ṭawāf* negatively, according to the preponderant view in this concern.

It is worth mentioning here that scholars have differed whether touching a marriageable woman invalidates ablution or not. Some say that it invalidates it, some assert that it does not invalidate it, and still some maintain that it invalidates ablution if it is done with sexual lust. And, Allah knows best.

Q. No. (317): What is the *Sharʿī* ruling concerning a person who reached Mecca at the afternoon of the day of *ʿArafah* and could not perform *Ṭawāful- Qudūm* (arrival circumambulation)?

A: This person has more than one choice. He can enter Mecca and perform *Ṭawāf* and say then go to Arafat where he stays even during the night then he can leave for Muzdalifah where he spends the night. He can also go to Arafat immediately and stay there until sunset then leave for Muzdalifah where he will perform the Maghrib and the *ʿIshāʾ* prayers and spend the night, then he can perform *Ṭawāf* and say on the Day of Sacrifice or even after that and no penalty slaughtering is required because of that if he assumed *Iḥrām* for *Ḥajj* only. If, however he assumed *Iḥrām* for *Ḥajj* and *ʿUmrah*, he should offer the *hady* required for *Tamattuʿ*. And, Allah knows best.

Q. No. (318): What are the mistakes that may be committed by some pilgrims when performing the different duties of *Ḥajj* and *ʿUmrah*?

A: These mistakes may be outlined as follows:

1. **Mistakes related to *Iḥrām*:**

The mistake that may be committed as regards *Iḥrām* is that the pilgrim surpasses the *Mīqāt* specified for him by the Sharīʿah without assuming *Iḥrām* from it. Whenever this happens, the pilgrim is to return to the *Mīqāt*- if he can do so- and assume *Iḥrām* from it or else he will have to offer a *fidyah*.

2. **Mistakes related to *Ṭawāf*:**

-A pilgrim may start performing *Ṭawāf* before the Black Stone. He may perform *Ṭawāf* inside the *Ḥijr* of Ismail (Ishmael), peace be upon him. This invalidates *Ṭawāf* because he will not be circumambulating the *Ka'bah* as he will be circumambulating a part of it because the *Ḥijr* is part of the *Ka'bah.*

- He may apply *ramal* - by moving quickly- when performing the seven circuits of *Ṭawāf*, and not during the first three circuits as required according to the *Sunnah*, and this ramal is to be applied to *Ṭawāful- Qudūm* (arrival circumambulation) in particular.

- He may compete with people to touch and kiss the Black Stone. It is better for a Muslim not to touch or kiss the Black Stone than to harm his Muslim brothers and sisters, especially with the fact that he can point toward it when he is in front of it.

- He may rub his body against the Black Stone seeking to obtain a blessing because of that. This is an innovation in the religion (*Bid'ah*).

- He may touch all the pillars or even the walls of the *Ka'bah* and rub his body against it. The Prophet (PBUH) did not touch except the Black Stone and the Yemenite Corner.

- He may specify an invocation for each circuit of *Ṭawāf*. It has been authentically narrated that the Prophet (PBUH) would recite *Takbīr* whenever he passed by the Black Stone and that he would say when being between the Stone and the Yemenite Corner in the last circuit,

"Our Lord! Give us in this world that which is good and in the Hereafter that which is good, save us from the torment of the Fire, and admit us to Paradise with Al-Abrār[1], O Almighty, O Most Forgiving, O Lord of the Worlds!"

- He may raise his voice while performing *Ṭawāf* to the extent that he disturbs and confuses the others who are performing *Ṭawāf* with him.

---

[1] Those who are obedient to Allah and follow His Orders strictly.

- He may compete with others to perform the two prayers attached to *Ṭawāf* at the *Maqām* of Ibrāhīm. It will be sufficient if he performs these two *Rak'ahs* at any place inside the *Haram*.

3. **Mistakes related to say:**

- When pilgrims climb As-Ṣafā and Al-Marwah, a pilgrim may face the *Ka'bah* and recite *Takbīr* while pointing with his hands as if he is reciting *Takbīr* for prayer. This is wrong because the Prophet (PBUH) would raise his hands in such a situation for invocation.

- A pilgrim may move quickly during all the phases of say, while this quick moving is done only when the pilgrim is between the two green flags.

4. **Mistakes related to the stay at *'Arafah***

- Some pilgrims may stay outside the boundaries of *'Arafah* until the sun sets then leave for Muzdalifah without staying inside the actual boundaries of Arafat. This is a big mistake because of which *Ḥajj* becomes invalid because *Ḥajj* is *'Arafah* as stated by the Prophet (PBUH). Therefore, every pilgrim must make sure that the place where he is to stay belongs to *'Arafah*.

- Some pilgrims may leave *'Arafah* before the sun sets. This is not permissible because the Prophet (PBUH) stayed at *'Arafah* until the sun had already set.

- A pilgrim may compete with others to climb the mountain of *'Arafah* and reach its top. There is no need for that because it will be deficient if he stays in any part belonging to *'Arafah*.

- He may face the mountain of *'Arafah* - and not the *qiblah* as required by the *Sunnah*- when invoking Allah.

- Some pilgrims may heap up sand and stones on the day of *'Arafah* in certain places. This has not been authentically proven as being recommended by the Sharī'ah.

5. **Mistakes related to Muzdalifah:**

Once they reach Muzdalifah, some pilgrims occupy themselves with picking up pebbles before performing the *Maghrib* and the *'Ishā'* prayers thinking that the pebbles with which the *Jamrahs* are to be thrown must be picked up from Muzdalifah. Rather, it is permissible to pick up such pebbles from any place in the Haram.

6. **Mistakes related to the throwing of pebbles**

Some pilgrims wrongly think that they throw devils when throwing the Jamrahs so they throw them furiously while invoking curses upon those devils. The throwing of pebbles has been prescribed for remembering Allah, and not for invoking curses upon devils.

- Some pilgrims may use for the throwing in question big pebbles or shoes or pieces of wood. It has been narrated that the Prophet (PBUH) said,

"O people! Do not kill one another! When you are to throw the Jamrah, throw (it) with (pebbles) like the stones of *khadhf* (i.e., small stones which are like beans)."[1]

Some pilgrims may compete with the others while throwing the *Jamrahs* - Some pilgrims may throw all pebbles all together. Scholars assert that if anyone does so, only one pebble is counted.

- A pilgrim may deputize someone to throw the pebbles instead of him though he is able to do it himself.

7. **Mistakes related to farewell circumambulation:**

- Some pilgrims may leave *Mīnā* before throwing the pebbles and perform *Ṭawāful- Wadā'* or farewell circumambulation then return to *Mīnā* and throw the pebbles then travel from there to his

[1] Narrated by Abū Dāwūd.

homeland. Thus, the last thing he does is throwing the pebbles while the Prophet (PBUH) said,

"Whoever makes pilgrimage to this House or performs *'Umrah*, let his last action be with the House,"[1]

meaning: let his last action be the circumambulation round the *Ka'bah*.

- After performing this *Ṭawāf*, some pilgrims may leave the Sacred Mosque while moving backward and making the *Ka'bah* in front of them. They claim that is this for glorifying the *Ka'bah* while this is an innovation in the religion.

- Some pilgrims may turn their faces toward the *Ka'bah* after finishing *Ṭawāful- Wadā'* and recite invocations with which they pay farewell to the *Ka'bah* at the gate of the Sacred Mosque. This is also an innovation in the religion, and it is sufficient for the pilgrim to pay farewell to the *Ka'bah* with the farewell circumambulation which is enacted for this. And, Allah knows best.

Q. No. (319): What is the excellence of visiting the Prophet's Mosque?

A: It is an act of the *Sunnah* that whoever makes pilgrimage to the Sacred Mosque heads for Medina to visit and perform prayer in the mosque of Prophet Muḥammad (PBUH). It has been narrated by Aḥmad that the Prophet (PBUH) said,

"A prayer performed in this mosque of mine is better than a thousand prayers performed in any other mosque except the Sacred Mosque, and a prayer performed in the Sacred Mosque is better than a hundred thousand prayers performed in any other mosque."

The mosque of the Prophet (PBUH) is one of the three mosques for which a person can set out on a journey especially for performing

---

[1] Narrated by At-Tirmidhī and Abū Dāwūd.

prayer therein. It has been narrated by Al-Bukhārī on the authority of Abū Hurayrah, may Allah be pleased with him, that the Prophet (PBUH) said,

"Do not set out on a journey except for three Mosques: The Sacred Mosque (in Mecca), the Mosque of the Messenger of Allah (in Medina), and the Aqsa Mosque (in Jerusalem)."

And, Allah knows best.

Q. No. (320): What is the excellence of visiting the Prophet's grave?

A: Visiting the grave of Prophet Muḥammad (PBUH) is one of the greatest acts that any Muslim who visits Medina is recommended to do. He is also recommended to salute the Prophet (PBUH) when standing beside his grave, because the Prophet (PBUH) said, as narrated by Aḥmad,

"Whenever someone salutes me at my grave, Allah restores my soul to me until I answer his salutation."

It is also recommended that whoever visits the Prophet's grave visits also the two graves of his Companions Abū Bakr and 'Umar, may Allah be pleased with both of them, and salutes them.

It is really a great blessing that the Muslim be near to the purest body of the dearest creature, Prophet Muḥammad, may Allah's peace and blessings be upon him! And, Allah knows best.

Simply by saying for example, "Peace be upon you, O Messenger of Allah".

'Umrah (Lesser Pilgrimage)

Q. No. (321): What is the *Shar'ī* ruling concerning *'Umrah*?

A: Generally speaking, according to Abū Ḥanīfah and Mālik, *'Umrah* is a *Sunah Mu'akkadah* or an affirmed act of the *Sunnah*, while Aḥmad

Ibn Hanbal says that it is an obligation prescribed in the form of an act of the *Sunnah.*[1] Still, Ash- Shāfi'ī asserts that *'Umrah* is to be performed obligatorily by whoever is to perform *Ḥajj* obligatorily. In other words, *'Umrah* is obligatory upon whoever meets the conditions which are to be met for *Ḥajj* to be obligatory.

Among those who maintain that *'Umrah* is an obligation are Umar, Ibn 'Abbās, Ibn 'Umar, Jābir, Ibnul- Musayyab, Ibn Jubayr, Al-Ḥasan al-Baṣrī, and others, may Allah be pleased with all of them. On the other hand, Ibn Mas'ud, may Allah be pleased with him, views that *'Umrah* is not an obligation and Mālik followed in his footsteps concerning this judgment. And, Allah knows best.

Q. No. (322): What is the difference between *Ḥajj* and *'Umrah*?

A: *'Umrah* is different from *Ḥajj* in the following:

- There is no stay at *'Arafah* in *'Umrah* No spending of the night at Muzdalifah is required in *'Umrah.*

- *'Umrah* contains no throwing of pebbles.

- There is no specific time during which *'Umrah* is to be performed, unlike *Ḥajj* which is to be performed in a specific time during the year. Thus, *'Umrah* can be per- formed throughout the year including the months of *Ḥajj.*

Accordingly, if a person assumes *Iḥrām* for *'Umrah* from the *Mīqāt* specified for him then circumambulates the *Ka'bah* in seven circuits then performs say between As-Ṣafā and Al- Marwah in seven phases, he will have performed a *'Umrah* completely with all its pillars. And after that he is to have the hair of his head shaved or shortened, thus

---

[1] By this Imam Aḥmad may have meant that *'Umrah* is such an act of the *Sunnah* that is so important and strongly confirmed by the Sharī'ah that it seems to be nearer to being an obligation than being an act of the *Sunnah*, And, Allah knows best.

finishing all the acts related to *'Umrah*. This is simply the difference between *Ḥajj* and *'Umrah* And, Allah knows best.

Q. No. (323): What are the pillars of *'Umrah*?

A: There are five pillars of *'Umrah* as follows:

1. Thick.

2. *Ṭawāf*.

3. *Sa'y* or going between As-Ṣafā and Al-Marwah.

4. Having the hair of the head shaved or cut short.

5. To consider arrangement when dealing with these pillars.

And, Allah knows best.

Q. No. (324): What are the *Mawāqīt* (times and sites) of *Iḥrām* for *'Umrah*?

A: *'Umrah* can be performed at any time throughout the year and the best time for performing it is Ramaḍān.

The *Mawāqīt* (pl. of *Mīqāt*) of *'Umrah* for those who come to Mecca from distant places such as Morocco and Egypt are the same *Mawāqīt* of *Ḥajj*, as a person who is to perform *'Umrah* should pass by any of the five *Mawāqīt* of *Ḥajj*: Dhul-Hulayfah, Al-Juhfah, Yalamlam, Dhāt 'Irq, and Qarn al-Manāzil. No one is to surpass these *Mawāqīt* without *Iḥrām* if he wants to perform *Ḥajj* or *'Umrah*.

Significant still, whoever is inside the Haram (the Sacred Precincts) and wants to perform *'Umrah* must go outside the Haram to assume *Iḥrām* for that. The nearest place in this regard is At-Tan'īm, which is known nowadays as the mosque of 'Ā'ishah, may Allah be pleased with her. And, Allah knows best.

Q. No. (325): How many times did the Prophet (PBUH) perform *Ḥajj* and how many times did he perform *'Umrah*?

A: It has been authentically narrated that the Prophet (PBUH) performed *Ḥajj* only one time and that was the *Ḥajj* known as the Farewell Pilgrimage. That was in the tenth year after Ḥijrah as explicitly cited in the narration of Muslim on the authority of Jābir, may Allah be pleased with him, when he said,

"The Messenger of Allah (PBUH) resided in (Medina) for nine years during which he did not perform *Ḥajj*, then he made a public announcement in the tenth year to the effect that he (PBUH) was about to perform *Ḥajj*. A large number of people came to Medina and all of them were eager to follow the Messenger of Allah (PBUH) and imitate his every action..."

to the end of the narration

As for *'Umrah* the Messenger of Allah (PBUH) performed it four times as authentically narrated in more than one Ḥadīth. For example, it has been narrated by Al-Bukhārī that Anas, may Allah be pleased with him, said,

"The Messenger of Allah (PBUH) performed *'Umrah* four times: (i) the *'Umrah* of Al-Hudaybiyah in (the month of) Dhul-Qa'dah when the polytheists held him back (from performing *Ḥajj*), (ii) the *'Umrah* (that he performed) in the next year when he made peace with them, (iii) the *'Umrah* of Al-Ji'rānah when he distributed the spoils of (the battle of) Hunayn, and (iv) the *'Umrah* (that he performed) with his (Farewell) *Ḥajj*."

Thus, the Prophet (PBUH) performed *Ḥajj* only once and *'Umrah* four times. And, Allah knows best.

Q. No. (326): Is it detestable to repeat performing *'Umrah*?

A: The majority of Faqīhs, including Abū Ḥanīfah, Ash- Shāfi'ī, and Aḥmad, are of the opinion that *'Umrah* can be performed throughout the year and that it is permissible for the Muslim to perform it even for a number of times every month. This is because *'Umrah* is a special act of obedience with which the Muslim is supposed to seek to draw nearer to Allah every now and then, especially that the Prophet (PBUH) said,

"Follow *Ḥajj* and *'Umrah* one after another, for they both remove sins and poverty as bellows remove the refuse of iron, gold, and silver."[1]

And, Allah knows best.

Q. No. (327): What is the excellence of performing *'Umrah* in Ramaḍān?

A: The Prophet (PBUH) encouraged Muslims to perform. *'Umrah* in the month of Ramaḍān in particular. He (PBUH) said,

"*'Umrah* in Ramaḍān is equivalent to a performance of *Ḥajj*."[2]

According to another narration of Muslim, he (PBUH) said that *'Umrah* in Ramaḍān is equivalent to a performance of *Ḥajj* with him (PBUH). And, Allah knows best.

Q. No. (328): If the performance of *'Umrah* in Ramaḍān is that great, so why did the Prophet (PBUH) not perform *'Umrah* in this month?

A: The Prophet (PBUH) performed *'Umrah* during the months of *Ḥajj* - and Ramaḍān is not one of them - in order to show that it is permissible for the Muslim to perform *'Umrah* during these months in particular, as the people during the pre-Islamic period used to prevent that claiming that it was one of the most abominable acts to perform *'Umrah* during the months of *Ḥajj*. Thus, he (PBUH) wanted to refute their wrong belief and show that what they prevented was lawful. Ibn Ḥajar commented,

"It seems that performing *'Umrah* in Ramaḍān is better on the part of people other than the Prophet (PBUH), as what he did (i.e., performing *'Umrah* during the months of *Ḥajj*, and not performing it

---

[1] Narrated by At-Tirmidhī.
[2] Narrated by Muslim.

in Ramaḍān) was to refute that pre-Islamic belief. It is also probable that he used to be occupied with worshiping Allah (during this month) with (acts of worship) more important than *'Umrah*. Also, (perhaps) he feared that he would put his followers to difficulty because if he performed *'Umrah* in Ramaḍān they would be keen to imitate him thus combining *'Umrah* and fasting. And, the Prophet (PBUH) would not perform a certain act (of worship) though he liked it lest it should be (regarded as) obligatory and lest that should be hard for them."[1]

And, Allah knows best.

[1] See *Fatḥ al-Bārī*, 3/605.

Marriage

Q. No. (329): What are the benefits of marriage?

A: There are many benefits and advantages that a person can get as a result of marriage. Some of these benefits are the following:

1. Complying with Allah's command.

2. Following the *Sunnah* of the Prophet (PBUH) and the line of conduct adopted by the Messengers before him. Almighty Allah says, *"and indeed We sent Messengers before you (O* Muḥammad*), and made for them wives and offspring"* [TMQ: 13: 38]

3. Assuaging one's lust and lowering one's gaze.

4. Protecting one's genitals against evil and immorality and helping women be modest and chaste.

5. Preventing abomination and *Zinā* from spreading among Muslims.

6. Producing abundant offspring so that the Prophet (PBUH) can feel proud of that before the other nations and Messengers on the Day of Resurrection.

7. Obtaining reward by virtue of having intercourse lawfully.

8. Loving what the Prophet (PBUH) used to love, as he said, *"I have been made to love perfume and women from among (the pleasures of) your world."*[1]

9. Producing faithful offspring that can defend Islam and its people and lands and be cooperative in righteousness and piety.

---

[1] Narrated by An-Nasāʾī and others.

10. Enjoying the affection, love, and mercy which Allah puts between spouses. This is in addition to many other benefits of marriage some of which only Allah knows.

And, Allah knows best.

Q. No. (330): Who are the unmarriageable women?

A: Unmarriageable women are women whom man is not allowed to marry. These unmarriageable women are divided into two sections: (i) eternally prohibited women, and these are not allowed for man to marry at any time forever; and (What is the Islamic attitude toward) temporarily prohibited women, and these are not allowed for man to marry in special cases, so when these cases are over, he can get married to them.

The eternally prohibited women are the following:

-Women prohibited because of kinship. They are seven: mothers, daughters, sisters, paternal aunts, maternal aunts, brother's daughters, and sister's daughters.

-Women prohibited because of affinity. They are four: the wife of father (stepmother), the mother of wife (mother- in-law), the daughter of wife (stepdaughter),[1] the wife of son (daughter-in-law).

-Women prohibited because of foster relationship. The Prophet (PBUH) said, "Suckling (i.e., foster relationship) prohibits that which delivery prohibits."[2] This means that women who are prohibited because of kinship relationship are also prohibited because of foster relationship on the part of the suckled male.

The temporarily prohibited women are the following:

---

[1] But to be unmarriageable, the man in question must consummate the marriage with her mother. So, if he conducts marriage to her and does not consummate it, it is permissible for him to marry her daughter.

[2] Narrated by Al-Bukhārī and Muslim.

-**Two sisters** in wedlock at the same time.

-**A woman and her parental or maternal aunt** in wedlock at the same time.

-**A married woman,** or a woman during her *'Iddah* (waiting period) as to another man. A man is not allowed to marry a married woman except when she is taken captive, as ordained by Allah. Besides, it is lawful for a man to marry a woman who is married to a disbeliever and has embraced Islam, because her embracing Islam separates between her and her disbelieving husband.

-**A woman who has been divorced three times** is not lawful for her husband unless she marries another one validly (i.e., not through the *Muḥallil*[1] marriage).

-**A polytheist woman** is prohibited unless she confesses Islam. Yet, this rule has an exception, which is that a Muslim can marry a Christian or a Jewish woman.

- **A woman who commits *Zinā*** is prohibited unless she shows repentance. And, Allah knows best.

Q. No. (331): What are the invalid forms of marriage?

A: The following are the invalid forms of marriage:

1. **The *Shighār* marriage**

The *Shighār* marriage is that a man exchanges his daughter or sister for another man's daughter or sister on condition that no reciprocation of mahr (Islamic dowry) is required.

2.**The *Muḥallil* marriage**

---

[1] See the glossary of this book.

The *Muḥallil* marriage is that a man marries a woman who has been divorced three times after the end of her waiting period (*'Iddah*) then divorces her so that she can reunite with her first husband.

3. The *Mut'ah* (temporary) marriage

The *mut`ah* marriage or temporary marriage is a personal contract between a man and a woman to cohabit for a limited period of time at the end of which she becomes automatically divorced, in return for a certain remuneration payable by the man.

This form of marriage was once lawful during the lifetime of the Prophet (PBUH) then Allah abrogated that permission on the tongue of His Prophet (PBUH) to be permanently prohibited until the Day of Resurrection.

4. The *'Urfi* (informal) marriage

This form of marriage refers to the phenomenon that has widely spread among the Muslim youth. For example, a man would establish a relation with his female colleague and have intercourse with her secretly, while both of them base this abominable relation on a mere piece of paper which falsely authenticates their relation and perhaps, they seek the testimony of some immoral persons who themselves are of the same nature and may be involved in similar relations. In this alleged contract of marriage, there is no *Walīyy* (legal guardian), though the latter is one of the main conditions of valid marriage according to the majority of scholars, and once it is not met the marriage in question is not valid. There is also lack of the condition of marriage announcement.

And, Allah knows best.

Q. No. (332): What are the qualities desired in a spouse?

A: The answer to this question includes the qualities desired in a wife and those desired in a husband. Both will be listed as follows:

The qualities desired in a wife

1. To be religious.

2. To be, along with religiosity, of wealth, family status, and beauty.

3. To be kind and affectionate.

4. To be a virgin.

5. To be obedient and trustworthy.

6. To be fertile.

The qualities desired in a husband

1. To be religious.

2. To know at least some part of the Qur'ān.

3. To have the ability to get married in respect to intercourse as well as the expenses of marriage and that of living after it.

4. To be gentle with women.

5. To be attractive to his woman, so that she may not feel disgust for him.

6. To be potent, so that the wife can conceive and have children, and this is one of the major objectives of marriage.[1]

And, Allah knows best.

Q. No. (333): What is the *Shar'ī* ruling concerning looking at a would-be wife?

A: When a man intends to propose to a woman, it is lawful for him to look at her, and there is no difference among scholars concerning

---

[1] The qualities desired in each spouse have been derived from related texts in the Qur'ān and the Sunnah.

this point.[1] But they have differed concerning the extent to which a man is allowed to look at the woman he wants to marry.

What matters here is that the majority of scholars maintain that it is permissible to look at the face and the hands only.[2] However, the Ḥanbalīs say that it is permissible to look at what often appears of a woman like her neck, hands, and feet, whereas Al-Awzāʿī views that he can look at whatever he wants to see from her except her *ʿawrah*. Also, Ibn Hazm and Dāwūd are of the opinion that it is permissible for him to look at her whole body. Of course, the last opinion means that this is to be done while she is wearing her clothes, and not naked as some may presume. And, Allah knows best.

Q. No. (334): What are the *Sharʿī* regulations related to a would-be wife?

A: These regulations can be listed as follows:

1. He should not look at her in private, but he should do that in the presence of some of her female *Mahrams* or some her male *Mahrams*.

2. He should not look at her with lust.

3. He should be sure that she would likely accept his proposal of marriage, or else he is not allowed to look at her.

4. It is not permissible for him to shake hands with her or touch any part of her body.

5. It is better to look at her before proposing to her, if possible, because he may not like her if he does that after proposing to her, and this may harm one or both of them.

6. It is permissible for him to talk to her with consideration of the relevant *Sharʿī* limits, because her voice which is heard during her

---

[1] *Al-Mughnī*, 6/553.
[2] *Fatḥ al-Bārī*, 9/182.

"normal" talking is not part of her awrah according to the preponderant view in this connection.

7. He should not sit with her repeatedly, as some men would sit with their fiancées every day.

8. It is not permissible for him to go out with her without a mahram, for this may lead to dislikeable and disgraceful consequences. And, Allah knows best.

Q. No. (335): What is the *Shar'ī* ruling concerning proposing to an engaged woman?

A: When a man proposes to a woman to take her in marriage, it is not lawful for anyone else to propose to the same woman, because the Prophet (PBUH) said,

"And a man is not to propose to a (woman) engaged to his (Muslim) brother until he marries (her) or leaves (her)."[1]

This means that he must not propose to her as long as she is engaged to another man, then if the latter marries her the former will not have any access to her, and if the engagement is revoked, he can propose to her.

Anyone who acts against this *Shar'ī* rule is sinful and has committed an act of disobedience (*Ma'ṣiyah*) as agreed upon by scholars.

However, if a man marries a woman while she is engaged to another man, the marriage is valid though the husband is sinful, because "not proposing to an engaged woman" is not a condition of the validity of marriage. Therefore, if this forbidden act is committed, it does not invalidate the marriage itself.[2] And, Allah knows best.

Q. No. (336): What is the *Shar'ī* ruling concerning proposing to a woman during her *'Iddah* (waiting period)?

---

[1] Narrated by Al-Bukhārī and Muslim.
[2] *Fatḥ al-Bārī*, 9/200

A: A *mu'taddah*, that is, a woman having a waiting period, normally has one of three cases, as follows,

1. **To have a waiting period as a result of her husband's death**, and in this case, it is not permissible for any man to propose to her explicitly, yet he can express his desire to marry her indirectly. One of the forms of such indirect reference to betrothal is what Ibn 'Abbās, may Allah be pleased with him, said when commenting on the words, ... if you make a hint of betrothal... He said, "A man may say, 'I want to marry, and I wish I could easily find a righteous woman."[1]

2. **To have a waiting period because of revocable divorce**, i.e., after the first or the second divorce, and in this case, it is not permissible for a man at all to propose to her whether directly or indirectly, simply because she is still a wife. Even an indirect reference to betrothal in this case is a violation of her husbands' right to taking her back and a way of encouraging her to refuse the revocation of the divorce.

3. **To have a waiting period because of irrevocable divorce**, i.e., after the third divorce, and in this case, it is not permissible for a man to propose to her directly. Yet, scholars have differed concerning the question whether a man can make an indirect reference to betrothal or not: some say this is permissible and some maintain otherwise. The first view may be more evident, and Allah knows best.

Q. No. (337): What are the pillars of marriage contract?

A: Simply, there are two pillars of marriage contract: proposal and acceptance. And, Allah knows best.

Q. No. (338): What are the conditions of the validity of marriage contract?

---

[1] Narrated by Al-Bukhārī and At-Tabari.

A: They are as follows:

1. **The permission of *Walīyy* (legal guardian)**

A woman's *Walīyy* is basically her father, or her brother, or her grandfather, or her parental uncle, or her paternal cousin.

2.**The acceptance of woman before contracting the marriage**

This means that if a woman is coerced to get married and the marriage is contracted while she does not accept it, the contract is to be revoked.

3. ***Ṣadaqah* (Islamic Dowry)**[1]

It is also called "*mahr*," and it is one of the conditions of the validity of marriage. The Mālikīs maintain that even if the spouses agree that there is no *mahr* the marriage will be invalid.

4. **Witnesses**

Most scholars maintain that witnesses are one of the conditions of marriage validity. And, Allah knows best.

Q. No. (339): What is the *Shar'ī* ruling concerning conditioning in marriage contract?

A: Conditioning in marriage contract can be divided into three sections:

---

[1] The word "Islamic" is attached here to the word "dowry" so that it may not be confusing as the word "dowry" - as well as the word "dower" is normally used by English-speaking people to mean "Money or property brought by a bride to her husband at marriage," while in Islam *Ṣadaq* is paid-by a husband to his bride. That is why either the word "mahr" or the word "*Ṣadaq*" will be used to refer to this "Islamic dowry".

1. **Conditions that must be fulfilled**, and these include, for example, the woman's conditioning that her husband must live with her honourably[1] or release her with kindness[2].

2. **Conditions that are not to be fulfilled**, such as a woman's conditioning that her co-wife must be divorced, because the Prophet (PBUH) said, as narrated on the authority of Abū Hurayrah, may Allah be pleased with him,

"It is not lawful for a woman (at the time of wedding) to ask for the divorce of her sister (i.e., the other wife of her would-be husband) in order to have everything for herself, for she will take only what has been written for her."[3]

Another similar condition is that a woman stipulates that her husband must not have intercourse with her. It is not obligatory to fulfil such conditions, as agreed upon by scholars.

Attached to this kind of conditioning is any stipulation that is in contradiction with the Qur'ān or the Sunnah, for the Prophet (PBUH) said,

"Whoever imposes conditions which are not in Allah's Book (Laws), his conditions will be invalid even if he should impose them a hundred times."[4]

3. **Conditions that are between this and that**, such as a woman's conditioning that her husband must not marry any other woman as long as she is his wife, or that he must not make her depart from his country, and the like. Scholars have differed concerning the permissibility of such conditions, but the preponderant view is that it is not permissible for a woman to impose such conditions, but her husband is to fulfil her conditions as long as they do not contradict

---

[1] See the Qur'ān: 4:19

[2] See the Qur'ān: 2: 229.

[3] Narrated by Al-Bukhārī and Muslim.

[4] Narrated by Al-Bukhārī and Muslim

the Qurʾān or the *Sunnah*. The Prophet (PBUH) said, "The conditions which are the worthiest in terms of fulfilment are those according to which you have been given legal access to women (through marriage).[1] And, Allah knows best.

Q. No. (340): Is there any limit of *Ṣadaq*?

A: Generally speaking, there is neither maximum nor minimum of the limit of *mahr*.

Scholars have agreed to the effect that there is no maximum limit of mahr, because there is no *Sharʿī* proof that specifies any such maximum limit of it. On the other hand, according to the most evident view, there is no minimum limit of mahr, as it is permissible to pay anything that has a material or immaterial value as mahr. And, Allah knows best.

Q. No. (341): What does confirm a woman's right to the whole *Ṣadaq*?

A: A woman has a full right to her whole *Ṣadaq* if any of the following take place,

1. If actual consummation of marriage takes place, the wife deserves the whole *Ṣadaq*. By "actual" we mean that once the husband consummates the marriage with his wife and "has intercourse with her," she deserves her whole *Ṣadaq* because the husband will have already obtained his own right by this actual consummation.

2. If one of the spouses dies before consummating the marriage, which is a valid one, the wife deserves the whole. *Ṣadaq*, as unanimously agreed upon by scholars,[2] as long as the *Ṣadaq* was appointed in the marriage contract, for the contract is not cancelled because of death.

---

[1] Narrated by Al-Bukhārī and Muslim.
[2] Bidāyat al-Mujtahid, 2/22.

3. If a correct *khalwah* (privacy) takes place between the spouses after contracting the marriage yet before consummating it, the woman deserves the whole *Ṣadaq*. "Correct *khalwah*" means that the husband and his wife live together after contracting a valid marriage in a place where they can. - sexually enjoy each other completely without fearing that anyone should enter as they do that, and on condition that neither of them has any natural, sensual, or legal impediment that prevents the undertaking of such enjoyment.[1]

However, some scholars, including Ibn ʿAbbās, maintain that she deserves only half of the *Ṣadaq* if the marriage is not consummated irrespective of the happening of such *khalwah.*

4. If the husband divorces his wife during his death illness to deprive her of inheritance before consummating the marriage, the woman deserves the whole *Ṣadaq*. This is according to the Ḥanbalīs.[2]

5. If a woman stays for a year at her husband's house before consummating the marriage and without having intercourse with her, she deserves the whole *Ṣadaq*. This is according to the Mālikīs, unlike the view of the majority of scholars.[3] And, Allah knows best.

Q. No. (342): What does confirm a woman's right to half of the *Ṣadaq*?

A: The wife has the right to get half of her *Ṣadaq* if she is divorced before consummation of the marriage and the *Ṣadaq* has been appointed in the marriage contract. Almighty Allah says,

﴿وَإِن طَلَّقْتُمُوهُنَّ مِن قَبْلِ أَن تَمَسُّوهُنَّ وَقَدْ فَرَضْتُمْ لَهُنَّ فَرِيضَةً فَنِصْفُ مَا فَرَضْتُمْ ﴿٢٣٧﴾﴾

---

[1] Ibn ʿĀbidīn, Radd al-Muḥtār, 2/338
[2] *Al-Mughnī*, 1/157.
[3] *Al-Fiqh al-Islāmī wa Adillatuh*, 7/292.

"And if you divorce them before you have touched (had a sexual relation with) them, and you have appointed unto them the Mahr, then pay half of that (Mahr)." [TMQ: 2: 237]

And Allah knows best.

Q. No. (343): What is the *Shar'ī* ruling concerning proclamation of marriage and how should marriage be proclaimed?

A: Proclamation of marriage is to publicize it and let people know that such and such a man has taken such and such a woman in marriage.

This proclamation of marriage is desirable according to the majority of scholars. However, Az-Zuhrī maintains that it is obligatory, and if a man marries a woman in secret, makes two men witness it, and orders them to keep this secret, the spouses must be separated.[1]

Marriage is proclaimed by women's beating *duff* (tambourines) and singing permissible songs. Such singing - on such an occasion is lawful as long as it is free from abominable and immoral things such as saying immoral words by immoral women or men, and as long as there are no musical instruments other than duff.

And, Allah knows best.

Q. No. (344): What are the abominable acts related to weddings?

A: These acts are:

1. The bride's visiting the hairdressers.

2. Women's seeing the awrah of the bride.

3. Persisting in celebrating weddings at hotels where abominable acts are committed.

[1] *Al-Mawṣū'ah al-Fiqhiyyah*, 5/262, Kuwait.

4. The bride's showing her adornment in public.

5. The newlyweds sitting together amongst strange men and women.

6. Some women may dance during the celebration.

7. Recording wedding parties through photographing and video-taping.

8. Exaggeration in the wedding banquet.

9. The newlyweds' neglecting prayer on their wedding day. And, Allah knows best.

Q. No. (345): What are the proprieties of wedding night?

A: The following are some of the proprieties that are to be considered at wedding night:

1. The bridegroom is recommended to greet his bride because this is apt to remove worry from her heart.

2. The husband is recommended to present to his bride some drink or sweet as an initiation of his kind treatment to her.

3. He is recommended to place his hand on her head and pray for her asking Allah to grant them blessing, as derived from the *Sunnah* of the Prophet (PBUH).[1]

4. He is recommended to perform two *Rakʿahs* along with his bride.

5. It is desirable that he purifies his mouth with *Siwāk* before entering upon her.

6. He is to recite *tasmiyyah*[2] and invoke Allah upon starting to copulate with her.

---

[1] Narrated by Abū Dāwūd and others.
[2] Tasmiyah is to say, "Bismillah (In the Name of Allah)".

And, Allah knows best.

Q. No. (346): What are the husband's rights upon his wife?

A: The husband's rights upon his wife can be pinpointed as follows:

1. To obey him.

2. To stay in the house (in principle) and not to leave it except with his permission.

3. To obey him when he calls her to bed.

4. Not to allow anyone to enter his house except with his permission.

5. Not to observe any voluntary fasting while he is present (i.e., not traveling) except with his permission.

6. Not to spend from his property except with his permission.

7. To serve him and his children.

8. To guard him as regards her honour, his children, and his property.

9. To be grateful to him and live with him honourably.

10. To adorn and beautify herself for him.

11. Not to remind him if she spends upon him and his children, as such reminding of favours is dispraised in Islam.

12. To be pleased with what he can afford and not to overburden him with what he cannot fulfil.

13. Not to do what may harm or annoy him.

14. To treat his parents and relatives kindly.

15. To be keen on living with him and not to ask for divorce except for a *Shar'ī* reason.

16. To mourn for him when he dies for four months and ten days, and this is also her *'Iddah* as a widow. And, Allah knows best.

Q. No. (347): What are the wife's rights upon her husband?

A: In answering this question, we may concentrate on certain rights as well as certain aspects of the comprehensive right of "living with one's wife honourably," as this right covers many aspects which can be regarded as independent rights. These rights or aspects can be pinpointed as follows:

1. To pay her *Ṣadaq*.

2. To support her financially.

3. To treat her honourably and kindly, and this includes that he should not harm her or delay her rights though he is able to fulfil them without hesitation.

4. To play with her and consider her stage of lifetime as the Prophet (PBUH) - the best example for all husbands - used to do with his wives.

5. To chat with her, as the Prophet (PBUH) would speak and listen to his wives.

6. To teach her religion and encourage her to obey Allah.

7. To overlook some of her mistakes unless this contradicts Islamic laws.

8. Not to harm her by slapping her face or finding fault with her.

9. If he should refuse to share the bed with her, he can do that only in the house.

10. To help her be modest concerning their private relation, that is, the husband should respond positively to his wife's desire when she needs him sexually in order to help her be modest and never think of any other illegal alterative.

And, Allah knows best.

Q. No. (348): What is the wisdom behind the legislation of polygamy?

A: The wisdom behind the legislation of polygamy represents - at the same time - the *Shar'ī* reasons that justify and permit polygamy. These matters or reasons of polygamy are known by all reasonable people. They include the following,

1. A man may be keen on increasing his progeny yet his "one" woman's menstruation, illness, postnatal bleeding, and other such hindrances may prevent him from achieving his goal as he wishes.

2. Men are in most cases - less than women in number and are prone to causes of death more than women are in many fields of life. If all men were to marry only one woman each, so many women would remain unmarried, and that might in turn lead them to immorality and *Zinā*.

This may be observed clearly in countries where wars are waged every now and then.

We may also remind our readers in passing this of the Prophet's words concerning the portents of the Hour:

"And women will increase in number, so much so that fifty women will be looked after by one man."[1] Yet this does not mean that one man will marry fifty women all together.

3. "All" women may be ready to get married yet "a few" men are ready to meet the requirements of marriage especially those related to financing.

4. A man may have a sexual ungovernable nature to the extent that he will not be satisfied by one woman only, so he is allowed to gratify

---

[1] Narrated by Al-Bukhārī and Muslim

such abnormally strong lust legally by marrying more than one woman.

5. A man may marry - in addition to his wife - a female relative of his if her husband dies or divorces her and she has no one to support her except a married man.

Yet still, some people may misapply this allowance to the extent that many wrongly consider it - i.e., marrying a woman for the pinpointed purpose - a kind of meanness and ingratitude. And, Allah knows best.

Q. No. (349): What is the Islamic attitude toward physical desires in general?

A: Almighty Allah created man as His vicegerent on earth in order that he might populate and rule it. Obviously, this purpose cannot be realized unless the human species perpetuates itself, living, thriving, cultivating, manufacturing, building, and worshiping its Creator. Accordingly, the Creator has placed certain appetites and drives in man so that he is impelled toward various activities which guarantee the survival of the species.

Among the appetites which an individual must satisfy for his personal survival is that of food and drink. The sexual appetite, however, is for the purpose of the survival of species. Thus, sex is a satisfaction and fulfilment. Human beings have responded to the demands of the sexual appetite in three different ways:

One way is to satisfy one's sexual need freely with whomever is available and whenever one pleases, without any restraints of religion, morality, or custom. This is the position of the advocates of free sex, for they do not believe in any religion. This philosophy reduces the human being to the status of an animal, and, if practiced universally, would result in the destruction of the family structure and society.

The second approach is to suppress, and try to annihilate, the sexual drive. This approach is advocated by certain worldly philosophies which lead toward monasticism and an escape from the world. Such advocacy of suppression of a natural appetite, or rather annihilation of its functioning, is contrary to Allah's plan and purpose, and is in conflict with the course of the natural order which requires the use of this appetite for the continuity of life.

The third approach is to regulate the satisfaction of this urge, allowing it to operate within certain limits, neither suppressing it nor giving it free rein. This is the stand of the revealed religions, which have instituted marriage and prohibited fornication and adultery. In particular, Islam duly recognizes the role of the sexual drive, facilitates its satisfaction through lawful marriage, and just as it strictly prohibits sex outside marriage and even what is conducive to it, it also prohibits celibacy and the shunning of women. This is the just and intermediate position. And, Allah knows best.

Q. No. (350): Is sexual perversion a major sin?

A: First of all, we must understand that in regulating the sexual drive Islam has prohibited not only illicit sexual relations and all ways which lead to them, but also the sexual deviation known as homosexuality. This perverted act is a reversal of the natural order, a corruption of man's sexuality, and a crime against the rights of females.

The spread of this depraved practice in a society disrupts its natural life pattern and makes those who practice it slaves to their lust, depriving them of decent taste, decent morals, and decent manner of living. The story of the people of Prophet Lūṭ (Lot) as narrated in the Qur'ān should be sufficient for us. Lūṭ's people were addicted to this shameless depravity, abandoning natural, pure, and lawful relations with women in the pursuit of an unnatural, foul, and illicit practice. That is why their Prophet, Lūṭ, peace be upon him, said to them,

﴿أَتَأۡتُونَ ٱلذُّكۡرَانَ مِنَ ٱلۡعَٰلَمِينَ ١٦٥ وَتَذَرُونَ مَا خَلَقَ لَكُمۡ رَبُّكُم مِّنۡ أَزۡوَٰجِكُمۚ
بَلۡ أَنتُمۡ قَوۡمٌ عَادُونَ ١٦٦﴾

"What! Of all creatures, do you approach males and leave the spouses whom your Lord has created for you? Indeed, you are people transgressing (all limits)!" [TMQ: 26: 165-166]

Any such abominable act is prohibited in Islam. And, Allah knows best.

Q. No. (351): What is the *Shar'ī* ruling concerning masturbation?

A: The pressing need to relieve himself of sexual tension may drive a young man to masturbation.

The majority of scholars consider it prohibited. Imām Mālik bases his judgment on the following verse,

﴿وَٱلَّذِينَ هُمۡ لِفُرُوجِهِمۡ حَٰفِظُونَ ٥ إِلَّا عَلَىٰٓ أَزۡوَٰجِهِمۡ أَوۡ مَا مَلَكَتۡ أَيۡمَٰنُهُمۡ فَإِنَّهُمۡ
غَيۡرُ مَلُومِينَ ٦ فَمَنِ ٱبۡتَغَىٰ وَرَآءَ ذَٰلِكَ فَأُوْلَٰٓئِكَ هُمُ ٱلۡعَادُونَ ٧﴾

"Those who guard their sexual organs except with their spouses or those whom their right hands possess, for (with regard to them) they are without blame. But those who crave something beyond that are transgressors."

[TMQ: 23:5-7]

He argues that a masturbator is one of those who "crave something beyond that".

On the other hand, it has been reported that Imām Aḥmad Ibn Hanbal regards semen as an excretion of the body like other excreta and permits its expulsion as bloodletting is permitted. Ibn Hazm holds the same view. However, the Ḥanbalīs permit masturbation only under two conditions: first, the fear of committing fornication or adultery, and second, not having the means to marry.

We may draw the attention of our readers to the idea that even if some scholars permit masturbation, this in addition to the conditions pinpointed above - must not become excessive or a habit, for in both cases it becomes harmful, and no harming is permitted in Islam neither to oneself nor to others.

Finally, we may also remind our readers of the Prophet's words,

"O young people! Whoever among you is able (to marry) should marry, and whoever is not able (to marry) is (recommended) to fast, as fasting diminishes his sexual power (positively)."[1]

This is better than indulging into such means as masturbation. And, Allah knows best.

Q. No. (352): What is the *Shar'ī* ruling concerning monasticism?

A: Just as Islam is against fornication and adultery and blocks all ways leading to them, it is also against suppressing the sexual urge. Accordingly, it calls people toward marriage, prohibiting *tabattul* or renunciation, which means remaining celibate and renouncing worldly activity for the sake of worship.

As long as he possesses the means to marry, the Muslim is not permitted to refrain from marriage on the grounds that he has dedicated himself to the service or worship of Allah and to a life of monasticism and renunciation of the world.

The Prophet (PBUH) noted a tendency toward monasticism among some of his Companions. Declaring this to be a deviation from the straight path of Islam and a rejection of his *Sunnah* (recommended practice), he thereby rid Islam's conceptual framework of such a Christian notion. It has been narrated that Abū Qulābah said,

"Some of the Companions of the Prophet (PBUH) decided to relinquish the world, forsake their wives, and become like monks.

---

[1] Narrated by Al-Bukhārī and Muslim.

The Prophet (PBUH) said to them with asperity, 'The people before you perished because of their asceticism; they made excessive demands on themselves until Allah brought hardships on them: you can still see a few of them remaining in monasteries and temples. Then worship Allah and do not associate anything with Him, perform *Ḥajj* and *'Umrah*, be righteous, and all affairs will be set right for you"

Abū Qulābah said that the following verse was revealed. concerning them,

﴿يَـٰٓأَيُّهَا ٱلَّذِينَ ءَامَنُوا۟ لَا تُحَرِّمُوا۟ طَيِّبَـٰتِ مَآ أَحَلَّ ٱللَّهُ لَكُمْ وَلَا تَعْتَدُوٓا۟ ۚ إِنَّ ٱللَّهَ لَا يُحِبُّ ٱلْمُعْتَدِينَ ٨٧﴾

"O you who believe! Make not unlawful the Ṭayyibāt (all that is good as regards foods, things, deeds, beliefs, persons, etc.) which Allah has made lawful to you, and transgress not. Verily, Allah does not like transgressors." [TMQ: 5:87]

Therefore, there is no monasticism in Islam. And, Allah knows best.

Q. No. (353): Why is it prohibited for a Muslim woman to marry a non-Muslim man, including Christian and Jewish men, while a Muslim man is permitted to marry a Christian or Jewish woman?

A: It is prohibited for a Muslim woman to marry a non- Muslim man, regardless of whether he is of the People of the Scripture (Jews and Christians) or not. Almighty Allah says,

﴿وَلَا تَنكِحُوا۟ ٱلْمُشْرِكَـٰتِ حَتَّىٰ يُؤْمِنَّ ۚ وَلَأَمَةٌ مُّؤْمِنَةٌ خَيْرٌ مِّن مُّشْرِكَةٍ وَلَوْ أَعْجَبَتْكُمْ ۗ وَلَا تُنكِحُوا۟ ٱلْمُشْرِكِينَ حَتَّىٰ يُؤْمِنُوا۟ ۚ وَلَعَبْدٌ مُّؤْمِنٌ خَيْرٌ مِّن مُّشْرِكٍ وَلَوْ أَعْجَبَكُمْ ۗ أُو۟لَـٰٓئِكَ يَدْعُونَ إِلَى ٱلنَّارِ ۖ وَٱللَّهُ يَدْعُوٓا۟ إِلَى ٱلْجَنَّةِ وَٱلْمَغْفِرَةِ بِإِذْنِهِۦ ٢٢١﴾

"And give not (your daughters) in marriage to Al-Mushrikūn till they believe (in Allah Alone) and verily, a believing slave is better than a (free) Mushrik

(idolater, etc.), even though he pleases you. Those (Al-Mushrikūn) invite you to the Fire, but Allah invites (you) to Paradise and Forgiveness by His Leave". [TMQ: 2:221]

Allah also says concerning the emigrant Muslim women,

﴿فَإِنۡ عَلِمۡتُمُوهُنَّ مُؤۡمِنَٰتٖ فَلَا تَرۡجِعُوهُنَّ إِلَى ٱلۡكُفَّارِۖ لَا هُنَّ حِلّٞ لَّهُمۡ وَلَا هُمۡ يَحِلُّونَ لَهُنَّۖ ١٠﴾

"Then if you ascertain that they are true believers, send them not back to the disbelievers, they are not lawful (wives) for the disbelievers nor disbelievers lawful (husbands) for them...} are them." [TMQ: 60:10]

Thus, while a Muslim man is permitted to marry a Christian or Jewish woman, a Muslim woman is not allowed to marry a Christian or Jewish man. There are many sound reasons for this difference. First, the man is the head of the household, the one who maintains the family, and he is responsible for his wife. And while Islam guarantees freedom of belief and practice to the Christian or Jewish wife of a Muslim, safeguarding her rights according to her own faith, other religions, such as Judaism and Christianity, do not guarantee the wife of a different faith freedom of belief and practice, nor do they safeguard her rights. Being so, how can Islam take chances on the future of Muslim women by giving them into the hands of people who neither honour their religion nor are they concerned to protect their rights?

A marriage between a man and a woman of different faiths can be based only on the husband's respect for his wife's beliefs; otherwise, a good relationship can never develop. Now, the Muslim believes that both Judaism and Christianity "originated in divine revelation," although later distortions were introduced into them. Accordingly, the Christian or Jewish wife of a Muslim lives under the protection of a man who respects the "basic" tenets of her faith, her scripture, and her prophets, while in contrast to this a Jew or Christian man does not recognize the divine origin of Islam, or its Book, or its Prophet (PBUH). How then could a Muslim woman live with such a man, while her religion requires of her the observance of certain worships, duties, and obligations, as well as refraining from certain things? It would be impossible for a Muslim woman to retain her respect for her beliefs as well as to practice her religion properly if she were opposed in this regard by the master of the house at every step. It is obviously impossible that two such people can live together in harmony and love. And, Allah knows best.

Q. No. (354): Why was the Prophet (PBUH) permitted to marry more than four wives?

A: The case of the Prophet (PBUH), who had nine wives, was exempted from the prohibition of marrying more than four wives by Allah for the sake of the propagation of the message of Islam during his lifetime and because of the need of the Muslim Ummah after his death. And, Allah knows best.

Q. No. (355): Why is it that justice among wives is a condition?

A: The main condition which Islam lays down for permitting a man to have more than one wife is confidence on his part that he will be able to deal justly and equitably with his two or more wives regarding food, drink, housing, clothing, and expenses, as well as in the division of his time between them. Anyone who lacks the assurance that he will be able to fulfil all these obligations with justice and equity is prohibited by Almighty Allah from marrying more than one woman. Almighty Allah says in this regard,

﴿وَإِنْ خِفْتُمْ أَلَّا تُقْسِطُوا۟ فِى ٱلْيَتَٰمَىٰ فَٱنكِحُوا۟ مَا طَابَ لَكُم مِّنَ ٱلنِّسَآءِ مَثْنَىٰ
وَثُلَٰثَ وَرُبَٰعَ ۖ فَإِنْ خِفْتُمْ أَلَّا تَعْدِلُوا۟ فَوَٰحِدَةً أَوْ مَا مَلَكَتْ أَيْمَٰنُكُمْ ۚ ذَٰلِكَ أَدْنَىٰٓ أَلَّا
تَعُولُوا۟ ﴿٣﴾﴾

"And if you fear that you shall not be able to deal justly with the orphan-girls, then marry (other) women of your choice, two or three, or four but if you fear that you shall not be able to deal justly (with them), then only one or (the captives and the slaves) that your right hands possess. That is nearer to prevent you from doing injustice." [TMQ: 4:3]

Also, the Prophet (PBUH) said,

"Anyone who has two wives and does not treat them equally will come on the Day of Resurrection dragging one part of his body which will be hanging down."[1]

The equal treatment mentioned here pertains to the rights of the co-wives, not to the love their husband feels toward them, for equality in the division of love is beyond human capacity and any imbalance in this regard is forgiven by Almighty Allah, who says,

﴿وَلَن تَسْتَطِيعُوٓا۟ أَن تَعْدِلُوا۟ بَيْنَ ٱلنِّسَآءِ وَلَوْ حَرَصْتُمْ ۖ فَلَا تَمِيلُوا۟ كُلَّ ٱلْمَيْلِ فَتَذَرُوهَا كَٱلْمُعَلَّقَةِ ١٢٩﴾

"You will never be able to do perfect justice between wives even if it is your ardent desire, so do not incline too much to one of them (by giving her more of your time and provision) so as to leave the other hanging (i.e., neither divorced nor married)". [TMQ: 4:129]

That is why the Prophet (PBUH) used to divide his time among his wives equally, and he said,

"O Allah, this is my division in regard to what I can control. Then (please) do not hold me accountable regarding what You control, and I do not control."[2]

referring to the attachment and affection which he felt for one particular wife. And, Allah knows best.

---

[1] Narrated by Ibn Hibban and others.
[2] Narrated by An-Nasāʾī and others.

Q. No. (356): Is it permissible for a man to marry his daughter who has come as a result of *Zinā* between him and her mother?

A: According to the majority of scholars, it is not permissible for a man to marry his daughter who has come as a result of his committing *Zinā* with her mother. This is simply because even such a daughter is included in the general meaning of the following verse, *forbidden to you (for marriage) are: your mothers, your daughters...* to the end of the verse. [TMQ: 4:23]

Not only this, scholars have differed as to the *Sharʿī* ruling concerning a man who has already married his *Zinā* - produced daughter: should he be killed or not? According to Aḥmad, he is to be executed.

Another ruling which is attached to this one is that a man is prohibited to marry his *Zinā*-produced sister, son's daughter, daughter's daughter, brother's daughter, and sister's daughter.

And, Allah knows best.

Q. No. (357): If a man conducts his marriage to a woman yet has not consummated the marriage yet, can his son marry her after him?

A: Scholars have unanimously agreed that in this case it is prohibited for the son of this man to marry this woman even though his father did not consummate his marriage with her, and that this prohibition is forever. If, however, a son marries a woman who was once married to his father, he is to be killed, and his property is to be taken from him. It has been narrated that *Al-Barāʾ*, may Allah be pleased with him, said that once he met his uncle and asked him where he was going. The man said, "The Messenger of Allah (PBUH) has sent me to a man who has married the wife of his father after him, to behead him and take his property.[1] And, Allah knows best.

---

[1] Narrated by Abū Dāwūd and others.

Q. No. (358): Does the prohibition of marriage because of foster relationship extend to the relatives of the male in question?

A: If a male is prohibited to marry any of certain females because of foster relationship, such as the woman who suckled him, her daughters, sisters, etc., this prohibition has nothing to do with this male's relatives. Accordingly, his foster sister, for example, is not a sister as to his brother. The general rule that governs this matter is that: those who suckle from one and the same breast are brothers (or sisters). This means that the brother of a person who suckled from a certain woman is not her son because he did not suckle from her as his brother did. This in turn means that the brother of the person who suckled can marry the daughter of this woman because she is marriageable to him even if she is unmarriageable to his brother. Important still, the term "relatives" here does not include the descendants of the person who suckles, as his son, for example, would not marry his (i.e., this person's) foster sister because she is a foster paternal aunt as to this son, and so on. And, Allah knows best.

Q. No. (359): Does it make any difference - as regards the prohibition of marriage - if a male suckles the breast- milk of a woman through a cup for example?

A: The prohibition of marriage which comes as a result of breast-milk suckling is the same whether the milk is suckled directly from a woman's breast or is milked in a cup, for example, then drunk. This is according to the view adopted by the majority of scholars. And, Allah knows best.

Q. No. (360): If a man married a woman, then another woman claimed that she suckled both of them, what is the *Shar'ī* ruling concerning this?

A: In this case the man and his wife must be separated as long as the woman who has stated that she suckled them is an upright Muslim woman and there is a probability that this suckling was possible.[1] It has been narrated that 'Uqbah Ibnul- Harith said that a black woman came and claimed that she had suckled both Uqbah and his wife. So, he mentioned that to the Prophet who turned his face from him and smiled and said, *"How (can you keep your wife) and it was said (that both of you were suckled by the same woman)?"*[2]

And, Allah knows best.

Q. No. (361): What is the *Shar'ī* ruling if a disbelieving man becomes a Muslim while being married to two sisters?

A: In this case he must divorce one of them, yet he can choose which of the two is to be divorced. It has been narrated that a man told the Prophet (PBUH) that he professed Islam while having two sisters in wedlock, and the Prophet (PBUH) said to him, "Choose which of them you wish (to keep in wedlock),"[3] meaning "and divorce the other one". And, Allah knows best.

Q. No. (362): If a man is to marry a woman who has been divorced three times and it is stipulated (by someone, like her first husband for example) that this man must marry her in the way of *Muḥallil* marriage, i.e., to marry her then divorce her especially for making her lawful again for her first husband, but this man marries her intending that this marriage is not a *Muḥallil* marriage, is this marriage valid?

A: If the man in question marries the woman in question because he really wants to marry her and thus conducts this marriage with this intention and not that of *Muḥallil* marriage, the marriage is valid because there is no intention of *tahlīl* (i.e., making her lawful for her

---

[1] This is because a woman who is twenty years old for example may claim that she suckled a man and a woman when they were two years old while these two are now in the same age of the woman in question.

[2] Narrated by Al-Bukhārī and others.

[3] Narrated by At-Tirmidhī and others.

ex-husband) and because the intention here is like any intention of lawful marriage.[1] And, Allah knows best.

Q. No. (363): What is the *Shar'ī* ruling concerning a man who marries a woman while intending to divorce her after a certain period of time?

A: This is done by many of those who travel abroad as it much happens that a man marries a woman belonging to the country to which he has travelled for the sake of having the right to stay in this country intending to divorce her when he is to go back to his homeland. Scholars say that this marriage is valid if he does not specify a certain period of time after which he will divorce her, because this man may intend something and does not do it or do something without intending it and in this case the action becomes disconnected with the intention.

Al-Awza'i however asserts that this marriage is a form of mut ah (temporary) marriage and is thus forbidden.

Al-Awza'i's view may be more evident especially with the fact that such a form of marriage involves much deceit and cheat and is not based on a real desire of conducting marriage which is prescribed and permitted in Islam. And, Allah knows best.

Q. No. (364): If a dissolute man proposes to a woman, is it permissible for a righteous man to propose to the same woman?

A: According to the most evident view in this regard, it is permissible for a righteous man to propose to this woman if she is righteous and religious, because much evil is expected to afflict her if she is left to marry such a dissolute man.[2] And, Allah knows best.

Q. No. (365): What is the *Shar'ī* ruling concerning a man who marries a woman during her *'Iddah* after the death of her husband?

---

[1] See Ibn Qudamam, *Al-Mughnī*, 6/648.
[2] See *Fatḥ al-Bārī*, 9/200.

A: They must be separated, and she is to complete her *ʿIddah* related to her first husband then spend another *ʿIddah* related to her second marriage if the second husband consummated the marriage with her, and she can receive her mahr if she is ignorant of the ruling of her marrying during her *ʿIddah*. If, however she married the second man while knowing that she was not allowed to do so, the ruler (and the judge) can either give her the mahr or deposit it in the public treasury as a kind of *Taʿzīr* (discretionary punishment) for what she did. And, Allah knows best.

Q. No. (366): Is it permissible for the second husband - in the previous question - to marry this woman after the two 'iddahs are finished?

A: It has been narrated in this regard that 'ʿUmar Ibn al-Khaṭṭāb, may Allah be pleased with him, prevents such marriage while ʿAlī Ibn Abū Talib, may Allah be pleased with him, says that it is permissible.[1] And, Allah knows best.

Q. No. (367): Is it permissible for a father to present his daughter to a righteous man to marry her?

A: This is permissible, and that was what the righteous man did with Prophet Musa (Moses), peace be upon him, when he said to him,

﴿قَالَ إِنِّيٓ أُرِيدُ أَنۡ أُنكِحَكَ إِحۡدَى ٱبۡنَتَيَّ هَٰتَيۡنِ عَلَىٰٓ أَن تَأۡجُرَنِي ثَمَٰنِيَ حِجَجٖۖ فَإِنۡ أَتۡمَمۡتَ عَشۡرٗا فَمِنۡ عِندِكَۖ ٢٧﴾

"I intend to wed one of these two daughters of mine to you, on condition that you serve me for eight years." [TMQ: 28: 27]

Also, it has been narrated on the authority of Ibn ʿUmar that ʿUmar Ibn al-Khaṭṭāb presented his daughter Hafsah to 'Uthman Ibn Affan

---

[1] Jamiu Ahkamin- Nisa', 3/229.

then to Abū Bakr, then the Prophet (PBUH) married her.[1] And, Allah knows best.

Q. No. (368): Is it permissible for a man to mediate for proposing to or marrying some woman?

A: It is permissible for the Muslim to do so. It has been narrated that the Prophet (PBUH) interceded for Mughīth with Barīrah to marry him. She said, "O Messenger of Allah! Are you commanding me (to do so)?" He (PBUH) replied, "I am only interceding for him." She said, "I have no need in him (as a husband)."[2] This Ḥadīth may also indicate that whoever is to intercede or mediate so that a man can marry a certain woman should not practice any form of pressure upon the woman in question. And, Allah knows best.

Q. No. (369): Does the *Walīyy* of a woman have any right to her *Ṣadaq*?

A: *Ṣadaq* is the right of a wife and not of her *Walīyy*. Almighty Allah says,

﴿وَءَاتُوا۟ ٱلنِّسَآءَ صَدُقَـٰتِهِنَّ نِحْلَةً ۚ ﴿٤﴾﴾

"And give to the women (whom you marry) their Mahr with a good heart." [TMQ: 4:4]

Allah also says,

﴿فَمَا ٱسْتَمْتَعْتُم بِهِۦ مِنْهُنَّ فَـَٔاتُوهُنَّ أُجُورَهُنَّ فَرِيضَةً ۚ ﴿٢٤﴾﴾

"So, with those of whom you have enjoyed sexual relations, give them their Mahr as prescribed." [TMQ: 4: 24]

There are other verses which indicate that a woman's *Ṣadaq* is her right and so it is not lawful for her father or any other one to take any part of this *Ṣadaq* without her permission. Unfortunately, a

---

[1] Narrated by Al-Bukhārī.
[2] Narrated by Al-Bukhārī

father would take the whole *Ṣadaq* of his daughter as if he was selling her and the *Ṣadaq* was the price. And, Allah knows best.

Q. No. (370): What is the *Shar'ī* ruling concerning the gifts and presents that a suitor gives to his fiancée if he wants to cancel his engagement to her?

A: If he gave her anything as mahr, she must give it back to him if the engagement is to be cancelled. This is because mahr is paid in return for his enjoying her through marriage, and this has not happened, so the mahr must be paid back. This is the view adopted by the majority of scholars.[1]

If the suitor gave his fiancé something as a gift or a present and now "she" wants to cancel the enjoyment, she must give him his gift or present back. This is because it is not fair that the suitor should suffer two forms of pain: the pain of cancelling his engagement and the pain of losing the value of his gift. On the other hand, if it is the man who wants to cancel the engagement, he has no right to get the gift back, also because it is not fair that the woman should suffer both the pain of cancelling her engagement and that of losing the gift in question. This is the fairest view in this regard.[2] And, Allah knows best.

Q. No. (371): What is the *Shar'ī* ruling concerning the house furniture and other such things that the bridegroom and his bride normally need to start a new marital life?

A: The husband is legally responsible for preparing the place in which he and his wife will live, and this is to be done in accordance with his capacity. Almighty Allah says,

﴿أَسْكِنُوهُنَّ مِنْ حَيْثُ سَكَنتُم مِّن وُجْدِكُمْ ۝٦﴾

---

[1] Bidāyat al-Mujtahid, 2/21.
[2] See Al-Ikhtiyārāt, 128.

"Lodge them where you dwell, according to your means."

[TMQ: 65:6]

﴿وَعَلَى ٱلْمَوْلُودِ لَهُۥ رِزْقُهُنَّ وَكِسْوَتُهُنَّ بِٱلْمَعْرُوفِ ۚ لَا تُكَلَّفُ نَفْسٌ إِلَّا وُسْعَهَا ۚ ﴿٢٣٣﴾﴾

"But the father of the child shall bear the cost of the mother's food and clothing on a reasonable basis. No person shall have a burden laid on him greater than he can bear" [TMQ: 2:233]

The wife however is not asked to prepare anything of this from her own property, and there is no proof which indicates that she must do that. Yet, if she willingly prepares something related to the furniture of the house or anything of the kind, there is no harm in this.[1] And, Allah knows best.

Q. No. (372): What is the *Shar'ī* ruling concerning a person who is invited to a wedding banquet while he is fasting?

A: In this case he or she must answer the invitation because the majority of scholars maintain that it is obligatory - unless there is some legal excuse to answer the invitation to a wedding banquet. It has been narrated on the authority of Ibn ʿUmar, may Allah be pleased with him, that the Messenger of Allah (PBUH) said,

"Whenever any one of you is invited to a banquet, he should go to it."[2]

Concerning a fasting person, when he comes to the banquet place, he has two options: either to break his fast and eat from it if the fasting is voluntary or to refuse to eat and he may instead pray for the person who has invited him. It has been narrated that the Prophet (PBUH) said,

---

[1] See Ibn Hazm, Al- Muhalla, 9/507

[2] Narrated by *Al-Bukhārī*.

"When any one of you is invited to a feast, he should accept it. He may eat if he likes, and he may abandon (eating) if he likes."[1]

If he wants to pray for the person who has invited him, he may say for example,

"O Allah! Bless for them that you have provided them, forgive them, and have mercy upon them!"[2]

And, Allah knows best.

Q. No. (373): What are the proprieties of having intercourse with one's wife?

A: The following may be the most important proprieties related to having intercourse with one's wife:

- It is desirable that the husband plays with his wife first, and this is known as foreplay.
- When he finishes with her, he should wait until she has been satisfied as well.
- He can have intercourse with her in any position he likes as long as it is done to her vagina.
- He can enjoy any part of her body except anal penetration.
- It is not permissible for a man to have intercourse with his wife during her period.
- He can have intercourse with her one time after another, yet it is desirable that he performs ablution before doing that for a next time.
- Both man and woman can be naked during the copulation.[3]
- It is not permissible for a wife to refuse when her husband asks her for intercourse.

---

[1] Narrated by Muslim and others.

[2] Narrated by Muslim and others.

[3] There is a false statement attributed to the Prophet (pbuh) in which he prevents husband and wife from getting naked during copulation as a camel and a she-camel would do (also while copulating).

- It is not permissible for any spouse to uncover the secrets of intercourse.
- When a husband wants to return from some journey, he should not surprise his wife and thus he should tell her about the date of his arrival.
- It is detestable for a husband to ejaculate outside his wife's vagina, as the Prophet (PBUH) called this "*hidden wa'd*[1]"[2] And, Allah knows best.

Q. No. (374): What is the *Sharʿī* ruling concerning contraception?

A: Contraception is legal as long as it is done according to the Sharīʿah. The first valid reason for employing contraception is the fear that the pregnancy or delivery might endanger the life or health of the mother. This can be indicated by past experience or the opinion of a reliable physician. Almighty Allah says,

﴿ وَلَا تُلْقُوا۟ بِأَيْدِيكُمْ إِلَى ٱلتَّهْلُكَةِ ﴿١٩٥﴾ ﴾

"And do not be cast into ruin by your own hands" [TMQ: 2: 195]

Another valid reason is the fear that the new pregnancy or a new baby might harm a previous suckling child, and in our modern time new methods of contraception are available which help a father and a mother to delay the pregnancy so that they may not harm their now suckling baby.

Interestingly enough, Imām Aḥmad maintains that contraception requires the consent of the wife, because she has a right both to sexual enjoyment (if the method to be used is avoiding her sexually or if it deprives her of sexual enjoyment) and to decide whether or not she wants a child. Also, it has been narrated that 'Umar, may Allah be pleased with him, forbade the practice of coitus interruptus

---

[1] *Wa'd* is burying alive a newborn girl, as the people used to do during the pre-Islamic period.

[2] Narrated by Muslim and others.

without the consent of the wife. This was, on the part of Islam, a noteworthy step toward establishing the rights of women in an age when they had no rights. And, Allah knows best.

Q. No. (375): What is the *Sharʿī* ruling concerning abortion?

A: Islam does not allow doing violence to pregnancy. Muslim Faqīhs unanimously agree that after the foetus has been completely formed and given a soul, aborting it is prohibited. This is because it is a crime which constitutes an offense against a complete, live human being even though it is still a foetus.

However, there is one exceptional situation. Faqīhs say that if it is reliably established - after the baby is completely formed that the continuation of the pregnancy would necessarily result in the death of the mother, then abortion must be performed. This goes in accordance with the general principle of the Sharīʿah concerning the choosing of the lesser of two evils. And, Allah knows best.

Q. No. (376): What is the *Sharʿī* ruling concerning a man who has married a fifth woman while having four in wedlock?

A: It is not permissible for a man to marry a fifth wife while having four wives in wedlock, and if he does, the marriage will be invalid. Mālik and Ash-Shāfiʿī assert that the legal punishment (of *Zinā*) is to be applied to him if he knew it was unlawful before doing it. And Az-Zuhrī says that he is to be stoned to death if he was aware of the ruling concerning this before doing it, and if he did that out of ignorance, the lesser of the two legal punishments (of *Zinā*), i.e., lashing, is to be applied to him, the woman in question is to take her *mahr*, and they must be separated and never be united again (in wedlock). And, Allah knows best.

Q. No. (377): Is it permissible for a man to keep more than one wife in one house?

A: In principle, he is to make a house for each wife because this is what the Prophet (PBUH) did. Ibn Qudāmah says that it is not permissible for a man to keep two wives together in one and the same house without their consent because this causes harm to them and stimulates jealousy and animosity between them.[1] And, Allah knows best.

[1] See Ibn Qudamah, *Al-Mughnī*, 7/26-27.

Ṭalāq (Divorce)

Q. No. (378): What are the categories of divorce according to the five rulings?

A: Divorce may be (i) obligatory (*Wājib*), (ii) recommended (*mandūb*), (iii) allowable (mubāḥ), (iv) detestable (*Makrūh*), or (v) prohibited (harām). This is what is meant by the "the categories of divorce according to the five rulings".

1. **Divorce may be obligatory**, and that happens when there is a breach between two spouses and the judge sends two arbitrators to check the nature of this breach then the two arbitrators judge that they are to be separated. In this case the husband must divorce his wife.

2. **Divorce may be recommended or desirable**, and this happens when the wife neglects fulfilling the rights of Allah upon her, as when she neglects prayer for example, and the husband cannot oblige her to fulfil such rights. Also, this happens when the woman is unchaste.

3. **Divorce may be allowable or permissible**, and this happens when it is required as a result of the woman's ill- conduct and ill-treatment.

4. **Divorce may be detestable**, and this happens when the divorce is done without any reason while the spouses in question are on good terms with each other.

5. **And divorce may be prohibited**, and this happens when a man divorces his wife while she is menstruating or divorces her during an interval between her menstruations and he has had sexual intercourse with her during this interval. This is called "*bidʿah* divorce," and it will be clarified soon, Allah willing. And, Allah knows best.

Q. No. (379): How is divorce expressed?

A: "Expressions of divorce" are the words or terms which a husband pronounces when aiming to divorce his wife. These expressions are either explicit or implicit or, in other words, they are either direct or indirect.

Explicit expressions of divorce are such expressions which refer to divorce directly, and no other meaning is determined through them. An example of this is a man's saying to his wife, "You are divorced," or "I have divorced you," and such direct and explicit expressions.

Therefore, once a man says any of those expressions to his wife, divorce takes place i.e., is effective whether he has intended it or not and whether he is serious or joking.

Implicit expressions of divorce are the words or terms which can refer to divorce and other things at the same time. An example of this is a man's saying to his wife, "Go to your family," or "I have become separated from you". Accordingly, if a man says any of such indirect expressions to his wife, divorce takes place "only" if he has intended it, otherwise it will not be effective. And, Allah knows best.

Q. No. (380): What is the *Shar'ī* ruling concerning triple divorce which is expressed all at one time?

A: A man may say to his wife, "You are divorced three times," or "You are divorced. You are divorced. You are divorced". According to the preponderant view in this regard, this effectuates only one time or one pronouncement of divorce, as that was applied like this during the time of the Prophet (PBUH). It has been narrated on the authority of Ibn ʿAbbās, may Allah be pleased with him, that

"(the pronouncement of) three divorces during the lifetime of the Messenger of Allah (PBUH) and that of Abū Bakr and two years of the caliphate of `Umar (was treated) as one. But ʿUmar Ibn al-Khaṭṭāb said, 'Verily the people have begun to hasten in an issue in which they are required to observe respite. So, if we had imposed this upon them, (that might have been better for them).' And he imposed it upon them."[1]

And, Allah knows best.

Q. No. (381): What is the difference between the *Sunnah* divorce and the *bid'ah* divorce (innovated divorce)?

A: **The *Sunnah* divorce** is the permissible divorce, and it goes as follows:

- that a man divorces his wife with one pronouncement of divorce,

- after her menstruation period ends,

- after she takes the ritual bath required after it,

- and before he has intercourse with her,

- then he leaves her without making any other pronouncement of divorce until her *'Iddah* (waiting period) expires.

He may revoke the divorce during her *'Iddah* without her consent or the consent of her *Walīyy* and no new mahr will be required in this case.

He may leave her until her *'Iddah* ends, and in this case, he must release her with kindness because she will have been divorced irrevocably. If he wants to marry her again after the end of her *'Iddah*, it is permissible for him to do so yet the marriage is to be contracted as if he is marrying her for the first time.

He may divorce her again - i.e., for the second time- and if he revokes this second divorce then divorces her for the third time, he will not be allowed to marry her unless she marries another man properly (i.e., not through the *Muḥallil* marriage as clarified in the

---

[1] Narrated by Muslim and others.

part dealing with marriage). After that, if the second husband divorces her, it is permissible for the first husband to marry her.

The *bid'ah* divorce is a prohibited divorce because it is innovated in the religion (and this is the meaning of "*bid'ah*"). It contradicts the previous legal way of divorcing, that is, the *Sunnah* divorce. To illustrate this, a man may divorce his wife during her menstruation or divorce her during an interval between her menstruations yet after copulating with her during this interval. This divorce is prohibited and whoever does it is sinful.

Nevertheless, this divorce is counted, that is to say: in spite of its being prohibited and its perpetrator is sinful, the *bid'ah* divorce is effective and one pronouncement of divorce is counted. But how should a man act if he divorces his wife in this manner?

If a man divorces his wife during her menstruation for example, one divorce is counted; if the divorce is revocable, i.e., if it is the first or the second divorce, he is to revoke the divorce then keep her until her period of menstruation ends then another period starts then ends then he can keep her if he wants and he can divorce her if he wants yet this must be done before having intercourse with her. And, Allah knows best.

Q. No. (382): What are the types of divorce?

A: Divorce can be any of the following types:

1. Divorce can be **explicit** or **implicit** according to the words with which it is expressed.

2. Divorce can be **instantly effective**, as when a man intends to effectuate divorce immediately with words such as "You are divorced," and divorce can be **contingent** on something, as when a man says to his wife, "You will be divorced if you drink milk," for example. It becomes effective only if the wife drinks milk, yet some scholars - including Ibn Taymīyah say that if the husband did not

intend divorce if she did what he conditioned divorce by (drinking milk in the example in question), the divorce is not effective, and some scholars maintain that it is regarded as a broken oath and thus an oath expiation is required. In all cases, the divorce becomes effective if he intends it.

3. Divorce can be ***Sunnah* divorce** or ***bid'ah* divorce** (as) explained in a previous answer).

4. And finally, divorce can be **revocable** or **irrevocable.** It is revocable after divorcing a deflowered wife for the first or the second time. And, divorce becomes irrevocable either after divorcing a deflowered wife for the third time, and this is called "*baynūnah Kubrā*" (major irrevocability of divorce), or when a man divorces his wife after contracting his marriage to her yet before consummating this marriage, and this is called "*baynūnah Ṣughrā*" (minor irrevocability of divorce). In *baynūnah Kubrā* the man in question cannot remarry his divorced wife except after she marries another man, while in *baynūnah Ṣughrā* he can marry her with a new contract and a new *Ṣadaq*. And, Allah knows best.

Q. No. (383): What is rajah (revocation of divorce) and what are its conditions?

A: *Raj'ah* is that a man takes his divorced wife back to wedlock without a new contract. Also, *raj'ah* does not require *Walīyy*, *Ṣadaq*, or the consent or knowledge of the wife, as unanimously agreed upon by scholars. Certain conditions must be met as far as *raj'ah* is concerned, as follows:

1. The divorce in question must be revocable, that is, a husband can take his wife back only if he has divorced her once or twice.

2. This revocation of divorce must take place during her *'Iddah.*

3. The divorce must be without remuneration ('Iwaḍ), because if it is with remuneration, it will be *Khul'* and not divorce.

4. The husband must have consummated the marriage, as maintained by some scholars.

A *Raj'iyyah* divorcee i.e., a woman whose divorce is revocable is to be treated like a normal wife except with regard to the obligation of dividing the husband's stay with more than one wife. Thus, any of the two spouses can inherit the other if the latter dies, as unanimously agreed upon by scholars. And, Allah knows best.

Q. No. (384): What is the *Shar'ī* ruling concerning the maintenance and lodging of a *Raj'iyyah* divorcee, i.e., a woman whose divorce is revocable?

A: Almighty Allah says,

﴿يَـٰٓأَيُّهَا ٱلنَّبِيُّ إِذَا طَلَّقْتُمُ ٱلنِّسَآءَ فَطَلِّقُوهُنَّ لِعِدَّتِهِنَّ وَأَحْصُوا۟ ٱلْعِدَّةَ ۖ وَٱتَّقُوا۟ ٱللَّهَ رَبَّكُمْ ۖ لَا تُخْرِجُوهُنَّ مِنۢ بُيُوتِهِنَّ وَلَا يَخْرُجْنَ إِلَّآ أَن يَأْتِينَ بِفَـٰحِشَةٍ مُّبَيِّنَةٍ ۚ ﴿١﴾﴾

"O Prophet! When you divorce women, divorce them at their 'Iddah (prescribed periods), and count (accurately) their 'Iddah (periods). And fear Allah your Lord (O Muslims) and turn them not out of their (husband's) homes, nor shall they (themselves) leave, except in case they are guilty of some open illegal sexual intercourse." [TMQ: 65:1]

The words "...turn them not out of their (husband's) homes, nor shall they (themselves) leave..." require that the woman in question has the right to reside in her husband's house during her *'Iddah*. The Prophet (PBUH) said in this regard,

"A woman has a right to maintenance and lodging if her husband can take her back (after divorce)."[1]

And Almighty Allah says,

﴿أَسْكِنُوهُنَّ مِنْ حَيْثُ سَكَنتُم مِّن وُجْدِكُمْ وَلَا تُضَآرُّوهُنَّ لِتُضَيِّقُوا۟ عَلَيْهِنَّ ۚ ﴿٦﴾﴾

[1] Narrated by An-Nasā'ī.

"Lodge them (the divorced women) where you dwell, according to your means, and do not treat them in such a harmful way that they be obliged to leave" [TMQ: 65:6]

Still, a woman who is divorced before consummating the marriage has the right to maintenance because Almighty Allah says as a general rule,

﴿وَلِلْمُطَلَّقَٰتِ مَتَٰعٌۢ بِٱلْمَعْرُوفِ ۖ حَقًّا عَلَى ٱلْمُتَّقِينَ ﴿٢٤١﴾﴾

"And for divorced women, maintenance (should be provided) on reasonable (scale). This is a duty on Al- Muttaqin (the pious)."

[TMQ: 2: 241]

This includes what is used in such cases of expenses and clothing.

As for the pregnant divorcee, she is to be provided with maintenance until she delivers her baby, because Almighty Allah says,

﴿ وَإِن كُنَّ أُو۟لَٰتِ حَمْلٍ فَأَنفِقُوا۟ عَلَيْهِنَّ حَتَّىٰ يَضَعْنَ حَمْلَهُنَّ ﴿٦﴾﴾

"And if they are pregnant, then spend on them till they deliver"

[TMQ: 65: 6]

And, Allah knows best.

Q. No. (385): What is the ʿ*Iddah* (waiting period) of a divorcee?

A: ʿ*Iddah* here[1] is the divorce prescribed period during which a divorcee is not allowed to get married. The ʿ*Iddah* of a divorcee differs according to her status, as follows:

[1] By "here" we mean to differentiate between a divorcee's ʿ*Iddah* and the "*Iddah* of a widow, as the latter is to wait for four months and ten days, and if she is pregnant her ʿ*Iddah* is that she must wait until she delivers her baby.

1. If a woman whose marriage has been consummated is divorced and this divorce is revocable and she is a woman who has menses, her *'Iddah* is three menstrual periods.

2. If she does not have menses due to her young age or old age, her *'Iddah* is three months.

3. If a woman is divorced before consummating the marriage, no *'Iddah* is required on her part.

4. The *'Iddah* of a pregnant divorce is to wait until she delivers.

Q. No. (386): What is the *Shar'ī* ruling concerning a man who says to his wife, "You are prohibited to me."?

A: According to the most evident view in this connection, this is not a form of divorce. Rather, it is to be treated like a broken oath for which the person in question is to expiate (as clarified in the section dealing with "oaths"). This is because Almighty Allah says,

﴿يَٰٓأَيُّهَا ٱلنَّبِيُّ لِمَ تُحَرِّمُ مَآ أَحَلَّ ٱللَّهُ لَكَۖ تَبۡتَغِي مَرۡضَاتَ أَزۡوَٰجِكَۚ وَٱللَّهُ غَفُورٞ رَّحِيمٞ ۝١ قَدۡ فَرَضَ ٱللَّهُ لَكُمۡ تَحِلَّةَ أَيۡمَٰنِكُمۡۚ وَٱللَّهُ مَوۡلَىٰكُمۡۖ وَهُوَ ٱلۡعَلِيمُ ٱلۡحَكِيمُ ۝٢﴾

"O Prophet! Why do you ban (for yourself) that which Allah has made lawful to you, seeking to please your wives? And Allah is Oft-Forgiving, Most Merciful. Allah has already ordained for you (O men), the dissolution of your oaths" [TMQ: 66: 1-2]

And, Allah knows best.

Q. No. (387): What is the *Shar'ī* ruling concerning a man who divorces his wife in himself without expressing this with words?

A: If a man divorces his wife in himself, i.e., without expressing this with words, this divorce is not effective according to the majority of scholars, because it has been narrated on the authority of Abū

Hurayrah, may Allah be pleased with him, that the Prophet (PBUH) said,

"Allah forgives my followers those (deeds) their souls may whisper or suggest to them as long as they do not act (on that) or speak (expressing it)."[1]

And, Allah knows best.

Q. No. (388): What is the *Sharʿī* ruling concerning a man who says about a certain woman before marrying her actually, "If I marry so and so, I will divorce her."?

A: Such a statement is not legally considered and does not have any effect as long as divorce is concerned. This is because the Prophet (PBUH) said,

"...and he has no (right to) divorce in that which he does not have (any right to do so)."[2]

This means that a man has no right to divorce a woman upon whom he does not have such a right. And, Allah knows best.

Q. No. (389): What is the *Sharʿī* ruling if a man gives his wife the right to divorce herself?

A: Most scholars say that the divorce will be effective if she divorces herself from him, while some others assert that it will not be effective because divorce is for men and not for women. And, Allah knows best.

Q. No. (390): If a man divorced his wife, then she married another man then the second man divorced her then the first husband married her again, would the first divorce be counted from the three acts of divorces after which divorce becomes irrevocable?

---

[1] Narrated by Al-Bukhārī and Muslim.
[2] Narrated by At-Tirmidhī and others.

A: This question comes in two possible cases:

- The first husband may have divorced her three times, and thus the divorce became irrevocable, then she married another man who divorced her later, then she remarried the first husband. In this case the first husband has a new right according to this new marriage to three times of divorce, as unanimously agreed upon by scholars.
- The first husband may have divorced her one time or two then she married another one who divorced her then she married the first husband again. Some scholars say that the first husband has the right to divorce her only the number of divorce allowances remaining from the first marriage, i.e., two if he divorced her once in the first marriage and one if he divorced her twice. This is the view of ʿUmar Ibn al-Khaṭṭāb, may Allah be pleased with him, and it has been adopted by Ash-Shāfiʿī as well. On the other hand, some other scholars are of the opinion that the second marriage to the first husband demolishes the first divorce or divorces and consequently the first husband has the right to divorce her up to three times irrespective of how many times he divorced her before. This view has been attributed to Ibn ʿAbbās, Ibn ʿUmar, Abū Ḥanīfah, and others. The second view may be more evident than the first one as it befits the spirit of the Sharīʿah, especially it is not logical that a man who divorces his wife three times - then remarries her after she marries another one and the latter divorces her has the right to divorce her three times while a man who divorces his wife with a "lesser" number of divorces then remarries her after she marries another one and the latter divorces her has the right to divorce her also with a "lesser" number of divorces. And, Allah knows best.

Q. No. (391): What is the *Sharʿī* ruling concerning a woman whose husband has been lost?

A: If a husband travels or goes out of his house for any other reason than is lost, his wife is to wait for four years then applies an *'Iddah* of a widow, i.e., four months and ten days, and after that she can legally marry another man. This judgment has been authentically attributed to 'Umar Ibn al-Khaṭṭāb, 'Uthman Ibn 'Affan, and Ibn 'Umar, may Allah be pleased with them.[1]

However, some scholars maintain that there is no legal reason for her so that she can wait for such a period of time as long as her absent husband has left for her what suffices her for living. Yet still, these scholars say that if she fears of seduction and temptation, she can ask a judge for nullifying her marriage.[2] And, Allah knows best.

Questions on Related Topics

Q. No. (392): Can woman demand dissolution of marriage (as in *Khul'*) without legal reason?

A: The Prophet (PBUH) said in this regard, "If a woman asks her husband for divorce without harm (inflicted upon her), she will be forbidden from the fragrance of Paradise."[3] And, Allah knows best.

Q. No. (393): Can a woman's husband keep her aiming to harm her?

A: Just as a woman is not allowed to ask her husband for divorce without legal reason, he is not allowed to keep her in wedlock if she demands dissolution of marriage for a legal reason; rather, he should release her. Almighty Allah says,

﴿وَإِذَا طَلَّقْتُمُ ٱلنِّسَآءَ فَبَلَغْنَ أَجَلَهُنَّ فَأَمْسِكُوهُنَّ بِمَعْرُوفٍ أَوْ سَرِّحُوهُنَّ بِمَعْرُوفٍۚ
وَلَا تُمْسِكُوهُنَّ ضِرَارًا لِّتَعْتَدُواْۚ وَمَن يَفْعَلْ ذَٰلِكَ فَقَدْ ظَلَمَ نَفْسَهُۥۚ وَلَا تَتَّخِذُوٓاْ

[1] See *Jāmi'al-Aḥkām an-Nisā'*, 4/199.
[2] See Al- Jami', 4/202.
[3] Narrated by At-Tirmidhī and others.

ءَايَٰتِ ٱللَّهِ هُزُوٗاۚ وَٱذۡكُرُواْ نِعۡمَتَ ٱللَّهِ عَلَيۡكُمۡ وَمَآ أَنزَلَ عَلَيۡكُم مِّنَ ٱلۡكِتَٰبِ
وَٱلۡحِكۡمَةِ يَعِظُكُم بِهِۦۚ وَٱتَّقُواْ ٱللَّهَ وَٱعۡلَمُوٓاْ أَنَّ ٱللَّهَ بِكُلِّ شَيۡءٍ عَلِيمٞ ﴿٢٣١﴾

"And when you have divorced women and they have fulfilled the term of their prescribed period, either take them back on reasonable basis or set them free on reasonable basis. But do not take them back to hurt them, and whoever does that, then he has wronged himself. And treat not the Verses (Laws) of Allah as a jest, but remember Allah's Favours on you (i.e., Islam), and that which He has sent down to you of the Book (i.e., the Qur'ān) and Al-Hikmah (the Prophet's Sunnah- legal ways - Islamic jurisprudence, etc.) whereby He instructs you. And fear Allah, and know that Allah is All-Aware of everything." [TMQ: 2: 231]

And, Allah knows best.

Q. No. (394): Is *Khul*ʿ counted as one divorce?

A: The majority of scholars maintain that *Khul*ʿ is itself divorce, yet their proofs in this regard are refuted, and according to the evident view *Khul*ʿ is *faskh* and not divorce. In marriage, *faskh*, literally meaning "nullification," signifies the nullification of marriage contract due to a legal reason.

*Khul*ʿ is *faskh* and not divorce because it has been authenticated that it is permissible to apply *Khul*ʿ after two divorces and thus a third divorce is possible after it. Therefore, if *Khul*ʿ were to be divorce, the allowed number of divorces would have been four.

This is what Ibn ʿAbbās, the interpreter of the Qur'ān, understood from the following verse,

﴿ٱلطَّلَٰقُ مَرَّتَانِۖ فَإِمۡسَاكُۢ بِمَعۡرُوفٍ أَوۡ تَسۡرِيحُۢ بِإِحۡسَٰنٖۗ وَلَا يَحِلُّ لَكُمۡ أَن تَأۡخُذُواْ
مِمَّآ ءَاتَيۡتُمُوهُنَّ شَيۡـًٔا إِلَّآ أَن يَخَافَآ أَلَّا يُقِيمَا حُدُودَ ٱللَّهِۖ فَإِنۡ خِفۡتُمۡ أَلَّا يُقِيمَا حُدُودَ
ٱللَّهِ فَلَا جُنَاحَ عَلَيۡهِمَا فِيمَا ٱفۡتَدَتۡ بِهِۦۗ ﴿٢٢٩﴾

"The divorce is twice, after that, either you retain her on reasonable terms or release her with kindness. And it is not lawful for you (men) to take back (from your wives) any of your Mahr which you have given them, except when both parties fear that they would be unable to keep the limits ordained by Allah (e.g., to deal with each other on a fair basis). Then if you fear that they would not be able to keep the limits ordained by Allah, then there is no sin on either of them if she gives back (the Mahr or a part of it) for her Al-Khulʿ." [TMQ: 2: 229]

Ibn ʿAbbās said, as narrated on the authority of Tawus,

"Giving back (the mahr or a part of it) is not divorcing."[1]

Another proof which confirms that *Khulʿ* is not divorce is that the husband has the right to revoke divorce unlike *Khulʿ* in which he has no such right unless the wife accepts it.[2]

Also, the *ʿIddah* of divorce is three menstrual periods or three months, as pinpointed earlier, whereas the *ʿIddah* required after *Khulʿ* is only one menstrual period as will be clarified soon.

Accordingly, if a husband applies *Khulʿ* to his wife ten times, he has the right to remarry her with a new contract before she marries another husband.[3] This means that an act of *Khulʿ* is not counted as from the allowed number of divorces, and Allah knows best.

Important still, *Khulʿ* is not to be counted as divorce even if the husband says that he has divorced his wife, as long as it is done "in return for remuneration paid by the wife". Still, it is not stipulated that it should be done with words expressing "*Khulʿ*" or "*faskh*" in particular. This is what has been derived from and indicated by texts and principles of jurisprudence.[4]

And, Allah knows best.

---

[1] Narrated by ʿAbdur-Razzāq.
[2] See Zadul-Ma'ad, 5/199.
[3] See Ibn Taymīyah, Fatāwā, 32/289.
[4] Ibid, 32/309.

Q. No. (395): What is the *'Iddah* of *Khul'*?

A: After applying *Khul'* the woman in question waits until she has one menstrual period then she can marry another man.

It has been narrated that Ar-Rubayyi' Bint Mu'awwidh applied *Khul'* with her husband then she went to Uthman Ibn Affan, may Allah be pleased with him, and asked him, "What *'Iddah* should I apply?" He said, "No *'Iddah* is prescribed upon you unless you are newly (married) to him, for, (if so), you are to wait until you have one menstrual period." He also said, "In this (judgment of mine) I follow the judgment of the Messenger of Allah (PBUH) concerning (the case of) Maryam al-Mughāliyyah who was a wife of Thabit ibn Qays Ibn Shammas and applied *Khul'* with him."[1] And, Allah knows best.

Q. No. (396): What is *li'an* and how should it be applied?

A: *Li'an* can simply be identified with the phrase "oath of condemnation". It is applied in the following case: if a man accuses his wife of committing adultery and she belies him, the judge applies *li'an* between them (in the manner pinpointed inside the book). It is called "*li'an*," which literally means "invoking curse," because the husband says, "I invoke Allah's curse upon myself if I am of those who tell lies".

According to the texts available concerning *li'an*, it is to be applied in the following manner:

- The judge starts with reminding the spouses in question of showing repentance before starting the *li'an* process.
- If they insist on applying *li'an*, the judge starts *li'an* with the husband and tells him to say four times, "I testify by Allah that I speak the truth concerning the adultery of which I have accused this wife of mine".

[1] Narrated by An-Nasā'ī and Ibn Mājah

- Then the husband testifies four times that he is one of those who speak the truth.
- Then the judge commands someone to place his hand on the husband's mouth, then he (the judge) tells him to be conscious of Allah, for the fifth testimony will definitely bring Allah's curse upon him if he is telling a lie about his wife. This is so that the husband may not bear the fifth testimony if he is a liar, because worldly punishment is much lighter than that of the Hereafter.
- If the husband insists, he is to say, "I invoke Allah's curse upon myself if I am of those who tell lies". Once he says that, he is saved from the legal punishment prescribed for *qadhf* (slanderous accusation).[1] If he with- draws his accusation, he is to be lashed eighty lashes.
- After that the judge tells the wife that she either applies her part of the *li'an* or the legal punishment of adultery (stoning to death) will be applied to her.
- To apply her part of the *li'an*, the wife testifies four times that he is telling a lie.
- Then the judge commands someone to admonish her and tell her that the fifth testimony will definitely bring.
- Allah's curse upon her if she is guilty, so that she may withdraw before bearing this testimony if she is guilty.
- After that she either withdraws her belying her husband and confesses her guilt, and in this case the legal punishment for adultery stoning to death will be applied to her; or she continues the process of *li'an* and says, "I will incur Allah's wrath if he speaks the truth". In the latter case she is saved from the punishment of *Zinā*. And, Allah knows best.

[1]The legal punishment which is to be inflicted to the person who commits *qadhf* is that he is to be lashed eighty lashes.

Q. No. (397): What are the consequences of *li'an*?

A: When *li'an* is applied between a husband and his wife in the manner pinpointed above, the following consequences result:

1. The two spouses are to be separated.

2. The wife becomes prohibited for the man forever.

3. The woman deserves her *Ṣadaq*, and so the husband is not to take anything from it.

4. The child is ascribed to the mother.

5. The woman and her son inherit each other. And, Allah knows best.

Q. No. (398): What is the *Shar'ī* ruling if a man accuses his wife of committing adultery, yet they do not submit the case to a judge?

A: Answering this question, Ibrāhīm An-Nakha'ī says, "She remains his wife,"[1] meaning that the case does not have the same consequences of *li'an* when a man accuses his wife of committing adultery then they apply *li'an* when she belies him. And, Allah knows best.

Q. No. (399): What is the *Shar'ī* ruling if a man says to his wife "I have not found you a virgin"?

A: If he means that she committed *Zinā* and so she lost her virginity because of that, no legal punishment is to be inflicted because of that and *li'an* is not to be applied either, because a woman may lose her virginity because of other causes than intercourse. If, however he means to directly accuse her of *Zinā*, then *li'an* is to be applied if she belies him. And, Allah knows best.

Q. No. (400): What is *Ẓihār* and what is its expiation?

---

[1] Recorded by 'Abdur-Razzāq in his *Musannaf* (12411).

A: *Ẓihār* is that a man says to his wife, "You are like my mother's back," meaning "You are prohibited to me".

If a man says to his wife, "You are like my mother's back," his wife becomes prohibited to him, and it is not permissible for him to have intercourse with her or enjoys any part in her body except after expiating for what he has said.

The expiation of *Ẓihār* is to be executed according to the "arrangement" specified by the Sharīʿah, and "arrangement" means that the husband in question is not allowed to switch to the next item representing this expiation except when he is not able to do the previous one, as follows:

1. First of all, he is to free a believing slave.

2. If he cannot do so, he is to observe fasting for two successive months without touching his wife.

3. And if he cannot do so, he is to feed sixty poor people.

And, Allah knows best.

Q. No. (401): What is the *Sharʿī* ruling concerning a man who says to his wife, "You are like my sister to me"?

A: This is neither divorce nor *Ẓihār*, because it has been narrated that a tyrant sent to Prophet Ibrāhīm (Abraham), peace be upon him, and asked him, "Who is (this lady) accompanying you?" meaning his wife. Thereupon Prophet. Ibrāhīm said that she was his sister, to the end of the Ḥadīth.[1] And, Allah knows best.

Q. No. (402): what is *Ilā'* and what are the cases in which it occurs?

A: *Ilā'* is that a husband swears that he will not have intercourse with his wife for a certain period of time. *Ilā'* has two cases:

---

[1] Narrated by Al-Bukhārī and Muslim.

1. That the period specified in the husband's oath is "less" than four months, and in this case, it is better for the husband in question to have intercourse with his wife and expiate for his oath. If he does not expiate for his oath and continues acting upon his *Ilā'*, the wife must remain until the specified period of *Ilā'* is over and she has no right to demand divorce.

2. That the period is "more" than four months, and in this case, he can have intercourse with his wife and expiate for his oath as well. If he does not have intercourse with her, she must remain patient until the period is over, then she can ask him to either have intercourse with her or divorce her.

When the specified period is over the husband is to be made to choose either to have intercourse with her or to divorce her. This is according to the view of the majority of scholars.[1] And, Allah knows best.

---

[1] See *Fatḥ al-Bārī*, 9/428.

Oaths and Vows

Q. No. (403): What are the divisions of oaths? A: There are three divisions of oath, as follows:

1. ***Al-Yamīn al-Laghw* (unintentional oath)**

This is an oath that a man takes without actually intending to swear, whether it is taken for confirming something or negating it, as when a man says, "No, by Allah," or "By Allah, you will eat with me".

This oath is not to be fulfilled and the person who takes it is not legally blamed, because Almighty Allah says,

﴿لَّا يُؤَاخِذُكُمُ ٱللَّهُ بِٱللَّغْوِ فِيٓ أَيْمَٰنِكُمْ وَلَٰكِن يُؤَاخِذُكُم بِمَا كَسَبَتْ قُلُوبُكُمْ ۗ وَٱللَّهُ غَفُورٌ حَلِيمٌ ٢٢٥﴾

"Allah will not call you to account for that which is unintentional in your oaths, but He will call you to account for that which your hearts have earned. And Allah is Oft-Forgiving, Most-Forbearing." [TMQ: 2: 225]

2. ***Al-Yamīn al-Ghamūs* (heinous oath)**

This kind of oath is a major sin, and it is that a man swears when telling a lie to deprive someone of his due right; it is the false oath. The Prophet (PBUH) said,

"He who swears falsely to take the property of a Muslim unlawfully, will meet Allah on the Day of Resurrection when He will be angry with him."

There is no expiation for this oath, because it is too heinous to be expiated, yet whoever takes such an oath must repent to Allah sincerely and give anything he might have taken unlawfully back to those from whom he has taken it.

3. ***Al-Yamīn al-Mun'aqidah* (deliberate oath)**

This oath is established when a person takes an oath concerning a certain thing that he will do in the future with the intention of swearing as well as of doing the thing in question.

This oath must be fulfilled, that is, by doing the thing specified in the oath, otherwise it will be a broken oath, and this requires an expiation. Still, the Muslim must remember here the Prophet's words,

"He who takes an oath then finds something better than that, should do that which is better, and let him expiate for his oath."[1]

And, Allah knows best.

Q. No. (404): What is oath expiation and what are the conditions obligating this expiation?

A: A person who has broken his oath and is legally asked to expiate for that can do so by doing "any" of the following:

1. To feed ten poor people on a scale of the average of that with which he feeds his own family.[2]

2. To cloth ten poor people.

3. To set a slave free.

If a person cannot do any of these three things, he is "to observe fast for three days".

To confirm not to repeat, you have no right to expiate a broken oath with the fasting of three days except after failing to use any of the first three choices: feeding ten poor people, or clothing them, or freeing a slave. And, Allah knows best.

---

[1] Narrated by Muslim and others.

[2] If you choose to feed ten poor people to expiate a broken oath, you must feed them, and it is not permissible that you pay the fiscal value of the food required for that. This is according to the view adopted by the majority of scholars, unlike the opinion of Abū Ḥanīfah who maintains that it is permissible to do so.

As for the conditions obligating this expiation, it should be known that this expiation of broken oaths becomes obligatory when the following conditions are met:

1. If the person who takes the oath is *mukallaf* (legally responsible).

2. If he does this willingly.

3. If he intends to fulfil the oath (i.e., if the oath is deliberate).

4. If the oath is concerning something that is intended to be done or not be done in the future.

5. If the man breaks his oath by doing what he has sworn to not do or not doing what he has sworn to do. And, Allah knows best.

Q. No. (405): What is the *Shar'ī* ruling concerning an oath which is taken by other than Allah?

A: An oath is to be fulfilled only when it is taken by Allah or any of His Attributes or Names. It has been narrated on the authority of Ibn 'Umar, may Allah be pleased with him, that the Messenger of Allah (PBUH) found ʿUmar Ibn al-Khaṭṭāb, may Allah be pleased with him, in a group of people and he was swearing by his father. So, the Messenger of Allah (PBUH) said, "Verily! Allah forbids you to swear by your fathers. If a person has to take an oath, let him swear by Allah or otherwise he is to keep quiet."[1]

It may be added here that swearing by other than Allah is an act of polytheism, for it has been narrated on the authority of Ibn 'Umar, may Allah be pleased with him, that the Prophet (PBUH) said,

"Whoever swears by other than Allah will have committed (an act of) disbelief or (an act of) polytheism."[2]

---

[1] Narrated by Al-Bukhārī and Muslim.
[2] Narrated by Al-Bukhārī and Muslim.

Accordingly, it is not permissible to swear by the Prophet, or by the *Ka'bah*, or by one's sons, or one's father, etc.

Still, if a person swears by Allah, you should accept that, for the Prophet (PBUH) said,

"Isa (Jesus), seeing a man stealing, asked him, 'Did you steal?' He said, 'No, by Allah, except Whom there is no god.' Isa said, I believe in Allah and doubt my eyes. "[1]

And, Allah knows best.

Q. No. (406): What is the *Shar'ī* ruling if one takes an oath concerning something then forgets it?

A: If you take an oath concerning something then forget it, no breaking of oath is counted against you. In other words, if you swore that you "would not do" a certain thing then you forgot that and "did" that thing forgetfully or by mistake, your oath is not regarded as a broken one, because Almighty Allah says,

﴿رَبَّنَا لَا تُؤَاخِذْنَآ إِن نَّسِينَآ أَوْ أَخْطَأْنَا ۚ ٢٨٦﴾

"Our Lord! Punish us not if we forget or fall into error." [TMQ: 2: 286]

And according to a Ḥadīth narrated by Muslim in this regard Allah said "Yes," (as responding positively to this invocation). And, Allah knows best.

Q. No. (407): Is the oath taken by a person based on his intention?

A: Any oath which a person takes is considered on the basis of his intention as regards its being effective or not. Thus, if a person takes an oath concerning doing something while intending to do some other thing, his intention is the criterion here. It has been narrated

---

[1] Narrated by Al-Bukhārī and Muslim.

on the authority of Abū Hurayrah, may Allah be pleased with him, that the Prophet (PBUH) said,

"An oath is to be interpreted according to the intention of the one who takes it."[1]

And, Allah knows best.

Q. No. (408): What is the *Sharʿī* ruling concerning a person who says "*In shā' Allāh* (Allah willing)" after swearing that he will do a certain thing?

A: In this case, his oath will not be considered a broken one if he does not do the thing in question. It has been narrated on the authority of Abū Hurayrah, may Allah be pleased with him, that the Prophet (PBUH) said that once (Prophet) Sulayman (Solomon), son of (Dāwūd) David said, "(By Allah) Tonight I will have sexual intercourse with one hundred (or ninety-nine) women each of whom will give birth to a knight who will fight in Allah's cause." And he did not say, "Allah willing." Therefore, only one of those women conceived and gave birth to a half-man. The Prophet (PBUH) added, "By Him in Whose Hands Muḥammad's soul is, if he had said, 'Allah willing,' (he would have begotten sons) all of whom would have been knights striving in Allah's cause."[2] And, Allah knows best.

Q. No. (409): What are the kinds of vow?

A: Vow is of two kinds:

1. **Absolute or unrestricted vow**, and it is that a man commits himself to do a certain act without conditioning it by a certain thing. For instance, a man may say, "I commit myself to offer two *Rakʿahs* for the sake of Allah."

---

[1] Narrated by Muslim.

[2] Narrated by Al-Bukhārī and others.

2. **Contingent vow,** and it is that a man commits himself to do a certain act and makes it contingent on the happening of some blessing or the removal of some calamity. For example, he may say, "If Allah cures my patient, I commit myself that I will feed a poor person." Such contingent vow is detestable in principle, as the Prophet (PBUH) said,

"A vow neither hastens nor delays anything, but by the making of vows, some of the wealth of a miser is taken out."[1]

And, Allah knows best.

Q. No. (410): What is the *Shar'ī* ruling concerning a person who vows to do a thing that Allah has not prescribed?

A: Whoever vows to do a thing that Allah has not prescribed or a legal thing that he cannot do, should leave it, yet he is to do an oath expiation. It has been narrated on the authority of Ibn 'Abbās, may Allah be pleased with him, that

"While the Prophet (PBUH) was delivering a sermon, he saw a man standing, so he asked about that man. They (the people) said, 'It is Abū Isrā'īl who has vowed that he will stand and never sit down, that he will never come in the shade nor speak to anybody, and that he will fast.' The Prophet said, 'Order him to speak, let him come in the shade, and make him sit down, but let him complete his fast."[2]

And, Allah knows best.

Q. No. (411): What is the *Shar'ī* ruling concerning a person makes a vow and does not specify it?

A: Whoever makes a vow and does not specify it, should do an oath expiation. For example, a man may say, "I make a vow that I will do

[1] Narrated by Al-Bukhārī and Muslim.
[2] Narrated by Al-Bukhārī and others.

something for Allah," without defining this thing. The Prophet (PBUH) said,

"The expiation of a vow which has not been named (i.e., specified) is that of an oath."[1]

And, Allah knows best.

Q. No. (412): What is the *Shar'ī* ruling concerning a person who makes a vow then dies?

A: If a person makes a vow, then dies, his *Walīyy* - who is normally one of his sons or his heirs in general is to fulfil that vow. It has been narrated on the authority of Ibn 'Abbas, may Allah be pleased with him, that

"Sa'd Ibn 'Ubādah asked the Messenger of Allah (PBUH) concerning a vow that his mother made then died before fulfilling it. The Messenger of Allah (PBUH) said, 'Fulfil it on her behalf."[2]

And, Allah knows best.

Q. No. (413): When does a vow become valid and when does it become invalid?

A: A vow becomes valid if it is made for doing something that would bring one near to Almighty Allah, and in this case, it must be fulfilled. On the other hand, a vow becomes invalid if it is made for doing something evil, so such a vow is not to be fulfilled yet an oath expiation is to be made. And, Allah knows best.

---

[1] Narrated by Abū Dāwūd and others.

[2] Narrated by Al-Bukhārī and Muslim.

Food and Drinks

Q. No. (414): What are the proprieties of drinking?

A: The following may be the most important of the proprieties related to drinking as derived from the Qur'ān and the Sunnah.

1. To recite *tasmiyah.*

2. To use the right hand.

3. To drink while sitting, because this is better, yet is it permissible to drink while standing.

4. To drink in three times during each you breathe outside the vessel from which you drink, because it is "more thirst-quenching, healthier, and more wholesome," as the Prophet (PBUH) said.[1]

5. Not to breathe into the vessel from which you drink.

6. Not to drink from the head of a bottle.

7. To start with those who are on the right side when giving people to drink.

8. To be the last to drink if you are the one who gives others to drink.

9. To praise Allah after drinking. And, Allah knows best.

Q. No. (415): What is the *Shar'ī* ruling concerning a part that has been cut from an animal while it is alive?

A: This part is to be treated as *maytah* (dead animals) are treated, i.e., it is prohibited for eating. It has been narrated that the Prophet (PBUH) said,

"Whatever is cut from a beast while it is alive is *maytah.*"[2]

---

[1] Narrated by Al-Bukhārī and Muslim.
[2] Narrated by Abū Dāwūd and Ibn Mājah.

And, Allah knows best.

Q. No. (416): What is the *Shar'ī* ruling concerning eating something impure?

A: Anything which is considered to be from among impurities, such as insects, is prohibited for eating. And, Allah knows best.

Q. No. (417): What is the *Shar'ī* ruling concerning eating imported meats?

A: It is lawful to eat imported meats, such as chicken and canned beef, if two conditions are met: first, the meat must be from the meats which are lawful for eating, and second, the animal, fowl, etc., to which the meat in question belongs must have been slaughtered according to the Islamic way.

It is worth mentioning here that some companies which export meats to Islamic countries would cheat concerning the label on which they declare that their meats have been slaughtered according to the Islamic manner of slaughtering while in fact the necks of their exported chickens, for example, are sound and carry no sign of slaughtering. That is why the Muslim must be careful when dealing with such companies or eating from such meats.

Finally, imported meats which originate with the People of the Scripture are lawful for us, as this is included in the general rule stating that their food is lawful for us. Still, these imported meats, i.e., of the People of the Scripture in particular, must not include any prohibited meat, such as the flesh of swine. And, Allah knows best.

Q. No. (418): Is it permissible to use something prohibited as a medicine?

A: Concerning the question of whether some of the prohibited food substances can be used as a medicine, there is a difference of opinion among scholars. Some do not consider medicine to belong to the category of a compelling necessity like food, and in support of their position they cite the following Ḥadīth,

"Assuredly Allah did not provide a cure for you in what He prohibited to you."[1]

Others consider the need for medicine equal to that of food, as both are necessary for preserving life. To support their view, these scholars argue that the Prophet (PBUH) allowed 'Abdur-Raḥmān ibn 'Awf and Az-Zubayr ibn al-'Awwām to wear silk because they were suffering from scabies.[2] Perhaps this latter view is closer to the spirit of Islam which is concerned with the preservation of human life. However, taking medicine containing some of the prohibited substances may be permissible only under the following conditions:

- The patient's life is endangered if he does not take this medicine.

- No alternative medication made from entirely lawful sources is available.

- The medication is prescribed by a Muslim physician who is knowledgeable and pious.

We may also remind our readers of the prohibition of using *khamr* as a medicine. The Prophet (PBUH) said when a man told him that he used wine as a medicine, *"It is not a medicine but a disease."*[3] He (PBUH) also said as a general rule,

---

[1] Narrated by Al-Bukhārī.

[2] The text of this Ḥadīth is quoted in the section entitled "Clothing and Ornaments".

[3] Narrated by Muslim, Aḥmad, Abū Dāwūd, and At-Tirmidhī. Narrated by Abū Dāwūd.

"Allah has sent down diseases and medicines, and has made a medicine for every disease. So, take medicine but do not use anything prohibited as a medicine."[1]

And, Allah knows best.

Q. No. (419): What are the animals prohibited to Jews and Christians?

A: In the divinely revealed religions, Allah prohibited to Jews the eating of many land and marine animals. The Qur'ān mentions some of the things which Allah prohibited to them. The cause of prohibition was to punish them for their transgressions and sins. Almighty Allah says,

﴿وَعَلَى ٱلَّذِينَ هَادُواْ حَرَّمۡنَا كُلَّ ذِي ظُفُرٖۖ وَمِنَ ٱلۡبَقَرِ وَٱلۡغَنَمِ حَرَّمۡنَا عَلَيۡهِمۡ شُحُومَهُمَآ إِلَّا مَا حَمَلَتۡ ظُهُورُهُمَآ أَوِ ٱلۡحَوَايَآ أَوۡ مَا ٱخۡتَلَطَ بِعَظۡمٖۚ ذَٰلِكَ جَزَيۡنَٰهُم بِبَغۡيِهِمۡۖ وَإِنَّا لَصَٰدِقُونَ ١٤٦﴾

"And unto those who are Jews, we forbade every (animal) with undivided hoof, and We forbade them the fat of the ox and the sheep except what adheres to their backs or their entrails, or is mixed up with a bone. Thus, we recompensed them for their rebellion (committing crimes like murdering the Prophets, eating of Ribā [usury], etc.). And verily, we are Truthful."

[TMQ: 6:146]

It may be assumed that Christians were also supposed to observe the same prohibitions since the Injīl (Gospel) declares that Prophet Isa (Jesus), peace be upon him, did not come to abolish the Law of Prophet Musa (Moses), peace be upon him, but to fulfil it. However, Christians made permissible things which had been prohibited in the Tawrāh (Torah), although not abrogated in the Injīl. Christians followed the teachings of Paul, who declared all foods and drinks permissible with the sole exception of the flesh of animals sacrificed

---

[1] For description of these you may refer to the Old Testament book of Leviticus, chapter eleven.

to idols. Accordingly, Christians permitted themselves the eating of pork, despite the fact that the text of the Tawrāh prohibits it until this day. And, Allah knows best.

Q. No. (420): What is the wisdom behind the prohibition of dead animals?

A: There are obvious reasons for this prohibition, as follows:

- Eating the flesh of a dead animal is repugnant to civilized taste and is considered by reasonable people in all societies to be contrary to human dignity.

- In whatever he does, the Muslim acts with a set purpose and intention. He is ordered to slaughter the animal he wants to eat to take him away from the category of dead animals. Almighty Allah does not desire that man should eat of what he did not intend or think of eating as is the case with the dead animal; conversely, slaughtering an animal or hunting it as game both require an intention followed by effort and subsequent action.

- If an animal died naturally, it is quite likely that it died of some acute or chronic disease, through eating a poisonous plant, or other similar causes; hence eating its flesh would probably be harmful. The same is the case when the cause of death is old age or starvation.

- By prohibiting the flesh of a dead animal to human beings, Allah provides a source of food to animals and birds, that, in the words of the Qur'ān, constitute communities (*umam*) like us. This is what actually happens, as carcasses of animals lying out in the open are devoured by birds and animals. And, Allah knows best.

Q. No. (421): What is the wisdom behind the prohibition of eating every animal that has been killed by strangling, by a violent blow,

by a headlong fall, or by the goring of horns, or of eating an animal that has been killed or partly eaten by a wild animal?[1]

A: The reasons why the mentioned categories of animals are prohibited can be the same reasons mentioned concerning animals that die naturally (i.e., dead animals as mentioned in the answer to the previous question). Yet still, it may be important in passing this to draw attention to the fact that a person should be kind to his animal and protect it from harm so that it may not be neglected until it is strangled, falls from a high place, or is gored in a fight with other animals. And, Allah knows best.

Q. No. (422): What is the wisdom behind the prohibition of the blood poured forth?

A: The reason for this prohibition is both that the drinking of blood is repugnant to human decency and that it may likewise be injurious to health. Also, during the pre-Islamic period, a person who felt hungry might jab a bone or a sharp object into the flesh of his animal, and collect and drink the flowing blood; thus, since piercing the flesh of a living animal injures and weakens it, Allah prohibited such a practice. And, Allah knows best.

Q. No. (423): What is the wisdom behind the prohibition of flesh of swine?

A: Since the pig relishes filth and offal, its meat is repugnant to persons of decent taste. Moreover, recent medical research has shown that eating swine-flesh is injurious to health in all climates, especially hot ones. Scientific research has also shown that pork carries a deadly parasite. Perhaps science may discover in the future things that will shed more light on the wisdom of this prohibition. In addition to this, there are some scholars who say that eating pork

---

[1] As mentioned in the Qur'ān (5:3).

frequently diminishes the human being's sense of shame in relation to what is indecent. And, Allah knows best.

Q. No. (424): What is the *Shar'ī* ruling concerning making use of the skin, bones, and hair of a dead animal?

A: The prohibition concerning the dead animal is limited to the eating of its flesh. That is why it is permissible for the Muslim to make use of its skin, horns, bones, and hair, for throwing them away is a waste-something which is not permitted. It has been narrated that Ibn 'Abbās, may Allah be pleased with him, said,

"The freed maidservant of Maymunah, the Prophet's wife, was given a sheep, and it died. The Prophet (PBUH) passed by its carcass and said, 'Why do you not take its skin to be tanned and used? They (the listeners) replied, 'But it is dead.' The Prophet (PBUH) said, 'What is prohibited is the eating."[1]

The Prophet (PBUH) made it clear that the way to purify the skin of a dead animal is to tan it. He (PBUH) said,

"The tanning of the skin is its slaughtering,"[2]

meaning that just as slaughtering makes the eating of the flesh of a sheep or a cow lawful, likewise tanning makes the use of the skin lawful. He (PBUH) also said,

"Tanning removes its impurity,"[3]

and

"If the skin is tanned, it is purified."[4]

---

[1] Narrated Al-Bukhārī and others.
[2] Narrated by Abū Dāwūd and An-Nasā'ī
[3] Narrated by Al-Hakim.
[4] Narrated by Muslim and others.

According to some scholars, including Ash-Shawkānī, the application of these latter hadiths is quite general, including the skin of the dog or the pig. And, Allah knows best.

Q. No. (425): What is the wisdom of the Islamic manner of slaughtering?

A: The wisdom of the Islamic rules of slaughtering is to take the animal's life in the quickest and most painless way. The requirements of using a sharp instrument and of cutting the throat relate to this end. That is why it is forbidden to slit the throat by using teeth or nails since this will cause pain to the animal and is likely to strangle it. It has been narrated that the Prophet (PBUH) said,

"Verily Allah has enjoined goodness to everything; so, when you kill, kill in a good way, and when you slaughter, slaughter in a good way. Thus, each one of you should sharpen his blade, and let the (would-be) slaughtered animal die comfortably."[1]

And it has been narrated on the authority of Ibn 'Abbas, may Allah be pleased with him, that once the Prophet (PBUH) saw a man who was sharpening his knife after laying down a sheep to be slaughtered, and he (PBUH) rebuked him saying,

"Do you intend to make it die twice? Why did you not sharpen your knife before laying it down?"[2]

Therefore, the main intent here is to be kind to the animal, which cannot express itself freely, and to spare it unnecessary suffering insofar as this is possible. And, Allah knows best.

Q. No. (426): What is the significance of mentioning Allah's name when slaughtering an animal?

---

[1] Narrated by Muslim.
[2] Narrated by Al-Ḥakim.

A: Mentioning the name of Allah to purify the act of slaughtering has a subtle significance. First, this practice is in opposition to the practice of idolaters and the people of pre- pre-Islamic period who would mention the names of their non-existent and false deities while slaughtering animals. That is why the believer is recommended to mention the name of the true God. Second, these animals, like human beings, are creatures of Allah, and like them they have life. When depriving an animal of its life by slaughtering it, the Muslim mentions the name of Allah as a declaration of the divine permission for doing so. And, Allah knows best.

Q. No. (427): What is the *Shar'ī* ruling concerning animals which are slaughtered for churches and Christian festivals?

A: If one does not hear from a Christian or a Jew that a name other than Allah's, such as that of Isa (Jesus) or Uzayr (Ezra), was mentioned at the time of slaughtering, the meat he offers is lawful. If, however, he hears him mentioning a name other than Allah's, it is prohibited, according to the opinion of some Faqīhs who argue that it falls under the heading of "what has been dedicated to other than Allah". Some others maintain that the food of the People of the Scripture has been permitted to us by Allah, who is aware of what they say when slaughtering an animal. It has been narrated that someone asked Abud- Darda', may Allah be pleased with him, whether he could eat the flesh of a lamb which had been given to him and which had been slaughtered for the Church of St. George. Abū Dardā' answered, "Are they not the People of the Scripture whose food is lawful for us and ours for them?" He then told the person (who had asked him) to eat it.[1] And, Allah knows best.

Q. No. (428): What is the *Shar'ī* ruling concerning hunting with weapons?

---

[1] Narrated by At-Tabari.

A: Two conditions must be met if the game is to be killed by a weapon. First, the weapon should pierce the body of the animal, making a wound. Therefore, death by mere impact does not render it lawful. It has been narrated that 'Adiyy ibn Ḥātim said,

"I asked the Messenger of Allah (PBUH) about the game killed with a mi'rad (a weapon) and he (PBUH) said, 'If you hurl the mi'rad and it pierces the game, eat it, but if it is killed by the blow of its side, do not eat it."[1]

This Ḥadīth proves that what makes the game lawful is that the body of the animal be pierced, even if the weapon is blunt. Accordingly, a game killed by a rifle or pistol, or the like is lawful as the bullet will penetrate its body even more deeply than an arrow, spear, or sword.

The second condition to be met when hunting with a weapon is that the name of Allah must be mentioned when hurling or striking with the weapon, as the Prophet (PBUH) instructed 'Adiyy ibn Ḥātim. And, Allah knows best.

Q. No. (429): What is the *Shar'ī* ruling concerning hunting with hounds and the like?

A: If hunting is done with a dog or falcon or the like, the following requirements are to be considered: first, it should be a trained animal; second, it should catch the game for its owner and not for itself, as the Qur'ān specifies; and third, the name of Allah must be mentioned while sending it for the chase. And, Allah knows best.

Q. No. (430): What is the *Shar'ī* ruling concerning a game which is found dead?

A: It may happen that although a game is struck by an arrow it may nevertheless escape. The hunter may find it dead some time-

[1] Narrated by Al-Bukhārī and Muslim.

perhaps even days - later. In such a case, the game is lawful as food under the following conditions:

- That it is not found in water. The Prophet (PBUH) said, "If you shoot an arrow and it kills (the animal), you can eat it. But if it is found in water, you do not know whether its death was caused by drowning or by your arrow."[1]
- That it has no wounds other than the wound inflicted by the hunter's arrow. ‘Adiyy ibn Ḥātim once asked the Prophet (PBUH), "What if I shoot an arrow and find the game the next morning with my arrow in it?" The Prophet (PBUH) replied, "If you know that your arrow killed it, and you do not find any wound inflicted by wild beasts, you may eat it."[2]
- That the game has not reached the stage of decay, as eating rotten meat is likely to be injurious. It has been narrated that the Prophet (PBUH) said to Abū Tha‘labah al-Khashnī, "If you shoot an arrow but the game disappears for three days, and you then come upon it, you may eat what is not decayed of it."[3]
- And, Allah knows best.

---

[1] Narrated by Al-Bukhārī and Muslim.
[2] Narrated by At-Tirmidhī.
[3] Narrated by Muslim.

Clothing and Adornment

Q. No. (431): What is the *Shar'ī* ruling concerning going to extremes in beautification by changing what Allah created?

A: Islam denounces such excesses in beautifying oneself as require altering one's physical features. The Qur'ān considers such alterations as inspired by Satan, who ... *will command them (his devotees) to change what Allah has created...* [TMQ: 4:119] And, Allah knows best.

Q. No. (432): What are the things required in the Muslim woman's dress?

A: The following things are required in the Muslim woman's dress:

1. It must cover all her body, yet scholars have differed concerning the covering of the face and the two hands; some say they must be covered as well while some others maintain otherwise.

2. The Muslim woman's dress must not be an adornment in its own right.

3. It must be thick so that it does not reveal what is beneath it.

4. It must be loose enough so that it does not portray any part of the body.

5. It must be neither incensed nor perfumed.

6. It must not be like men's wear.

7. It must not resemble the dresses of disbelieving women.

8. It must not be a dress of distinction, i.e., a dress which is worn for the sake of ostentation, pride, and fame. And, Allah knows best.

Q. No. (433): What is the *Shar'ī* ruling concerning tattooing, shortening the teeth, and undergoing surgery for beautification?

A: The Messenger of Allah (PBUH) cursed the person who tattoos and the person who is tattooed, the person who shortens teeth and the one whose teeth are shortened.[1]

As for cutting or shortening the teeth, the Prophet (PBUH) cursed both the men and the women who do it and the women who request it. If a man does it, he incurs even a greater curse. Similarly, the Prophet (PBUH) prohibited widening the spaces between the teeth. It has been narrated that he (PBUH) cursed "... women who widen the gaps between their own or others' teeth for the sake of beauty, changing what Allah has created."[2]

As far as beautification surgeries (known as plastic surgeries) are concerned, some scholars are of the opinion that it may happen that a person has an unusual physical defect which attracts the attention of others to the point of inflicting physical and psychological pain every time he meets people. In this case, he may treat the defect and thus alleviate the embarrassment which made his life miserable. Allah the Most Merciful has imposed no hardship on us in religion. Thus, it is not permissible to undergo any surgery for the sake of beautification unless it is needed to eliminate pain or distress in the meaning expressed above. And, Allah knows best.

Q. No. (434): What is the *Shar'ī* ruling concerning plucking the eyebrows?

A: One of the extremes of beautification prohibited by Islam is *nams*, which means removing the hair of the eyebrows by plucking in order to thin or shape them. The Prophet (PBUH) cursed both the women who do the plucking and those who have it done."[3]

According to some Ḥanbalīs, if the husband approves of it, the removal of facial hair (other than that of the eyebrows) and the use

---

[1] Narrated by Muslim.
[2] Narrated by Al-Bukhārī and Muslim.
[3] Narrated by Abū Dāwūd.

of powder, creams, and other beauty aids are permitted to women, as this is part of feminine adornment. It has been narrated that once a woman asked ʿĀʾishah, may Allah be pleased with her, "What if a woman removes the hair from her forehead to please her husband?" ʿĀʾishah replied, "Remove what is harmful from yourselves (you women) whenever possible.[1]" And, Allah knows best.

Q. No. (435): What is the *Sharʿī* ruling concerning wigs and hairpieces?

A: The addition of any other hair, real or artificial, to one's own hair which is normally done by wearing wigs and hairpieces is forbidden in Islam. It has been narrated on the authority of ʿĀʾishah, may Allah be pleased with her, and others that "the Messenger of Allah (PBUH) cursed the *wasīlah* and the *mustawsīlah.*[2] *Wasīlah* denotes a woman whose profession is making wigs and hairpieces, and *mustawsīlah* is a woman who uses them. Men are prohibited such things to an even greater degree. And, Allah knows best.

Q. No. (436): What is the *Sharʿī* ruling concerning dyeing the hair?

A: This is an aspect of beautification which relates to dyeing the grey hair of the head or the beard. It has been narrated by Al-Bukhārī on the authority of Abū Hurayrah, may Allah be pleased with him, that the Prophet (PBUH) said,

"Jews and Christians do not dye their hair, so be different from them."

This is not a command but only a recommendation, as is evident from the actions of the Companions, such as Abū Bakr and Umar, who used to dye their hair, while others, such as ʿAlī, Ubayy Ibn Ka'b, and Anas did not.[3]

---

[1] Recorded in *Fatḥ al-Bārī*, the book on clothing.
[2] Narrated by Al-Bukhārī.
[3] Recorded in *Fatḥ al-Bārī*, the book on dyeing the hair.

Still, it should be known that if a man is of a very advanced age, with white hair and beard, it would hardly be appropriate for him to use black dye, as on seeing the snow-white hair of the aged father of Abū Bakr, the Prophet (PBUH) said, "Change this, but avoid black."[1] On the other hand, Az-Zuhrī said, "We dyed our hair black when the face looked young, but discarded it when the face became wrinkled and the teeth decayed."[2] And, Allah knows best.

Q. No. (437): What is the *Shar'ī* ruling concerning letting the beard grow?

A: It has been narrated on the authority of Ibn 'Umar, may Allah be pleased with him, that the Messenger of Allah (PBUH) said,

"Be different from polytheists; let the beard grow and trim the moustache."[3]

The purpose here, as the Ḥadīth states, is to be different from the polytheists. Also, shaving the beard is an affront to the masculine nature, as it is an attempt to resemble women, while the beard is an integral part of masculinity and a distinctive feature of the male sex.

A large number of Faqīhs consider shaving the beard to be prohibited on the basis of the Prophet's command. They say that this command to let the beard grow renders it an obligation, especially because it is for the purpose of being different from non-Muslims, since maintenance of this distinction from those who do not believe is obligatory for Muslims.

Some modern scholars, however, permit the shaving of the beard under the impact of events in response to public opinion.

Between these two views, there is a third view which is that shaving the beard is legally detestable. This opinion is attributed to Ayyad as

---

[1] Narrated by Muslim.
[2] Narrated by Ibn Abū Asim.
[3] Narrated by Al-Bukhārī.

mentioned by Ibn Ḥajar in *Fatḥ al-Bārī* but of no one else. And, Allah knows best.

Q. No. (438): What is the *Shar'ī* ruling concerning the keeping of statues in the Muslim home?

A: Islam has prohibited the keeping of statues in the Muslim home. By statues is meant complete, solid figures which have not been disfigured or otherwise defaced. Their presence in a house is considered sufficient to drive away angels, who represent Allah's mercy and His pleasure, as the Messenger of Allah (PBUH) said,

"Assuredly angels do not enter a house in which there are statues (or figures)."[1]

Also, according to the commentary of scholars, a person who keeps statues in his house is similar to unbelievers who keep and venerate idols in their homes. And, Allah knows best.

Crimes and Legal Punishments[2]

Q. No. (439): What is the *Shar'ī* ruling concerning a Muslim who does not reveal the faults of another Muslim?

A: It is recommended that the Muslim conceals the faults committed by another Muslim as long as this does not help in inflicting any evil upon any Muslim. It has been narrated on the authority of Abū Hurayrah, may Allah be pleased with him, that the Prophet (PBUH) said,

[1] Narrated by Al-Bukhārī and Muslim.

[2] This section also includes questions on *diyah* (blood money) as related to crimes and the legal punishments attached to them.

"And he who conceals (the faults) of a Muslim, Allah will conceal his faults in the world and in the Hereafter"[1]

And, Allah knows best.

Q. No. (440): When is killing permitted?

A: Islam ordains that no one is to be killed except for a just cause and that this is to be determined and carried out through Islamic *Sharī'ah*. And, Allah knows best.

Q. No. (441): What is the *Shar'ī* ruling if a group of people kill one person?

A: If a group of people kill one person, all of them are to be executed. It has been narrated by Mālik on the authority of Sa'id Ibnul-Musayyab that 'Umar Ibn al-Khaṭṭāb, may Allah be pleased with him, killed a group of people, five or seven, because they killed one man. Umar said, "Even if the inhabitants of Sana' helped one another (in killing) him, I would kill them all."[2] And, Allah knows best.

Q. No. (442): What are the types of killing?

A: There are three types of killing:

1. Intentional killing, which is also known as "deliberate murder," and it is that a person intentionally kills a man whose life is not to be harmed using a thing which is most likely supposed to kill.

2. Semi-intentional killing, and it is that a person strikes another with a thing which does not usually kill.

3. Unintentional killing, which is that a person kills another by mistake when doing something allowed such as hunting. And, Allah knows best.

---

[1] Narrated by Muslim.

[2] Narrated by Al-Bayhaqi and others,

Q. No. (443): What are the conditions obligating *qiṣāṣ* (retaliation)?

A: There are certain conditions which, if met, obligate *qiṣāṣ*, as follows:

1. The killer must be *mukallaf* (legally responsible).

2. The killed person must not be one of those whose blood can be lawfully shed.

3. The killed person must not be a son of the killer.

4. The killed person must not be a disbeliever and the killer a Muslim.

5. The killed person should not be a slave and the killer free. And, Allah knows best.

Q. No. (444): When is *qiṣāṣ* established?

A: *Qiṣāṣ* is to be established or confirmed by either of two things: confession and the testimony of two upright witnesses. And, Allah knows best.

Q. No. (445): What are the conditions of fulfilling *qiṣāṣ*?

A: *Qiṣāṣ* cannot be fulfilled except when the following three conditions are met:

1.The person to whom *qiṣāṣ* is to be applied must be *mukallaf.*

2. Those who have the right to have it fulfilled must agree to its fulfilment.

3. The *qiṣāṣ* must not extend to someone other than the criminal, so if a pregnant woman is to be executed, she is to be granted respite until she delivers her baby and feeds him with the first product of breast milk. And, Allah knows best.

Q. No. (446): What is the killing obligating *diyah* and what are the types of *diyah* as related to this connection, i.e., killing?

A: Scholars have agreed that *diyah* is a must in killing by mistake (unintentional killing) and semi-intentional killing, and that it is required in intentional killing only if the perpetrator does not meet any of the conditions of *Taklīf* (legal responsibility) as when he is under puberty or insane. It is also a must in intentional killing in such cases as when a free person kills a slave.

Diyah is of two types: *mukhaffafah* (lightened) and *mughallazah* (hardened).

1. *Diyah mukhaffafah* (lightened blood money) is that which is paid in case of killing by mistake or unintentional killing. It has been narrated on the authority of Amr Ibn Shu`ayb through his father who narrated through his father that the Messenger of Allah (PBUH) judged that the *diyah* required for killing a person by mistake is to be a hundred camels (as follows): thirty bint *mahkads*[1], thirty *bint labūns*[2], thirty *ḥiqqahs*[3], and ten *ibn labuns*[4].[5]

2. *Diyah mughallazah* (hardened blood money) is that which is paid in case of semi-intentional killing. The value of *diyah mughallazah* (hardened blood money) is one hundred camels forty of which are pregnant, as judged by the Prophet (PBUH) concerning semi-intentional murder.[6] This kind of *diyah* is to be paid from the property of the criminal alone.

As for *diyah* in intentional killing, it is paid if the *Walīyy* of the murdered person chooses that the killer is not to be killed, i.e., when he takes the option of compensation and not that of retaliation. This *diyah* is to be paid according to the amount on which the two parties reconcile. The Prophet (PBUH) said, "Whoever commits intentional murder, his (case) is to be in the hands of the awliyā' (plural of

---

[1] *Bint makhāḍ* is a one-year-old she-camel.
[2] *Bint labūn* is a two-year-old she-camel.
[3] *Ḥiqqah* is a three-year-old she-camel.
[4] *Ibn Labūn* is a two-year-old male camel
[5] Narrated by Abū Dāwūd and Ibn Mājah.
[6] Narrated by Abū Dāwūd, Ibn Mājah, and An-Nasā'ī.

Walīyy) of the killed person. They can (have the killer) killed if they wish, and they can take diyah if they wish, and (in this case diyah) is: thirty *ḥiqqahs*, thirty jadh'ahs[1], and forty pregnant she-camels. And what they reconcile on will be theirs (i.e., if they agree to increase the diyah, the increase will be theirs)[2] And, Allah knows best.

Q. No. (447): What are the crimes to which legal punishments are connected and what is the legal punishment of each crime?

A: According to the Qur'ān and the *Sunnah*, there are certain punishments for certain crimes. The legal punishments which are known as hudud are connected to the following crimes: *Zinā* (adultery or fornication), *qadhf* (slanderous accusation), theft, drinking *khamr* (intoxicants), *muharabah* (also *harabah*, waging war against Allah and His Messenger and doing mischief), and apostasy.

A person who commits *Zinā* is either *muḥsan* or non- *muḥsan*. A *muḥsan* person is one who has experienced sexual intercourse through a valid marriage, whereas a non-*muḥsan* person is one who has not married yet; a virgin. If a *muḥsan* person, who is free and legally responsible (*mukallaf*), commits *Zinā* willingly, he is to be stoned to death.[3] In case of a non- *muḥsan* person, he is to be flogged with a hundred stripes and be exiled for one year. If a slave, male or female, commits *Zinā*, no stoning to death is to be applied to him or her. He or she is to be lashed with fifty lashes. And if a man has intercourse with another man, and this is known as sodomy, the two men are to be executed whether they are *muḥsan* or not.

The legal punishment of *qadhf* is that the person who commits it is to be flogged with eighty lashes.

---

[1] Jadh'ah is a four-year-old she-camel.

[2] Narrated by At-Tirmidhī and Ibn Mājah.

[3] Accordingly, this punishment is not to be inflicted to a person who is insane, immature, or a slave.

If a person drinks *khamr* willingly while knowing that what he drinks is *khamr*, he is to be flogged with forty lashes, and the ruler or the judge - can increase it up to eighty lashes if he sees that this is befitting.

The legal punishment of a person who commits theft is that his hand is to be cut off. Concerning the punishment of harabah, Almighty Allah says,

﴿إِنَّمَا جَزَٰٓؤُاْ ٱلَّذِينَ يُحَارِبُونَ ٱللَّهَ وَرَسُولَهُۥ وَيَسۡعَوۡنَ فِي ٱلۡأَرۡضِ فَسَادًا أَن يُقَتَّلُوٓاْ أَوۡ يُصَلَّبُوٓاْ أَوۡ تُقَطَّعَ أَيۡدِيهِمۡ وَأَرۡجُلُهُم مِّنۡ خِلَٰفٍ أَوۡ يُنفَوۡاْ مِنَ ٱلۡأَرۡضِۚ ذَٰلِكَ لَهُمۡ خِزۡيٞ فِي ٱلدُّنۡيَاۖ وَلَهُمۡ فِي ٱلۡأٓخِرَةِ عَذَابٌ عَظِيمٌ ٣٣﴾

"The recompense of those who wage war against Allah and His Messenger and do mischief in the land is only that they shall be killed or crucified or their hands and their feet be cut off on the opposite sides, or be exiled from the land. That is their disgrace in this world, and a great torment is theirs in the Hereafter." [TMQ: 5: 33]

Some scholars say that, "or" which is mentioned between the items of punishment in the verse, means that the ruler can choose from these items of punishment what he sees as most befitting. Whereas most scholars maintain that "or" here signifies variation, in the meaning that the punishment varies according to the crime committed, and that these items of punishment are according to the "arrangement" of the crimes and do not signify choosing; for example, if they kill and take property, they are to be crucified[1], and so on according to the crime committed. And, Allah knows best.

Q. No. (448): What is the *Shar'ī* ruling concerning discretionary punishment (*Ta'zīr*) which is based on taking property?

---

[1] This example has been taken from the judgment of Ibn 'Abbās in this regard as narrated by Ash-Shāfi'ī in his Musnad.

A: According to Mālik and Abū Yusuf, it is permissible that the ruler (or the judge) punishes a person by taking his property or part of it. Ibnul-Qayyim said that the Prophet (PBUH) applied a discretionary punishment to the effect that he deprived a person of his share in the booty. It has also been narrated by Aḥmad and others that the Prophet (PBUH) said concerning *Zakāh*,

"Whoever pays it seeking to receive a reward (from Allah) will receive its reward, and if any person withholds it, we shall surely take it (from him) in addition to half of his property..."

And, Allah knows best.

Q. No. (449): What is the *Shar'ī* ruling concerning a person who spoils the crop of another?

A: If a person, while irrigating his own crop, spoils the crop of another person because his irrigation is done more heavily than what is normally done, he is liable for this ruined crop. However, if water is poured from an unknown spot, he is not to be held responsible for that. In general, whenever a crop is drowned because of him, he is to guarantee that. And, Allah knows best.

Q. No. (450): What is the *Shar'ī* ruling concerning a physician who causes harm to a person while medicating him?

A: There is no difference between scholars concerning the judgment that if a person who has no medical experience tries to medicate someone and causes harm to him, he is to be held responsible for that according to the harm he has caused. It has been narrated that the Prophet (PBUH) said,

"If a person practices medication and no one knows that he has ever practiced it before, he is responsible (for any harm he may cause)."[1]

And, Allah knows best.

---

[1] Narrated by Abū Dāwūd and others.

Q. No. (451): Is the legal punishment of *khamr* drinking the only punishment in this regard?

A: A person who drinks *khamr* is to be lashed with forty lashes which can be increased up to eighty lashes. In addition to this punishment, the Prophet (PBUH) is reported to have said a number of hadiths concerning *khamr* and drunkenness, including the following:

- "A habitual *khamr* drunkard will not enter Paradise."[1] "Allah has cursed *khamr*, the one who drinks it, the one who serves it, the one who sells it, the one who buys it, the one who wrings it, the one for whom it is wrung, the one who carries it, and the one to whom it is carried." [2]
- "*khamr* is the mother (i.e., source) of evil things. So, whoever drinks it his prayer will not be accepted for forty days, and if he dies while it is in his abdomen, he will die (as stray) as (the people of the pre-Islamic period of) ignorance."[3] And, Allah knows best.

Q. No. (452): Is it permissible to invoke Allah against a person who drinks *khamr*?

A: This is not permissible. It has been narrated on the authority of Umar, may Allah be pleased with him, that during the lifetime of the Prophet (PBUH) there was a man called `Abdullah whose nickname was "*himar* (donkey)," and he used to make the Messenger of Allah (PBUH) smile. The Prophet (PBUH) lashed him because of drinking (*khamr*). And one day he was brought to the Prophet (PBUH) on the same charge and was lashed. On that, a man among the people said, "O Allah! Curse him! How frequently he has been brought (to the Prophet on such a charge)!" The Prophet (PBUH) said, "Do not curse

---

[1] Narrated by Ibn Mājah.
[2] Narrated by Abū Dāwūd and others.
[3] Narrated by At-Tabarani.

him, for by Allah, I know for he loves Allah and His Messenger."[1] It has also been narrated on the authority of Abū Hurayrah, who said,

"A drunkard was brought to the Prophet (PBUH) and he ordered that he be beaten (lashed). Some of us beat him with their hands, some with their shoes, and some with their garments (twisted in the form of a lash). When that drunk had left, a man said, 'What is wrong with him? May Allah disgrace him!' The Messenger of Allah (PBUH) said, 'Do not help Satan against your (Muslim) brother."[2]

And, Allah knows best.

---

[1] Narrated by Al-Bukhārī.
[2] Narrated by Al-Bukhārī and Abū Dāwūd.

Jurisdiction

Q. No. (453): What is the *Shar'ī* ruling concerning jurisdiction in general?

A: Jurisdiction is a collective obligation or *farḍ kifāyah*, in the meaning that if some Muslim in a certain place is assigned by the ruler for judging people, that will be sufficient for all the other Muslims in this place as to the obligation of judging between people.

Another aspect of the "obligation" related to jurisdiction is that the ruler "must" assign persons- according to the need of the country he rules - to judge between people. This is because the Prophet (PBUH) used to judge between people, and he also sent 'Alī to Yemen for the same job. Also, the Rightly- guided Caliphs used to judge between people and appointed judges in the countries under their rule.[1] And, Allah knows best.

Q. No. (454): Who is to judge between people?

A: In his *Fatḥ al-Bārī*, Ibn Ḥajar, may Allah have mercy upon him, mentions that, according to Abū 'Alī Al-Karabisi, a follower of Ash-Shāfi'ī, there is no difference between scholars that the worthiest of people as regards the right to judge between them is a person who has the following qualities:

-To be of well-known excellence, truthfulness, knowledge, and piety.

-To be a good reciter of the Qur'ān and know most of its rules and rulings.

-To be well aware of the *Sunnah* of the Prophet (PBUH) and memorize most of it.

---

[1] Manarus- Sabil, 2/453.

-To be well aware of the statements and traditions related to the Prophet's Companions and those related to their successors (*Tabi''un*) and the points of agreement and difference therein.

-To be a person who follows guidance concerning any matter first in the Qur'ān then, if he is not guided to any solution therein, he it to search it in the *Sunnah* then the fatwas delivered by the greater Companions.

-To be a person who always studies (religious knowledge and other related items of knowledge) with the people of knowledge and consult with them.

-To preserve his tongue, abdomen, and genitals against evil.

-To be able to understand the speech of litigants.

-To be reasonable and not to follow his vain or personal desires, i.e., to be objective.

After that the great scholar concludes with these words,

"Though we know that there is no one on earth who can enjoy all these qualities, yet we do assert that the best of people and the nearest of them to perfection must be sought (for this job)."[1] And, Allah knows best.

Q. No. (455): What are the ways of authenticating a suit?

A: A suit can be authenticated or confirmed through three ways: confession, bearing testimony, and taking oath.

1. Confession

If a person who is legally responsible (mukallaf) willingly confesses that he has done a certain thing, the judge must deliver his judgment in the case in question according to this confession. It has

---

[1] *Fatḥ al-Bārī*, 13/146

been narrated that the Prophet (PBUH) stoned Ma'iz and Al-Ghamidiyyah after their confessing the crime of adultery.[1]

2. Testimony

A suit can be authenticated and confirmed through the testimony of witnesses, and it is an individual obligation (*fard 'ayn*) on the part of any person who is called for testimony. Important still, testimony is accepted only from those who are Muslim, mature, insane, and upright.[2]

3. Taking oath

If the plaintiff fails to present any item of proof and the defendant denies the right in question, the plaintiff will have nothing in this

---

[1] Narrated by Muslim.

[2] The quorum of testimony is defined according to the case in which testimony is sought and this itself is determined according to the right claimed.
Rights are of two sections: the rights of Allah and the rights of humans.
The rights of humans are of three types:
1. A type in which two male witnesses are accepted, and it concerns things which have nothing to do with property such as marriage and divorce.
2. A type in which two men or a man and two women or one witness and the oath of the plaintiff are accepted, and it concerns things connected with property such as selling.
3. A type in which two men or one man and two women or four women are accepted as witnesses, and it concerns things which are not seen by men in normal cases, such as suckling, child delivery, and internal defects of women.
The rights of Allah, however, do not stand for the testimony of women, as Az-Zuhri says, "No person is to be flogged as a legal punishment except with the testimony of two men."
These rights are of three types:
1. A type in which not less than four men are accepted as witnesses, and it concerns Zinā. Almighty Allah says, and those who accuse chaste women, and produce not four witnesses, flog them with eighty stripes... [TMQ:24:4]
2. A type in which two men are accepted as witnesses, and it concerns things for which there are legal punishments other than Zinā, according to the aforementioned statement of Az-Zuhrī.
3. A type in which one man is accepted, and it concerns the seeing of Ramaḍān crescent.

regard except the oath taken by the defendant. The Prophet (PBUH) said, "The proof is to be presented by the plaintiff and the oath is to be taken by the defendant."[1]

And, Allah knows best.

Q. No. (456): What is the *Shar'ī* ruling concerning a person's seeking to be a ruler or a judge?

A: It has been narrated that Abdur-Rahman Ibn Samurah, may Allah be pleased with him, said,

"The Prophet (PBUH) said (to me), O Abdur- Rahman! Do not seek to be a ruler, for if you are given authority on your demand then you will be held responsible for it, but if you are given it without asking (for it), then you will be helped (by Allah) in it..."[2]

Seeking to be a judge is similar to seeking to be ruler. And, Allah knows best.

Q. No. (457): What is the *Shar'ī* ruling concerning a person who judges between people while feeling angry?

A: It is not for a person to judge between people while he is in any angry mood. It has been narrated that Abdur-Rahman Ibn Abū Bakrah said,

"Abū Bakrah wrote to his son who was in Sijistan, 'Do not judge between two persons when you are angry, for I heard the Prophet (PBUH) saying, 'A judge should not judge between two persons while he is in an angry mood."[3]

And, Allah knows best.

---

[1] Narrated by At-Tirmidhī.
[2] Narrated by Al-Bukhārī, Muslim, and others
[3] Narrated by Al-Bukhārī, Muslim, and others

Q. No. (458): Does a judge's verdict change the truth as to the legality or illegality of things?

A: A judge's verdict does not change the truth as to the legality or illegality of things. It has been narrated that Umm Salamah, the wife of the Prophet (PBUH), said that once the Messenger of Allah (PBUH) heard the clamour of some contenders at the door of his apartment. He went to them and said,

"I am a human being, and the claimants bring to me (the dispute) and one of them may be more eloquent than the others. Thus, I may judge him to be on the right and decide in his favour. So, If I, by my judgment, give someone (the undue share) out of the right of a Muslim, I will be giving him a portion of Fire. There- fore, he may burden himself with it or abandon it."[1]

And, Allah knows best.

Q. No. (459): What is the *Sharʿī* ruling concerning a person who judges between people while he is not qualified to do so?

A: Scholars have stated that it is not permissible for a person to judge between people as long as he is not qualified for that. They also assert that if such a person judges between people, he will be sinful and his judgment is not to be effective whether it is in conformity with the truth or not, because such conformity with the truth will come accidentally and not according to a well-established verdict which has been given on the basis of some *Sharʿī* origin. And, Allah knows best.

Q. No. (460): In what exactly should a judge equal between two contenders?

A: He should treat them equally in five things: in letting them enter upon him, in letting them sit before him, in receiving them, in

---

[1] Narrated by Muslim and others.

listening to them, and finally in judging between them concerning the case in question. And, Allah knows best.

Q. No. (461): What is the *Shar'ī* ruling concerning the testimony of a blind man?

A: According to Mālik and Aḥmad, it is permissible for a blind person to bear testimony concerning a case in which he testifies for something he "heard" as long as he can identify the voice in question. Thus, his testimony is permissible in cases related to marriage, divorce, trade, endowment, confession, and the like, whether he witnessed the case in question when he was blind or when he was endowed with eyesight then became blind thereafter. Ibnul-Qasim said,

"I said to Mālik, (What about the case in which) a man hears his neighbour divorcing his wife from behind a wall (without being able to see him)? (Can) he testifies to that (divorce) as he identified the voice?" Mālik replied, His testimony is permissible (i.e., effective)" The Shāfi'īs say that a blind person's testimony is permissible only in certain things including lineage and death.

Finally, Abū Ḥanīfah asserts that a blind person's testimony is not acceptable in principle. And, Allah knows best.

Dealings and Transactions

Q. No. (462): What are the forbidden forms of trade?

A: Everything is lawful to sell as long as this is undertaken according to the consent of the seller and the buyer and as long as the item in question or the form of selling is not forbidden by the Sharīʿah. The forbidden forms of trade can be listed in brief as follows:

1. **Business monopoly**: As monopoly means concentration of supply in one hand, it leads to exploitation of the consumers and the workers, and it has, therefore, been declared unlawful by the Prophet (PBUH). Huge trusts, cartels, and monopolies should not exist in Islamic society. The monopoly-dominated economic order betrays lack of harmony between private and social good and is, thus, a negation of the principle of maximum social advantage which the Islamic society sets out to achieve.

2. **Speculative business based on selfish interest**: Speculation means buying something cheap in bulk at a time and selling it at a high price at another and, thus, controlling the market to achieve personal gains.

3. **Interest transactions:** All transactions involving interest are forbidden in Islam.

4. **Transactions similar (in nature) to gambling**: Any monetary gain which comes too easily, so much so that one does not have to work for it, is unlawful. The principle on which the objection to gambling is based is that you gain what you have not earned, or lose by mere chance. Dice, lottery, prize bonds, and horse race betting are to be held within the definition of gambling.

5. ***Munābadhaḥ* and *Mulāmasaḥ***: *Munābadhaḥ* means that the seller should throw the cloth to the buyer before he has carefully examined it. The very act of throwing the cloth will mean that the

bargain has been struck. *Mulāmasaḥ* means touching the cloth without examining it, i.e., the buyer was just supposed to touch the cloth to strike the bargain. Both these forms of transaction were prohibited because in either case the purchaser could not carefully examine the things sold to him, and the bargain was likely to prove unduly disadvantageous to one side.

6. ***Muzābanah:*** It is the exchange of fresh fruits for dry ones in a way that the quantity of the dry fruits is actually measured and fixed, but the quantity of the fresh fruits to be given in exchange is guessed while it is still on the trees.

7. ***Mu'āwamah:*** It consists in selling the fruit on the trees in one, two, or three years even before it has made its appearance. It is prohibited because like *Muzābanah* it is also a leap into the dark. Such transactions may result in bitterness and frustration.

8. ***Gharar*** (Aleatory Trade): This includes every form of trade that includes unawareness and risk. In other words, it is to sell a thing which one does not have in one's possession, nor expects to bring it under one's control, e. g., fish in the river, or birds in the air.

9. ***Bay' al-Ḥasāh* (Sale by means of pebbles):** In his commentaries on Ṣaḥīḥ Muslim (10/156), Imām An-Nawawi says that there are three interpretations for what is meant by the pebble trade or *Bay' al-Ḥasāh:*

- The purchaser tells the seller that when he will throw a pebble on his goods, the sale contract will be confirmed for such and such a price.

- The seller tells the purchaser that on whatever thing a pebble thrown by him falls will be sold to him.

- The seller tells the purchaser that he has the right to cancel the trade he has transacted with him only until he throws his pebble.

10. ***Bay' al-Muḍṭar*** **(Trade conducted by force)**: It is to buy something forcibly or to purchase something when its owner is compelled under stress of want to dispose it off.

11. **Sale over the sale of another**: When one person has sold goods to another, a third person should not upset the bargain trying to sell his own goods to the latter, offering them at lower rates or pointing out the defect in the goods already sold to him by the former. And, Allah knows best.

Q. No. (463): What are the things which are not to be sold?

A: There are certain things that the Muslim is not allowed to trade in, as follows:

1. *Khamr*, and this includes all kinds of intoxicants.

2. Carcass, swine, and idols.

3. Dogs.

4. Statues and other similar things related to creatures having souls.

5. Unripe fruit and unripe corn. And, Allah knows best.

Q. No. (464): What are the divisions of *Khiṣār* (choices in business dealings)?

A: There are three divisions of *Khiṣār*, as follows:

1. ***Khiṣārul-Majlis*** **(the *Khiṣār* connected to the transaction place):** This *Khiṣār* is established on the part of the two contractors in question from the time they contract the transaction until they separate (physically), unless they agree that there is no *Khiṣār*, or cancel it after the contraction, or one of them cancels it thus cancelling his own right (to *Khiṣār*) yet not the right of the other contractor.

2. ***Khiṣārush- Sharṭ*** **(the *Khiṣār* based on a condition):** This division of *Khiṣār* is that the seller or the buyer or both of them set a condition

that *Khiṣār* - i.e., the right to confirm or cancel the transaction in question is effective during a specific period, and this *Khiṣār* is valid even if this period should be long.

3. ***Khiṣārul- 'Ayb* (the *Khiṣār* caused by defects):** This division of *Khiṣār* means that if a man buys a defective commodity yet he does not discover this defect except after he and the seller separate the transaction place, he has the right to return the commodity to the seller. And, Allah knows best.

Q. No. (465): What is *Salām* and what is the *Shar'ī* ruling concerning applying it to something that is not possessed?

A: *Salām* is terminologically defined as selling something whose price is paid in advance, and it is to be delivered later.

It is not stipulated that the person who is to deliver the thing which has been bought through *Salām* has this thing in his possession at the time of the deal. And, Allah knows best.

Q. No. (466): What is the description of a legal partnership?

A: A legal partnership exists when there is consent between two or more people who agree that each of them will pay a specified amount of his property whereby, they seek to have profits on condition that each of them will receive from these profits what is tantamount to what he has paid and that he will share with the others - also according to his proportion - in the expenses and the like. Such partnership is permissible as long as there is consent no matter whether the share of one of the partners is too small and the share of another one is very big. This is because it is like a form of trading which is undertaken on a basis of consent, tolerance, and good-heartedness.[1] And, Allah knows best.

---

[1] See As-Saylul-Jarrar, 3/246-248.

Q. No. (467): What is *Muḍārabah* (sharing venture) in Islam and what is the *Shar'ī* ruling concerning the labourer who violates the agreement?

A: In Islam, *Muḍārabah*, which is also called *qirāḍ*, is a contract which is conducted between two persons who agree that one of them will pay to the other a sum of money in cash in order to trade therein and the profits will result from this are to be shared between the two according to the proportions upon which they both agree.

Muḍārabah is permissible whether it is applied with certain restrictions or without such restrictions, and the labourer - i.e., the person who receives the money to trade in - is not liable for the money unless he transgresses or violates the conditions agreed upon. Ibnul-Mundhir said,

"They (scholars) have agreed that if the owner of the money forbids the labourer to sell on credit, i.e., sale based on delay of payment, and the labourer does otherwise, he is to be held liable for the money.[1]"

And, Allah knows best.

Q. No. (468): What is *Ijārah*, and in what is it permissible?

A: *Ijārah* can be defined as a contract granting use or occupation of an item of property during a specified period in exchange for a specified rent. This also applies to hiring someone for doing a certain job for specified wages.

Ijārah can be applied to everything which can be used with the remaining of its *'ayn* (object, substance), i.e., the thing used should not disappear as a result of *Ijārah*. To illustrate this, a man can use an apartment for a specified time, and this is included in *Ijārah*, but

---

[1] Al- Ijma, 125.

he cannot make use of a small quantity of water in a utensil by drinking them and call this *Ijārah*.

Thus, everything which can be used with the remaining of its *'ayn* can be hired or leased as long as this is not forbidden due to some *Shar'ī* reason.

Also, the rented object must be known, i.e., defined, and so must be the remuneration, which is to be paid, the period of rent, and the kind of work or use for which this thing is rented or hired. And, Allah knows best.

Q. No. (469): What is the Islamic attitude toward demanding debts and paying them back?

A: Whenever the Muslim demands his due debts back, he should do that in a good way as tolerance is a characteristic of Islam and Muslims. It has been narrated on the authority of Abū Hurayrah, may Allah be pleased with him, that the Prophet (PBUH) owed somebody a camel of a certain age. When he came to demand it back, the Prophet (PBUH) said (to some people), "Give him (his due)." When the people searched for a camel of that age, they found none but found a camel one year older. The Prophet (PBUH) said, "Give (it to) him." On that, the man remarked, "You have given me my right in full. May Allah give you in full!" The Prophet (PBUH) said,

"The best amongst you are those who pay the rights of others in a good way."[1]

Also, if an indebted person is insolvent and thus does not have money to pay his debt back, the creditor is recommended to give him time until he becomes able to repay.

---

[1] Narrated by Al-Bukhārī, Muslim, and others.

Concerning paying debts back, it has been narrated on the authority of Abū Hurayrah, may Allah be pleased with him, that the Prophet (PBUH) said,

"Whoever takes people's property with the intention of repaying it, Allah will repay it on his behalf (i.e., will help him repay it), and whoever takes it in order to spoil it, then Allah will spoil him."[1]

This means that the Muslim should be keen on paying his debts back and never think of spoiling any money he may have borrowed from people. And, Allah knows best.

Q. No. (470): Why is *Ribā* prohibited?

A: In his *Al-Ḥalāl wa-l-Ḥarām fī al-Islām* Al-Qaraḍāwī says that Islam strictly prohibits *Ribā* because it is deeply concerned for the moral, social, and economic welfare of mankind. Muslim scholars have given sound arguments, explaining the wisdom of this prohibition, and recent studies have confirmed their opinion, with some additions and extensions of their arguments.

Then Al-Qaraḍāwī quotes what Imām Ar-Razi said in his *Tafsīr* of the Qur'ān in this regard, as follows,

"**First**, *Ribā* requires the taking of interest appropriating another person's property without giving him anything in exchange, because the one who lends one *dirham* for two *dirhams* gets the extra *dirham* in exchange of nothing. Now, a man's property is for (the purpose of) fulfilling his needs and it has great sanctity, according to the Ḥadīth, 'A man's property is as sacred as his blood."[2] This means that taking it from him without giving him anything in exchange is prohibited.

Second, dependence on interest prevents people from working to earn money, since the person with dirhams can earn an extra *dirham*

---

[1] Narrated by Al-Bukhārī.
[2] Narrated by Abū Nu'aym.

through interest, whether at once or at a later date, without working for it. The value of work will consequently be reduced in his estimation, and he will not bother himself to take the trouble of running a business or risking his money in trade or industry. This will lead to depriving people of benefits...

Third, permitting the taking of interest discourages people from doing good to one another as required by Islam. If interest is prohibited in a society, people will lend to each other with good will, expecting back no more than what they have loaned, while if interest is made permissible the needy person will be required to pay back more on loans (than what he has borrowed), and this will weaken his feelings of good will and friendliness toward the lender.

Fourth, the lender is very likely to be wealthier and the borrower poorer. If interest is allowed, the rich will exploit the poor, and this is against the spirit of mercy and charity."[1]

After that Al-Qaraḍāwī says that in a society where interest is lawful, the strong people benefit from the suffering of the weak. As a result, the rich become richer and the poor poorer, creating socio-economic classes in the society separated by wide gulfs. Naturally this generates envy and hatred among the poor toward the rich, and contempt and callousness among the rich toward the poor. Conflicts arise, the socio-economic fabric is rent, revolutions are born, and social order is threatened.

Then Al-Qaraḍāwī concludes this part with the words: "Recent history amply illustrates the dangers to the peace and stability of nations inherent in interest-based economies.[2]" And, Allah knows best.

---

[1] Ar- Razi, Tafsir, 7/4.

[2] *See Al-Ḥalālu wal-Ḥarāmu fil-Islām*, chapter four, the section dealing with "Transactions".

Q. No. (471): What are the divisions of Ribā?

A: *Ribā* is divided into two sections:

1. ***Ribā an-Nasā'ah***, or interest on lent money. This is the interest that the lender stipulates that the borrower must pay in return of the delay of payment. This kind of *Ribā* is prohibited according to the Qur'ān, the *Sunnah*, and the consensus of Muslim scholars.

2. ***Ribā al-Faḍl***, or interest based on superiority, and it is the taking of a superior thing of the same kind of goods and giving more of the same kind of goods of inferior quality, e.g., dates of superior quality for dates of inferior quality in greater amount. This kind of *Ribā* is prohibited as well according to the Sunnah and consensus of scholars. And, Allah knows best.

Q. No. (472): What is *muzara'ah* (crop-sharing) and is it lawful absolutely?

A: *Muzāra'ah* is terminologically defined as giving a piece of land to a person to cultivate it against half of what it will produce or the like of that. There is no harm that the expenses be shouldered by the owner of the land which is to be cultivated in the way of *Muzāra'ah* or by the person who is to cultivate it or by them both.

The Prophet (PBUH) forbade his Companions, may Allah be pleased with them, to practice another form of crop-sharing which clearly involves great uncertainty and risk, and is contrary to the spirit of justice. It went that the landowner would give out his land conditional to his getting the produce of one part of it and the cultivator the produce of the remaining part or perhaps half, or to the owner's getting a specified weight or measure of the grain produced and the cultivator the rest. But sometimes one part of the land produced a crop while the other did not, so that one of the two would receive nothing or very little, while the other would take everything or most of the produce. Similarly, if the total produce did not exceed the specified weight or measure, the owner would get everything while the cultivator would get nothing. And, Allah knows best.

Q. No. (473): What is *Musāqah*?

A: *Musāqah* is to give certain trees to a person to water and take care of them in exchange for part of the crop of these trees. It has been narrated on the authority of Ibn 'Umar, may Allah be pleased with him, that the Messenger of Allah (PBUH) contracted with the people of Khaybar (the trees) on the condition that he would have half of the produce in fruits and harvest.[1] And, Allah knows best.

Q. No. (474): What is the Islamic attitude toward *Iḥyā' al-Mawāt* or cultivation of barren land?

A: *Iḥyā' al-Mawāt* is cultivating a barren land so that it can be fertile and productive. This kind of cultivation generally concerns such barren lands which have no known owners. Thus, if a barren piece of land is not known to have any owner, a person can water and watch it until it becomes fertile, and this makes him its owner.[2]

Islam encourages Muslims to cultivate barren lands. It has been narrated by Al-Bukhārī on the authority of 'Ā'ishah, may Allah be pleased with her, that the Messenger of Allah (PBUH) said,

"He who cultivates a land that does not belong to anybody is more rightful (to own it)."

After that Al-Bukhārī says, "Urwah said that "Umar gave the same verdict during his Caliphate."

There are other Ḥadīths giving the same meaning and judgment. And, Allah knows best.

---

[1] Narrated by Al-Bukhārī, Muslim, and others.

[2] See *Fatḥ al-Bārī*, 5/18.

Q. No. (475): What is the *Shar'ī* ruling concerning *rahn* or mortgaging?

A: *Rahn* is putting up collateral connected to a debt so that it can be used for taking one's due in full if the indebted person cannot pay the debt back.[1] It has been narrated that the Prophet (PBUH) purchased food grains from a Jew on credit and mortgaged his iron armour to him.[2]

Interestingly enough, it is not permissible for the mortgagee to benefit from the mortgaged thing because of the general rule stating that whenever a loan brings about interest this becomes a form of *Ribā*. However, if the mortgaged thing is a thing that can be taken as a mount or if it can be milked, the mortgagee can mount or milk it if he spends on it, as the Prophet (PBUH) said, "A person can ride the mortgaged animal because of what he spends on it, and he can drink the milk of a milch animal as long as it is mortgaged."

Also, mortgaging becomes ineffective once the mortgaged thing is returned to the mortgagor according to the mortgagee's will. And, Allah knows best.

Q. No. (476): What is the *Shar'ī* ruling concerning wadi ah or trusts deposited for safekeeping?

A: Whenever a man entrusts his Muslim brother with something to keep it from him, it is desirable that he accepts that as long as he knows that he is able to keep it well, because this is a form of cooperation in righteousness a piety that Islam encourages. Also, the entrusted person must give the entrusted thing back when he is asked to do so.

Yet it should be known that there is no liability on the part of the entrusted person concerning the entrusted thing except when he is responsible for ruining or losing it. It has been narrated that the

---

[1] See *Fatḥ al-Bārī*, 5/140.
[2] Narrated by *Al-Bukhārī*.

Prophet (PBUH) said, "Whoever is trusted with a trust, there is no guarantee on him."[1] And, Allah knows best.

Q. No. (477): What is the *shari* ruling concerning *Ḥawālah* or transferring the right to collect a debt?

A: *Ḥawālah* is transferring the right to collect a debt from one person to another. This happens when the troubled person transfers this right to another person from whom the creditor can get his money back. Islam allows *Ḥawālah* because it is something that people need to do to solve some problems that may result as regards payment of debts. Thus, if "A" is indebted to "B" yet "C" is indebted at the same time to "A", the *Sharī'ah* allows "A" to make "B" collect his money from "C", who is indebted to "A". "B" must accept the transfer of the right to collect the debt in question if "C" is well-to-do. And, Allah knows best.

Q. No. (478): What is the *shar'i* ruling concerning *'Ārīyah* or lending things for use?

A: *'Ārīyah* is something whose owner allows others to use without receiving any remuneration for that.

It is legally desirable to give something to others to use as *'ariyah*. However, whenever a person gives something to another person to use as *'Ārīyah*, the latter must give it back to him after making use of it, and there is no guarantee on his part except in case of negligence. Also, a person who receives a *'Ārīyah* is to guarantee it if the person who gives it to him stipulates that he should guarantee it. And, Allah knows best.

Q. No. (479): What is the *Shar'ī* ruling concerning *Luqāṭah* or findings?

---

[1] Narrated by Ibn Mājah.

A: *Luqāṭah* refers to every kind of property which has been lost by someone and is prone to losing and forfeiture and whose owner is unknown.

Whenever a person finds any kind of property, he must identify its type and number then make an upright person testify to that then keep it and make a public announcement about it for one year. After that, if a person tells him of a distinctive sign that proves his being its owner, he is to give it to him, even if this happens after the passing of one year; otherwise, he can make use of it.

It is also worth mentioning that whoever finds an eatable thing in his way, can eat it; and whoever finds a trivial thing which no one would yearn to have, can take it and utilize it.

Moreover, any *Luqāṭah* which is found in the Haram can be picked up only for making a public announcement of it forever, and it is not permissible for anyone to possess it after the passing of one year as normally done with items of *Luqāṭah* found elsewhere. And, Allah knows best.

Q. No. (480): What is the *Shar'ī* ruling concerning *laqīt* or foundling?

A: *Laqīṭ* is a child who is under the age of puberty and who is found astray in a street (or any similar place) and whose lineage is not known.

Picking such a child up is a collective obligation or *Farḍ kifāyah*, and it is one of the forms of cooperation in righteousness. If there is any money with him, it is to be spent on him, otherwise his spending is to be on the public treasury.[1]

If a foundling dies and leaves inheritance yet no heirs, his inheritance is to be taken by the public treasury. The same ruling

---

[1] See Al- Irwa', 1573.

applies to his *diyah* (blood money) if he is killed and a *diyah* is to be paid for that.

And if a person, male or female, claims that a certain foundling belongs to his or her family, he is to be ascribed to the lineage of this person as long as this attribution is possible. If two or more people claim that he belongs to them, the foundling is to be ascribed to the person who presents proof that supports his claim. And, Allah knows best.

Q. No. (481): What is the *Shar'ī* ruling concerning *shuf'ah* (pre-emption)?

A: *Shuf'ah* or pre-emption can be simply defined as the right to purchase something before others.

It has been narrated on the authority of Jābir Ibn Abdullah, may Allah be pleased with him, that the Prophet (PBUH) gave a verdict regarding *shuf'ah* in every undivided joint thing (property), but if the limits are defined (or demarcated) or the ways and streets are fixed, then there is no pre-emption.[1]

Therefore, whoever has a partner in a land, a garden, a house, or anything of the kind, should not sell his share until he lets his partner know that he wants to sell it. If he sells it before informing his partner, the latter is worthier of the purchased object. And, Allah knows best.

Q. No. (482): What is the *Shar'ī* ruling concerning *hibah* (gifts and presents)?

A: *Hibah* is that a person puts another in possession of something that he owns without remuneration.

---

[1] Narrated by Al-Bukhārī and others.

Islam encourages *hibah* and warns Muslims against depreciating things that they may receive as gifts or presents. It has been narrated that the Prophet (PBUH) said,

"Exchange presents (and gifts) so that you may love one another."[1]

It is recommended that when a person receives something as a present or a gift, he may reward the person who has given it to him in any suitable way by giving him something in return. Islam also encourages that one's relatives and neighbours are worthier of one's gifts and presents, especially when they are in need of these gifts and presents. And, Allah knows best. Still, the Muslim should not give preference to one of his children over another when he gives them gifts.

Finally, no gifts are to be given to State officials. A State official here refers to any person who has been appointed by the State to be in charge of a certain job, such as ministers, managers, etc. No employee of the kind is to receive a gift or a present because it may be given to him as a bribe. Were he not appointed in the position in question, he would not in most cases be given such gifts. And, Allah knows best.

Q. No. (483): What is the *Shar'ī* ruling concerning waqf (endowments)?

A: *Waqf* can be defined as keeping some property and spending what comes out of it in the form of profits and the like - in the cause of Allah. Allah has legislated waqf and made it a means through which His servants can draw near to Him. Among the religious texts that encourage waqf is the verse in which Allah says,

﴿لَن تَنَالُواْ ٱلۡبِرَّ حَتَّىٰ تُنفِقُواْ مِمَّا تُحِبُّونَۚ وَمَا تُنفِقُواْ مِن شَيۡءٖ فَإِنَّ ٱللَّهَ بِهِۦ
عَلِيمٞ ٩٢﴾

[1] Narrated by Al-Bayhaqi.

"By no means shall you attain righteousness unless You spend (in charity) of that which you love" [TMQ: 3:92]

There are two types of *waqf*:

1. Family-oriented endowment, and this is the endowment which is specified for one's relatives.

2. Charitable endowment, and this is the endowment which is specified for any of the various forms of charity spending as well as spending in the cause of Allah in general.

It is valid to endow everything which can be lawfully sold and purchased and from which people can benefit with the existence of its object, unlike things whose objects or substances cannot exist except for short times such as food, drinks, and the like. And, Allah knows best.

Q. No. (484): What is the *Shar'ī* ruling concerning *wakalah* (authorization)?

A: *Wakalah* is that a person authorizes another to replace him and act as if he was him whether absolutely or under certain restrictions. The legality of *wakalah* is supported by the Qur'ān, the Sunnah, and consensus of scholars.

As a general rule, everything which a person can permissibly undertake by himself is permissible as to be undertaken by another person whom this person authorizes to act on his behalf concerning this thing.

A person who is authorized to act on behalf of another must be truthful and so he must be up to the responsibility which he has incurred as a result of this authorization. Therefore, as an authorized person is just like an entrusted person, he is not to guarantee the thing concerning which he has been deputized except in case of negligence. And, Allah knows best.

Q. No. (485): What is the *Shar'ī* ruling concerning *Ja'alah* (a contract of achieving an expected benefit)?

A: *Ja'ālah* is a form of contract conducted between a person who needs to obtain some expected benefit, such as bringing something lost, and a person who is ready to achieve this benefit. An "expected" benefit means that the lost thing for example is expected to be found if some effort is exerted for getting it. According to this contract certain remuneration for doing the job in question is to be defined. *Ja'ālah* also applies to such things as defining a certain compensation for a person for helping one's son to memorize the Qur'ān, or for curing him, and the like. This is legal.

As far as the contract of *Ja'ālah* is concerned, it is not stipulated that the two parties of the contract be present, as it could be done between the owner of the lost thing and "any" person who may bring it later on.

Moreover, the contract of *Ja'ālah* can be cancelled by one of the two parties of the contract, and it is for the person who is do the job to cancel the contract before starting to do it or after that as long as he accepts to cancel the defined remuneration.

Finally, it may be worth mentioning that some scholars, including Ibn Hazm, do not approve of *Ja'ālah* contracts. And, Allah knows best.

Q. No. (486): What is the *Shar'ī* ruling concerning *Waṣiyyah* (wills and bequests)?

A: In Islam, *Waṣiyyah* is that a person gives or leaves property by will to another person, yet the latter is to possess the bequeathed property after the death of the former.

Scholars have differed concerning the *Shar'ī* ruling concerning *wasiyyah*. Some scholars, including Ibn Hazm, say it is obligatory upon whoever has property whether it is little or much. Some others, including, Az-Zuhrī, assert that it is obligatory for a person's parents as well as for his relatives who will not inherit him. And still some other scholars, including the Four *Imāms*, that it can be obligatory, or desirable, or allowable, or prohibited, or detestable according to the conditions and circumstances in which the bequest is made. They say that it becomes obligatory when a person must fulfil a certain *Sharʿī* right - such as paying *Zakāh* or performing *Ḥajj* - but he has not fulfilled this right yet when death approaches him; it becomes desirable when it is made for drawing near to Allah and for one's kith and kin as well as righteous people; it is allowable (*Mubāḥah*) if it is made for a rich person whether this person is a relative of the person who makes the bequest or not; it becomes prohibited if it causes harm to the inheritors of the person who makes this *wasiyyah*; and finally, *Waṣiyyah* becomes detestable if the property of the person who makes it is little while he has an inheritor or inheritors who need this property; and it becomes also detestable if it is to be made for an immoral or disobedient person or for a person who will most probably use the money in performing acts of disobedience.

The amount of property that can be bequeathed is one third, and one third is much as the Prophet (PBUH) said to Sāʿd Ibn Abū Waqqas, may Allah be pleased with him.[1]

It should be known that no bequest is to be made for an heir, as the Prophet (PBUH) said.[2] And, Allah knows best.

Q. No. (487): Islam sanctifies work and condemns lethargy, but is there any case in which begging is allowable?

A: First of all, it has been narrated that the Prophet (PBUH) said,

"Anyone who begs from people in order to increase his wealth will have his face scratched on the Day of Resurrection, and will eat

[1] Narrated by Al-Bukhārī, Muslim, and others.
[2] Narrated by Ibn Mājah and others.

burning stones from Hell. So let him reduce it (his punishment) or let him increase it as he pleases."[1]

He (PBUH) also said,

"He who begs without need is like a person holding a burning coal in his hand."[2]

Still, the Prophet (PBUH) was aware of situations of necessity. If a person is forced, under the pressure of need, to ask for financial help from the government or from individuals, he is blameless. The Prophet (PBUH) said,

"Begging is similar to scratching the flesh off your face. So, if someone wants to save his face, he should avoid it, except for asking from the ruler or asking in case of dire need."[3]

Again, it has been narrated that the Prophet (PBUH) said to shower,

"O Qubaysah! Asking (for money) is not permissible except in three cases: (i) for a man who takes it upon himself to pay Ḥamālah[4], as he may ask people for help until the designated amount is received and then he should stop asking; (ii) for a man who suffers calamity and loses his property, as it is permissible for him to ask until he is able to stand on his own feet; and (iii) for a man who is starving, until three reliable persons from his community say, "That man is reduced to hunger,' (as then) it is permissible for him to ask until he is able to stand on his own feet."

After that the Prophet (PBUH) said, "Except for these, O Qubaysah, begging is fire; it is like eating fire."[5] And, Allah knows best.

---

[1] Narrated by At-Tirmidhī.
[2] Narrated by Al-Bayhaqi.
[3] Narrated by Abū Dāwūd and An-Nasā'ī
[4] *Ḥamalah* is an amount of money paid for making peace between two quarrelling parties.
[5] Narrated by Muslim.

Q. No. (488): What is the *Shar'ī* ruling concerning having a job related to dancing and other erotic arts?

A: Islam does not permit sexually exciting dancing or any other erotic activity, such as suggestive or obscene songs, provocative dramas, and every type of such rubbish-like things which some people may affiliate to arts or progress.

Almighty Allah says,

﴿وَلَا تَقْرَبُوا۟ ٱلزِّنَىٰٓ ۖ إِنَّهُۥ كَانَ فَٰحِشَةً وَسَآءَ سَبِيلًا ﴿٣٢﴾﴾

"And come not near to the unlawful sexual intercourse. Verily, it is a Faḥīshah (i.e., anything that transgresses its limits [a great sin]), and an evil way (that leads one to Hell unless Allah forgives him)." [TMQ: 17: 32]

This indicates that not only *Zinā* is forbidden, but anything which brings one near to it is also forbidden, including the things referred to above. This is because provocative dances and songs are included in the expression "coming near *Zinā*," especially with the fact that these things can easily tempt, excite, and lead people toward such a sin.

Finally, Islam does not allow that a Muslim contributes to undertaking any of such abominable acts and works. And, Allah knows best.

Q. No. (489): What is the *Shar'ī* ruling concerning making statues and similar articles?

A: Islam prohibits the acquisition of statues and even more strongly the making of them. However, drawing, painting, and photography are either permitted or at worst disapproved, depending on what comes closest to the spirit of the Islamic legislation. Their subject matter should not be sexually provocative, as, for example, the erotic parts of the female body or a man and woman in a state of intimacy, and should not be of someone sacred or respected, such as angels or prophets. And, Allah knows best.

Q. No. (490): What is the *Sharʿī* ruling concerning price manipulation?

A: In Islamic perspective the market is to be free and permitted to respond to the natural laws of supply and demand. Thus, when the prices became high in the Prophet's time and the people asked him to fix prices for them, he replied,

"Allah is the One Who fixes prices, who withholds, who gives lavishly, and Who provides, and I hope that when I meet Him none of you will have a claim against me for any injustice with regard to blood or property."[1]

This means that unnecessary interference in the freedom of individuals is injustice and that one should meet Allah free from blame for such a thing. If, however, any artificial forces, such as hoarding and manipulation of prices by certain. merchants, interfere in the free market, public interest takes precedence over the freedom of such individuals. Under such circumstances price control becomes permissible in order to meet the needs of the society and to protect it from greedy opportunists by thwarting their schemes.

Scholarly researchers have concluded that, depending on the nature of the circumstances, price control may at times be unjust and prohibited, and at other times may be just and permissible. If price control compels people to sell their goods at a price which is not acceptable to them or denies them the reasonable profit permitted by Allah, it is prohibited. But if price control establishes equity among people, for example, by forcing sellers to accept a price equal to that commanded by other comparable commodities and

[1] Narrated by Aḥmad and others.

restraining them from taking more than this, then it is allowed, for this is necessary. And, Allah knows best.

Q. No. (491): What is the *Shar'ī* ruling concerning hoarding?

A: Freedom for individual and natural competition in the marketplace is guaranteed by Islam. Nevertheless, Islam severely condemns those who, driven by ambition and greed, accumulate wealth at the expense of others and become rich by manipulating the prices of food and other necessities. That is why the Prophet (PBUH) denounced hoarders, saying,

"If anyone withholds grain for forty days out of the desire for a high price, Allah will renounce him." [1]

He (PBUH) also said,

"If anyone withholds goods until the price rises, he is a sinner."[2]

And exposing the selfish and greedy mentality of hoarders, the Prophet (PBUH) declared,

"The man who hoards goods is evil. If prices fall, he is grieved, and if they rise, he is happy."[3]

Thus, on the basis of the aforementioned texts and other ones, scholars have deduced that hoarding is prohibited under two conditions: first, that hoarding at a given time is injurious to the people of the country in question, and second, that the hoarder's aim is to force the price up in order to make more profit. And, Allah knows best.

Q. No. (492): Is brokerage permissible?

---

[1] Narrated by Aḥmad and others.
[2] Narrated by Muslim.
[3] Recorded by Ar- Razi in his Jami'.

A: Brokerage is permissible as long as it is a sort of fair mediation and connection between the buyer and the seller, which facilitates a profitable transaction for at least one of them or for both according to Islamic laws and without any helping in such forbidden forms as price manipulation, hording, or interference in the free market.

Nowadays, middlemen have become more necessary than at any time in the past because of the complexities of trade and commerce, which involve all types of exports and imports, and wholesale and retail sales and purchases; brokers play a very important role in keeping things moving. There is nothing wrong, therefore, with the broker's charging a commission for his services. The commission may be a fixed amount or proportional to the volume of sales or whatever is agreed upon among the parties involved. It has been narrated by Al-Bukhārī that Ibn Sīrīn and others saw nothing wrong with commissions charged by brokers, and that Ibn ʿAbbās said,

"There is no harm if one person says to another, 'Sell this robe, and if you sell it for more than such and such a price, you can keep the extra amount."

In the same narration Ibn Sīrīn said,

"There is nothing wrong if one person says to another, 'Sell it for this price and keep the profit,' or "The profit will be shared between you and me.' The Prophet (PBUH) said, 'Muslims must abide by their terms."[1]

And, Allah knows best.

Q. No. (493): What is the *Sharʿī* ruling concerning frequent swearing when undertaking some transaction?

A: The sin of deceiving is greater when the seller supports it by taking a false oath by Allah or any of His Attributes, and still a much

---

[1] Narrated by Al-Bukhārī and others.

greater sin is committed if the person in question swears by other than Allah or any of His Attributes. The Prophet (PBUH) said,

"Whoever swears by other than Allah will have committed (an act of disbelief or (an act of) polytheism."[1]

And, the Prophet (PBUH) said that merchants should avoid. swearing in general and, in particular, in support of a lie, saying,

"Swearing (may) produce a ready sale but blots out the blessing."[2]

He (PBUH) disapproved of frequent swearing in business transactions because first, it is probably done to deceive people, and second, because it takes away one's glorification of the name of Allah from one's heart. And, Allah knows best.

Q. No. (494): What is the *Shar'ī* ruling concerning withholding full measure?

A: One way of defrauding the customer is to measure or weigh incorrectly. The Qur'ān emphasizes this aspect of business transactions, i.e., giving full measure and full weight, and includes it among the ten obligations described in the last part of the chapter of *Al-An'am*; Almighty Allah says,

﴿ وَأَوْفُوا۟ ٱلْكَيْلَ وَٱلْمِيزَانَ بِٱلْقِسْطِ ۖ لَا نُكَلِّفُ نَفْسًا إِلَّا وُسْعَهَا ۖ ﴿١٥٢﴾ ﴾

"And give full measure and (full) weight, in justice; We do not burden any soul beyond what it can bear..." [TMQ: 6:152]

Therefore, the Muslim must try to do justice in measuring and weighing as accurately as it is humanly possible, although absolute accuracy in this regard may not be attainable. And, Allah knows best.

---

[1] Narrated by Al-Bukhārī and Muslim.
[2] Narrated by Al-Bukhārī.

Q. No. (495): What is the *Shar'ī* ruling concerning insurance companies?

A: This question must be concerning the present-day companies which issue life insurance and insurance against hazards and accidents. What is the Islamic ruling concerning such companies?

First of all, suppose that a person takes out insurance for twenty thousand dollars and dies soon after paying the first premium, his beneficiaries are then entitled to the entire sum of twenty thousand dollars. Had this been a business partnership, they would have been entitled only to the amount of the premium which was paid plus the profit on it. Again, if the insured person fails to pay his premiums after having paid a few of them, according to the terms of insurance in these companies he will lose all or a great part of what he has already paid. This is an invalid condition.

The argument that the two parties, the insured and the insurance firm, enter into this contract willingly in accordance with their respective self-interest carries no weight, and so do the lender and the borrower on interest and two gamblers. The mutual agreement of the two parties has no validity in a transaction which is not based on justice and equity, and which is not devoid of ambiguity or exploitation. Moreover, since justice, with no harm either to oneself or others, is the ultimate criterion here, a transaction is invalid if it stipulates that in certain situations one party is to take all, with no benefits guaranteed to the other. And, Allah knows best.

Q. No. (496): What is the *Shar'ī* ruling concerning partnership in raising animals?

A: Partnership in raising animals is quite common in Muslim countries, especially in villages. One of the partners puts up all or a part of the price of some livestock and cattle, while the other partner raises them; the two then share the yield and the profits of this joint venture.

This partnership is entered into on the basis of purely commercial purposes, e.g., raising calves for beef or cows and water buffalo for milk production. It is supposed here that one partner contributes the price of the animals and the other contributes the effort, that is to say, the management and supervision. The expenses of feeding, watering, and the like are borne by the joint partnership and not by one partner alone. After a sale is made, the feeding expenses are deducted from the proceeds before dividing up the profits in the agreed-upon proportions. It is not just that one partner alone be required to bear all the feeding expenses without receiving any commensurate return, while the profits are divided between the two; this point is quite clear.

Another aspect of this partnership is the same as the first except that the partner who manages the business also bears the feeding expenses and in return benefits from the milk or makes use of the animals in the field for ploughing, irrigating, or planting; this is the situation when large animals are involved. Shaykh Yusuf Al-Qaraḍāwī says that this contract may involve no harm, although it may not be possible to balance exactly the cost of feed with the benefits derived from milking or working the animal or animals in question, so that there is an element of uncertainty about it. He adds that the element of risk is negligible, and there are other examples of such contracts which are permitted by the *Sharīʿah*. It has been narrated, concerning mortgages, that the Prophet (PBUH) stated the permissibility of using an animal which is mortgaged for riding or milking, saying,

"One can ride the mortgaged animal because of what one spends on it, and one can drink the milk of a milch animal as long as it is mortgaged."[1]

Here, Al-Qaraḍāwī concludes, if this type of mortgage is allowed for people's mutual benefit, with the possibility that the expenses of

---

[1] Narrated by Al-Bukhārī.

feeding may be more or less than the benefit derived from the animal by using it for riding or milking, then there may be no harm in allowing a similar arrangement in the case of partnerships in raising animals, as the needs of people are better served in this manner.

However, if the partnership is in raising young calves which cannot be used for work or for milk stipulating that the price be paid by one partner and the feeding expenses by the other, the rules of Islam do not permit such an arrangement. The partner who bears the cost of feeding is the only loser, as he receives no return in the form of work or milk, while the other partner has the clear advantage. And, Allah knows best.

Inheritance

Q. No. (497): What are the rights related to the property which is to be inherited?

A: While laying down the rules for the distribution of the estate of the deceased person, the first principle to be observed is that the property both movable and immovable can be distributed after meeting the following obligations:

- funeral expenses;

- clearing off the debts incurred by the deceased person;

- and payment of bequest, if any, to the extent of one third of the total assets.

And, Allah knows best.

Q. No. (498): Who are the persons who are not to get inheritance?

A: Four persons cannot get inheritance:

1. A fugitive slave who has fled away from his master.

2. A person who has murdered his predecessor (who is to be inherited) intentionally or unintentionally

3. A person who professes a religion other than Islam.

4. A person living in *dār al-ḥarb* (a place or country which is in a state of war against Islam) cannot inherit the property of a person living in *darul-Islam* (a place or country of Muslims and where Muslims have control) and vice versa. And, Allah knows best.

Q. No. (499): Who are the recipients of inheritance in Islam?

A: According to Islam, heirs are divided into three classes:

dhawul- fara'id, dhawū al-Arḥām, and *'asabahs.*

Dhawul-fara'id are those persons who have a right to definite shares in assets left by the deceased person, such as father and mother.

Asabahs are the relatives in whose line of relationship no female enters, such as son; when *dhawū al-Arḥām* have received the respective shares, the remainder of the assets falls to their share (and son is the first to get the remainder in order of succession).

Dhawū al-Arḥām are the relatives who are connected through females, such as daughter's son, but it is in extremely rare cases that they get any share in the inheritance.

And, Allah knows best.

Q. No. (500): Who are the recipients of one half of the property left by a deceased person?

A: One half is the share of five heirs:

- Husband, if his wife has no children.

- Daughter.

- Son's daughter, because she is to take the share of the daughter.[1]

- Full sister and paternal sister.

And, Allah knows best.

Q. No. (501): Who are the recipients of one-fourth?

A: This is the share of two heirs:

- Husband, if his wife has children.
- Wife, if her husband does not have children.

And, Allah knows best.

Q. No. (502): Who are the recipients of one eighth?

---

[1] See Al- Ijma, 79.

A: This is the share of one heir, who is the wife whose deceased husband has children. And, Allah knows best.

Q. No. (503): Who are the recipients of two thirds?

A: This is the share of four heirs:

Two daughters (or more) and two granddaughters (daughters of the son) (or more). Two full sisters and two paternal sisters.

And, Allah knows best.

Q. No. (504): Who are the recipients of one third?

A: This is the share of two heirs:

Mother, if she is not excluded (from this share by means of *hajb* or exclusion).[1]

Two or more of maternal brothers and sisters.

And, Allah knows best.

Q. No. (505): Who are the recipients of one sixth?

A: This is the share of seven heirs:

Mother, with the existence of son or brothers (or sisters). Grandmother, when mother is not alive. Ibnul-Mundhir has stated that scholars unanimously agree that grandmother has one sixth if the deceased person has no mother.[2]

- One maternal brother or sister.

- Son's daughter with the existence of daughter.

- Paternal sister with the existence of full sister, and by her taking one sixth that will make two thirds of the total property, just as in the case of son's daughter with the existence of daughter.

---

[1] Hajb or exclusion from inheritance or from a certain share.
[2] See Al-Ijmā‘, 84.

- Father with the existence of son.

- Grandfather when there is no father.

And, Allah knows best.

Q. No. (506): What is the difference between *hajb nuqsan* (decrease-based exclusion) and *hajb hirman* (deprivation-based exclusion)?

A: *Hajb nuqsan* or decrease-based exclusion is that the share of one of the heirs is decreased because of the existence of another heir. This can be illustrated through the following cases which represent the conditions in which this type of *hajb* is applied:

- Husband is excluded from the share of one half to the share of one fourth with the existence of a child of his deceased wife.
- Wife is excluded from the share of one fourth to that of one eighth with the existence of a child of her deceased husband.
- Mother is excluded from the share of one third to that of one sixth with the existence of a descendent of the deceased person, such as his or her son.
- Son's daughter is excluded from the share of one half to the share of one sixth with the existence of daughter of the deceased person.
- And finally paternal sister is excluded from the share of one half to that of one sixth with the existence of full sister.

***Hajb hirman* or deprivation-based exclusion** can be simply expressed as "disinheritance" as far as this very meaning is concerned. It is that a person is excluded from inheritance as a whole because of the existence of a certain person. This type of *hajb* is established on two bases:

(a) Every person who belongs to the deceased person through a certain person does not inherit with the existence of this person. To illustrate this, a son's son does not inherit with the existence of a son, with the exception of a mother's sons because they inherit along with her though they belong to the deceased person through her.

(b) The nearer to the deceased person is given precedence over the farer. For instance, a son excludes his brother's son. If two heirs are of the same degree, as when they are brothers of the deceased person, then the one whose relation to the deceased person is stronger is to be given precedence. In the given example (of brothers), a full brother is to be given precedence over a paternal brother, and so on.

Yet still, there are six persons who are not included in *hajb hirman*, as they inherit in all cases though *hajb nuqsan* may be applied to them as clarified above. These six persons are: son, daughter, father, mother, husband, and wife. And, Allah knows best.

Q. No. (507): What is the *Shar'ī* ruling concerning the inheritance of *khuntha* (intersex)?

A: In Arabic a *khuntha* is a person who may have both genitals of a male and a female or none of them. If it is evident that he is a male (i.e., nearer to the male sex or sexual characteristics of male), then he is to be treated as a male is treated in inheritance and vice versa. If neither state is evident, then the person in question to be treated as having the worse condition. To illustrate the latter case, if a woman dies and leaves behind a husband, a mother, a sister, and a paternal *khuntha*, in this case if the *khuntha* is treated as a male, he will take a share less than that he will take if treated as a female, and so he is to take the share of a male (i.e., a paternal brother) because it is less than the share of a female (i.e., a paternal sister).

If a *khuntha* is regarded once as a male and another as a female to find out his condition as to the inheritance in question, and he is to inherit according to one of the two cases and be deprived of the inheritance according to the other, he is to be treated also according to the worse condition, which is "deprivation" here. An example of this is: A woman dies and leaves behind a husband, a full sister, and a paternal *khuntha*. If the *khuntha* is treated as a female, she will inherit, and if the *khuntha* is treated as a male, he will not inherit. In this case, the *khuntha* is to be treated as a male. And, Allah knows best.

Q. No. (508): What is the *Shar'ī* ruling concerning the inheritance of a foetus?

A: According to Abū Ḥanīfah and some Mālikīs, the share of four sons or four daughters the bigger amount thereof is to be kept aside for the foetus and the rest of the heirs are to be given the least shares as a way of taking precautions. According to Abū Muḥammad, the share of three sons or the share of three daughters - the bigger amount thereof is to be kept for the foetus. And still, according to Abū Yusuf, the share of one son or one daughter - the bigger amount thereof is to be kept for the foetus. This may be the most evident view among these three views, because in most cases only one son or one daughter is delivered. If a verdict concerning the inheritance of a foetus is based on this third view, the judge must take a guarantor from the heirs because the pregnancy may result in more than one baby. And, according to some other views the distribution of inheritance is to be left undecided until the delivery takes place.

Another important matter in this regard is that every heir whose share does not change because of the change of the delivered baby - i.e., whether it is a male or a female baby - is to be given his or her share in full. For example, if a man dies and leaves behind a grandmother and a pregnant woman, the grandmother is to be given one sixth of the property because her share in the inheritance will not change whether the delivered baby is a male or a female. And, Allah knows best.

Q. No. (509): What is the *Shar'ī* ruling concerning the inheritance of a lost person?

A: "Lost person" here refers to anyone who has been lost and no news is available about his whereabouts, and it is not even known whether he is alive or dead, and a judge gives a verdict that he is (considered legally to be) a dead person. According to Mālik and Ash-Shāfiʿī, a lost person is judged as being a dead person if he is lost for four years if he has been absent on a journey where he is most probably prone to destruction, as when he is absent for this period of time after some attack of enemies for example.

As far as inheritance is concerned, a lost person is not to be inherited by anyone except after his death has been proven or a verdict has been given to the effect that he is regarded as dead after being absent for a certain period of time as pinpointed above. And, Allah knows best.

Q. No. (510): What is the *Sharʿī* ruling concerning the inheritance of an apostate?

A: If an apostate dies or is killed or joins a *dār al-ḥarb* (a place or country which is in a state of war against Islam) and a judge gives a verdict that he has joined such a place, some scholars maintain that the part of his property that he earned during his being a Muslim is to be distributed among his Muslim heirs and what he earned during his apostasy is to be taken by the public treasury (*Bayt al-māl*). Some others are of the opinion that both earnings are to be distributed among his Muslim heirs. Yet scholars unanimously agree that what he earned "after joining" *dār al-ḥarb* is to be considered as fay (war booty gained without fighting).

On the other hand, the apostate himself is not to inherit from any Muslim relative of his.

Interestingly enough, according to Ash-Shāfiʿī, Mālik, and the more famous view of Aḥmad in this regard, an apostate is not to inherit or be inherited and his property is to be taken by the public treasury. And, Allah knows best.

Q. No. (511): What is the *Shar'ī*? ruling concerning the inheritance of a captive?

A: "Captive" here refers to a Muslim who has been taken by force as captive by people who are in war against Muslims.

As far as inheritance is concerned, such a captive is to be treated just like other Muslims, that is, he is to inherit others and be inherited by others. If he apostatizes, he is to be treated as an apostate, and if his life or death is not known, he is to be treated as a lost person (as clarified in a previous answer). And, Allah knows best.

Q. No. (512): What is the *Shar'ī* ruling concerning the inheritance of a group of people who die together?

A: A group of people may die together, as when their boat is drowned, and there is a family relationship which connects them, yet it is not known who among them died first. In this case all of them are to be regarded as having died at the same time, the property of each one of them is to be given to his living inheritors, and these deceased persons are not to inherit one another, i.e., the distribution of the inheritance of any one of them is not to be affected by his relation to any of the other deceased people and only the living heirs are to be treated as the only heirs of the person in question. And, Allah knows best.

Q. No. (513): What is the *Shar'ī* ruling concerning the obligatory bequest?

A: If a person has a descendant heir[1] (like his son) and this descendent dies during this person's lifetime, he must make a bequest for the children of this descendant with an amount equal to that which the dead descendant would receive if he did not die, or with some part of his property up to one third of it, and one third is

---

[1] A descendant heir here means that the heir in question is both a descendant of the deceased person and one of his inheritors at the same time, such as his son.

much as the Prophet (PBUH) said[1] when speaking about bequests. This is called "the obligatory bequest". If such a person dies before making a bequest for his descendant's children, they are to be given out of his property an amount equal to that which he was to bequeath during his lifetime. This is because it is a debt on his part, and if he dies before writing his bequest in this regard, this debt is not to be cancelled because of his death.

It may moreover be said that a descendant - who is referred to in the obligatory bequest - contributes - in many cases - to making the wealth of his father, so it is a sign of justice that his children be given out of this wealth. And, Allah knows best.

Q. No. (514): What are the conditions obligating the obligatory bequest?

A: There are two conditions which obligate the obligatory bequest and without them it is not a must that such a bequest be made:

1. The descendent heir in question must not be one of those who deserve a share in the inheritance, and if he deserves even a small share, no bequest will be obligatory in this case. An example of this is that a man may die and leave behind a daughter and the sons of his son who died during this man's lifetime. In this case the son's sons deserve inheritance, so there is no obligatory bequest for them.

2. The deceased person must not have given the descendent heir in question any part of his property without remuneration - as a gift for example - equal to the amount he would make in an obligatory bequest. Yet, if he gave him less than that, he is to be given what completes the amount ordained for such a bequest. And, Allah knows best.

---

[1] Narrated by Al-Bukhārī, Muslim, and others.

Q. No. (515): What is the way of distributing inheritance with the obligatory bequest?

A: The following steps may be followed for distributing inheritance properly and correctly when there is an obligatory bequest, i.e., when a descendant heir is to be given the right of his dead father for example:

1. The share of the son of the deceased person who died during the life of the latter is to be defined as if he was present at the time of distribution.

2. After that the share of the dead son is to be taken out of the property and given to his descendant who deserves the obligatory bequest.

3. Then the remainder of the property is to be distributed among the real heirs each according to his or her *Shar'ī* share.

These steps can be applied to the following example:

A woman has died leaving behind a husband, a maternal brother, and a daughter of her daughter who died during her (the deceased woman's) life. The inheritance can be distributed as follows:

- Originally and if the dead daughter were to be alive, the husband would take one-fourth of the property, the remainder would go to the daughter, and the maternal brother would be excluded by the daughter.
- If the share of the dead daughter was to be given to her living daughter, the latter would take more than one third of the property. Therefore, she is to take only one third (as the bequest is not to exceed this limit) and the rest, which is also one third, is to be distributed between the husband (who has already taken one third as his ordained share) and the maternal brother, who is to take a share after the new amendment. And, Allah knows best.

Conclusion

All praises are due to Allah, who has helped me to compile, abridge, arrange, and translate the contents of this book. I hope that it has been helpful to our dear readers and that they have found it easy, smooth, and inclusive.

I ask Allah to bless my effort, to make it purely exerted for His Sake, to help whoever reads this book to benefit from it, and to forgive any mistake I may have committed during any stage of work. Amen!

Glossary[1]

Adhān: Prayer call.

A.H.: After Ḥijrah (the Prophet's emigration to Medina).

Allāhu Akbar: It literally means "Allah is Greater" and this consequently means that Allah is "greater" than "everything," so it is normally translated as "Allah is the Greatest".

Al-yamīn al-ghamūs: Heinous oath.

Al-yamīn al-laghw: Unintentional oath.

Al-yamīn al-mun'aqidah: Deliberate oath.

Anṣār: Plural of Ansari, who is one of the Companions of the Prophet (PBUH) from the inhabitants of Medina who embraced Islam and supported it and who received and entertained the Muslim emigrants from Mecca and other places.

Anṣāri: One of the Anṣār.

Aqīlah: As far as blood money (*diyah*) is concerned, this term normally refers to the relatives of the person who has committed a crime that requires the payment of blood money, yet it concerns the "male" relatives who are in addition to this - "mature," "sane," and "well-to-do," and who adopt the same religion of the person in question.

***`aqiqah***: *Aqiqah* refers to the sacrificing of one or two sheep when a child is born, as a token of gratitude to Almighty Allah. Also, the animal slaughtered for the newly born is called *`aqiqah.*

---

[1] N.B. Some of the transliterated terms in this glossary have been typed with capital initials and some others have been typed with small initials, each according to the way it is typed inside sentences, e.g., Ansari and badanah.

`asabah: Relatives in whose line of relationship no female enters.

'Aṣr: Literally meaning "afternoon" and usually used with "Prayer" as "The *'Aṣr* Prayer" to refer to the prayer whose due time starts with the afternoon.

'Awrah: Certain parts in the body that must be covered, and they differ according to the gender. And, awrah can be translated in brief as "private parts".

Ash-Shām: The region now covering Palestine, Jordan, Lebanon, and Syria.

As-Ṣalāh Al-Ibahimiyyah: It literally means "The Ibrāhīmi Invocation of Blessings," and it is a form of invocation that is recited after the *tashahhud* at the end of prayer. It is an act of the *Sunnah* related to prayer, or one of its pillars according to some fight views. It reads, *"Allahumma salli ala Muḥammad wa ala 'Alī Muḥammad. Kama sallayta ala Ibrāhīm wa ala 'Alī Ibrāhīm. Wa barik ala Muḥammad wa ala 'Alī Muḥammad. Kama barakta ala Ibrāhīm wa ala 'Alī Ibrāhīm fil-alamin. Innaka hamidun majid.* (O Allah! Send Ṣalāh (graces, honors, blessings, mercy, etc.) on Muḥammad and on the family of Muḥammad as You sent Ṣalāh on Ibrāhīm (Abraham) and on the family of Ibrāhīm. And bless Muḥammad and the family of Muḥammad as You blessed Ibraham and the family of Ibrāhīm in the world. Verily, you are Praiseworthy and Honourable.)"

awliyā': Plural of *Walīyy.*

badanah: (Plural *budn)* A cow, an ox, or a camel which is driven to be offered as sacrifices by pilgrims at the sanctuary of Mecca.

Banu: Literally means "sons of".

bid'ah: Innovation in the religion.

bint labūn: Two-year-old she-camel.

bint makhad: One-year-old she-camel.

Bint: Literally means "daughter of".

dār al-ḥarb: A place or country which is in a state of war against Islam.

dār al-Islām: A place or country of Muslims and where Muslims have control.

dhawū al-farā'id: These are those persons who have a right to definite shares in assets left by the deceased person.

dhawū al-arḥām: Relatives connected through females.

dhikr: The word *dhikr* literally means "mentioning" or "remembering" and both meanings are connected to mentioning the name of Allah or remembering Him in general through any way of praising, glorification, etc. The plural "*adhkar*" refers to any group of invocations or words of glorification or praise said for this purpose.

dhimmī: A non-Muslim living under the protection of an Islamic government.

dīnār: The basic gold unit of currency *dirham*: The basic silver unit of currency.

diyah mughallazah: *Diyah mughallazah*, literally meaning "hardened blood money," is the blood money which is paid in case of semi-intentional killing.

diyah mukhaffafah: *Diyah mukhaffafah*, literally meaning "lightened blood money," is the blood money which is paid in case of killing by mistake or unintentional killing.

diyah: *Diyah* is the money or property paid because of some crime that a person has committed, and it is to be paid to the victim in question or to his *Walīyy*.

Fajr: Literally meaning "dawn" and usually used with "Prayer" as "The *Fajr* Prayer" to refer to the prayer whose due time starts at dawn.

Faqīh: A scholar specialized in *Fiqh*.

fard 'ayn: An individual obligation which is to be fulfilled by every Muslim, such as prayer. Compare "*farḍ kifāyah*" *farḍ kifāyah*: It means that if one Muslim does it in a certain place that will be sufficient for all the other Muslims. To apply this to *Adhān* (prayer call) for example, if a Muslim pronounces it, that will be sufficient for the other Muslims (in the mosque) and thus it is not obligatory that everybody there pronounces it.

farsakh: About two miles.

faskh: In marriage, *faskh*, literally meaning "nullification," signifies the nullification of marriage contract due to a legal reason.

fatāwā: Plural of *fatwa*.

fatwā: A legal opinion or verdict normally given by a learned person who is specialized in religious knowledge.

fidyah: It literally means "ransom," and it is a penalty slaughtering which is prescribed upon any pilgrim who commits any of the things forbidden in *Iḥrām* or neglects any duty related to *Ḥajj*.

Fiqh: The science dealing with Islamic jurisprudence in all aspects: worship, marital affairs, transactions, etc.

fiqhī: Pertaining to *Fiqh*.

ghurrah: The *diyah* (blood money) of a foetus, and it is a male slave or a female slave.

Ḥadath: *Janābah* is usually referred to as *Ḥadath akbar* or major ritual impurity, but *Ḥadath* applies to both *Janābah* and *Ḥadath asghar* or minor impurity that is usually caused by urination, excretion, or passing wind.

Ḥadīth Ḥasan Ṣaḥīḥ: Technically, it can be directly translated as "agreeable, authentic Ḥadīth".

Ḥadīth Ḥasan: Though it literally means "good Ḥadīth," it can be technically translated as "agreeable Ḥadīth," and it belongs to the accepted group of hadiths (mostly comprising agreeable and authentic hadiths).

Ḥadīth musnad: A Ḥadīth is graded as *musnad* when it is narrated with a complete chain of transmitters from the narrator to the Prophet (PBUH) himself.

Ḥadīth: Any of the statements of the Prophet (PBUH), i.e., his sayings, deeds, and approvals, etc.

hady: An animal (a camel, a cow, a sheep, or a goat) offered as a sacrifice by pilgrims.

hajb: Literally meaning "exclusion" *hajb* is that a certain person is excluded from inheritance as a whole or from a certain share in it because of the existence of a certain person among heirs.

Ḥajj: Literally, the word "*haj*" means "heading for a scarified and glorified place with the intention of visiting". This literal meaning of *Ḥajj* can also be used to refer to *Ḥajj* in *Sharʿī* terminology, as it in the latter means: to head for the Sacred House in Mecca with the purpose of worshiping Allah and performing certain prescribed duties including visiting certain sacred places.

Ḥanafīs: This word generally refers to the followers and proponents of Imām Abū Ḥanīfah's school of Fiqh. Sometimes it is used to refer to Abū Ḥanīfah's views. In other words, when it is said, "The Ḥanafīs maintain that..." it can mean "Abū Ḥanīfah maintains that...".

Ḥanbalīs: This word generally refers to the followers and proponents of Imām Aḥmad Ibn Hanbal's school of *Fiqh*. Sometimes it is used to refer to Ibn Hanbal's views. In other words, when it is said, "The Ḥanbalīs maintain that..." it can mean "Ibn Hanbal maintains that....".

harabah: *Harabah* is that a group of Muslims in a Muslim land cause chaos, shed blood, rob property, dishonour people, and destroy crops and cattle, thus defying the religion, morals, and laws.

Ḥaram: The word haram refers to the sacred precincts in Mecca, and sometimes it is translated as "Sanctuary".

Ḥijrah: It literally means "emigration" and in this book it refers to the Prophet's emigration to Medina.

ḥiqqah: Three-year-old she-camel.

hirz: Especially as far as theft is concerned, *hirz* is a thing in which money and other items of property are kept, e.g., safes for keeping money, storehouses for keeping commodities, etc.

Ḥudūd: The legal punishments or penalties that have been enjoined by the Sharīʿah concerning certain acts of disobedience so that they may not be committed again. *Iʿtikāf*: It literally means "to adhere or devote oneself to something," and terminologically as far as the *Sharīʿah* is concerned it means "confining oneself in a mosque for worshiping Allah, Glory be to Him".

ibn labūn: Two-year-old male camel.

Ibn: It literally means "son of".

idtiba: Uncovering the right hand, and it is an act of the Sunnah related to *Ṭawāf* (circumambulation).

Ifrād: *Ifrād* is that a person assumes *Iḥrām* for *Ḥajj* "alone".

Iḥrām: The state of ritual consecration during which the pilgrim is forbidden to do certain things such as wearing stitched clothes and cutting his hair or nails.

Iḥṣār: It literally means "prevention," and it refers to the state when a pilgrim is prevented by illness or some enemy for example - from completing the duties of *Ḥajj* or *ʿUmrah.*

Ijtihād: Personal Reasoning: a secondary source of Islamic Law.

Ilā': *Ilā'* literally means "swearing" and terminologically is that a husband swears that he will not have intercourse with his wife for a certain period of time.

Imām: Often rendered as "leader" and in this meaning in particular it can be used in different contexts, e.g., Imām Mālik and Imām in prayer, as in the former it refers to a leading and pioneering scholar and in the later it refers to a person who leads people in congregational prayer.

'Id: Islamic feast.

ʿIddah: The prescribed period during which a divorcee or a widow is not allowed to get married.

Id al-Aḍḥā: Sacrifice Feast.

Id al-Fiṭr: Fast-breaking Feast.

Iqāmah: Immediate prayer call.

ʿIshā': Literally meaning "night" and usually used with "Prayer" as "The *ʿIshā'* Prayer" to refer to the prayer whose due time starts at night about twenty-three minutes after sunset.

Istiftāḥ: As far as prayer is concerned, this word is normally attached to the invocation with which prayer is "commenced" (and this is what is meant by "*Istiftāḥ*") after the first *Takbīrah* and before recitation of *Al-Fātiḥah.*

Istikhārah: Asking (Allah) for proper guidance, and this is normally done by invoking Allah with certain words after performing two *Rak'ahs*, according to the Sunnah of the Prophet (PBUH). See Ḥadīth No. 263, Vol. 2, Ḥadīth No.391, Vol. 8, and Ḥadīth No. 487, Vol. 9, Sahihul-Bukhari.

Istisqā': Request for rain, and this is normally done by performing a two-*Rak'ah* prayer and invoking Allah for rain. This prayer is called "the *Istisqā'* Prayer".

jadh`ah: Four-year-old she-camel.

jallalah: This term refers to animals that are fed with impurities, and this includes camels, cows, sheep, and the like. It is prohibited to eat these animals.

jam Ta'khīr: It literally means "delay combination," and it is the opposite of *jam taqdim* or advancement combination, e.g., to perform both the *Maghrib* and the *"'Ishā'"* prayers during the time of the *"'Ishā'"* Prayer.

jam Taqdīm: It literally means "advancement combination," and it is to perform any of the *Zuhr* and the *'Aṣr* prayers or the *Maghrib* and the *'Ishā'"* prayers during the time of the first of them, i.e., to perform the *Zuhr* and the *'Aṣr* prayers during the time of the *Zuhr* Prayer or to perform the *Maghrib* and the `*'Ishā'* prayers during the time of the *Maghrib* Prayer.

Jamrah: There are three places where pebbles are thrown in *Ḥajj*. Each of these places is called *jamrah*, which is a small stone-built pillar in a walled place. The three *Jamrahs* are situated at *Mīnā*, and they are known as *Al-Jamrah Al-Kubra* or the Big *Jamrah*, *Al-Jamrah Al-Wusta* or the Medium Jamrah, and the *Al-Jamrah As-Sughra* or the Small *Jamrah*.

Janābah: See the term Ḥadath in this glossary.

Jihād: Fighting in the cause of Allah or any kind of effort exerted for keeping Allah's Word superior. It is regarded as one of the pillars of Islam.

Jināyah: *Jināyah* represents any act which is committed or omitted in violation of a law forbidding or commanding it and for which punishment is imposed upon conviction.

Jumu'ah: Friday, and it is usually attached to the *Jumu'ah* (Friday) Prayer which is performed on Friday at the time of the *Zuhr* (Noon) Prayer.

Ka'bah: A square stone building in the Sacred Mosque in Mecca and toward it all Muslims turn their faces in prayer.

Khalā': the place where people relieve themselves (i.e., urinate or defecate).

khalwah: *Khalwah* literally means "privacy," and correct *khalwah* is that a husband and his wife live or be together after contracting a valid marriage in a place where they can sexually enjoy each other completely without fearing that anyone should enter as they do that, and on condition that neither of them has any natural, sensual, or legal impediment that prevents the undertaking of such enjoyment.

khamr: Any intoxicant is included in the general Arabic term '*khamr*'.

khatib: The person - usually the Imām - who delivers the *Khuṭbah* or religious sermon on such occasions as the *Jumu'ah* (Friday) Prayer and the *'Id* (Feast) Prayer.

khitbah: *Khitbah* or engagement is that a man presents a proposal of marriage seeking to marry a certain woman.

khuff: Socks made from thick fabric or leather.

Khul': This is the right of woman in demanding the dissolution of marriage. *Khul'* literally means putting off or taking off a thing. It is a kind of facility provided for the wife in securing divorce from her husband by returning a part or full amount of the bridal gift (mahr).

khuntha: In Arabic a *khuntha* is a person who may have both genitals of a male and a female or none of them. It can be simply expressed as "intersex".

Khuṭbah: The religious sermon delivered on such occasions as the *Jumuʿah* (Friday) Prayer and the 'Id (Feast) Prayer.

Li'an: *Li'an* can simply be identified with the phrase "oath of condemnation". It is applied in the following case: if a man accuses his wife of committing adultery and she belies him, the judge applies *li'an* between them (in the manner pinpointed inside the book). It is called "*li'an*," which literally means "invoking curse," because the husband says, "I invoke Allah's curse upon myself if I am of those who tell lies".

Maghrib: Literally meaning "sunset" and usually used with "Prayer" as "The Maghrib Prayer" to refer to the prayer whose due time starts at sunset.

mahr: Check the term "*Ṣadaq*" up in this glossary.

mahram: It generally refers to a woman's husband or any of her unmarriageable male relatives, and when the term is related to a man it refers to any of his unmarriageable female relatives; also a man's wife may be called his mahram.

Mālikīs: This word generally refers to the followers and proponents of Imām Mālik's school of Fiqh. Sometimes it is used to refer to Mālik's views. In other words, when it is said, "The Mālikīs maintain that..." it can mean "Mālik maintains that...".

Mas'a: The place where the *Saʿy* or going between As-Ṣafā and Al-Marwah is performed as one of the prescribed duties of *Ḥajj* and *ʿUmrah*.

mawla: In this book this word refers to the "freed slave" of the person to whom he is attached, e.g., the mawla of Ibn 'Abbas.

mawqudhah: An animal that has been killed by a violent blow.

maytah: Every animal that dies without killing or slaughtering is generally called "*maytah*".

Mīqāt: This term refers to the time when and the place where a pilgrim assumes *Iḥrām* for *Ḥajj* or *ʿUmrah.*

mu`awamah: It consists in selling the fruit on the trees in one, two, or three years even before it has made its appearance.

mudarabah: *Muḍārabah*, which is also called *qirāḍ*, is a contract which is conducted between two persons who agree that one of them will pay to the other a sum of money in cash in order to trade therein and the profits will result from this are to: be shared between the two according to the proportions upon which they both agree.

mu'taddah: A woman having a waiting period (*ʿIddah*).

Mu'takif: A person who is in a state of *i'tikaf* or who stays and confines himself in a mosque for worshiping Almighty Allah.

Mu'adhdhin: A prayer caller.

mudd: A measure of two thirds of a kilogram approximately. It may be less or more than that, because four *mudds* equal one *Sāʿ* and the latter equals three kilograms approximately.

Muḥallil: The *Muḥallil* marriage is an invalid form of marriage which is that a man temporarily takes a woman in marriage, has sexual intercourse with her, and then divorces her to go back to her ex-husband's bond after the termination of her waiting period.

muḥrim: A person in a state of *Iḥrām*, and it can be used as an adjective in this book, e.g., "*muḥrim* woman".

muḥsan: A *muḥsan* person is one who has experienced sexual intercourse through a valid marriage, whereas a non- *muḥsan* person is one who has not married yet; a virgin.

muḥṣar: A person in a state of *Iḥṣār*.

mukallaf: Legally responsible.

Mulāmasaḥ: *Mulāmasaḥ* means touching the cloth without examining it, i.e., the buyer was just supposed to touch the cloth to strike the bargain.

Munābadhaḥ: *Munābadhaḥ* means that the seller should throw the cloth to the buyer before he has carefully examined it. The very act of throwing the cloth will mean that the bargain has been struck.

munkhaniqah: An animal that has been killed by strangling.

Muṣallā: Prayer place.

Muṣḥaf: A copy of the Qur'ān whether written in the form of a book, typed in a file, recorded on a tape, etc.

mūsinnah: Two-year-old cow.

Musnad: Collections of hadiths arranged not in accordance with the subject matter but under the name of the person who transmitted them from the Prophet (PBUH). An example of such collections is the *Musnad* of Imām Aḥmad Ibn Hanbal.

Mut'ah: The mut ah marriage or temporary marriage is a personal contract between a man and a woman to cohabit for a limited period of time at the end of which she becomes automatically divorced, in return for a certain remuneration payable by the man. This is an invalid form of marriage.

mutaraddiyah: An animal that has been killed by a headlong fall.

Muzābanah: It is the exchange of fresh fruits for dry ones in a way that the quantity of the dry fruits is actually measured and fixed, but the quantity of the fresh fruits to be given in exchange is guessed while it is still on the trees.

Nabīdh: *Nabidh* generally refers to water which is sweetened with dates, raisins, and the like.

Nāṭiḥah: An animal that has been killed by the goring of horns.

Nisāb: The minimal amount of wealth which obligates *Zakāh* as specified by the *Sharī'ah*, e.g., the *Nisāb* of gold is twenty dinars (85 grams of 24-karat gold).

nusuk: This term has more than one meaning, as sometimes it is used to refer to the sacrifice offered in *Ḥajj* and *'Umrah* and sometimes it is used to refer to the rituals of these two acts of worship.

(PBUH): A formula literally meaning "Peace be upon him," and it is specified to be put in this form - (PBUH) - only when referring to Prophet Muḥammad.

qadhf: *Qadhf* is that a person accuses another of committing adultery or fornication. It can be expressed as "slanderous accusation".

Qawāmah: This term refers to the protection and maintenance which men enjoy as regards their relation to women.

qiblah: The direction toward which all Muslims turn their faces in prayer; it is the direction toward the *Ka'bah* in Mecca.

Qirān: It is that a person assumes *Iḥrām* for performing both *Ḥajj* and *'Umrah*.

qiṣāṣ: Retaliation, and some render it as "the law of equality in punishment," and this is included in the word "*qiṣāṣ*" itself.

raj'ah: It literally means "taking back" and terminologically is that a man takes his divorced wife back to wedlock without a new contract during her waiting period. It can simply be expressed as "revocation of divorce".

***raj`iyyah***: A *raj`iyyah* woman or a *raj'iyyah* divorcee is a woman whose divorce is revocable. Check the term "rajah" up in this glossary.

rajm: The stoning of a *muḥsan* person (male and female) who commits adultery.

Rak'ah: Unit of prayer.

ramal: To move quickly in the first three circuits of circumambulation round the *Ka'bah* and walk normally in the remaining four circuits.

Rikāz: This is a term that refers to treasures buried before the Islamic era

Sā': One *Sā'* equals three kilograms approximately.

Sa'y: This term refers to one of the pillars of *Ḥajj* and *'Umrah*, and it is that the pilgrim goes seven times between the two mountains called As-Ṣafā and Al-Marwah starting with As- *Ṣafā* and ending with Al-Marwah.

Ṣadaq: *Sadiq*, also called "mahr," is terminologically the obligatory bridal money (or any form of property and the like) given by the husband to his wife at the time of marriage.

Ṣadaqah: This word originally refers to alms which are paid or given out voluntarily, and it has been used in the Qur'ān and the *Sunnah* in certain contexts as referring to *Zakāh* or Obligatory Alms.

Ṣaḥīḥ: The word "Ṣaḥīḥ" literally means "authentic" or "sound"; and it is sometimes connected to the names of the books mainly containing collections of authentic hadiths such as the Two Ṣaḥīḥs of Al-Bukhārī and Muslim where there are the most authentic versions of Ḥadīths.

Ṣalāh: Islamic Prayer.

Shāfi'ī: This word generally refers to the followers and proponents of Imām Ash-Shāfi'ī's school of Fiqh. Sometimes it is used to refer to Ash-Shāfi'ī's views. In other words, when it is said, "The Shafi is maintain that..." it can mean "Ash-Shāfi'ī maintains that...".

Shar'ī: Pertaining to the *Sharī'ah* (Islamic Law).

Sharī'ah: Islamic law which contains all the ordinances that Almighty Allah has prescribed for Muslims.

Shighār: The *Shighār* marriage is that a man exchanges his daughter or sister for another man's daughter or sister on condition that no reciprocation of *mahr* (Islamic dowry) is required. This is an invalid form of marriage.

Siwāk: Cleaning stick for teeth, and Muslims use it especially when it is time to perform prayer according to the Sunnah of the Prophet (PBUH).

Ṣiyām: Islamic Fasting.

suhur: A meal taken at night before the *Fajr* Prayer by a person who intends to observe fast the next day.

sunnah mu'kkadah: An affirmed act of the *Sunnah*.

Sunnah: The original meaning of the word is "way" or "path to be followed," but it is used as a technical term for all the authentically transmitted words, actions, and sanctions of the Prophet (PBUH).

sutrah: An object that is to be placed before a performer of prayer to prevent anyone or anything from passing right before him and to prevent him from looking at things that may be beyond it so that he may not be distracted from his prayer.

ta`zir: A discretionary punishment which is enjoined by the ruler (or the judge) concerning a crime for which the Shariah has not specified a legal punishment, or for which the Shariah has specified a certain legal punishment yet when this punishment is to be applied the conditions of implementation are not met, such as having sex with a woman without intercourse (as in kissing and caressing) and stealing something whose value is less than the value which obligates cutting the hand.

Tabi': One- year- old calf.

Tabi'ah: One- year- old cow.

Tafsir: Exegesis of the Qur'ān.

tahlilah: An act of declaring the Oneness of Allah normally by saying "*Lā ilāha illā Allāh* (There is no god but Allah)".

tahmidah: An act of praising Allah normally by saying "*Al-Ḥamdu lillāh* (Praise be to Allah)".

Takbīr: To say "*Allāhu Akbar* (Allah is the Greatest)".

Takbīrah: An act of saying "*Allāhu Akbar* (Allah is the Greatest)".

Takbīrat al-Iḥrām: The act of *Takbīr* that is said at the very beginning of prayer and by which all the sayings and acts which are not related to prayer become prohibited.

Ṭalāq: *Ṭalāq* or divorce is simply "dissolution of the marriage union". It can also be defined as "the dissolution of marriage, or the annulment of its legality by the pronouncement of certain words".

Tamattu': It is that a person assumes *Iḥrām* for performing *'Umrah* during the months of *Ḥajj* then performs *Ḥajj* during the same year in which he performed *'Umrah*.

Tarāwīḥ: The night prayer of Ramaḍān.

Tarjī': This term is related to *Adhān* (prayer call) and it is to utter the two testifications of faith (*Shahādatan*) twice for each quietly before uttering them, also twice for each, loudly. The *Shahādatan* is (1) *'Ashhadu allā ilāha illā-llāh* (I testify that there is no god but Allah) and

(2) *Ashhadu anna* Muḥammad*an rasul-ullah* (I testify that Muḥammad is the Messenger of Allah).

tarwiyah: This term refers to the eighth day of Dhul-Ḥijjah. It is said that *tarwiyah* here is derived from the Arabic word "*riwayah*," which means "narration" or "relating" and this day is called "the Day of *Tarwiyah*" in this sense as the Imām "tells" pilgrims about the *Manāsik* or prescribed duties of *Ḥajj* and *ʿUmrah* on it. It is also said that the word *tarwiyah* is derived from the Arabic word *irtiwa'*, which means "quenching one's thirst" because pilgrims would quench their thirst with water on this day and collect it at *Mīnā*.

Tasbīḥah: An act of glorifying Allah normally by saying *Subhanallah*, which means "Glory be to Allah!" or "How far from imperfection Allah is!".

tashahhud: A religious formula that is recited at the first sitting as well as at the last sitting in prayer. The first sitting is that is done after performing the first two *Rakʿahs* in the *Zuhr*, *ʿAṣr*, *Maghrib*, and *ʿIshāʾ* prayers. The last sitting is the one done after the second *Rakʿah* in the *Fajr* Prayer, after the third *Rakʿah* in the *Maghrib* Prayer, and after the fourth *Rakʿah* in the *Zuhr*, *ʿAṣr*, and "*ʿIshāʾ*" prayers. *Tashahhud* starts with the words, "*At-tahiyyatu lillahi as-salawatu wat-Ṭayyibāt* ([All] the compliments [as well as] the prayers and the good things are due to Allah.)".

Tashrīq: *Tashrīq* literally means "airing," and this term is always connected to the days known as "the Days of *Tashrīq*," which are the three days following Id al-Aḍḥā (Sacrifice Feast). They are called "the Days of *Tashrīq*" because pilgrims used to "dry" the meat of their sacrificial animals and make it dried slices during these days.

Taslīm: It is the salutation done at the end of prayer or, in other words, the salutation with which prayer ends. It is normally done by saying "*As-Salāmu ʿalaykum wa raḥmatullāh* (Allah's peace and mercy be upon you)".

tasmiyah: To say, "*Bismillāhi r-raḥmāni r-raḥīm* (In the Name of Allah, the All-Merciful, the Ever-Merciful)".

Ṭawāf: The act of circumambulation the *Ka'bah* in Mecca.

Uḍḥiyah: *Uḍḥiyah* is a camel, a cow, or a sheep which is slaughtered on the Day of Sacrifice and the three days of *Tashrīq* as a way of drawing near to Almighty Allah. The Day of Sacrifice is Id al-Aḍḥā or Sacrifice Feast, and the three days of *Tashrīq* are the three days following this Day of Sacrifice.

Ummah: This word is usually translated as "nation", yet it is used here in its Arabic form as its meaning is capable of more than that. For, it refers to the nation of Prophet Muḥammad (PBUH) in all times and places as well as to those who believe in him from among jinn or even the inhabitants of any other planet.

'Umrah: The word *'Umrah* is derived from the Arabic word "*itimar*" which means "visiting". And, in *Shar'ī* terminology as an act of worship *'Umrah* is to visit the sanctified *Ka'bah*, circumambulate it, perform the *Sa'y* or going between As-Ṣafā and Al-Marwah, then have the hair of the head shaved or cut short.

uqiyyah: One *uqiyyah* equals forty *dirhams*.

Walīyy: Legal guardian, and in cases such as retaliation and reception of blood money, the *Walīyy* normally refers to the heir of the victim.

wasq: One *wasq* equals sixty *Sā''s* and one *Sā'* equals 3 kilograms approximately.

witr: The word *witr* literally means "odd" and it is usually attached to the *Witr* Prayer which is a form of prayer that is performed in an odd number of *Rak'ahs*, and it is an affirmed act of the Sunnah (sunnah *mu'kkadah*) which is to be performed every night.

Zāhirīs: A school of Islamic jurisprudence (*Fiqh*) named after Ibn Ḥazm az-Zāhirī.

Zakāh: *Zakāh* is the name of what man takes out of his property in a certain amount that is specified by the *Sharī'ah* as a right of Allah which is to be paid for the poor and the other recipients of *Zakāh*. It is called *Zakāh* because it purifies both the soul and the property of whoever pays it, especially with the fact that the Arabic word "*Zakāh*" means "purity," "growth," and "blessing". *Zakāh* is the second obligation in Islam after Prayer (*Ṣalāh*).

Zakātul-Fiṭr: This is Fast-breaking obligatory alms, and this form of *Zakāh* is to be paid after breaking fast at the end of the month of Ramaḍān.

Ẓihār: *Ẓihār* can be defined as regarding one's wife as the back of one's mother. This is expressed when a man says to his wife, "You are like my mother's back," meaning "You are prohibited to me".

Zinā: Adultery or fornication.

Zuhr: Literally meaning "noon" and usually used with "Prayer" as "The *Zuhr* Prayer" to refer to the prayer whose due time starts at noon.

Transliteration Table

Arabic Character	Symbol
أ/ء	a/ʾ
ب	Ab
ت	T
ث	J
ج	H
ح	Kh
خ	D
د	D
ذ	Dh
ر	R
ز	Z
س	S
ش	Sh
ص	_s
ض	_d
ط	_t
ظ	_Z
ع	ʿ
غ	Gh
ف	F
ق	Q
ك	K
ل	L
م	M
ن	N
هـ	H

ة	h/t
و	W
ي	Y
...◌َ	a
...◌ِ	i
...◌ُ	U
...ا/آ	ā
وُ	ū
◌ِي	ī
وَ	Aw
يَ	Ay

www.ingramcontent.com/pod-product-compliance
Lightning Source LLC
Chambersburg PA
CBHW050520240926
51846CB00003B/636
* 9 7 8 8 1 1 9 9 4 6 4 5 7 *